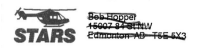

MW01105216

Once Lived a Village

STEVEN KASHUBA

Trafford
PUBLISHING

Order this book online at www.trafford.com/07-0251
or email orders@trafford.com

Most Trafford titles are also available at major online book retailers.

Note for Librarians: A cataloguing record for this book is available from Library
and Archives Canada at www.collectionscanada.ca/amicus/index-e.html

Printed in Victoria, BC, Canada.

ISBN: 978-1-4251-1841-9

*We at Trafford believe that it is the responsibility of us all, as both individuals
and corporations, to make choices that are environmentally and socially sound.
You, in turn, are supporting this responsible conduct each time you purchase a
Trafford book, or make use of our publishing services. To find out how you are
helping, please visit www.trafford.com/responsiblepublishing.html*

*Our mission is to efficiently provide the world's finest, most comprehensive
book publishing service, enabling every author to experience success.
To find out how to publish your book, your way, and have it available
worldwide, visit us online at www.trafford.com/10510*

 www.trafford.com

North America & international
toll-free: 1 888 232 4444 (USA & Canada)
phone: 250 383 6864 ♦ fax: 250 383 6804 ♦ email: info@trafford.com

The United Kingdom & Europe
phone: +44 (0)1865 722 113 ♦ local rate: 0845 230 9601
facsimile: +44 (0)1865 722 868 ♦ email: info.uk@trafford.com

10 9 8 7 6 5 4 3

ENDORSEMENTS

Steven Kashuba's portrayal of the life and times of an immigrant family in Canada is very compelling. His descriptions and explanations are vivid and the obstacles he encountered while searching for his ancestral village are most intriguing. This is a must read for those interested in gaining a better understanding of recent history.

Paul J. Byrne, Ph.D., President & CEO
Grant MacEwan College, Edmonton

Preserving the story of one's heritage is important. Once Lived a Village does just that in a masterful way. It is a story of two people who left their ancestral homeland never to return. It would be their son who journeyed to the Soviet Union in search of his roots and his grandfather's village. What happened during this and subsequent trips to Ukraine and Poland is gripping. And, the story of who guided him to his grandfather's burnt-out village is shocking! I highly recommend this book to anyone interested in their heritage.

Hon. Gene Zwozdesky,
Minister of Education (2006)
Province of Alberta, Canada

———

DEDICATION

This book is dedicated to two special people who touched my heart in very different but special ways. Ilze Kreislere, the daughter of my cousin Mariann Straupeniece, was born and raised in Broceni, Latvia. She had recently graduated from a medical academy as a specialist in gastroenterology, married and had a bright future ahead of her. Sadly, she was taken from us at a very early age. The other person is my Aunt Oksana Kaszuba-Dutkevich. Even though I had never met her, she continues to capture my interest and imagination. Like so many other young mothers living in Poland, she wanted a better life for herself and her family and set out to work in France in 1938. Unfortunately, the war broke out in 1939 and she was never heard from again. To all those who have met and come to know these two individuals, I share in your sorrow.

Steven Kashuba

ACKNOWLEDGEMENTS

I must thank God who gave me the spirit and power to write this book and fulfill my ambitions; for guiding and protecting the multitudes of immigrants, my parents among them, who came to Canada in search of freedom while setting down roots in a new and often hostile land.

I would also like to thank all those individuals who gave me encouragement and constructive advice. In the process of writing and editing the book, I got some special input and support from John and Glenda Benson, John and Sonia Shalewa, Veronica Izsak, Trevor Watt, Jars Balan, Lisa Grekul and Andrij Makuch. Throughout, I relied very heavily upon information received from my parents, especially my mother whose recollections of Plazow were critical to the story.

Of course, the telling of the story would not be possible without those journeys to Poland, Latvia and Ukraine where I interviewed various members of my extended family about their experiences over the last half of the 20th century. In particular, I want to extend my special thanks to my Aunt Anna Grokh whose memories of her childhood in Poland, work in Germany as an Ostarbeiter and deportation to Soviet Ukraine are of great interest. As well, I want to thank my cousin, Izabela Kopczacka of Plazow, who helped me find the location of my grandfather's torched village.

Finally, I want to thank Sharon, my wife, soul mate, and confidant, for her encouragement to write this story, for putting together the Kaszuba/Groszko family tree, and for editing the final draft of the manuscript.

PROLOGUE

The title of the book *Once Lived a Village* immediately conjures up a vision of a village that once lived but for whatever reason no longer exists. It is this image that raises many questions and ultimately adds to the intrigue of the story.

In recent years and within many cultures the world over, there has been an increased amount of interest expressed by individuals in their heritage. Perhaps some of this interest was triggered within me by a book written by Arthur Hailey entitled *Roots,* a poignant story about a black American who could not rest until he had exhausted his search for his ancestry in a continent far removed from America.

My search for dad's ancestral village began while I was on a teaching assignment with the Department of National Defense in Germany. Even today, a journey to Russia by car from Germany is not without some risk; in 1967 it was a difficult undertaking and even downright dangerous. Never out of range of the ever-present KGB, military police and People's Deputies, there was no shortage of surveillance. In the end, it was nearly as difficult to get out of Soviet Ukraine as it was to get into Soviet Russia. In fact, it would not be until the dawning of a new millennium that I would finally find my way to the village of Plazow and learn the heart-wrenching truth about the village of Grohi. The reason for this delay is very simple; the Soviet authorities expelled me from the Soviet Union in 1967 for a period of twenty-five years.

Over that period of twenty-five years, I could not get out of my mind how my parents left their homeland in search of a new life in Canada. Besides the obvious economic considerations, there were a number of other common threads that caused people to leave their homeland. Perhaps the most important single force was called *freedom.* Andrij and Eva Kaszuba came to

Canada with Polish passports but as ethnic Ukrainians whose dream of a free and independent Ukraine seemed always to be in their hearts and minds. They were not alone in taking this momentous decision to emigrate. During this period in history, millions of young people in Europe also took the decision to leave their place of birth for a destination that they, all too often, knew very little about. In retrospect, this period in history saw a phenomenon that we will likely not see again in our lifetime—the out-migration of a sizeable percentage of Europe's population.

The final chapter of this story might have been written when Ukraine gained its independence in 1991, *not so much with a bang but with a whimper.* But, as a new millennium dawns and the results of government policies are tabulated, the concept of a democratic state for Ukraine, as we know democracy in the West, seems to be as elusive as ever. In the end, one thing seems certain; you cannot dismantle a totalitarian state over night. The *Russian Bear's hold on Ukraine may be loosening but it is still there— tenaciously hanging on.*

Consider for a moment, *in light of today's mass communications capability*, is it conceivable that any individual or group of individuals would attempt to put forward a political movement that would have as its basic tenet world domination? Would bolshevism, communism, or fascism have a chance of taking root today? *Then, consider how the birth of these political movements changed the course of history.* As catastrophic as these world events were, it is the view of many that the world today is a much better place in which to live because of them or in spite of them.

This is a story of the trials and tribulations of one family carried along on currents of national and international upheaval. It is a story of a search for my roots and reflects just how the family was torn apart by national and international conflicts—especially so because their place of birth happened to fall in a region coveted by a number of nations.

Yes, there once was a village by the name of Grohi. The question is, why and by whom was it wiped off the face of the earth?

INTRODUCTION

To capture the impact of significant events on my family, the story is presented in four Parts. PART 1, *LAND OF ONION DOMES* opens in Germany where I sought permission from Canadian authorities to travel to the Soviet Union. Canada's Prime Minister at that time was The Honourable Lester B. Pearson and it would be from his office that I would receive approval for the trip. Travel to any *one* Soviet Bloc country would have been challenging, however, travel to *several* Iron Curtain countries was never without a considerable amount of apprehension and risk. Taking stock of my adventures and sometimes misadventures, I was happy *not* to have ended up in a Siberian work gang.

PART 2, *WHERE IT ALL BEGAN* deals with the first part of the 20th Century and describes why my father joined the Austrian Army during World War I. Unable to find meaningful work immediately following the war, he took a decision to serve with Commander-In-Chief Petliura's Army with the hopes of establishing an independent West Ukrainian National Republic. When this initiative failed, he reluctantly joined Marshal Pilsudski's Polish Home *Army*. However, marriage brought a new set of circumstances where the challenge became one of economic survival leading to a decision to emigrate to Canada.

PART 3, *FROM DREAMS TO REALITY* deals with the challenges that Andrij and Eva experienced in overcoming the obstacles to the dreams they had for themselves and for their children. In particular, the story describes how Eva moved Andrij away from the customary patriarchal model of a family, so prevalent in the Old Country, to one where she played an increasingly significant role in determining the direction in which the family would move.

PART 4, *A SEARCH FOR THE VILLAGE* turns the clock forward from my momentous journey to the Soviet Union in 1967 to Ukraine's Declaration of Independence in 1991. It is a curious fact that my period of expulsion expired at just about the same time that Ukraine gained its independence! Yes, the search for my dad's village is full of surprises. Some say that truth is often stranger than fiction. The story of *Once Lived a Village* is testimony to this belief.

A NOTE ABOUT TRANSLITERATION

Transliteration is the process of substituting letters or words of one language for those of another. Since the story takes place in Canada, Poland and Ukraine, significant *family* and *place* names are spelled *as they might appear in the subject country.* The best example is the spelling of my family name; Kashuba in Canada and Ukraine but Kaszuba in Poland. In *Austrian* Galicia, the village of Plazow might have been spelled as Plaziv and Lubaczow as Lubachiv. A number of other examples of transliteration appear in the story.

ABOUT THE COVER

On the cover is a recent photograph of the Ukrainian Greek Catholic Church *(Dormition of the Blessed Virgin Mary)* in Plazow, Poland. First constructed in 1728 and re-built in the nineteenth century after it was lost to a fire, it stood witness to life in a small community that reflected a peaceful co-existence among Ukrainians, Poles and Jews. Today, despite the scars of armed conflict and ethnic tensions during the first half of the 20th century, it continues to portray a serene, *albeit sorrowful,* majesty as it stands witness to the plight of Ukrainians who at one time formed up the majority in the region. In 1945 many of its parishioners were rounded up by Polish nationalists from nearby towns, held captive in the church and then forcefully deported to Soviet Ukraine. Surviving parishioners long for the day that they might once again inhabit their ancestral village and revitalize the church.

CONTENTS

PART 1

LAND OF ONION DOMES

1

Zweibrucken, Germany

The Journey Begins

My dad always referred to it as *The Old Country*. He never talked much about it but when he did his eyes would light up and his five-foot-ten frame would suddenly seem much taller; like that of a career soldier.

As brief as were these glimpses of his childhood, I must give him credit for developing within me a curiosity about his place of birth; a place that he proudly called *the land of onion domes*. As I was completing my second year of teaching in an Edmonton high school, I reflected upon my heritage and shared my thoughts with Henry Ward, the school principal. I had heard of his interest in the derivation of family names and this gave me an opportunity to discuss mine. When I told him of my interest of going to Europe one day in search of my roots, he thought for a moment before responding, *"Why don't you write a letter to Jo Yamamoto?"*

"A letter to Jo Yamamoto? Who is Jo Yamamoto?"

"Jo is one of our teachers on leave to teach in a DND school in Germany." He then went on to explain Canada's role in the North Atlantic Treaty Organization (NATO) and the procedure a teacher would use in applying for a teaching position with the Department of National Defense, adding, *"why don't you give it some thought?"*

I took Henry's advice and wrote a letter to Jo Yamamoto who was on a teaching contract in RCAF 3-Wing, Zweibrucken, Germany. At the same time, I contacted the Department of National Defense in search of upcoming postings and application procedures.

Sometimes, we all experience that feeling of starting out on some sort of journey as though pushed by an external force. Surely this was one of them. Even my closest associates were surprised to learn that I had formally applied for a DND posting in Europe. Having taken the initial step, I knew that the

Above:
Bohdan Khmelnitsky, astride a horse with bulowa in hand, rises from the middle of the Sofiyska Ploshcha in Kyiv. The statue, with the domes of St. Michael in the background, commemorates Khmelnitsky's battles with the Poles in the Mid-17th century. Source: Dreamstime.com

Left:
A symbol of Russia: St. Basil's Cathedral in Red Square, Moscow. Source: Dreamstime.com.

The Union Jack, Canada's flag for over 100 years, is emblematic of Canada's membership in the British Commonwealth. However, it was not officially proclaimed until December 18, 1964—just in time to be replaced.

Adopted by Parliament on December 15, 1964 and effective February 15, 1965, the Maple Leaf was proclaimed the official flag of Canada by Her Majesty Queen Elizabeth II.

Known as The Yukon, the CC-106 was used for long-haul transport by Squadron 412 of the Royal Canadian Air Force.

Dominion Curling Champions, 1962,
Bonnie Doon Composite High School, Edmonton, Alberta.
Wayne Saboe, Ron Hampton, Rick Aldridge,
Mick Adams and in the centre, Steven Kashuba, Coach.

4

ultimate prize might well be a teaching position in France or Germany; a springboard to travel to the Soviet Union. However, I soon discovered that making a request for a two-year posting to Europe was one thing, being nominated by the School Board was quite another. The competition for a limited number of teaching positions that opened up each year with the DND was fierce, to say the least. Not only that, but I also discovered that some specialties were in greater demand than were others. Finally, the appointments had to have an appropriate geographic distribution across Canada. In essence, I was now competing with teachers from all regions of Canada as well as with those who might well be able to speak a language in addition to the two official languages of French and English.

When I received the letter of rejection from the Edmonton Public School Board, I was not surprised. The only thing that it did for me was make me all the more determined. To add to my challenge, DND informed me that a particular candidate approved by local school districts could be rejected by the military as a result of failing a physical examination or a security check. For the moment, I was prepared to put aside my involvement in curling, baseball, and golf. I was even willing to give up my brand new Ford convertible, purchased not only for the purpose of enhancing my stature in the community but with the opposite sex as well only to find out that the only thing my car attracted was the local police and speeding tickets.

As 1964 came to a close, I planned my re-application strategy for a teaching position in Europe. It was a time when the petroleum industry in Alberta got an economic shot in the arm with the announcement that Great Canadian Oil Sands in Fort McMurray would be increasing its production capacity and a new pipeline would be constructed to feed the refineries in Edmonton. But, the talk was not all of energy. Canada seemed to be at the forefront of new technological developments and author Marshall McLuhan hit the technological jackpot when he published his book entitled *Understanding Media: The Extension of Man*, in which he stated that *the Medium is the Message*; a catch phrase that would stay with Canadians for a very long time.

Led by Prime Minister Lester B. Pearson, perhaps the most interesting challenge to Canadians was not one of economics but rather the debate as to whether or not the Canadian flag, which embodied the Union Jack of Great Britain, should be replaced by a *made-in-Canada* flag. In fact, Canadians got an early Christmas present when on December 15, 1964, after months of bitter debate, the Pearson government forced a vote on the *single red maple leaf with red bars* design. Not everyone was happy with having to give up the British Union Jack.

In a way, I wanted to give myself a Christmas present in 1964 when I made my second application for a Department of National Defense teaching position in Europe. Only this time I supported my application with a couple of letters of support from community leaders and pointed out that '...*I love my work with the Edmonton Public School District and see this posting as enhancing my educational experiences...'* and concluded with, *'if unsuccessful in my application, I will be leaving the district for another position.'* This approach *seemed* to work because I was soon informed by Edmonton Public School Board's selection committee that my specialties in business education, mathematics, and physical education tipped the scales in my favour. As I made my plans in the winter of 1965 for the impending trip to Europe, it occurred to me that much of my interest in national and international affairs seemed to be limited to that of Canada and the United States. Only on rare occasions did I see the need to embrace the news from faraway places such as Europe, the Soviet Union or the Middle East. That, however, was about to change. My outlook was about to take on an international flavour.

Canada was taking its rightful place in the international economic community when Lyndon Johnson, the president of the United States, and Canadian Prime Minister Lester B. Pearson signed a far-reaching auto pact in Austin, Texas. Pearson predicted that the agreement would help to create 50,000 new jobs in Canada and solidify Canada's position as the second most affluent nation among the industrialized countries of the world, right behind the United States, as determined by the Organization for Economic Cooperation and Development. Even more significant for many Canadians was the news on February 15 that the old Red Ensign was about to be hauled down from flagpoles in all parts of Canada and replaced with the new Maple Leaf flag. I visualized the military bases in Europe now having to fly the Maple Leaf. Somehow, all of this did not seem quite right with me. Like so many other Canadians, I had become attached to the Union Jack.

Meanwhile, I soon discovered that travel to Europe with the armed services required more than an approval of an application. There were those security checks followed by a battery of physical examinations. Soon, it seemed as though the last hurdle had been overcome except, of course, for all of those inoculations and vaccinations for diphtheria, tetanus, typhus and malaria. Even as my application was confirmed in writing, I had to admit that I would really miss curling, baseball, and those televised baseball, NHL and NFL games, soon to be beamed in colour. The only consolation seemed to be that I was being posted to Marville, France. *'Better than Germany,'* I thought, *'at least I can speak a few words of French. The only words I know in German are auf Wiedersehen, Berlin and Adolf Hitler.'* As the date of my departure came closer and closer, I was reminded of my fear of flying. To ease the pain, I decided to drive the first leg of the journey from Edmonton to Trenton, Ontario with Allen Karabonik, who was headed for Ottawa. As we drove through the prairie provinces, I marvelled at the checker-board colors of the grain fields and just how hard our pioneers worked to reach this stage of development in agriculture. What a contrast to 1931 when my mother traveled through the very same region to the sight of drifting soil and crop failures!

The military plane which was to take me to France was a turbo-prop version that had all of its seats re-configured so that all of the passengers faced towards the rear of the craft. It was the contention of the military brass that the survival rate of passengers, in the event of a major disaster, was far greater in this position as opposed to the alternative. Somehow, all of this did not make me feel any better about flying. Having boarded the aircraft, it did not take long to discover that many of the passengers were not military personnel; some were teachers while others were school administrators and they came from all regions of Canada. You could sense the excitement in the air as some were returning to Europe after a summer holiday in Canada while others were leaving the familiarity of Canada for Europe and an uncertain future. The ten-hour flight to Marville, France was uneventful. However, it was the beginning of a different kind of an education.

Before leaving for Europe, I spent a considerable amount of time educating myself about the countries that I planned to visit. Naturally, there were those Western European countries of France, Germany, Italy, Spain and Portugal--all of which encouraged tourism. Not so, however, with the Soviet Union. I knew little about Poland, Russia, Belarus, and the Ukrainian Soviet Socialist Republic. Since these countries fell under the grasp of the hammer and sickle, information about them was relatively inaccessible to the West. As a result, it was this mysterious corner of the world that held the most intrigue for me. In the meantime, I had to admit that I received very little encouragement from my parents about my plan to visit relatives and practically had to steal a couple of letters which had the return addresses of an uncle and an aunt in a village by the name of Buzk. Once again, I realized just how little I knew about the homeland of my parents. However, there *was* one thing I did understand and that was their condemnation of the communist way of life where villagers spied on their neighbours and the state police controlled the lives of its citizens.

While thinking about the future, I was not prepared for what awaited me in Marville. We landed in dense fog and, as I made my way to the officers' barracks with other passengers, the fog seemed to envelope everyone and everything around me and made me think about the battles that took place in this region. An exterior light on the terminal building that appeared far away was actually just a few yards away. Then, there was the smell; a dank, musty smell. I could not identify the source of the oppressive smell but concluded that it had something to do with conflicts gone by. I had visions of bravery and of sacrifice and of human misery and suffering. The outside temperature may have been in the fifties, but I felt cold and alone with my thoughts.

Sitting over a late dinner in the Officers Mess, conversation came easily with officers of the air force and with fellow teachers who held the honorary rank of Flight Lieutenant. Unlike your typical talk in Canada, our discussions took on a European flavour interspersed with references to the Canadian scene. Marville was a supply depot for the Canadian Armed Forces in Europe and a part of Canada's ongoing commitment to the North Atlantic Treaty Organization. The next morning, with little to do on the air base until school opening, a couple of teachers rented a car and headed for Belgium while others took in the local sights. One or two of the teachers had been posted to Marville the previous year and were not in a hurry to leave the air base. They preferred to participate in activities in the Officers Mess.

I had only been on the base for two days when I got quite a surprise. A military courier came by my quarters and informed me that the base commander wished to have a word with me. 'Well,' I thought, 'there is nothing like having a word with the top dog on the base.' Upon arriving at headquarters, I was promptly ushered into the General's office.

"Nice to meet you, Flight Lieutenant Kashuba," were his first words. "Please have a seat." Being a school teacher and carrying the honorary rank somehow made me feel important. After exchanging a few pleasantries about my flight, my job and my family, the General got right to the point. "I don't know whether this is good news or bad news. I have a telegram in my possession from headquarters in Ottawa which, in part, reads,

'PLEASE ADVISE FLIGHT LIEUTENANT KASHUBA THAT EFFECTIVE IMMEDIATELY, HE IS BEING TRANSFERRED TO CANADIAN FORCES BASE, ZWEIBRUCKEN, GERMANY. STOP. UPON ARRIVAL AT 3-WING, HE IS TO REPORT TO THE BASE COMMANDER. STOP.'

Well, what is your reaction, sir?"

A thousand thoughts went through my head before I could answer. Who was responsible for this transfer? Why? As I considered his question, I could hear the General saying, "It must be nice to know someone in a position of power. It sure looks like the Base Commander at 3- Wing had a hand in this!"

It wasn't long before I found out that the base commander at 3 Wing Zweibrucken might well have had a role in the transfer. Apparently, General Don Laubman was an avid curler and, perhaps, he decided to strengthen his curling team. Being from the city of Edmonton, he was likely aware of my interest in competitive curling and that I had coached the Bonnie Doon High School curling team to a national championship in 1963 while at the same time serving as the coordinator of junior curling in Edmonton. From this I concluded that The Royal Canadian Air Force played by a different set of rules. Rank played an important part in decision-making and a base commander had certain powers and privileges. Still, I thanked my lucky stars. Anyone who was acquainted with the role of the North Atlantic Treaty Organization in Europe knew that a posting to the Fighter Wing of the RCAF in Zweibrucken was a plum. Suddenly, this made the transfer to Germany all the more palatable.

It was late August and I had the option of flying or bussing from Marville to Zweibrucken. Since I wanted to see and learn more about France and Germany, I elected to take a military bus. The route to Zweibrucken first took us through Verdun which is often considered to be a *warrior town* because of its long history in military affairs. It was here in 1916 that one of the greatest battles of the war took place, thereby saving Paris from destruction. Next, the pastoral and undulating countryside took us through the historical city of Metz. Located at the confluence of the Mosel and Seille rivers, it was first colonized by the Romans and along with Verdun played an important role in both world wars. Approaching the Rhine Valley in Germany, I visualized Montgomery and Bradley as they closed in on the last German stronghold towards the end of World War II for, in order to defeat Germany, the Allies had to cross the Rhine and capture the Ruhr. This was essential and yet somehow seemed formidable. The sprawling industrial Ruhr Basin covered 4,000 square miles and contained coal mines, oil refineries, steel mills and armament factories.

Perhaps it was on a day like today that Field Marshal Montgomery at 6:10 on the evening of Tuesday, March 27, 1945 coded a message to General Eisenhower, '*Today I issued orders ...for the operations eastwards which are now about to begin. My intention is to drive hard for the line of the Elbe using the Ninth and Second Armies. Canadian Army will operate...to clear Northeast Holland and West Holland and the coastal area to the north of the left boundary of the Second Army...*' Who is to say that this was not one of most significant decisions of the war in an effort to bring it to a successful conclusion? Even twenty years later, the sights and sounds of the war seemed very real. No matter where I looked, there was evidence of the devastation of war. Devastation that looked senseless. Evidence of what war can do to a people and her nation.

I recalled how my parents would join their friends to talk about their childhood and how difficult it was to live in the border region of two would-be nations, Poland and Ukraine. I could visualize the dilemma of the people living in this area. How many times had those living in this very region changed their nationality and their allegiance? For those living in the Ruhr Valley, one day it might be French only to revert back to German after a major battle. Then another war and it was back to speaking French once again. Perhaps they had become accustomed to conflict and learned to appreciate one another as human beings rather than combatants in military conflict. Or, could it be that the question was far more complex? Did some of the residents harbour feelings of resentment? Guilt? Could they have done more to preserve harmony?

It seems odd that so many thoughts could flood one's consciousness in so short a period of time. Upon entering Germany, there seemed to be evidence of increased economic vibrancy. As the military bus entered the small city of Zweibrucken, I felt a certain amount of apprehension and found it difficult to suppress the feeling that this had been the staging ground for many battles during the two world wars. It was difficult not to think of the nearby city of Reims in northeast France which was perhaps the most important city in Europe in 1945. For centuries, battles had raged about this strategic crossroad. It was here that the Supreme Headquarters of the Allied Expeditionary Forces was tucked away in a back street and it was here that Dwight D. Eisenhower took some momentous decisions in his drive for the capture of Berlin. No doubt Eisenhower heard well his mission '... *you will enter the continent of Europe and, in conjunction with the other United Nations, undertake operations aimed at the heart of Germany and the destruction of her armed forces...*' But, it might also have been the very moment that Russian Generals had the same urge to get on with the attack on Berlin, Hitler's stronghold. In fact, we *did* learn after the war that Marshal Georgi Zhukov's huge army group was scheduled to take the City but would not do so until the go ahead was received from Josef Stalin in Moscow.

The Canadian military base in Zweibrucken was commonly referred to as a Fighter Wing and was located on a relatively high plateau. At its entrance one could discern an imposing concrete bunker damaged by artillery and bombs during World War II. The entry gate into the base was closely guarded and every person entering the base had to identify himself and provide, if requested, the necessary documentation. Once clearance was received, an individual was given a salute and asked to proceed. Since this was an airborne division for the training of fighter pilots, there was plenty of noise as the F-104 jets kicked in their *after-burners*. The smell of jet fuel hung heavily in the air and those fighter jets were noisy, very noisy. Looking around, I could imagine how the Nazi regime had earlier prepared for war by constructing a variety of defences for this region and for all of Germany–the Gustav Line in Italy, the Atlantic Wall along the European coast, and the Siegfried Line at Germany's western borders.

Judy, sitting in a bus seat next to me, had earlier told me that she was a registered nurse on her way to the Canadian air base to join the staff at the military hospital. *"I wonder,"* I asked of no one in particular, *"what was it like to be a nurse in Berlin when the Marshal Zhukov Army smashed its way into Berlin?"*

"Of course," she replied, *"our jobs here are much different. Every time I come back to Germany after a vacation in Canada, it is difficult to think about the war without feeling sorrow. I had an aunt who was with the Red Cross in Berlin when the Russian Army attacked Berlin in mid-April of 1945. For her, it was not a pleasant experience. To this day she has nightmares about the atrocities committed by Russian soldiers."*

"Yes," I replied, *"that is not to say that the Germans were kind and gentlemanly when they attacked Poland and Russia. Or, to say that their treatment of European Jews was fair and just. And what of their treatment of women–especially during the siege of Leningrad?"*

In discussing matters related to World War II, it was always interesting to note how Canadians and Americans tended to think about the atrocities committed by Russian soldiers when they conquered Berlin. It seemed that NATO member countries at times forgot that Russia fought on the side of the Allies and that it was not until after the war that relations between the west and east had deteriorated. Or, was it that some of these people were remembering the Bolshevik Revolution of 1917 when thinking about modern-day Russia?

Any other thoughts I may have had about the war were quickly pushed to the back of my mind. This was not a time to dwell on the past. Better to think about the present and what the future held in store for me. Everything was a new experience for me. The very structure of the military captured my imagination. As a teacher and school administrator I thought, *'wouldn't it be nice to have that kind of a structure in the classroom? In the school? And, to command that kind of respect!'* I thought about the role of the military where leadership was responsible for the enunciation of those lean and simple statements of policy consistent with beliefs and values, vision and strategy. I concluded that policy gave practical meaning to values and that it was the role of the military to carry out these policies. But then, what would a school be without discipline problems and without some flexibility in its structure? How else would young people express themselves? After all, wasn't the war fought for those very freedoms? Freedom of speech, association, and worship?

As I settled into my duties at Schoenblick High School, I began to plan my trip to the Soviet Union. I wanted very much to share my travel plans with those around me while at the same time I knew that open discussion about my plans might make it more difficult to obtain a travel visa to an Iron Curtain Country. After all, it was my expectation that military authorities would look upon my request to travel to Russia with a degree of suspicion. Yet, the attraction to travel to my ancestral homeland was very strong. I wanted to experience first-hand what life must have been like for Andrij and Eva when they were young and how things had changed under the yoke of communism.

Once I got settled into the routine of a military base, I quickly learned that there were advantages to being attached to the Royal Canadian Air Force, particularly in the Officers Mess, the heartbeat of the base. It was here that officers would gather for their meals and for purposes of socializing. A mug of beer cost five cents and an ounce of an aperitif a mere ten cents; a fraction of the cost of the same drinks *on the economy*. In addition, one could sit in on a game of gin rummy or challenge someone to a game of billiards. I had all of the privileges of an officer in the air force while at the same time retaining my civilian status. For certain, I had the best of two worlds. In the fall of the year I was inspired enough by the upcoming Canadian Grey Cup football classic to write the lyrics for a song entitled *Gonna Ride That Bluebomber Train*. The song and our skit did little to affect the outcome of the football game which was broadcast over Services Network Radio from a feed directly from Canada. On November 27, the Hamilton Tiger-Cats defeated the Winnipeg Bluebombers 22 - 16.

During my first few months in Germany, the talk was of the new Canadian flag, the federal government's plan to merge the armed forces, and the military's role with the United Nations as a peace keeping force. All of these initiatives touched the very fabric of the military base. On another occasion I found myself saying to a close friend Brian Laird, *"why don't we go out on the economy tonight for dinner? Maybe visit a German gasthaus for some real German beer?"* Brian did not need much coaxing, even though he knew that the price of beer in downtown Zweibrucken was considerably higher than in the Officers Mess. Arriving at a gasthaus, I was surprised to learn that Brian spoke a considerable amount of German and seemed to know his way around a menu while at the same time not hesitating to enter into a conversation with the locals. As we sat over a beer, Brian must have sensed my thoughts, saying, *"You know, this is my third year in Germany. I asked for an extension of my contract so that I might get to know Germany better."*

"Where did you learn your German? Formal classes?"

"No. Actually, as time went on I found that many German words seem to have the same derivation as do English words. In other cases, I try my German on the German nationals who work as civilians on our base. When this fails, I improvise. I use gestures."

From downtown Zweibrucken we headed to another gasthaus located in a small village some twenty kilometres in the countryside. Being a newcomer and not knowing how the local Germans would take to our presence, we took a table somewhat removed from the locals. To my surprise, the frau who owned the gasthaus was most pleasant. *"Amerikaner?"*

"Nein," Brian responded. *"Ich bin ein kanadisch."*

That seemed to bring a smile to her face for I was soon to learn that Canadians seemed to be received with less animosity than were our American neighbours. In part, this seemed to be because Canada was not a super power and, as a result, far more acceptable to the German psyche than was the United States. Clearly, the locals did not object to being in the company of Canadians and, perhaps, looked upon the Americans as being the occupiers of their country. With this kind of a warm welcome, it was not uncommon for Brian and me to enter into a discussion with German war veterans. Conversation came easily. In many cases, the memories of the war were very much with those we befriended. Some even spoke openly about Nazism and Adolf Hitler while others talked about their role on the Eastern Front. One elderly veteran recounted stories about the German wehrmacht and the use of their blitzkrieg. No topic about the war was really taboo given an appropriate location and circumstance. There was, however, one notable exception–any discussion about the treatment of Jews by the Germans during World War II seemed to be off limits. It was as if each was trying to put these images out of their mind.

The evening at the gasthaus did much to heighten my desire to learn more about the German people and about the two world wars. This particular outing was a good springboard to more experiences in Zweibrucken and provided me with a thirst for travel to other parts of Europe and, in particular, to Eastern Europe. I felt that my upcoming journey would, in many respects, be the antithesis to that taken by my parents when they immigrated to Canada.

My parents left Poland knowing that they would never return whereas in my case, I *would* return to Canada once my assignment was over. To help me accomplish my objectives, I decided to enrol in a German language class being offered on the military base. The course was ideal for my purposes in that it dealt with the history of Germany, the German language, and with German customs. It seemed as though I had a bit of a head start on other students in that I already spoke a second language. My next challenge would be to find out if my knowledge of Ukrainian would be a bridge to understanding the Russian language. I knew that I would soon make use of this knowledge.

In testing the local cuisines, I did not limit myself to those in Germany. France was merely a stone's throw away and Jim Thatcher, a foreign language teacher on the base, took great pleasure in introducing me to French wine and food. The garlic-laced and wine-rejuvenated escargot, a delicacy frequently served in the Voge Mountains, quickly became a favourite of mine. It was not unusual to find German sounding names in this part of France. In fact, in one of the restaurants a Frau Mueller told us that at her *ripe* age of seventy-six she had changed her allegiance several times. First, it would be the Germans that would control this area only to be pushed back and the area would revert back to France. Despite the frequent changes on the political front, the locals did not waste much time speculating on what might have been, seemingly happy just to be alive.

"You know, Etienne," explained Frau Mueller, using the French Etienne rather than the English Steven, *"it was only twenty years after the signing of the Treaty of Versailles which ended World War I that Germany invaded Poland which formally launched World War II. That only tells me that treaties are not worth the paper they are written on."* She then went on to explain how one of the provisions of that treaty was to limit the armed forces in Germany to 100,000 men and the deprivation of the ingredients of war--tanks, heavy guns, and aircraft. *"It's too bad,"* she added, *"that the coalition which won the war did not survive for a very long period of time. The feeling that World War I was a war to end all wars was coined by a person who knew little about human nature."*

I thanked Frau Mueller for her insightful thoughts saying that it would be unusual to enter into this kind of a discussion in Canada. She smiled wistfully at me as if to say that she could do without having experienced the horrors of the great wars. *"You see, Etienne,"* she explained, *"I have had the misfortune to live through those horrible times. I know first hand the horrors of war!"*

"It seems," added Thatcher thoughtfully, *"that the most striking characteristic of foreign policy in the decade after the First World War was the tendency for each of the former allies to concentrate on its own interests. Russia made a separate peace with Germany. President Wilson of the United States played an important part at Versailles, but Congress did not share his enthusiasm for foreign affairs, and in 1920 the Senate declined to ratify the treaty, leaving America outside the newly formed League of*

Nations." However, Canada *was* among the many nations that gathered in Geneva to witness the birth of the League.

France went to war in 1914 hoping to recover the provinces of Alsace-Lorraine. She lost 1,335,000 men. One-third of the Frenchmen under thirty were killed or crippled. Not only did France lose a high percentage of her men, she also spent untold fortunes in preparation for war. Near the very restaurant where we socialized was the Maginot Line, which consisted of 23 artillery forts, 35 infantry posts, 295 interval casements and blockhouses, and scores of minor defences. France began the construction of the Line in 1929 with the belief that it would be impassable to major military movement. In response, the Germans began the construction of the Siegfried Line which, in their estimation, would create an impenetrable line of defence between Germany and the nations of France, Luxembourg, and Holland. The history of war shows us that both, France and Germany were wrong, very wrong.

War veterans living in and around Zweibrucken still harboured many memories of World War II, a war unlike any other—ever. Many German successes during the war were attributable to the use of a quick-strike force commonly known as the blitzkrieg, the art of infiltration and shock action. Hitler, in particular, was fond of the value of psychological dislocation. Deep in thought about the war, Jim Thatcher asked, *"what chance would a peace-loving nation have against Germany in 1939? What chance did Poland have? How long did it take the Allies to fully prepare for the German juggernaut?"*

In small communities surrounding the Canadian Air Base, the locals showed less curiosity in me than I showed in them. Frankly, I was mesmerized by the whole notion of a world war; a world conflict of such great magnitude. To those with whom I had an opportunity to exchange a few thoughts, I soon discovered that the first thing that they wanted to know was my country of origin. When told that I was a Canadian and associated with the *flugplatz* at 3-Wing, their ears often perked up. However, when they discovered that I was a civilian, they seemed to lose some of their interest in me. One thing was certain, however, most Germans had an abiding appreciation for war veterans, regardless of the country they represented. For the die-hard Nazi sympathizers, I discovered that they had an appreciation for heroism, even for the soldiers of the First Ukrainian Front which made the initial and final attack on Berlin in World War II.

As I reflected on the meaning of armed conflict, I had to admit that Zweibrucken was right in the middle of a lot of history and with each passing day I found myself becoming more and more immersed in European history. In particular, I thought about the conditions imposed upon Germany after World War I which helped to propel Hitler to power. Yet, as I observed the industriousness of Germans as they went about their daily tasks, I began to understand why even the Ostarbeiters, albeit grudgingly, developed an abiding respect for their oppressors. *For, despite its checkered history, I found that there was a lot to like about Germany.*

14

2.

Intourist

The key to all travel to the Soviet Union

Increased knowledge of Russia's role in the two world wars heightened my resolve to journey to the Soviet Union. As a general rule, those who served in highly sensitive military areas were prohibited from traveling to Iron Curtain countries, however, those assigned to less sensitive areas could, with approval, undertake such travel. Being a civilian, I assumed that there would be no military reason for denying me a visa to the Soviet Union. On the other hand, I had to acknowledge that Fighter 3-Wing was located in close proximity to several highly armed American military bases, not the least of which was Ramstein. Would this particular circumstance make the Soviets sufficiently suspicious as to give my application a second look? Would a Soviet agent dig deeper into my file for any suspicious activity?

The point was driven home in the case of two American students who had flown to Moscow earlier that spring. Justice seemed to come quickly and the verdict was guilty; ten years in a work camp in Siberia. And the charge? Involvement in the black market or what the Soviets called the *underground economy*. The defendants claimed that they were innocent; that they were framed and their lawyers immediately appealed. Still, the whole incident made me nervous. And, even though the sentence was being appealed, did not take away from its severity. Even my travel agent in Zweibrucken, who worked closely with *Intourist,* the only official Soviet travel agency licensed to pre-charge travelers to the Soviet Union for accommodation, air fare, gasoline coupons, and rail travel, was not overly enthusiastic about my plans. But, I could understand that. It would have been unusual to find *any* German who was in love with anything Russian. What made matters even worse was the prevailing suspicion held by Soviet officials that civilians coming into their

15

country were more apt to be involved in intelligence and counter-intelligence activity than were military personnel.

Tourists who motored to the Soviet Union could only drive on certain highways and these were clearly spelled out by the Soviet authorities in their Intourist booklets. Travel near any military installation was forbidden and accommodations were strictly limited to Intourist hotels. Above all else, the use of listening devices and cameras near any *sensitive* location was strictly *verboten*. Motorists had to have in their possession a valid international driver's license and automobile insurance. In the event of car trouble, the guide provided a list of cities which had auto service centres. Most important for me was the list of American and Canadian Embassies or Consulates in the countries that I would be visiting. Unfortunately, the use of credit cards was not in vogue in Iron Curtain countries. Still, it was comforting to know that most countries would accept American currency and, for those tourists willing to risk it, the black market trade in American currency was rumoured to be very lucrative.

"Steven," suggested Bill Montgomery who had traveled widely in Europe, *"any trip to the Soviet Union is fraught with danger. You will stick out like a sore thumb and may well become a target for the unscrupulous. After all is said and done, there is one thing that you must never ever do when you get to Russia."*

"And what might that be," I asked.

"The black market in the countries you plan to visit is very much alive. The hottest item of barter is, of course, the American dollar. And, it is the one infraction that Soviet officials love to use when making an arrest. The evidence would be right there before their eyes."

It seemed that Soviet authorities preferred to have all visitors bring the almighty American dollar with them and exchange these at prescribed rates. The reason for this was obvious—the government wanted to reap the benefits of the spread between the pegged rate and the market rate of exchange. It also appeared that the enforcement of this legislation was not consistent from country to country. For example, it was said that the authorities in Warsaw often turned a blind eye to this kind of activity as if to thumb their collective noses at the Kremlin. On the other hand, the same infractions would be treated much more harshly were they to occur in Moscow.

Even though my trip to the Soviet Union was one year away, I could not get it out of my mind when I motored with two University of Alberta students to Norway and Sweden during the spring of 1966. But, these thoughts were quickly put on the back burner when I got back to Zweibrucken. Being a golf nut, I hit the practice tee every day for a couple of weeks at the American airbase in Ramstein with the hopes of competing, as an amateur, on the European Professional Golf Tour. In those days, a handicap of six or seven was not too shabby when taking into consideration that Germany, France and Switzerland did not have that many top-notch amateur golfers. In the pro-am in Ramstein, my pro and I came in second, in the Swiss Open in St.

Moritz I won the amateur low medal championship and followed this up with the low net score for amateurs in the French Open Golf Championship held in Evian, France. Were these tournaments to take place in Canada or the United States, it is doubtful that my golf scores would have qualified for any prizes. But, what was nice about my experiences was the opportunity to meet some of the world's greatest golfers. I caddied for Alan and Harold Henning, both of whom played on the American PGA Tour.

There is one other memory I cherish from that summer. I competed in the European Military Services Golf Championship in Heidelberg, Germany. In the fourth and final round I led the pack at level par with but a few holes to play. That's when it all happened; first the trees got in the way and then the sand traps did me in. By the time the smoke cleared, all I could do was to finish fifth.

With school opening in the fall of 1966, I began the process of getting my documentation in order for the Soviet trip by reviewing a couple of unclassified intelligence reports from an American military base. If I had imagined that something very sinister was always taking place in the Soviet Union, I was very disappointed. It appeared as though the procedures in place for travelers to Soviet Union countries, having regard for the system of government, were consistent with expectations. In fact, it looked as though Communist Countries encouraged foreign visitors and the biggest prize seemed to be the American dollar.

It soon became obvious to me that the official Soviet government line about travel in Eastern Europe was somewhat at variance with what individual travelers were saying. Soviet literature described a host country's system of government in glowing terms. In fact, the presentations were so good that I felt as though I was about to travel to nothing more than democratic states. Of course, I knew that this was not true and that these were totalitarian states where your every move would be monitored. As well, I discovered that developing a travel route was easy so long as you stayed within the guidelines of permissible routes.

The shortest route from Zweibrucken to Moscow would have been through Berlin, located in East Germany, officially known as the Deutsche Demokratische Republik. However, Berlin was divided into four zones of Great Britain, France, the United States and the Soviet Union and travel through the City en route to Warsaw would have been difficult, if not impossible. Looking back, it was in 1961 that the citizens of Berlin were shocked to find that their beloved city suddenly had a dividing wall right through its centre. One point of entry into East Berlin was the Brandenburg Gate where West Berliners might be able to enter under the scrutiny of machine guns. Another famous point of entry was Check Point Charlie. I had no desire to tackle either of these entry points so early in the journey. Better to leave it for the re-entry to Germany. For the moment, the best route to Moscow would have to be via Vienna, Prague, and Warsaw.

Prior to submitting my proposed plan to the local travel agency, it first had to be submitted to the Royal Canadian Air Force (RCAF) authorities for approval. Although I was confident that approval from the RCAF would be forthcoming, I was also made aware that my biggest hurdle would be getting approval from the Soviet Intourist authorities, first in Germany and then in Moscow where their first question would be, '...*why are you planning to travel to the Soviet Union alone?*'

When I put this question to the Intelligence Officer at 3-Wing, he responded by saying, "*You know, there are a number of circumstances that can make travel in a foreign country down-right dangerous. Among these could be car trouble, being arrested for a minor offence without any witness to support your side of the story, the problems with communication in a foreign country, and even some clandestine work by the KGB to drum up a fictitious charge against you. Traveling alone can accentuate any of these problems.*"

"*Are you trying to dissuade me from going,*" I countered cautiously.

"*Not at all sir, I just want to make it clear that this trip is not without risk. It would be very easy for a Russian agent to believe that you are some sort of a spy on a special mission despite your protests. Besides, shortly before you leave and once final clearance is available, you will need to have a briefing session with our military brass.*" Having regard for this kind of a reservation, I asked a fellow educator, John Gavinchuk, if he would like to accompany me on the journey. After some thought, he said, "*why not, after all, my family came to Canada from Western Ukraine.*" This took a lot of weight off my shoulders since I could now get into the final stages of planning knowing that I had a trusted friend to join me on the trip.

Once we provided the travel agency with the proposed day-to-day travel itinerary and received their initial approval, the plan was then submitted to Intourist for their review and approval. The difficult part was yet to come when the plan would be submitted to the Russian authorities. I tried to imagine what information would be of interest to Soviet authorities. Would it be the birth place of my parents? Their citizenship? Would it be the place of residence of my extended family in Soviet Ukraine? Perhaps they would want to examine my statements as to the purpose of my trip, my political affiliations, my work history, and my work on a military base. I assumed that unless the Soviet authorities were able to get all of the necessary information, my entry to the Soviet Union would be denied. I suspected that they would handle my application for travel in the normal way—with a great deal of suspicion. After all, that *was* the very purpose for their national security system.

Since the Iron Curtain Countries did not have a free market economy, I was required to pay in advance, in American currency, for accommodation, meals, insurance and Intourist guides in Czechoslovakia, Poland, Russia, Belarus, and Ukraine. With the Canadian dollar being at par with the American dollar, the up-front cost of the trip was over $1,500. In those days, that was a considerable amount of money.

With the arrival of spring in 1967, Canadians kicked off their centennial celebrations with a museum train which started its cross-Canada journey in Victoria. Canadians on the Base also formalized their plans to mark this very special occasion. The city of Winnipeg was putting its final touches on hosting the Pan-American Games at which time Canada's centennial would be recognized while at the same time, Montreal was readying itself for Expo '67. There was news for hockey fans as well when it was announced that the National Hockey League would be expanding from six to twelve teams. The world seemed to be unfolding as it should, perhaps too smoothly. The first sign of any problem came in late May when John Gavinchuk informed me that he was not able to get clearance to travel to the Soviet Union. And, it did not surprise me that John had mixed emotions about this news. Maybe he was even relieved with the news. As I considered this development, I could not help but wonder if my application would be refused as well.

By mid-June the students at Schoenblick High School began writing their final examinations just about the time that teachers wrapped up their educational programs for the year. At the same time, the final plans for my trip were in place including all matters related to medical and automobile insurance. It was now time for a briefing by the Base's military brass. After brief introductions, legal counsel Major Townsend did not mince his words. *"Lieutenant,"* he opened, *"let me tell you a little bit about the purpose of this briefing session. First, as far as anyone is concerned in an Iron Curtain Country, you are an officer of the Canadian military. Second, and as a result of your rank, you have a variety of privileges when abroad. But, this does not come without added responsibility. As a result, everything that you do and everything that happens to you not only reflects on this Base but also on the Canadian military and Canada itself. In other words, your responsibility not only extends to Canada, but to NATO as well. As a result, we want to arm you with the best information possible. You and I know that you may never need this crucial information if all goes well. However, let me hasten to add, in the Soviet Union your credentials will be scrutinized and even challenged."*

As I listened to Major Townsend with thoughts of the Soviet Union, I couldn't help but think about a couple of lines of an anti-establishment song written by Vladimir Vysotsky entitled, *Ya Nye Lyublyu* (I Don't Like), *I don't like cold cynicism or people reading my letters, Looking over my shoulder, I don't like myself when I'm afraid...* which led me to ask, *"do you believe that I will be at risk traveling alone?"*

"Yes, I believe you will be at a bit of a disadvantage traveling alone. On the other hand, we do know that policing in the countries you intend to visit is very thorough which should be of some comfort to you. The citizenship of your parents could present a problem. The Soviet authorities will already have some information before them; information about the correspondence that has taken place between your parents and their friends and relatives in Soviet Ukraine. From this they will be able to determine the political leanings of your family and the likelihood of any anti-Soviet sentiment. So,

as you can see, this will present you with a special set of circumstances as well as for the Soviet authorities. Maybe even some potential difficulties."

Major Church, the chief legal counsel for the base, traced in detail how the sons and daughters of immigrants to Canada can be claimed as citizens of the country from which the parents had earlier emigrated. *"In your case,"* he concluded, *"it would appear that Poland or Soviet Ukraine may have some interest in your citizenship. After all, your parents did come to Canada with Polish passports."*

As the briefing progressed, I could not help but be impressed with how much information the military brass had about my family and my own background and that much of this information had found its way to Russian authorities prior to their reviewing and approving my application. Of interest to me was the latest intelligence report about the difficulties experienced by Canadian and American military personnel while on assignment in an Iron Curtain Country. It seemed to me that very little of this kind of information found its way into the newspapers of Western Countries, perhaps because it was filed under the category of *Secret*. Besides, Soviet authorities were not in the habit of releasing sensitive information. They were more likely to seek this kind of information, not share it.

"Just a few words, Lieutenant," continued Major Townsend, *"about the most common ways that westerners get in difficulty in Russia. Remember, unlike Canada, the Soviet Union does not have a free market economy. However, many of its residents long for western goods. In fact, many of these same people come by western currency, often by illegal means, and are looking for a destination for this currency. Often, some of this currency ends up in the hands of travelers who exchange personal goods for this currency. Sometimes, the possession of these goods is illegal in Russia. So, let me stress--do not sell, exchange, trade, barter, give away, or buy any goods that fall into this category."*

Since I had heard that the most common goods smuggled illegally into Russia were personal items of clothing, candies, chewing gum, pens, pencils, and electronic gadgets, I raised a question about this. Townsend once again cautioned me about this adding that, in his view, the matter of personal items being bartered was less serious than might be the case of electronic gadgets. As the briefing progressed, it began to appear as though the reasons for not going to Russia far outnumbered those that would be in support of the trip.

When I contacted Intourist as to their understanding about the items I should not bring into Russia, their answer was brief and to the point. They referred me to the Intourist Brochure, adding *"Russian authorities do not want you to have in your possession any photographic, electronic listening devices, tape recorders, sophisticated cameras, firearms, or any objects or substances that would lead the KGB or their military personnel to believe that some sort of illegal or questionable activity or enterprise is being planned."*

The one thing that struck me as being important was the military's description of the agency that would likely monitor my movement in the Soviet Union, the KGB. The acronym stood for *Komitet Gosudarstvennoy Bezopasnosti or Committee for State Security*; a committee created for the first time in 1917 under another name but one that went through several notable changes until 1954 when after the death of Josef Stalin it was changed to KGB. It was impressed upon me that no matter what the name, the agency was always a secret organization whose secrets were rarely fathomable by ordinary mortals.

Since Canadian Intelligence knew that a tourist traveling in the Soviet Union could come under external surveillance, it was up to Intelligence to alert that person that a KGB agent would, in all likelihood, consider a tourist to be an enemy of the state. As a result, it would be the responsibility of a KGB agent to discover where a tourist spends his time and with whom. The aim of this surveillance was to discover whether or not a tourist was engaged in anti-Soviet activity. What made the task easier for the KGB is that an Intourist agent or guide would be assigned a tourist in most, if not all over-night stops. Also, NATO Intelligence was aware that KGB agents carry out their activities secretly and, therefore, conduct their activities very discreetly and quietly. *"Remember,"* I was told, *"every person who comes under surveillance is given a special name. Therefore, even in the presence of an agent, you would not be aware that you are the object of a conversation."*

It was quite apparent that the Soviet Union was opposed to tourists getting involved in what we would term to be a free market economy or the black market because it smacked of capitalism and was contrary to the philosophy of the October Revolution and would undermine the whole economic life of the country should it take hold. The KGB, I was informed, was a formidable force; an empire of nearly 400,000 officers inside the Soviet Union, 200,000 border troops, and an army of informants. Not only that, but it was also common knowledge that it had over 200 million citizens ready to do its bidding, not only within its own borders but even in instances when its citizens traveled abroad. In fact, in many cases the only way a Soviet citizen could get a visa to travel abroad was to agree in advance to do the KGB's bidding. It was not uncommon for a Soviet citizen to spy on a neighbour or to falsely testify against a relative. Worst of all, I was warned that *"the threat of arrest is always there..."*

Since each stop in the Soviet Union had to be planned in advance, I had to anticipate just how much time I wanted to spend in each section of the country and each major city. Having completed this exercise, and with the final goodbyes to staff and students, I had little left to do but ensure that my Volkswagen Variant would be in tip-top running condition, my passport and personal papers all in order, and the final clearance from Canadian authorities. I made a final visit to the local Post Exchange store and purchased some writing supplies, personal items of clothing such as shirts, blue jeans, golf shirts, briefs, and socks, a tape recorder, a camera, and gum, even though I was aware that most of these would be on the prohibited list.

Knowing that this information would be of value when crossing borders, I made a list of all of the items I would be taking. My passport, visa, travel coupons, currency, maps, emergency telephone numbers at the airbase and the Canadian Embassy in Moscow, and NATO contact numbers. I practiced some common Russian phrases even though I knew that my Intourist guides would be able to speak English; after all, that was one of the requests I made. Knowing the rudiments of the Ukrainian language and the Cyrillic alphabet made it rather easy to learn some Russian. I hoped that the trip would help me accomplish two important goals; to make contact with my relatives in Soviet Ukraine and in Poland and to witness, first hand, the devastation of the war.

As the date of departure got closer, I felt mentally and physically ready for the journey. Basically, the school year had ended on June 20 and all formal classes were behind me. The only thing missing was approval from Ottawa. Each succeeding day brought the same response from Base Security, *"Sorry, nothing today."* On June 26, I made the decision that I would abort the trip if clearance did not come before June 28. To delay the trip would mean that my proposed entry into Czechoslovakia would be out of synch. This delay would affect my scheduled arrival in every city en route and may well leave me without an Intourist guide in these centres. In fact, there were moments when I thought it best that the trip would be cancelled for this very reason.

I guess I should not have worried. True to form, at 0830 hours on the morning of June 27, I received a telephone call from the office of the Base Commander. All kinds of thoughts raced through my mind and not too many were positive. I knew that the call was about my impending trip to Russia. The distance from my quarters to the Office of the Base Commander was some 200 hundred yards but I covered the distance in a flash. Did I fail the security check? The news, however, was good. I could tell by the smile on the face of the Security Chief. His manner as he greeted me confirmed my suspicion. The answer to my request, I was certain, would be in the affirmative.

Sergeant Bileau handed me, unopened, a telegram from the Prime Minister's Office in Ottawa. But, before I could open the letter, he said to me that the Security Chief wanted to have a word with me. *"Flight Lieutenant Kashuba,"* was the opening statement from the Security Chief, *"we have the news that you have been waiting for. Still, I must say to you that it is not too late to change your mind. The general feeling here at headquarters is that you should not be encouraged to go."*

"Thank you, Sir," I responded. *"However, my mind is made up, even though I really do appreciate the reservations expressed by your office. My bags are packed."*

"In that case, sir, go ahead and read the telegram."

The telegram from the PMO was brief and to the point,

"Flight Lieutenant Kashuba. Stop. This is to inform you that your planned trip to the Soviet Union has been approved. Stop. Please ensure that the final details have been reviewed with rcaf 3-Wing officials..."

With that, the Base Commander summarized it this way, *"Lieutenant, it is my duty to reiterate some of the things we discussed in the formal briefing session. You are well aware of the potential dangers of travel in Iron Curtain Countries. You are also aware that Russia has its espionage network operating not only in its own country, but in Germany as well. Once the Russian Embassy is aware of this clearance to travel, you may well come under the surveillance of another nation even while here. You can easily be the victim of a false charge or the object of some kind of international intrigue. You know how to contact the Base if you run into any difficulty. Bon voyage."*

On the night before my journey was to begin, I was joined by friends from the base for an evening out at a local pizzeria. Sipping our drinks while waiting for our pizzas, I could not help but notice the furtive looks from a guy sitting in a booth next to ours. In my mind, the local restaurants were frequented by locals and by NATO servicemen. Somehow, neither this individual nor the female with him fit that mold. Not only was he keeping on eye on me, but it seemed as though he wanted to eavesdrop on our conversation. When I made mention of this to Dr. Phil Furey, an Australian medical doctor on assignment on our Base, he was quite philosophical about it all saying, *"...just disregard him; I'll keep an eye on him."*

When the dark-haired stranger and his female companion left, I approached the bartender and asked him about the couple. *"You mean the couple in the booth next to yours?"*

"Yes, yes. The dark, heavy set guy and the blond gal. Can you tell me anything about them? Their nationality?"

"Never saw them before. The only thing I can tell you is that they came in right behind you and wanted this particular booth. Their nationality? It was not German. Nor was it American. The guy, in particular, had a distinct foreign accent. Maybe an Eastern accent."

Was this a coincidence or was someone interested in my movements? Interested perhaps in the company I kept and in my drinking habits? The image of his physical features, his foreign accent, and his manner of dress were all filed away in my mind. So was the appearance of his female friend. *Somehow, I felt that this kind of incident would repeat itself. The only question was where and under what circumstances.*

3.

Welcome to the Soviet Union, Comrade

"It's a riddle wrapped in a mystery inside an enigma"
(Winston Churchill)

Sitting under the glare of the lights in the *interrogation room* while waiting for the arrival of yet another Soviet official was not easy. Although the room did have one small window, the chair seemed hard and the atmosphere unfriendly. My whole life seemed to flash before me as I pondered my fate and the events that led to my present circumstance. Would it be this lonely border crossing between Soviet Ukraine and Czechoslovakia that would see my undoing? There seemed to be a strange irony to the events as they unfolded. After all, the border crossing was near the Ukrainian border city of Uzhorod whose derivation came from the word *snake*, reminding me somehow of my interrogator. I wondered if this was the way that so many before me were questioned, cross examined and then sent to some place in *Siberia* never to be heard from again. *My mind wandered back to where my journey into the Soviet Union began.*

It seemed such a short time ago that in Zweibrucken I had checked my itinerary which was developed with the assistance of Intourist. My plan called for my first stop after leaving Austria to be a hotel in the heart of Prague, Czechoslovakia on July 2, 1967. That left me a couple of days in which I would have to get all of affairs in order before leaving the comfort and safety of the military base in Zweibrucken. As an afterthought, I decided to take with me the telegram that I had received from the Prime Minister's Office. One never knew when that kind of a document may prove to be of value. After all, not everyone travels to another country with the permission of the highest office in the land. Once again, I had checked my luggage to make sure that everything I had packed was in order and that nothing more was included. It occurred to me that it would not be out the realm of possibility that a prohibited object

24

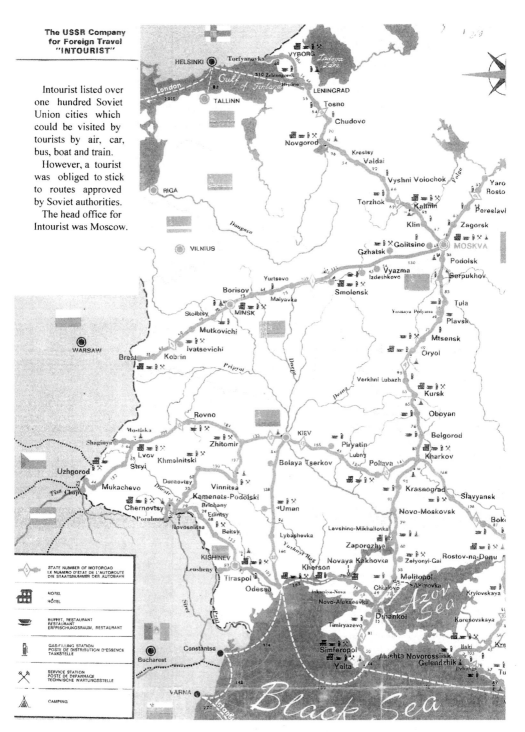

The USSR Company for Foreign Travel "INTOURIST"

Intourist listed over one hundred Soviet Union cities which could be visited by tourists by air, car, bus, boat and train.

However, a tourist was obliged to stick to routes approved by Soviet authorities.

The head office for Intourist was Moscow.

STATE NUMBER OF MOTOROAD LE NUMERO D'ETAT DE L'AUTOROUTE DIE STAATSNUMMER DER AUTOBAHN	
HOTEL HÔTEL	
BUFFET, RESTAURANT RESTAURANT ERFRISCHUNGSRAUM, RESTAURANT	
GAS-FILLING STATION POSTE DE DISTRIBUTION D'ESSENCE TANKSTELLE	
SERVICE STATION POSTE DE DEPANNAGE TECHNISCHE WARTUNGSSTELLE	
CAMPING	

Intourist Travel Map, approved in Moscow by the USSR Company for Foreign Travel, 1967. Tourists were restricted to travel on designated highways.

would find its way into my luggage placed there by someone else. I had an early breakfast with a few close friends, left a copy of my itinerary with Base Security and mailed one copy to my family in Edmonton before setting my sights on Vienna, Austria.

Leaving the Base on Sunday, June 30, my schedule called for an overnight stop in Vienna, one of the world's great cities; the city of Schubert, Strauss, Haydn, and Mozart. I had been to this beautiful city on two or three other occasions, one of them to attend the 1966 world hockey championships. However, I knew that the purpose of this trip would be quite different. I could not help but think about a movie I had recently seen that reminded me of Russia. The name of the movie was Dr. Zhivago, a poignant love story set in Russia during the Bolshevik Revolution. Images popped into my head about life in Siberia and how the human spirit was able to overcome so many obstacles and hardships. In my mind, I hoped that these images would not be a harbinger of things to come.

Looking up, I could see the directional sign which would take me to the Mannheim Autobahn. It was along this section of the national autobahn network that Adolf Hitler would land his aircraft during World War II and, escorted by military police astride their motorcycles, pay a visit to nearby military installations. It would now be the same area that the Americans would occupy and control from the nearby Ramstein Air Base which was the home of American singer Elvis Presley while he served his country in Germany. As I reflected on the journey before me and tried to keep pace with the traffic on the autobahn, it was very evident that Germany was very much a different country from what it had been when my dad's train took him through Berlin and the northern part of the country thirty-nine years earlier.

As the minutes and hours went by, I suddenly realized that traveling alone had its advantages. Living in Germany for two years made me realize just how crowded was the nation. Little wonder that Hitler wanted more land for his country's people. As I listened to the hum of the Volkswagen, I certainly did not miss the constant and incessant noise ever surrounding me on the military base. In addition, life on a military base meant that one was constantly in the presence of other people and it is for this reason that I began to appreciate the opportunity to spend some time with my own thoughts. My Blaupunkt radio became my constant companion and that is the way it would be for the next month. I recalled that on previous visits to Vienna, the trip seemed rather long. Not so this time. I arrived in Vienna much sooner than I had planned. That evening I was made welcome at an American military base. The officers' quarters were comfortable and the American officers were a friendly lot.

I always had a deep appreciation for Vienna. Interestingly, the dual monarchy called the Austro-Hungarian Empire was born in 1867, the same year as was Canada. Earlier, the Holy Roman Empire passed away and was replaced by the Empire of Austria in 1806. Ruled by the Habsburgs, the

Empire included Germans, Romanians, Czechs, Slovaks, Hungarians, Poles, Italians, Croats, Slovenes and Serbs. After World War I, the non-German peoples established their own nations while the German members of the Reichstag, the Imperial Parliament, proclaimed the Republic of German-Austria in November of 1918. Throughout this period of time, the city of Vienna played a pivotal role.

Even though July 1 was a holiday for Austrians, I did manage to get some valuable information at the American Military Base in Vienna. By virtue of its proximity to the Czech border, an agent in the travel agency knew a lot about travel in Iron Curtain Countries. In providing me with travel information, he seemed less than enthusiastic about my travel plans. His polite wishes were limited to *'good luck'* and *'have a nice trip'*. The only direct advice came over breakfast in the Officers Mess when Major Ramiriz said to me, *"Whatever you do, stay away from those Russian broads. They'll have your lunch and eat it too."* He seemed like an officer who knew what he was talking about. The Major further explained that he was in the Security Detachment and he knew how quickly an American can get into a jam in Russia. He left me with *"Remember, when you step on their soil, you fall under their jurisdiction. Be sure to obey their laws and you'll have no problem. A lot of what you hear about Eastern Bloc countries is grossly overblown; misrepresented."* His remarks did much to assuage any misgivings I may have had about my trip. I thanked him for his timely advice.

With lingering memories of Austrian Schnitzel, cordon bleu and Strudel, I left Vienna early on July 2. Vienna seemed to be unusually busy for such an early hour. In a way, I was glad that Ramiriz did not try to stuff me with too many security details, even though I could tell that he wanted to. As I zeroed in on the Czech border, I recited in my own mind the expectations that Intourist had of international travelers while in the USSR. I had my international driver's license and my CDN *Royal Canadian Air Force* vehicle plates in conformity with the International Road Traffic Convention. I felt quite secure with my knowledge of the speed limits in countries I would be visiting and the speed limits in zones where none were posted. In some cities, the speed limit would be 60 kilometres per hour and as low as 20 kilometres per hour at marked pedestrian crossings. Interestingly, my travel brochure indicated that it was illegal to drive a vehicle during the night with headlights on high beam. In fact, in some cities one was compelled to drive only with the *park* lights illuminated. In Czechoslovakia, I would be able to purchase additional automobile and liability insurance from a national insurance firm by the name of Ingosstrakh.

The countryside outside of Vienna was shrouded in a light fog which gave me an eery feeling. The light drizzle and Eastern European appearance to some of the vehicles headed towards Vienna told me that these vehicles were not built in the west. They looked, well, sort of weird. As I approached the border, a cold chill ran up and down my spine. It would be a scene that I would long remember and one that I had never seen before. As far as the eye could see to the left, a coiled barb wire fence-barrier was in plain view. Some sixty yards beyond the first fence was another coiled barb wire fence. Between the two fences was what the authorities loved to call *no man's land*; a buffer zone between Austria and Czechoslovakia. It was a common belief that Czech authorities would show no hesitation in using their weapons in this zone. To the right were two sentry posts and two more to the left. As I approached the security gate manned by no fewer than a dozen guards, I could see that the high-powered machine guns of the sentries trained directly at the windshield of my car.

As I brought my car to a stop, my mouth felt very dry. I looked around for some indication of welcome, perhaps a smile or an acknowledgment in the way of a nod. None was forthcoming. When I took a closer look at the guards located in the sentry posts, I was chilled by the sight of those machine guns trained directly upon me as I gingerly stepped out of my car. My legs seemed a little weak as if they didn't want to behave. I hoped that the guards did not recognize my anxiety. They exuded a no-nonsense approach to their duty. I could see that it would be very difficult to do anything other than to obey all commands. I watched nervously as an official approached my vehicle saying, *"Welcome to the Soviet Union, Comrade."* His demeanour was stern but his command of the English language seemed impeccable. *'How is it,'* I asked myself, *'that he automatically addressed me in English?'*

As the border guards examined my documentation, I was reminded of an incident the previous year en route to Baden Baden from Zweibrucken. By taking a shortcut through Biche, France I was able to cut about 40 kilometres from my trip. The purpose of my trip was to compete in a military golf tournament A border guard peered into my golf bag, took out a golf club, shook it, looked it over thoroughly, and asked me its purpose. I tried to explain in French but it appeared as though we were not communicating. He obviously knew sweet-tweet about golf. He took out another club and shook it. Somehow, both made a distinct rattling sound, perhaps from sand particles that found their way into the hollow shafts of the clubs. He must have thought that I was smuggling something into France. Why else would he cut off the rubber tops off each grip and peer into the hollow shaft of each? When he was satisfied that they contained nothing more than sand pebbles, he replaced the clubs into my bag with the command, *"proceed."*

"But, but what about my clubs. You've ruined them."

Somewhat irritated, he once again signalled me to proceed. I was about to ask him to replace the grips on each club. However, I thought better of it and proceeded on my way to the Canadian military base near the Black Forest in Germany. My *tipless* golf clubs were quite a conversation piece at the golf tournament! Just thinking about this incident brought a little bit of humour to my mind and made the border crossing just a little bit less stressful. Communicating with the border guards was not the easiest exercise I've ever had. Other than the one official who spoke English to me, the others conversed in German and in Czechoslovakian. Still, between the three languages I managed to respond to their questions. Finally, an official said *"ein moment bitte"* and left. He was back in a few minutes with a wan smile and an order to *"proceed comrade and have a good time in Russia."*

That's all there was to it. No tourist information, maps or booklets. No advice about the route to take or the road conditions. Any assistance in this regard would obviously go beyond the terms of reference for his office. As I drove away, the palms of my hands seemed sweaty as little tingles ran up and down my spine. I knew that those machine guns were still trained on my head. The paved highway leading into Czechoslovakia along the highlands east of the Vltava River Valley, which is a tributary of the famous Elbe River system, was much narrower than the highways to which I was accustomed. In fact, the change of scenery from Austria to Czechoslovakia was dramatic, to say the least. Although both were quite pastoral in nature, one could easily discern that the standard of living was considerably lower in this Iron Curtain country than was the case in Germany or Austria.

There were all manner of vehicles on the Czech highway. The cars looked chunky and small while the trucks looked like they came directly out of a Soviet factory. Along the highway there appeared to be constant reminders of war. It seemed that these kinds of scars were long ago repaired in Germany and in France. Here, it was as if nothing had changed since the defeat of the German wehrmacht in March of 1945; perhaps the Czechs wanted to keep it this way so as to provide a constant reminder of the horrors of war and the plight of the German Armies. It was difficult not to reflect upon the enormous losses that the Ukraine Front had suffered when it had reached the upper Vistula in March of 1945. Twenty five years later it was as if time had stood still. The smell of war seemed still to hang in the air and my thoughts turned back in time to September 1, 1939 when Germany attacked Poland, becoming the flashpoint for World War II. I was also reminded of how Hitler had earlier annexed this very region of Czechoslovakia.

It wasn't until I had reached the industrial city of Brno that I was able to put the thoughts of the war behind me. Well, maybe not completely behind me, but at least enough so that I could enjoy the sights, sounds and smells of Czechoslovakia. And yes, the countryside did smell of animals, farmyard manure, chickens, domesticated geese, pigs, vegetables, and industrial factories. During earlier times this region was known as Moravia and the city of Brno possessed many historical buildings and interesting museums. To the east is the Napoleonic battlefield with its Memorial to Peace and baroque palace where the ceasefire was signed.

To help me break up the fatigue of the drive, I pulled my Volkswagen into a farmer's driveway. *"Dzien dobry,"* I greeted the farmer working his garden. He seemed startled by my greeting, as though it were an uncommon experience. Still, he listened intently to me. It didn't take long for us to enter a rather lengthy, but awkward, conversation about farming and the economy in Czechoslovakia. He told me his name was Igor Braznovic and that he owned the small garden plot. I wanted to know who owned the larger plots of agricultural land nearby. However, before he could answer, we were suddenly interrupted by two military policemen who pulled in beside my Volkswagen. I guess they wanted to know why I had stopped and whether or not I was having car problems. I knew that this was my invitation to keep moving. Although their actions were efficient and not menacing in any way, I could see that they were used to giving commands without being challenged. When I told them that I was from Canada working in Germany and that I loved the countryside and the local people, they seemed to acknowledge my remarks. On impulse, I stuck out my hand to shake hands with one of the officers. He looked at me and then at my outstretched hand, shrugged his shoulders and shook my hand. The second officer did the same even though he looked somewhat suspiciously at my gesture of friendship. Looking into my rear-view mirror, I could see the two officers and the farmer watching me as I drove away. To me, it was a symbolic meeting of west and east. I smiled as I tuned my Blaupunkt to a local radio station. My destination would be the Intourist Hotel in the beautiful city of Prague.

As I proceeded towards Prague, it occurred to me that my parents were born and raised in Galicia, which was almost directly east of this part of Czechoslovakia. Although I wasn't certain, I assumed that this region would be a lot like the Galicia that my parents had left behind. Not far from here, and almost directly west, was the German city of Nuremberg, the site of the World War II criminal trials. Thinking about the Soviet Union, I knew that the communist system had groups of people's inspectors at every enterprise, collective and state farms and state institutions as well as inspection posts at lower units. Someone once said to me that there are about ten million such inspectors, many of whom were workers, engineers, technicians, and employees elected at general meetings. I had already noticed that members of the people's inspection groups saw to it that I was on schedule and stayed on my planned route.

It was evident that the ideological differences between Canada and the Soviet Union were as wide as was the global geography. Suddenly, I wished that I did not have to follow a pre-determined route. Still, I was very much looking forward to my first Soviet interpreter-guide so that I might begin to unravel, in my own mind, what Winston Churchill had meant when he said that, *'the Soviet Union is a riddle wrapped in a mystery inside an enigma.'* The time had come, I thought, to remove some of that mystery. I was looking forward to my first meal in Czechoslovakia; maybe some steaming boiled potatoes and sausages, mountains of caviar, and some mushrooms followed by a shot of their brandy and finally, some Armenian cognac washed down with Georgian tea from the samovar.

The Czech language is similar to Slovak, Polish, and, in many ways, the Ukrainian language. Both the Czechs and Slovaks used the Czech literary language until the middle of the 19th century, when a separate Slovak literary language based on the speech of the Slovak peasantry was created. The distinguishing features of Czechoslovakia are the two mountainous regions;

one partly enfolded by the Carpathian Mountains *(which stretch into Ukraine)* and the other the lowlands which are an extension of the Plain of Hungary. Coal and iron are of primary importance to the highly industrialized nation. Most of the fertile soils are found in Moravia and Slovakia. Of the fourteen million people living in the country, sixty-five percent were Czech or Slavic while thirty-five percent were Hungarians, Ukrainians, Germans, and Poles. Most embraced Roman Catholicism as their religion while at the same time the ruling communists saw the country as being atheistic in composition.

As I approached Prague, the federal capital of the Czechoslovakian Republic, I could see why its inhabitants were so proud of the city of over one million souls. It appeared to be much cleaner than was the city of Brno. Knowing that I would be using the local currency in Prague, I tried to re-orient my thinking to their terminology of crown, loruna, and hellers. The crown was pegged to the Soviet rouble and had an exchange rate of 7.14 crowns to the American dollar. However, a rate of about 16.09 crowns to the American dollar was being extended to tourists and reflected the importance of western currency to the economy of the country and the health of the black market.

Czechoslovakia was comprised of two provinces, Czech and Slovak. Both were formerly ruled by the Austrian Habsburgs and only came into existence as a political entity in 1918 at the close of World War I. The independence of the new nation was confirmed by the Treaty of St. Germain in 1919 between the Allies and Austria. However, after the German dictator Adolf Hitler rose to power in 1933, Germany claimed the Sudetenland on the pretext that it was a German-populated district. During the next few years, the expanding power of Germany in Europe was accompanied by increased pressure by the Hitler regime to include Czechoslovakia within the German *lebensraum* or living space. Through military and political manoeuvring, Czech and Slovakia came mainly under German control in 1939, with lesser parts being annexed by Hungary and Poland.

The trip from Vienna to Prague was less than 200 miles, a distance similar to that of Edmonton to Calgary with a driving time of slightly more than three hours. Yet, the trip took a full day. I entered Prague from the northwest having come up the Vltava *(the Moldau in German)* River. Prague was the chief commercial and industrial centre and the cultural capital of Czechoslovakia, is noted for book publishing and boasts Charles University which was founded in 1348. Falling in love with the city was easy. It was hard to believe that so beautiful a city or that so many architecturally-designed buildings could exist in an Iron Curtain country. I was particularly taken with the famous Karluv Most *(Charles Bridge)*, built in the 14th century and later embellished with statues of saints.

Having checked into my Intourist hotel located in the beautiful Vaclavske Namesti *(Wenceslas Square)*, I was met by my guide, a tall dark-skinned twenty-two year old Czech medical student by the name of Natasha. She did not give me the appearance that she was Czechoslovakian at all. But, in her flawless English, she insisted that she was. To me, she looked like she might be of Italian heritage or an Italian tourist in Prague. In short order she had me under tow and showing off Old Town which was traversed by crooked streets and contained architectural relics of Bohemian grandeur. The New Town was our next stop and, with its commerce and industry, provided quite a contrast to the Old Town. Natasha then took me to the west side of the river where a part of the city was called the Lesser Town, with a number of baroque palaces. Above this section was the Hradcany Castle, formerly the residence of the kings of Bohemia. *"The city of Prague,"* declared Natasha," *dates back to the 9th century. By the 14th century, Prague had become the second largest city in Europe behind Paris."* She then went on to explain that during World War II the city was occupied by German forces from March, 1939 until May, 1945. It would be one year after my visit that the city would once again be the scene of turmoil when, in August of 1968 the Soviet troops invaded Prague amid massive demonstrations.

As I continued to assimilate the beauty of the city, I was in a state of mild but pleasant shock. I never suspected that a city in Czechoslovakia could be so beautiful. I loved its people, too. To me, they seemed to be somewhat different from the Slavs I had known. They were more like the Ukrainians from the Black Sea region of Ukraine. From Odessa or from the Sea of Azov region which is closer to countries such as Turkey and Greece where its inhabitants are darker-skinned than are those of central Ukraine. The women, in particular, seemed to be more beautiful than I had imagined. *"Are you a fan of the Beetles,"* asked Natasha.

Her question caught me off guard. Her near-perfect English intrigued me and her voice seemed to have a slight Scottish brogue sound to it. I wondered how she came by it. I couldn't imagine her being educated in Scotland. Yet I could sense that her education did have a British influence. *"Yes,"* I replied. *"I was really weaned on Beetle music. Naturally, at first I was a fan of country and western. Have you heard of Hank Williams and Johnny Cash?"*

"No, I haven't. Are they classical singers?"

I could tell from her quizzical look that she was not into country music. Although I enjoyed my conversation with her about music, it seemed as though she wanted to get on to another topic. *"Are you a member of the Communist Party,"* I asked her.

"Yes, I am. Otherwise I would not be here tonight showing you our beautiful Prague. All Intourist guides, I imagine, are members of the Communist Party."

"Do you believe in their ideology?"

"Of course I do. Don't you believe in the principles of the Communist Party?"

"What about democracy, democratic principles, and our system of

government in Canada and the United States? What do you know of these?"

"Well, sir," impishly replied Natasha, *"I know enough about democracy to know that it is not an acceptable form of government for our country. Our government wants control over the production and distribution of goods and services; an equitable distribution of our wealth. In your country eighty-five percent of the wealth is in the hands of fifteen percent of its residents. That would be unacceptable to us."*

I could see that Natasha was well prepared for my questions and seemed to have all of the party-line answers. Consequently, I dropped any further discussion about democracy and communism. It seemed that she was too ready to try to change my beliefs rather to listen to anything positive that I might have to say about democracy. She did make it quite obvious that she was an active member of the Communist Party and wanted very much to adhere to the principles of communism. I couldn't quite make up my mind whether or not she was trying to convert me. Suddenly, she wanted to tell me about the Great Patriotic Struggle. In Canada, we always called it World War II, but not so in the Soviet Union, it seemed. *"Do you enjoy military service,"* she ventured.

"Well," I replied, *"What makes you think that I am in the military?"*

It was obvious that she wanted to discuss matters pertaining to the military. She was not satisfied with my response that I had little to do with the military. Finally, and with great reluctance, she gave up on her attempt at separating me from any information about military operations in Germany. As we continued our tour of Prague, I found it to be a very attractive and friendly city. The park on the banks of the River Elbe seemed to envelope us as we took a seat on a bench on a leafy promenade. There seemed to be no shortage of young people walking in the park. This, to a large degree, came about because very few residents had their own car. I noted that the males generally liked to wear leather jackets and the girls seemed to favour stockings and heeled shoes. Many listened to transistor radios and nibbled dried vegetables or a *moroznic,* which was their version of ice cream. Perhaps as was typical of young people elsewhere, the males seemed to be watching the girls while the girls demurely shied away. Natasha broke the silence by asking me what I was thinking about.

"Oh, nothing really. Except that it almost feels to me as though I had been here before. As though I were on my way home. Yes, I feel that these people are no strangers to me." The words I put to my thoughts even surprised me. I then went on to explain to her that despite our political differences, I had a great deal of respect for the Soviet Union and its people. *"But,"* I concluded, *"I cannot accept your politics."*

When I got back to the hotel that evening, I replayed the day's events in my mind much as I had watched hockey replays on Hockey Night in Canada. I felt like a Foster Hewitt doing a television replay in a hockey game between the Toronto Maple Leafs and the Montreal Canadiens. 'Yes,' I concluded, '*dealing with Natasha is much like a hockey game featured on Hockey Night in Canada. Like a seasoned hockey player, she portrayed a variety of subtle moves.*' It struck me that my guide knew much more about me than I did about her. The question was, how did she get this information? Could I conclude that each of my guides would have advance information about my past? About my political leanings? For certain, tomorrow would be another day and I would have to make a few moves of my own. '*Who knows,*' I concluded, '*but that influence is a two-way street.*'

"*You have about thirty minutes in which to have dinner,*" said the Intourist clerk at the front desk. I noted that her English was not nearly as good as that of Natasha. Still, I was surprised to learn that so many who worked at the Intourist hotel could speak English. But then, why not? After all, many of their clients were English, were they not? How could a local or national resident afford their exorbitant prices? I knew that if I did not join the other guests for dinner, I would have no dinner at all that evening. If there were restaurants nearby, I did not see them. Besides, I had already paid for the meal in hard currency.

The hotel's dining room was stately. So were my hostesses. There seemed to be a greater number of them than there were dinner guests. They seemed to stand around a lot. Stoically. '*How like a communist operation,*' I thought. With the pace of a snail being the norm, I worried that they might not get to me at all before closing time. Maybe they were using delaying tactics; a sort of work-to-rule procedure. The food, to my surprise, was much like that of Germany. Schnitzels seemed to be the order of the day and their heavy, black bread was superb. And, the red wine could have been from the Mosel in Germany. As the evening wore on, I noticed that the patrons tended to mingle. Earlier during the dinner hour I was joined by a young couple. This would have been an unusual occurrence in Canada yet seemed to be an acceptable practice here. They spoke a little English. I mixed my English with a little bit of Ukrainian and we got along just fine. The more schnapps we drank, the easier was our ability to communicate.

"*What do you make of the communist way of life,*" asked Igor. For some reason, just about everyone I met seemed to be named Igor or Natasha. Perhaps this was simply a coincidence. But then, maybe these were pseudonyms for another name and not their real names. Maybe it was a code name or a name given these folks by the Communist Party.

"*Yes,*" I replied, trying my best to be diplomatic, "*there is much to be admired about the communist way of life. They have accomplished much in the field of science. In the field of sports. In hockey.*" I could see that the remarks had struck a chord. They warmed to the conversation and seemed to descend upon me like locusts on a hot summer's night in Alberta. They suddenly wanted to pump all kinds of information into me about the advantages of their way of life. I could tell that they knew very little about democracy and about America. And, what they were able to tell me about politics in the western world didn't seem to wash. To get away from them, I asked Natasha if she would like to dance. To my surprise, she accepted. Not only that, but I also thought that she wanted to dance far too close to me. The faint smell of her perfume seemed irresistible. When I got to my hotel room, I felt that I had left them much too late and after far too many drinks.

Morning came too early, far too early. Since I did have some flex time, I called Intourist in Prague to tell them that I would be spending another day in Prague before leaving for Warsaw. After I had made the arrangements, I had some doubts about the change of plans. Perhaps it would have been better to stay on schedule. Still, I thought about all of those check points that Intourist had established. Why not throw these out of kilter? It was a pity that Natasha was committed to spend the day with another tourist. I knew that it would not be the same without her.

The second day of my stay in Prague was quite a contrast to the first day. I got the feeling that my activities were being monitored by at least one member of the local militia. I suppose they wanted to know why I would want to spend another day in Prague. I spent most of the day in and around Wenceslas Square. There was plenty to see. The place was really alive during the daytime. I was surprised to see the number of western-like shops in the downtown area. I found that most of these were strictly for tourists. The local people simply could not afford the goods offered for sale in these shops. Besides, most shop owners wanted hard currency for their goods. In fact, they seemed only to be interested in American currency. It would be here that I would have my very first lesson about the workings of the black market. Many entrepreneurs on the street seemed to be able to speak English. I noted that they used a variety of means to get my attention. For certain, they were much more interested in me today, now that Natasha was not with me. Some wanted to sell something. Others wanted to exchange their currency or Russian roubles for American currency. The exchange rates they were quoting were several times higher than was the official exchange rate.

As I continued with my sightseeing, I was ever cognizant of the watchful eye of a member of their militia. I recalled my briefing session at Zweibrucken and recalled the words of Major Tremblay, 'Remember, nothing is really as it seems. You will encounter some of the most sophisticated means of spying upon you that has ever been developed. A gesture or an innocent remark may well find its way to an unintended target. Always use caution as though your every remark is being recorded. Act as though you are being filmed. Maybe, just maybe, you are.' Going over the previous night's conversation, I wondered whether I might have said something that would have tweaked their interest.

To understand the pervasiveness of Communism in selected republics of the USSR, one would have to compare the percentages of Russians in the total population before World War II and after World War II. Some statistics of this particular ethnic mix became available by 1965 and showed that in Ukraine the percentage doubled from about eight percent to over sixteen percent and in Latvia from twelve percent to well over twenty-six percent. On the other hand, the percentage increase was relatively slight in Belarus from just under eight percent to slightly over eight percent.[1] Why then, were the increases so large in Ukraine and Latvia? Did this reflect a Soviet policy at *russification*? If that were the case, why only the small increase in Belarus?

It seemed to me that this influx of Russians was directed at specific sections of these nations. These were not your ordinary everyday Russians that found their way into these Soviet satellite nations. They formed up a part and parcel of the KGB. I was convinced that most of them were from the military and, from what I was able to discern, this intrusion was considerable in cities such as Prague, Warsaw, Minsk and Kyiv; cities that were on my planned itinerary. As well, I was not surprised to learn that Western Ukraine was a region ripe for this kind of influx of Russians–a region that was annexed in 1939 and where there were few Russians up until that time but, according to intelligence reports, were cropping up in all West Ukraine centres.

But then, this movement of peoples was not constrained to Russia or to Russians. The same report shows that military and non-military personnel from republics such as Poland, Belarus and Ukraine ended up in republics such as Kazakhstan and especially in the eastern regions of the USSR–some went willingly while others were forcibly re-located. Many were peasants while others were skilled workers and graduates of higher educational institutions. Various subtle methods were used to re-locate individuals and families. Some were simply directed where they were to go because of the interests of the state. If Prague were an example, it seemed that the reason for their presence was quite obvious; it was none other than control. Russians coming to a republic would use Russian as the language of communication while Ukrainians going to Kazakhstan would be forced to use a language understood in that republic–Russian. All of this seemed as though it were a master plan to *russify* all USSR republics.

Early the next day I set my sights on Warsaw. My planned trip would take me from Prague to Wroclaw, Lodz and Warsaw. The distance to be traveled was about 300 miles; a trip that would take six hours, or so I thought.

---

1   Naulko, V. I. Etnichny sklad naselennya Ukrayinskoyi RST (Ethnic Composition of the Population of the Ukrainian SSR) Kyiv, 1965, pp. 12 - 13.

4.

Postwar Poland

"Poland has not yet perished..."
First line of Polish national anthem

I left Prague feeling that I had made a new friend, glad that my introduction to the Soviet Union took place in a country so friendly as Czechoslovakia. The two-lane paved road leading out of Prague was busy with morning traffic mixed with farmers shuttling their farm tractors and horse-drawn wagons along the same road. I felt as though I was caught in a time warp watching life unfold at a snail's pace. By ten in the morning I was within striking distance of the Polish border and very much prepared to see more barbed wire fence, border guards, and security checks. I would not be disappointed.

Even though the Polish border guards did not speak English, they acted as though they expected my arrival as they checked my credentials. Perhaps they had access to my file and were aware that my parents immigrated to Canada from Poland. As a youngster, I remember listening to my parents converse with others in Polish when the occasion called for it, at the same time noting the similarities between Ukrainian and Polish. Even these infrequent moments of exposure to the Polish language helped me with communication at the border crossing. However, when an official listened to my attempts at speaking Polish, I noted that he could not suppress a chuckle.

The number of vehicles crossing the border into Poland was small but that did not seem to hasten my clearance. A guard excused himself and went inside the guardhouse to make a telephone call. Would that call be to Moscow or to Warsaw? Looking around I could see the barbed wire and the border guards with their usual machine guns. Finally, another official came back and, to my surprise, addressed me in English, *do you know, comrade, the conditions under which you will be traveling in our country?*

"Yes," I told him, *"I am aware of speed limits, school zones, prohibited zones, and conduct when approached by a police officer."*

He did not seem to be satisfied with my responses. *"No, no Pan Kashuba. I am asking about our laws. About our currency. About buying and selling on the illegal black market and about our government."* After further discussion, he seemed satisfied with my answers. But, abruptly, he stuck a finger in my face, *"Pan Kashuba, my documents say that your parents were born in Plazow, Poland. Is that correct?"*

"Yes, they were born in Galicia."

"Well, never mind. It is all a part of Poland now. Welcome to Poland, comrade."

Leaving the border crossing behind me, I reflected about his remarks and had to conclude that he exhibited about as much enthusiasm as a mannequin with a personality to match. His questions did surprise me and confirmed that Iron Curtain countries were quite willing to lay claim to the citizenship of an emigrant from Poland *if it suited their purpose.* I suppose they did this because many expatriates had recently become an excellent source of American currency, a much needed commodity. The fact that security at the border had information about me and my family was not a surprise to me either. Knowing the communist way of life and the role of the KGB, I expected no less. In a way, all of this made me feel important. Thinking ahead to Russia, I knew that their files would be no less thin; neither would be their interest in me.

Poland derived its name from Polanie or *plains* people who settled in northern Europe before the birth of Christ. Over the years, Poland has had its share of political problems. The nation was partitioned in 1795 among Russia, Prussia, and Austria. It reappeared once again in 1918 after World War I. During World War II, much of Poland was destroyed and was just now being rebuilt in an attempt to recapture its rich architectural and artistic heritage. One could almost sense the tensions within the country among factions advocating greater freedom and flexibility and those opposing it. With the presence of the powerful secret police apparatus, it wouldn't take much provocation to be arrested and detained without trial.

Immediately that I crossed the border, the changes in the countryside, mode of travel, the manner in which small farmers worked the land and their pace of work really hit home. Why there were not more vehicular accidents on Polish roads was a mystery to me. Time and time again and without warning, a horse-drawn wagon would pull out onto the main highway. The drivers seemed oblivious to the oncoming traffic. Fortunately for me, the horses never seemed to be spooked or to panic in the midst of the sudden appearance of my Volkswagen. Out of all of this chaos there seemed to develop some sort of order. As time went on, it all seemed so natural and commonplace, as though this was the way it was meant to be.

Fine, I thought. Now I can concentrate on my journey and try to enjoy my trip. It all gave me an opportunity to take my mind back to the days that my

A typical highway in Poland showing vehicular traffic and horse-drawn wagons, 1967.

ancestors roamed this land. Names of regions of Poland and the major cities that I heard dad talk about popped into my head. I knew without driving very far into Poland that this region was famous for its sugar beets, hogs, cattle, rye and potatoes. To the east was the cattle country and to the south lay the industrial region of Katowice and Krakow. Soon, I would be in the Lodz industrial region to be followed by the industrial region of Warsaw. Perhaps the biggest difference between this and the region from whence my parents emigrated was that more dairy farms would likely be evident in the Plazow region and, of course, the absence of industry.

Earlier, my journey from Prague took me almost directly east to the industrialized region of Katowice in Poland. At this point the two-lane highway swung north towards the city of Warsaw. As I left the Katowice region, the pace of activity seemed to slow to a snail's pace. Local farmers seemed to have little respect for vehicular traffic, treating cars as though they were a blight on their kingdom. Even though I carried considerable auto insurance, I drove with great care. I knew that any kind of a mishap would delay my progress on the long journey.

Naturally, the Communist-produced Intourist Guide Book would never make mention of the Black Madonna, Jasna Gora, or the Mother of God, but it did indicate that the small city of Czestochowa would be a good place to stop for a late lunch. Since it was not listed as a place of a stop-over in my itinerary, I was not compelled to check in with authorities. No doubt the Soviet surveillance over me would be far more stringent once I reached Russia. The small towns near Czestochowa reminded me of the province of Quebec where the spires of Catholic Churches stood out, reaching heavenward. At the entry to one such community I stopped at the edge of the road to take a photograph of a prominent-looking local church just as a multitude of faithful were leaving Sunday Mass. My concentration was broken just before I clicked the shutter of the camera. In Polish, I heard someone say, *"why have you stopped here?"*

From the tone of his voice it was obvious that he did not expect an answer. It was both an admonition and a command. I looked at him and he looked at me. I followed his gaze as it switched to my Volkswagen. Then, the answer occurred to me. In my mind flashed a picture of the Nazi blitzkrieg overrunning Poland in 1939. I had the vision of all of those foreigners in this man's land. I offered my apologies, quietly got into my Variant and drove away without taking a photograph, all the while reminding myself of another line in Poland's national anthem, '*...that which foreign force has seized...*' Even with his gruff manner, he left me with the impression that he loved the soil beneath his feet and had a special reverence for God. It appeared obvious that he looked upon me as being a foreigner from Germany. Perhaps, in many ways, he was typical of post-war Poles. As for me, it was hard not to admire his attitude.

Restaurants seemed to be as scarce as hen's teeth but I did spot one nearly at the end of the town. To my surprise, the inside reminded me of the typical German gasthaus; a gasthaus that one might expect to find in Zweibrucken. On the perimeter of the bar area, surrounded by higher stools, were two or three tables and a couple of booths. Since the service was rather slow, I struck up a conversation with a bartender by the name of Hans. Shortly, a young couple by the name of Karl and Maria Buchinski joined in our conversation. They seemed to be full of questions, saying at the outset that they had noticed my *machyna (Volkswagen)* parked out front and knew that I was a tourist. They wanted to know about the car's license plate and the country of origin, saying that they were aware that D stood for Deutschland and P for Poland. When I told them that I was from Canada serving on a military base, their questions became even more inquisitive. They joined me for a light lunch of bigos, made of sauerkraut, chunks of beef and vegetables, dark rye bread and Zywiec beer. I paid for the meals in American currency and got back what seemed to be an awful lot of Polish currency (zloty). This re-affirmed the power of the American dollar and reflected an exchange rate considerably higher than the official rate of exchange.

My thoughts about the currency were interrupted when the couple asked me if I would consider staying the night with their family. For whatever reason, I accepted their invitation while at the same time telling them about my obligation to stay only at designated hotels. The couple, in their mid-twenties, lived a short distance north of Czestochowa with their parents on what appeared to be a *dacha* or a small farming operation. Knowing that large tracts of land were prohibited, I concluded that this was their garden plot. The family home looked very Germanic to me, right down to the woodwork in the hallway and the scattered rugs in the family room. The home even had indoor plumbing and electricity.

We spent the evening talking about politics and the war. They all appeared to be very interested in Canada and the United States and my work in Germany. At first I thought that the information that I was providing them was common knowledge. Not so. As a result, I concluded that the Polish nation was being fed a *cleanitized* diet of misinformation from the Communist State. The family felt that their nation was expending too much money on the military which was structured after the Soviet model. According to their laws, each Pole was subject to the decision of the Defense Committee of the Council of Ministers, and in times of emergency could be called up for active duty. This law, I was told, applied to those males between the ages of eighteen and fifty and females between the ages of eighteen and forty. When I asked them about their political leanings, they indicated that they belonged to a group named *Znak* which was headquartered in Krakow. The purpose of the organization was to advance the proposition that a distinction should be made between the State and the Communist Party and that faithful Catholics could establish a working relationship with the State without admitting the atheistic ideology of the other.

If there was any limitation to the topics which could be discussed, I did not detect it. Our conversation was free-wheeling and no topic, it seemed, was sacred. For sure, their wine and liquor were as good as anything I had tasted in Canada, all of which likely added to our desire to talk about our respective countries. Having gone through a considerable amount of wine, beer and liqueur, we finally turned in at one in the morning. The bed that someone in the family gave up for me was comfortable and the goose-down quilt was sumptuous. As I slipped into slumber land, I couldn't quite make up my mind whether our conversations were generated by curiosity or by some other motive. I hoped that I had not shared any sensitive information with them. In the end, I concluded that I had none to offer them.

Consistent with my plan, I was up early in the morning, and after a breakfast of hot porridge, my hosts bade me farewell. I left them a package of chewing gum and a couple of ballpoint pens. They seemed to be very happy with the small gifts. As I left Czestochowa, I recalled Karl saying to me that Poland's economy remained in a veritable nightmare of managerial and production chaos and that *shortages of the most elementary items were evident everywhere.* As well, Karl was of the opinion that this region of Poland was turning into an environmental disaster whose magnitude could only be imagined and that the great River Vistula was being polluted by salinity and other industrial wastes. Trees in local forests were being threatened by poisonous runoff from a chemical plant, deforestation throughout the country was causing a dangerous drop in the local water table, and the air in cities such as Krakow and Katowice was thick with the soot from smoke-belching stacks and steel mills.

Along the route I spotted a farmer tending to a rather large garden of potatoes and beets. Since there was considerable room to pull off the road, I took the opportunity to stop for a chat. *"How is the crop of potatoes?"* I asked him in my best Polish. He looked surprised while at the same time looking as though he needed a bit of a rest. It didn't take too much to draw him into a conversation as we talked about his garden plot and the vegetables he grew in it. It was apparent that his family had lived here for many years and even though he longed, or so it seemed from our conversation, for a democratic government, he did not seem to be too unhappy with his present circumstance. As I pulled onto the highway, I peeked into my rear-view mirror to see if there was any traffic. In the distance and traveling in the same direction was a car that looked at lot like that driven by Karl and Maria.

As I proceeded to Warsaw in light traffic, I kept an eye out for the car as I recalled stories of the pervasiveness of KGB operations. In fact, the same car, now in heavier traffic was still tailing me. Traveling through a small village, I suddenly made a turn to the right without as much as a signal. I watched as the suspicious car passed and although I could not be certain, the driver looked very much like Karl. When I resumed my trip to Warsaw, the car was nowhere to be seen. *Perhaps,* I thought, *the incident is a stark reminder of the nature of informing in a communist state and how the KGB used this technique to their advantage.*

However, I could not get the incident out of my mind. I reflected upon the characteristics of communism and how Soviet policies were introduced beginning in December of 1922. For, it was at this time, consistent with Lenin's theories of governance, that foreign affairs, army and navy, foreign trade, finance and communications were all centralized in Moscow. This centralization was reached through the Communist Party and Stalin transformed the Party through arrests, exiles, purges and executions. As someone once said, *'he appointed and he removed.'* It was this system of informing that seemed to drive the Party. It was said that in order to safeguard yourself, you had to inform on a friend. For example, if one person made some derogatory remarks against the government or a party official, you were compelled to immediately go to the police. You *had* to protect yourself because the critic might have been sent by the police in the first place simply to test you! In the event that you did not go to the police, you would be arrested for being *an enemy of the people.*

As I approached the city of Warsaw, I recalled that it was nearly 28 years ago on August 31, 1939 that Hitler had given his Generals their secret orders. Hidden by trees along a road on the German side of the frontier, a fictitious Polish attack on a German radio station would be used as an excuse to attack Poland. It was on this occasion that the tanks and motorized infantry crashed through the Polish lines. Hitler unveiled a new kind of warfare that Hitler's Generals had perfected in Spain. The Poles were no match for the superior armour of the Nazis. Their communications linkages shattered by the lightning advance, thousands of Poles retreated or were captured and herded into prison camps by the victorious Germans.

The Nazi blitzkrieg, coupled with Hitler's special arrangement with Russia wherein Poland was partitioned between the two powers, facilitated a simultaneous Russian invasion from the east destroying the partially mobilized Polish Army in barely more than a month. The persecutions of Jews began in the towns and villages and even the oldest women were examined with a whip to see if they were useful as workers. After millions of Jews were killed under the most appalling of conditions, the last survivors of the Warsaw Ghetto put up a bitter struggle.

It wasn't until I approached the centre of Warsaw that I began to realize just how much damage Hitler inflicted upon this once beautiful city. All of the scars were still there; at least that's what it looked like to me. The closer I got to the heart of the city, the greater was the horror of destruction. My Intourist Hotel was right downtown which gave me an opportunity to view the sights first hand. To my surprise, the city had done two things—on the one hand, many of the buildings destroyed by war were left in that condition as a lasting monument to the horrors of war while on the other hand the Poles had completely rebuilt many of the downtown buildings retaining much of the pre-war architectural design. Somehow, the buildings, even though they looked statuesque, continued to look very communistic in appearance.

Since Warsaw was annihilated during the war and rose like a phoenix from the ashes, it was essentially a post-war city. In place of what might have been an aging population, it now boasted a population of younger people thereby weakening many of its centuries-old traditions and taking on many of the attributes of a modern western city. For me, the city epitomized a blend of old and new.

The Poles that I met in the hotel, which was within a stone's throw of the giant Palace of Culture and Science, were much more upbeat than were their country cousins. To make matters even more pleasant, I had the advantage of an Intourist guide for the duration of my stay in the city. Much like my guide in Prague, Justyna told me that she was a university student majoring in modern languages with English being her second language. By this time I knew the inflated value of the American dollar on the street and hoped to put it to good use living 'high off the hog'. In showing me around downtown Warsaw, Justyna must have read my mind when she said, "Yes, comrade. First, it was the Nazi army that inflicted considerable damage upon our beautiful city. Then, towards the end of the war, the Nazis did it again to us because of our underground resistance. Finally, it was the turn of the Russians to destroy what was left when they routed the Germans."

"Yes, it's too bad that these belligerent forces didn't fight their battles somewhere else. Maybe the Sahara Desert. Or, how about the moon?"

My attempt at a little bit of humour was somehow lost on my guide. She seemed to be pre-occupied with her own thoughts about Warsaw. "Remember, Pan Kashuba," continued Justyna, "many visitors come here from the West. Most bring western goods with them. Sometimes, small items of consumer goods or clothing. They then sell them on the black market. Or they barter with these goods."

"Is there anything wrong with that?"

"No, I suppose, if you don't mind spending some time in our jails. At any rate, it is my duty to tell you that the laws of our country prohibit you from engaging in this kind of illegal activity. To do so is a crime against the state punishable by our laws."

"I am not interested in selling or trading any goods," I assured Justyna. "The purpose of my visit to Warsaw is to walk on the same soil that my parents walked before coming to Canada."

"Yes, I did note that your parents were born in Eastern Poland."

"Actually," I reminded her, "my purpose in coming to Poland is to better understand the land and its people. And, I might add, I have a deep and abiding appreciation for this land and its peoples, be they Polish or Ukrainian."

Justyna, although taken aback by my reference to the ethnic Ukrainians, struck me as representing the heart and soul of the nation. On the one hand I found that she wanted to apologize for the condition of the city and the poverty evident everywhere while at the same time being ever ready to defend her city. I asked Justyna to join me for dinner that evening. I was glad that she accepted my invitation. The menu for foreign tourists surprised me. I had hoped to be served a typical Polish dinner; perhaps some pierogies and Hungarian goulash. What I got seemed to be totally American. Even though we had limited choice from the menu, the basic meal was sufficiently comprehensive--made up of borsch, meat, potatoes, deep rye bread, schnitzel, gravy, those ever-present mushrooms, an assortment of other vegetables, and a sumptuous dessert tray. I opened my meal with a Polish beer, tried some of their red wine, and finished the meal with a cognac. Justyna ate very sparingly. She did not even finish one glass of wine. No matter, I soon felt very much at home and Justyna, for all I knew, could have been the girl next door. Well, almost.

Listening to music provided by a small band, I was jolted out of my daydream when I heard Justyna remark, "I understand, Pan Kashuba, that you have an important role in the military." I thought for a moment about her question. Why did my guides always assume that I did something special in the military? Was she curious or was it required of her that she ask me? If the latter were true, why, then were her questions so direct and without any semblance of subtleness?

"Well, Justyna, permit me to ask you a question first. Are you a card-carrying member of the Communist Party?"

"Yes, of course. I think you know the answer. My work as a member of the Party allows me to attend a university. From this, I have some assurance that I will have a job once I graduate."

I could see that she was not prepared for my next question when I asked, "to whom do you report your findings, Justyna?"

From her evasiveness, I could see that pursuing the matter further would be useless. She denied having to report to anyone. No doubt she knew that I did not believe her. Seeing that the flow of information would be one way, I decided to change my question to one about the educational programs in Warsaw and how young people were able to afford to attend a post-secondary school institution. She seemed much more comfortable with this kind of a discussion. When the band struck up a Viennese waltz, I asked Justyna for a dance. She declined, saying that she was not permitted to dance with a tourist.

Once finished with dessert, we planned the balance of the evening. Justyna had a map of the downtown region of the city and showed me the route we could take by auto to see the heart of Warsaw. She made it clear that she was not to stay out longer than 2300 hours. With that, she excused herself for a moment. Out of the corner of my eye I noticed that Justyna made a bee-line for the lady's room. When she emerged in a few moments, I watched as she made a brief telephone call. Even with my limited knowledge of the role of guides, I suspected that the call was not to her mother. On the contrary, it was likely to a ranking officer of the party or the local secret service police. Maybe even the KGB.

The next day came all too early. Sitting over breakfast, the first thing I missed was an English newspaper and the latest information about the impending crisis in Egypt and Lebanon. I also wanted to get the latest scores in the major leagues of baseball. As I was thinking about what might have been, I could sense the gentle smell of perfume.

"Good morning, Pan Kashuba," was Justyna's greeting. Her showing up at the restaurant surprised me. I knew that she was not compelled to spend another day with me. Besides, after the previous night, I thought that I might want to spend a little bit of time on my own.

"You look good this morning," was my opening line as Justyna smiled demurely. Not only that, but I suspected, from the scent of her perfume, that she liked all things Western. Conversation on this day came more easily and, as the morning wore on, I was glad that Justyna was my guide. She knew a lot about the city and the history of Poland and Galicia. She even knew a great deal about Canada. And, she seemed to know a lot about me. Try as I might, I could not get any personal information from her. It was as if she wanted to keep her personal life just that. For, in the final analysis, who was to say that she was a student. Or Polish for that matter. She could have been a girl from Moscow on the payroll of the KGB.

To my surprise, Justyna gave me a big hug as we said our goodbyes saying, *"Pan Kashuba, I wish you luck in searching out your family. Please drive carefully, especially when you reach Russia."* I had to admit that behind that inscrutable but gentle face beat the heart of a compassionate girl. If nothing else, she made me feel like a cad and just a little bit guilty. I had it in my mind that she was no more than a communist lackey. I believe that I was wrong.

After bidding Justyna adieu, I was approached by a stranger at the entrance to my hotel. Having become accustomed to the East Europeans, it was obvious that he knew that I carried American currency with me. Without hesitation and in broken English, he asked me if I would like to exchange some American currency for Polish zloty. It was here that I discovered that the exchange rate on the American dollar was several times that of the official rate. Knowing how little I would have to pay locally for any Polish goods that I wanted to purchase, I decided that I would have to guard against exchanging too much of my hard currency. Since Soviet laws prohibited me from taking Polish zloty out of Poland, I did not want to accumulate too much Polish currency. I also knew that I would have difficulty in spending all of it in Poland in the short time available to me. In fact, carrying too much Polish zloty on my person could lead to another problem should I be confronted by local police and asked to explain the source of those funds.

As I left Warsaw that morning, I felt that it was a pity that I could not spend more time in the historic city. I was beginning to develop a liking for the historical aspects of the city and for its people. The fact that my parents spent their childhood relatively near Warsaw somehow made me feel at home. My excitement and apprehension heightened as I set out for the next leg of my journey to the land of enchantment, Russia. I reflected on my decision of the previous day to present Justyna with a couple of souvenirs that I had purchased in Warsaw. Somehow, I felt that bringing them with me across the border into Russia would be more trouble than they were worth. I was not surprised when Justyna accepted the souvenirs. She left me with some important advice, "...*the Russian authorities will not treat you lightly should you get involved in any wrongdoing.*" I promised Justyna that I would exercise more care in the future. As brief as was our time together, I got the impression that she was a fun-loving and gentle human being.

As I set my sights on Russia, I felt comfortable with the knowledge that German engineering in my Volkswagen Variant would not let me down. It was hard not to reflect on what the Soviet planners and ideologues had done to Poland. There were the high rise buildings for families that were supposed to be a panacea for the workers. The planners were wrong on all scores. The apartment buildings and industrial installations projected an ugly and grimy scene. Instead of a socialist city, they created a monstrosity. After twenty years of Soviet-enforced Marxism-Leninism, the quality of life in Poland seemed to be steadily deteriorating. It appeared as though too many Poles were losing their will to struggle for a better life.

Horror stories about shopping expeditions by a Polish housewife seemed legendary. It was not uncommon for her to quit work around two o'clock to go shopping for food and various household items. She would sometimes stand in a queue at the butcher shop to buy meat with her ration card, only to find that the government-operated shop would have run out of meat before her turn came up. So what does she do? She rushes to another shop to queue up again only to experience the same kind of frustration. When she gets home, she will have to walk up the stairs to her apartment on the fifth floor because the elevator is out of order or the state is on an energy conservation kick and the electricity has been temporarily turned off. Then, she has to cook dinner, serve it, wash the dishes, and put the children to bed. No wonder that many housewives dreaded the thought of tomorrow. They knew what awaited them!

Myron Sologowski, a Polish professor I met in Warsaw, put it in perspective for me when he said, *'...for the husband, life is not all that bad. Most of the life's burdens fall heavily on the women. Feminism does not exist in Poland and the women think only of survival. Men concentrate on going to work in their factory or office. It is a situation where the men go to a work place but not always to work. You do not have to accomplish anything to get paid by the state.'* This defined the state of communism very well for me. It was clear that Poland would need a change in government before it had any hope of changing the mind set of its people.

For those who had access to American currency, they could shop for anything they wanted in the Pewex, the dollar stores. This, in itself, caused frictions in a fragile society. In the midst of all of this, the rate of alcoholism in Poland was very high. At a typical liquor store, queues formed up in the morning for the early afternoon opening. On average, each Pole drank eight quarts of pure alcohol per year. Much of the drinking was stress-related which tended to decrease productivity. The official communist newspaper, Trybuna Ludu *(People's Tribune),* often chastised its readers for these drunken binges. In one article, the paper claimed that people trusted each other less and less. This mistrust seemed to permeate everything, including my presence as a tourist in Poland.

Farming, much as it was in Alberta in the 1920s, was hard work and many young people ended up fleeing the land en masse. Still, on my journey I ran across a number of what I would conclude to be prosperous farmers, albeit a relatively small number. Their homes, too, reflected this phenomenon, not to mention their love for fine thoroughbred horses and automobiles, many of which carried the Mercedes logo.

As I continued my journey to the Polish border I became convinced that the Poles *admired the West and its customs.* Poland desperately wanted western technology and seemed to be drawn like a magnet to the western culture. It was not uncommon to see Poles watching American television programs such as Grease with John Travolta. Notwithstanding, censorship restrained Polish writing and the arts--except, it seemed, at Warsaw's Grand Opera and the Ballet Theatre where excellent concerts were the norm. The Poles portrayed a great hunger for *consumer goods* which reflected a reaction to denials of material goods for as long as twenty years after World War II. The wait for a small apartment just large enough for a couple and two children was as long as a dozen years. Financially, this was accomplished through multiple jobs, moonlighting on government time during working hours, *bartering* for goods and services, *bribery,* and the colossal black market in foreign currencies and imported or smuggled merchandise. But, no matter how small the home, the hospitality of the Poles was legendary.

My destination on this particular day was Minsk, Belarus which, for all intents and purposes, was a part and parcel of Mother Russia. Traffic was slow and many sections of the highway were being repaired, often using old road building equipment and technology. The countryside was beautiful as were the small country-like cottages. Throughout, I was able to observe the older women, steeped in tradition, looking after two or three cows while they grazed along the highway. *'Too bad,'* I thought, *'sooner or later the world will come crashing in on them and they will then have to pay a price for their reluctance to embrace change.'* I stopped for lunch along the road and struck up a conversation with three elderly women herding their cows on the lush grass bordering the pavement. All three spoke Ukrainian which reflected an historical fact; this Ukrainian-inhabited region was once a part of the former Austrian Galicia. My mom's village was not all that far from here.

As I resumed my journey to the Belarus border, I had to admit that were it not for Intourist and the tourism policies of the Soviet Union, I might have steered a course directly for the village of Plazow. But, that was not to be.

5.

Belarus: The Tragedy of History

*A piece of land standing on the way of
a journey from Warsaw to Moscow*

It was late afternoon when I entered Kuznica at the Belarus border crossing en route to the historic city of Brest. The border crossings from Poland into Belarus were never easy because the train gauge was 24 cm wider in Belarus than in Europe making it necessary to change the wheels on each incoming train. Although this started out as a defensive measure against invasion, it was now a labour-intensive operation and a drawback to international trade. The sights at the border looked familiar enough–barbed wire, a stretch of no-man's land, a couple of lookout towers which also acted as pillboxes, and tight security everywhere. An official peered at me intently and demanded, in Russian, *"your passport and visa, please."*

As I presented my documents for inspection, several other border guards appeared on the scene. This being my entry into Mother Russia, I was not surprised that the officials wanted to thoroughly inspect my car and luggage. In the guard house, I could see an official going over a document on his desk while making a telephone call. I overheard one guard say to another, *"...this is the Canadian military officer that we have been expecting."*

Their line of questioning was precise and deliberate. They wanted to know how much and what currency I was bringing into the Soviet Union. Then, the questioning turned to any consumables that I would be bringing to Belarus and whether it was my intention to leave any gifts with anyone in the Soviet Union. Finally, there were those questions about my automobile, insurance, personal belongings, accommodations, gas coupons, Intourist documentation, and personal identification. As I carefully placed each item on a table, an official made a few notes. Another officer pointed to an item and asked, *"what is this?"*

The question caught me off guard. I could tell by the inflection in his tone that he might have discovered something that I should not be bringing to Russia. *"Why, that's a tape recorder,"* I replied. The officials seemed not to know what a tape recorder was. After further discussion, one was heard to say, *"Aha, a magnetaphone, that's what it is. Comrade, this instrument is forbidden in the Soviet Union."*

"Why is it forbidden," I asked him, trying to sound indignant.

"It's the law," was his firm reply. More discussion amongst the officials. *"Well, Comrade, you have two options. We can destroy this magnetaphone right here or we can send it to your place of exit from the Soviet Union."*

Not wanting to get separated from my tape recorder, I elected to have it repackaged and sealed. I signed the note and that I would not open the package while in the Soviet Union. This decision, as expedient as it was, saddened me. I realized that my exit point would be Uzhorod, Ukraine and that I would not be able to tape any of my impressions of Russia or Ukraine nor would I be able to record any interviews. *"Yes, Comrade,"* I heard him say, *"we will allow you to take the magnetaphone with you through Russia. But remember, do not open the package."*

Once that task was completed, an official turned his attention to currency, comparing the amount of currency I was bringing into Belarus with previous claims. The tone of his interrogation took on a more urgent tone when he asked me, *"...how is it Comrade, that you are carrying all of this Polish currency?"* When I explained that the Polish currency came from a state-operated currency exchange kiosk in Warsaw, he seemed not to believe me. *"You see,"* he explained, *"if you did exchange American currency for Polish zloty at the official rate of exchange, you would have far fewer zlotys. Your documents are not in order. You are required to keep a record of all of your financial transactions."*

I listened intently to his admonition and asked him if I had done anything illegal.

"Maybe you have. Maybe you didn't. What happened in Poland is not our concern. What happens in Belarus and in Russia in the next couple of weeks is our concern." He went on to explain to me that I should not be involved in the black market and to do so is a crime and is punishable under the laws of the land. *"It has been our experience,"* he added, *"that foreigners coming to Russia like to sell or give away certain items. I notice that you are bringing several packages of gum, chocolates, candy, pens, pencils, and shirts with you. Are all these for your consumption?"*

The official looked at me with a great deal of suspicion when I told him that all of those items were for my consumption and that I needed several changes of underclothing, blue jeans, shirts, sweaters, and jackets since I would have little opportunity to take the soiled ones to a dry cleaning firm. He seemed offended by my remarks, asking me whether it was my opinion that Russia did not have clean water. Waiting for final clearance, I noted that it was now 1900 hours, nearly two hours since I first arrived at the border.

When asked about the delay, an official informed me that my file was being updated with their Moscow Bureau. Finally, it would be an English-speaking agent that would address me, *"you are required to check into Intourist hotels on your route and fuel your auto only at designated fueling stations. Do not take photographs of factories, military installations, communes, or any other sensitive locations."*

When I asked the official if I would be able to make it to Minsk, a distance of 300 kilometres, that evening, he checked his watch then looked at me, saying, *"Nyet."*

"Can I stay in a hotel between here and Minsk?"

More discussion and more delay. From the amount of time it took the officials to check out my request and phone Hotel Brest, I was sorry that I had bothered. Finally, an official gave me his approval and provided me with an address of the hotel in Brest, adding, *"it is a pity that the construction of the new Intourist Hotel in Brest is not yet complete."*

Security was tight, not only at the border crossing but also en route to the city of Brest. As I entered the city of Brest, I wondered as to what it was about this region that made it so difficult for foreign powers to conquer. The land was flat and looked agricultural in nature, interspersed with marshland. When I checked into Hotel Brest, it was obvious that the manager was expecting me. When I told him I was hungry, he gestured in the direction of a small adjoining restaurant where I was served Russia's famous black rye bread, cured ham and cheese. I washed this down with a beer and checked in for the night. My guest room had the barest of essentials, a single bed with a squeaky spring and a common bathroom down the hallway.

As the sun began to set, I peered out into the street. To my surprise, there were no street lights. Everything was in darkness. In a park across the street I saw a group of young people, male and female, engaged in some sort of discussion and breaking out, from time to time, in what sounded like a patriotic song. Out of curiosity, I asked the night clerk about the activity. He informed me that the young people had gathered at the Brest Fortress which featured a massive rock at the side of which were carved scenes featuring soldiers. Perhaps influenced by drink, they sounded very happy. At the stroke of midnight, the group seemed to vanish as though into thin air. Despite their earlier youthful exuberance, I was impressed with how quietly the group dispersed. When I finally turned in, the silence of the city enveloped me.

The next morning over breakfast I was joined by three truckers for a bowl of steaming porridge, soft boiled eggs, *very soft,* cured bacon, *nearly raw,* and black Russian bread that was heavenly. Coffee was not on the menu; they were all tea drinkers. Having wolfed down their breakfasts, they all lit up and puffed away at their foul smelling cigarettes.

As a small country, Belarus has been described as being flat, dull, and marshy; *a piece of land standing in the way of a journey from Warsaw to Moscow.* It boasts wide stretches of unbroken birch groves as well as plenty of arable land. For centuries, nations such as Russia, Poland, Lithuania

A Belarus farmer about to fertilize his plot of land using barnyard manure.

and Germany showed a great deal of interest in Belarus and fought many ferocious battles in an attempt to conquer her. As a result, Belarusians had suffered terribly over the years. In World War II the small country lost a quarter of its population and most of its cities. This destruction was evident in Brest, which at one time had a population of over a quarter million. Much of it lay in ruins on the day of my visit.

The one thing that struck me was the countless number of memorials in honour of those who fought in the Great Patriotic War. Yet, despite the loss of all of those who defended her, it is interesting to note that hundreds of thousands were later purged or sent off to Siberia for alleged collaborations. There were no memorials for these heroes.

Belarus is noted for its timber milling, glass-making, boat-building, and railroad building. Because the language is so much like the Russian and Ukrainian languages, any sense among the Belarusians that they were a distinct people was very slow to emerge. In 1922, Belarus was controlled by the Bolsheviks and became a founding member of the USSR. In the years which followed, Belarus was encouraged to develop its language and culture. Unfortunately, Belarus was stuck between Germany and Russia and, as a consequence, was witness to several major battles during World War II. The Germans were routed in 1944 with great losses on both sides. After the war, Belarus became one of USSR's most prosperous republics and Minsk became the heartbeat of the country.

Driving through the marshland, I could see why even the Tatars were among the few conquerors who failed to make Belarus a battlefield. Unlike the armies of Poles, Swedes, Lithuanians, Germans, and Great Russians who all traversed this flat land, the Tatars avoided the region as though it were a plague. Maybe the Tatars were smarter.

It was Georgi Kurleyko, the manager of Hotel Brest who told me that the most important food in Belarus was the potato, *"...our second bread."* He even broke into a song commemorating the potato; a song entitled *Bulba Bulba* (Potato, Potato). *"It was the Lithuanians and the Poles who brought a Roman Catholic influence to this region,"* offered Georgi. *"Many people say that we are quieter and a little more reserved than are the Ukrainians and the Russians."*

If that were the case, then Georgi had not convinced me. He was very talkative and outgoing. Certainly, he would not be a good candidate for the KGB. While in Brest, I discovered that the bear was a popular hero in legends and that the Belarusians considered the bear to be a friend of man. Now I could see why the Russian circus always came to Edmonton with the dancing bears as its central theme. Georgi went so far as to tell me that residents in Brest have an annual bear holiday called Kamayeditsa. *"From time to time,"* said Georgi, *"I join other local people, eat a dish of potatoes and beans and lie on the grass imitating the movements of a bear!"*

'Yes Georgi,' I thought, *'you are keeping bad company. Not only are you acting like a bear, you are beginning to look like one.'*

Upon arriving at Hotel Yubileynaya in Minsk, I registered at the desk and was informed that my guide, a statuesque girl by the name of Tanya, was already waiting for me. She greeted me with *"good afternoon, Comrade Kashuba,"* and I immediately noted just how well she constructed each sentence in English and how clear was her pronunciation. She told me that she was a sports enthusiast enrolled in sports medicine at the local university. Knowing a little bit about the history of Minsk and the role of its residents during the war, I was not surprised to find that my guide wanted *me* to know a lot more about *her* city and the local war heroes. As I sat down for dinner, I wished that the staff in the restaurant displayed a little more enthusiasm.

"Minsk's population is now approaching one million," explained Tanya, *"but during the Great Patriotic War it had fallen to less than one hundred thousand. When the city was recaptured by the Soviet Army in 1944, not even one building was left standing."* The uniformity of the newly reconstructed buildings was somewhat softened by its wide streets. Tanya seemed determined to provide me with a brief history of the region from the frequent destructions by fire to sacking by Crimean Tatars in 1505, ruin by the French in 1812, damage in World War I by the Germans and Poles. However, when I asked her if she was aware that in the outlying district of Kurapaty, it is estimated that Josef Stalin murdered a staggering 900,000 innocent people between 1937 and 1941, she seemed not to hear me.

Not only was Tanya anxious to tell me about the history of Minsk and Belarus, she was also more than willing to tell me about communism. Anxious to get away from a lecture on communism, I asked her, *"why is your country called White Russia?"*

"Well, it is the colour of our people and the purity of our winters," she replied.

Sensing that I did not want to hear more about politics, Tanya turned back to her City. *"When the Red Army re-took Minsk in July 1944, only about 40,000 of the 237,000 people survived,"* she informed me. *"The main industry of Minsk at the present time is the manufacture of watches, bicycles, ceramics, and trucks. And, our most important food is the potato,"* she added as an afterthought. *"About 120 kilometres from Minsk is our Belarusian forest. It is here that you will find our strongest character, the bison or the zubr. Well, no, maybe it is the bear that is the toughest. Anyway,"* continued Tanya, *"the pine forest has seen its share of heartache and cruelty. It is here that wartime partisans built camps that served as their centres of operation. Over a dozen brigades operated out of here. Why, they even had their own hospital."*

Tanya then took me to the Khatyn monument to see how the burning of that famous village and the massacre of its people was memorialized on plaques along with an inventory of the total destruction of 209 towns and 9,200 villages and the death of 2,200,000 people. It was only then that I began to understand why this fragile young woman continued to be haunted by the images of a wartime trauma.

When I told Tanya that I was a bit of a sports buff, she promptly took me to the Palace of Sports. The life-like statues were moot testimony to the accomplishments of Belarusian youth. As a westerner, one would rarely appreciate this because athletes attending world-class events all represented the USSR or Russia. Rarely, if ever, would a foreigner actually know or suspect that a particular athlete came from one of the Soviet satellite nations such Belarus. Mother Russia did not like to share this kind of glory with its so-called *equal partners*.

That evening, Tanya joined me for dinner. It didn't seem to take her long to get into the bubbly, albeit guardedly, and use this as an excuse to tell me about the smallest of the Soviet Union's fifteen constituent republics, Moldavia. *"It is from here,"* she whispered, *"that we get our very best wines."* By the time that we finished the first bottle of wine, and I seemed to be drinking all but one glass of it, we were discreetly joined by a young man.

"Excuse me," said the young man to us both, *"my name is Igor. I am sitting at that table and overheard some of your conversation. I wonder, might I join you?"*

'Well,' I thought to myself, *'I really don't want you to join us,'* but then I heard myself saying, *"Sure, why not."*

Our conversations started out slowly enough as though we were heavyweight fighters looking for a good body shot. There was small talk about our home towns, Germany and the Royal Canadian Air Force. All the while, I was trying my best to take the measure of the guy. Was it an accident that he joined us? As we proceeded with our meal and another bottle of wine which Igor ordered, Tanya seemed to be drinking more while Igor was merely sipping his drinks. They both looked like they could handle their drinks. Several got up to dance to the music of a live band. I was glad when Tanya accepted my invitation to dance. She was a good dancer but kept her distance for the first number only warming to the situation after the third dance. Even as we danced, Tanya did not miss the opportunity to ask questions of me. With the gentle way in which she squeezed my hand, I wished that I had something of importance to share with her. At the same time I could hear a voice within me saying, *'Do not take any remark, gesture, inflection, question, no matter how innocent, to be simply small talk. Consider every word and when you are asked a question, answer it with another question. Seek clarification.'*

By late evening, I noted that Igor's questions got more and more pointed and most had to do with the military--inter-continental ballistic missiles, nuclear plants and the fire-power of the Ramstein military base. Since I knew little about the military, I found that the more evasive were my answers the more convinced was Igor that I was hiding something. As the midnight hour approached, I went on the offensive. *"Comrade,"* I asked him, *"do you enjoy your job? Is it your job to squeeze information out of visitors to your beautiful country?"*

My direct question seemed to catch him off guard. He denied being charged with any responsibility by his superiors in carrying out a surveillance operation saying that he only wanted to extend a hand of friendship. However, I was not convinced that ours was a chance meeting. I sensed that he knew Tanya and that the two of them formed a team; a cell and that Igor worked for Intelligence. After the exchange with Igor, I suddenly noted that Tanya had disappeared and her place was taken by another young woman who introduced herself as Ludmilla. We toasted our respective countries. We toasted hockey and we toasted Elvis Presley and rock and roll music, upon which they seemed hooked. We even told jokes about ourselves and our countries. I know that the punch lines often suffered in their translation but that seemed not to matter. With that, I bade them goodnight. It was Igor who asked me if I wanted Ludmilla to show me the way back to my flat. Whatever else, this girl looked to me as though she had loose morals or no morals at all.

When I awoke the next morning, I checked through my flat to make sure that there were no hidden microphones. Nothing obvious. Still, I had this suspicion that someone had gone through my suitcase. The items of clothing and personal belongings were not packed in quite the same way that I remembered. However, nothing seemed to be missing. I concluded that my mystery guest was a most inquisitive person.

As I left Minsk on the highway that would take me to Moscow, I knew that I would get some time to reflect upon the events of the previous night. Only then would I be able to make any sense of it.

6.

Moscow: The Hot Seat of the Cold War

*Russia—land of the Tsars, Lenin, Stalin,
Gorbachev and the Bolshoi Ballet*

Rubble and barbed wire, the visible remnants of The Great Patriotic War, met my gaze in every direction as I left Minsk bound for Smolensk, Russia. After the war, survivors lived in churches, barns, and sheds–anywhere that would provide them a roof over their heads. I marvelled at how Belarus continued to retain its timeless atmosphere. Horse-drawn wagons moved on rubber tires in a land that was flat--in stark contrast to 1941 when German troops moved through this region on their relentless march on Stalingrad and Moscow and, much like Napoleon in 1812, the Nazis lost legions of soldiers. Perhaps Igor put it best the previous night when he said, *'the fate of battles are not decided by orders from superiors but rather by that intangible force called the spirit of the army. The spirit of the people.'* Yes, it was one thing for Hitler to march forward to what seemed certain victory; however, the retreat back to Germany, when defeat was snatched from the jaws of victory, was devastating!

Driving through the peaceful and quiet countryside, I had to admit that Igor was not your ordinary soldier. He brought to life some of the great battles during the Great Patriotic Struggle, particularly the fight for Stalingrad in August of 1941 when Zhukov's forces launched a massive counterattack, cracked the German line and encircled the Nazi invaders. *'A total of over two million lay dead and wounded. Much like the army of Napoleon, Hitler never fully recovered,'* concluded Igor.

As I watched a cycling team in the distance, I did the unthinkable; on impulse and with great care, I unwrapped my tape recorder that was sealed by officials at the border crossing. I could not resist the urge to record my thoughts as I watched, first one cyclist leading the pack only to be replaced by another; training, perhaps, for the next international competition. The traffic was light, mostly army-type vehicles and transport trucks and the scenery had a consistency to it–spruce, muskeg, agricultural land and very flat throughout. By late afternoon I reached the valley of the Dnepr River *(Dnipro in Ukrainian and Dnieper in English)* and the Russian border; however, in contrast to earlier border crossings, this one was modest and did not have all of the security of previous border crossings. In contrast to the seeming isolation of Belarus, the last few kilometres to Smolensk reflected increased activity in agriculture and industry. Years ago the region was on a trade route between Moscow and the West and between the Baltic and Black seas. Located on the south bank of the Dnepr River, central Smolensk continued to be surrounded by an ancient wall, albeit in need of repair.

As I entered Smolensk, I was flagged down by a military policeman. In fact, this was the third such occurrence since leaving Minsk. Yes, my progress was closely monitored as I heard the policeman say, *"...can I see your documents please?"* For the most part, I found the Soviet police to be courteous and it was not unusual for them to ask if I was enjoying my trip. I had no reason to believe that these pleasantries were self-serving or insincere. In fact, I took some comfort in these questions knowing that should I have a problem, I could rely on the military police for assistance.

Hotel Smolenskaya served as the Intourist hotel and, as I checked in, the manager introduced me to my guide, Svetlana, a foreign languages student from the University of Moscow. As I enjoyed a late supper with her, she seemed bound and determined to tell me about the merits of the communist way of life. However, it was not so much the ancient wall, the town square or Svetlana that got my attention; it was what happened in the nearby Katyn Forest in 1940, for it was here that the bodies of nearly 6,000 Polish reservist officers, who had been imprisoned by the Soviet occupation troops in Poland in 1939, were discovered in four mass graves. It was also in this forest that the Nazis massacred 130,000 Soviet prisoners of war. At the time, the Soviets blamed the Nazis for the atrocities while the Nazis placed the blame for the Polish massacre squarely on the shoulders of the Soviet Union. *The truth would not be told until after the breakup of the Soviet Empire in 1989.*

That night, the thought of being within striking distance of Moscow, with its population in excess of nine million, likely contributed to my inability to get a full night's sleep. I was looking forward to testing its reputation as a friendly yet surly, beautiful yet grey and bleak, and flashy yet suburban metropolis. The outskirts of Moscow were riddled with billboards, many of which were politically inspired, full of platitudes about the Soviet way of life and banners that exhorted the visitor to *Keep High the Banner of Proletarian Internationalism.* As I got closer to Central Moscow and the Kremlin, vehicular traffic became increasingly heavy and there seemed to be construction activity everywhere.

Muscovites refer to spring as the *rasputitsa* or mud season and love the sight and smell of crab apple blooms. Throughout spring and summer, lovers,

Workers undertaking construction upgrades in Moscow, 1967.

young and old, like to walk in Gorky Park along the river and take in a puppet show, a songfest, a boat ride, or a visit to an illegal fortune-teller. I promised Svetlana that I would take her advice and *taste Moscow's ice cream at the railway station, visit a place of worship and listen to church music and take in the agricultural exposition.* It seemed that new buildings were everywhere; many along Kalinin Avenue were skyscrapers. By the time I had checked into the Intourist Hotel it was nearly midnight. What I liked about the location of my hotel was that it was close to a popular restaurant, Slavyansky Bazaar as well as Gorky Park, one of the city's most popular parks of culture and rest. It would not be until the following morning over breakfast that I would meet my guide, Katyryna Kalinkova, a young lady who looked as though she belonged in the Bolshoi Ballet. Her first question was, *"where would you like to start your tour, Comrade Kashuba?"*

Shortly after breakfast, Katyryna had me at the Moscow State University where she took me directly to the Department of Languages. Of course, the regular university academic year was over but that did not decrease the amount of frenetic activity on the campus. There was a great deal of nervous energy in that many students were preparing for the upcoming proficiency examinations. For those who passed the examination, it would be like winning a jackpot because their program would be fully subsidized by the state. Several females that I met wanted to gain admission into medicine while most males sought entry into an engineering program. Most were from other Soviet Republics and several of them indicated that their father had served their Motherland during the Great Patriotic Struggle. As our visit to the languages department was concluding, Katyryna seemed startled

58

when I told her that I was interested in the work of the KGB. It would not be until after she made a telephone call that she would point out that formal training for the KGB took place nearby. As a result of my expressed interest, we drove to the Moscow State Institute of International Relations. Security was very tight. After all, this was where the Soviet Union trained most of the functionaries for the Soviet Ministries of Foreign Affairs and Foreign Trade. According to my guide, it was the KGB that helped to ensure that Russia's socialistic society continued to be based on a privileged and all-powerful bureaucracy. To sanctify its power, the hierarchy glorified the memory of Lenin, the founder of the new state, whose writings were paraded as being universal and eternal.

As the afternoon waned, the level of my excitement did the opposite; I was very much looking forward to a new experience, Swan Lake and the Bolshoi Ballet. While waiting to get into the theatre, I concluded that the Russians were much like Canadians; they were hearty, quick to speak, unreserved in their opinions, and very hospitable. To those I met who did not speak English, communication seemed not to be a problem. They made every effort to understand my Ukrainian while I returned the compliment by trying my best to understand their Russian language. The similarities between Ukrainian and Russian were many and I certainly had no problem getting by on the streets of Moscow.

The Bolshoi Ballet & Opera's theatre dominates Teatralnaya ploshchad and an evening there remains one of Moscow's best nights out. As I entered the theatre with Katyryna, the atmosphere in the glittering, six-tier auditorium was electric. She told me that the ballet and opera companies had several hundred artists between them under the directorship of Boris Grigorovich, a name that Muscovites revered as Canadians might a Maurice *The Rocket* Richard in professional hockey. The tickets to Swan Lake cost me five American dollars. What a bargain!

Attending the Bolshoi Ballet was a thrill for me but it was obvious that this was not the first time for Katyryna. She told me of her very first visit to the world-renowned ballet and how her father, during intermission, escorted her up to the front for a look at the instruments in the orchestra pit. The following day I had the pleasure of seeing more of the pure elegance of the Bolshoi Ballet when I visited the ballet school where lean-limbed youngsters live in a secular cloister dedicated to the art.

Only those who have had the pleasure of seeing a Moscow Circus would understand and appreciate why I loved the state circus in Moscow. The city had two separate circuses but the one I took in was the Old Circus *(Stary Tsirk)* in a modernized 19th century building. The first half of the show was a mix of dance, cabaret and music before the animals and acrobats reasserted themselves. *"You know,"* said Katyryna, *"the state circus has over a hundred companies and 13,000 employees. In fact,"* she continued, *"the state circus has a school especially dedicated to training young people for a life in the circus. Many are selected when they are very young, leave home, and are supported by the state throughout their career."*

"Have you every considered a career in the circus?"

"Only in my dreams. My parents would never allow it."

Following the Swan Lake performance, Katyryna and I went to a nearby restaurant for a light snack. To this day, there is one thing that still sticks out in my mind and that is the taste of Moscow bread. It is sour, fragrant, and very dark. I liked it for its vitamin-rich vitality and there is no doubt that it is the most delicious bread I have ever tasted; all as good as the bread that I was served in Brest. Of course, that is not to say that I didn't enjoy a drink or two. It did not take me too long to embrace their vodka and Georgian wines. However, being accustomed to German beer, it was difficult to enjoy Russian beer. Their limp and languid garden salads didn't turn me on either, but that could be because Canadians love their garden salads enriched with popular salad dressings.

After a couple of full days in Moscow, I thought that I might expand my horizons and take the underground to Moscow's 175-acre National Economic Achievements Exhibition which displayed Soviet accomplishments in virtually every field from atomic energy to copper mining. Even more than that, I wanted to talk to the average *Joe citizen* on the street. As events unfolded, the next two days would prove to be very intriguing. Stand on almost any street corner and you will see a tourist trying to make a deal with a Muscovite, proof that the black market was a booming industry. Even though both parties likely knew that it was illegal, didn't seem to deter them. At first I resisted the idea of selling any more items of souvenirs, gum, pens and pencils. However, once I could determine that I was not selling to an undercover agent, I tried my luck. I must say, business was never better!

I spent most of the next day simply riding the fabulous subway system of Moscow, the first leg of which was completed in 1935 and spread far and wide enabling me to visit five airports at the outskirts of Moscow as well as the space training centre known as Zvesdny Gorodok *(Star City)*. In my travels within Moscow, no sight was as awe inspiring as was Red Square highlighting the glory of St. Basil's Cathedral, the Kremlin, and Lenin's tomb. I got off the public transit system long enough to visit the GUM Department Store and Lobnoye Mesto where officials once proclaimed new laws and passed sentences for a variety of crimes. The GUM Department Store was very crowded and I wondered why the Russian *babushkas* didn't make better use of underarm deodorant.

Later in the day I came back to Red Square to recall the story of *War and Peace* and the burning of the city in 1812 when three-fourths of the city was destroyed. What Russian could forget the words of Napoleon when he barely escaped with his life saying '...*to burn one's own city...a demon inspires these people...'* Naturally, the Muscovites thought this deed to be holy and continue to be inspired by the memory of it.

At dusk I walked across the road and through the square, passing beneath a statue of Lenin who seemed to be pointing the way to an uncertain future, much like me, I suppose. Later, as I relaxed in my hotel room before going down to the ballroom for a late dinner, I had ambivalent feelings about Russia, wondering about the stories I had heard about Soviet spies. Could it be that this barren-looking hotel room harboured hidden microphones and miniature cameras? Where *would* these devices be hidden? I examined every possible nook and cranny in my hotel room and concluded that the KGB had outsmarted me. If these instruments of invasion of privacy were in my room, they had to be well camouflaged; perhaps buried in the telephone, electrical outlet, or deep inside a panel of the wall.

There seemed to be an unusually large number of guests In the formal dining room. Looking around, I spotted two individuals who had the appearance of tourists. When we made eye contact, they motioned to an empty seat, introducing themselves as Adelio d'Amonti of Sudbury, Canada and Jim Jantz of New York. Both said that they were recent graduates of a university and were holidaying in Moscow as a part of their graduation presents. At least that's what they told me. Since I did not know too many young people who would be sufficiently adventurous to want to travel to the Soviet Union, they immediately got my attention. When I asked of Adelio, *why Moscow,* he looked at me saying, *"...you're beginning to sound a lot like my mother."* It didn't take me long to take a liking to them both, especially Adelio.

Just as we were finishing our meal, a Russian approached our table, introduced himself as Vladislav Mokilov and asked us if he and his female companion by the name of Tetyana Sokilska could join us. Before I could answer, Jim Jantz said *yes.* Both spoke English, saying that they were employees of the Soviet government. As the conversation flowed back and forth, it certainly seemed to me as though I had seen a similar scenario in Minsk. Vlad, in particular, seemed very interested in what I had to say. *'Could their interest be,'* I thought, *'because I came to Moscow from a military base?'* If the interlopers had any intention of seeking sensitive information from me, I disarmed them in a hurry by saying that I knew nothing about the military, about military installations or nuclear energy and quickly turned the conversation to other matters such as western sports and politics. Somehow, they both seemed relieved and welcomed the opportunity to talk about their proud city. It was no surprise to learn that these were real human beings with families, often far removed from Moscow. And, even though they eventually admitted that they *were* in the military, I found that their hopes and dreams were no different than were those of a farm boy from High Prairie. As we toasted one another, each expressed a hope for long-lasting peace.

As the band struck up a Beatles song entitled, *Love, Love Me Do,* Tetyana seemed to sense my interest in the song and, to my surprise, asked me if I wanted to dance. There went my theory that Russian women were shy! During the dance, we managed to chat a bit at which time she told me that she was from Sevastopil, studying to be a lawyer. When I asked her where she learned to speak English, she thought for a moment before answering that it was at Moscow State University. *"Why English,"* I asked her. Again, a long pause before saying that in many cases a knowledge of English could lead to increased contacts with people from the west and, ultimately, an opportunity to travel to an English-speaking country. *"Perhaps,"* I asked her, tongue in cheek, *"to escape from Russia to a democratic state?"* She did not respond but, from the increased tension in her body as we danced cheek to cheek, I suspected that I had struck a sensitive nerve.

The next day, Adelio, Jim and I took the underground to Moscow's 175-acre National Economic Achievements Exhibition. We strolled from exhibition to exhibition; from pavilion to pavilion and, throughout the day, we tasted foods from different regions of the Soviet Union. Unlike the Calgary Stampede or Edmonton's Klondike Days, the exhibition grounds in Moscow were squeaky clean. This made the experience doubly pleasurable!

�֎

During the day we met people from all over the Soviet Union. Communication seemed not to be a problem. The Russians, I found, were not overly nationalistic. When they found out that Adelio and I were from Canada and Jim from the United States, they seemed not to be able to differentiate. To them, we were from the West, that's all that seemed to matter.

My arrangement with Intourist was that I would provide their office with a brief report at the end of each day as to the places I had visited. It was their contention that they could provide a better service to those tourists who came after me if they had information as to what was of interest to visitors such as myself. I saw it another way. To me it was simply a case of Soviet authorities trying to monitor my movements. And, since I knew that my guide, along with other agents of the state would be able to monitor all of my movements, I saw no real reason for the reporting procedure. At the same time, I knew that I might need a favour from Intourist in the future and I really wanted to curry their favour. As a result, I provided their office with a full report at the end of each day. Naturally, my reports were quite favourable to the state.

Adelio and I spent the next day simply hanging out around the downtown area and the Intourist Hotel. We noticed that foreigners were frequently exchanging souvenirs and personal items for Russian roubles and artefacts on the street and in the lobby of the hotel, often in the plain view of Russian officials. This would be the second time that I would stuff my blue blazer sports jacket with just a few more pens and pencils and try my hand at bartering. In the process, I found that most of the individuals with whom I was dealing were actually other tourists from outside of Moscow and even from other countries, especially, as it turned out, from Poland and Yugoslavia. At the end of the day I had accumulated over three hundred Russian roubles and the biggest sale turned out to be my blue blazer, sold to a Polish tourist for US$75!

62

Prominently-placed signs portraying the virtues of communism, Moscow, 1967.

Spending all of those Russian roubles was not easy. I didn't want to burden myself with the purchase of Russian souvenirs and my accommodation and meals were already looked after. As a result, I decided to use the funds to take in more of what Moscow had to offer in the realm of arts and culture.

The next day Adelio confirmed that he would be taking a flight to Frankfurt, and right out of the blue I asked, *"why don't you consider driving back to Germany with me?"* To tell you the truth, I did not expect that his answer would be in the affirmative. After all, it was my plan to visit relatives in Soviet Ukraine and his presence may present a problem. But, it was too late. Adelio seemed very enthusiastic about my invitation. That afternoon, I telephoned the Moscow's Intourist office to find out whether or not Adelio would be able to change his travel plans. Intourist indicated that the request was most unusual and would require a more thorough review. I concluded that if permission were granted, a number of changes in accommodations and flight patterns would have to be made.

To my surprise, Intourist officials approved our request the very next day. However, to put into effect the change of travel plans with Intourist and with Air Canada would take nearly one week. This gave me sufficient time to drive to Leningrad, a city created by Peter the Great which provided Russia with a window on the West. The elegant buildings along the wide Neva River and along canals provided a stark contrast to the *onion domes* of Moscow. Leningrad is laden with history, all the way from the autocratic tsars who fell at the hands of its workers and soldiers in March of 1917 to the world famous Hermitage, one of the world's great art galleries. This was the city of the tsars' superb Winter Palace and the Kirov Ballet which rivals Moscow's Bolshoi Ballet.

The serfs in Leningrad, interestingly enough, were emancipated in 1861, just five years after Austria emancipated the serfs in Galicia. With the in-migration of so many peasants after this date, the city became a focus of political and social unrest. All of this led to *Bloody Sunday* on January 9, 1905 when a strikers' march to petition the Tsar in the Winter Palace resulted in a considerable amount of bloodshed. A wave of patriotism in 1914, at the outbreak of WW1 resulted in a name change from St. Petersburg to Petrograd. The Bolshevik revolution of 1917 took place here and led to the end of the Monarchy. Petrograd was renamed Leningrad after Lenin's death in 1924 and became the hub of Stalin's 1930s industrialization program.

It took Germany only two and one half months in 1941 to reach Leningrad after it had attacked the USSR. Since the city was the birthplace of Bolshevism, Hitler hated it and swore to wipe it off the map. His troops besieged it from the 8th of September in 1941 to January 27th in 1944. The city lost between 500,000 to a million of its residents and managed to survive only because it had a winter *Road of Life* across frozen Lake Ladoga to the east. Leningrad was reconstructed after the war but did not regain its pre-war level in population until 1960.[2]

As I wound my way back to Moscow I reflected on an incident which repeated itself several times. Before I came to Russia the most common lament was, '...*the Russians will only show you what they want you to see...*' Today, I concluded that many westerners underestimate the hospitality of the Russian. I was invited to more than one private apartment in Russia, with or without my Intourist guide. These ranged from the untidy studios of the average worker to unsanctioned artists, as well as the modest studios of old pensioners. I also visited the higher class digs in new high-rise apartments– all as a result of informal friendships.

I have tasted the symbolic Russian bread and salt and indulged myself in their ritual feasts of steaming boiled potatoes and sausages, mounds of caviar and plump forest mushrooms chased down with shots of powerful vodka and Armenian cognac. Everywhere that I went in Moscow I found that young people were especially curious about western ways. They were far more knowledgeable about Canada than I thought they would be and were far more open in their conversation than I thought they should be.

One thing was for certain; the communists were the most organized force of our time. The party had complete control over its people and, it seemed, over me. I found that there were groups of people's inspectors at every enterprise, collective and state farm, and state institution along with

---

2   It would not be until 1991 that Leningrad, through a free and democratic vote, would change its name back to St. Petersburg even though the surrounding areas continue to call their geographic region the Oblast of Leningradsky.

inspection posts at all levels of endeavour–be it workshop or production sections. By some estimate, there were ten million inspectors in the Soviet Union. They consisted of workers, engineers, technicians, employees elected at general meetings. As Vlad told me, *"...it is the people's inspection groups that ensure that party and state policy are correctly implemented by offices and enterprises concerned..."*

There appeared no end to surprises for me. Many of them had to do with bureaucracy and red tape. I discovered that each citizen is registered with the militia where he lives and carries a passport which he must produce to identify himself. In the event that he goes on a trip to another locality and stays overnight, he must report his presence to the local militia. If he registers in a hotel, the passport is deposited with the manager who is responsible for notifying the police authorities. What's interesting about this process is that peasants do not have passports and must not spend a night away from their villages except with the special permission of the local militia. It seemed that no matter where one turned, he was hemmed in by numerous checks, controls and bureaucracy.

Throughout my journey, local authorities and party workers assisted and closely watched over my schedule and itinerary. From time to time I got the impression that the authorities thought that I had some sort of a dark purpose in the country. Katyryna and I spent a lot of time philosophizing.

"In Canada," I told Katyryna, *"our industry was created by rail while I have heard that river transport played a major part in the development of your regions."*

"Yes, this is especially true in pre-revolutionary Russia. Rivers carried nearly one-fourth of our freight before the Revolution and still carry five percent. The Soviet Union possesses twenty five percent of the world's fresh water, a very important commodity. I do know that the Great Lakes in Canada have a considerable amount of fresh water as well, but Siberia's Lake Baikal, which is over a mile deep, contains a fifth of all the world's supply."

I asked Katyryna about Russia's favourite thirst quencher, the beery-tasting kvass. She informed me that it is made from the fermenting of mixed cereals and, in fact, did contain a small amount of alcohol. *"On the other hand, our vodka came to us from the West in the 16th century."*

Many visitors to Moscow talked about taking an icon back home. For whatever reason, I could not get excited about such a possibility. I did learn, however, that the most famous icon of old Russia was the Virgin of Vladimir. This icon has inspired the faithful for several centuries. Soldiers bore it into battle. Even Tsar Ivan the Terrible carried it against the Tatars on his siege of Kazan. In the final analysis, the icon was not Russian at all; it was a Byzantine import, painted in the 12th century in Old Constantinople *(Istanbul)*.

For Adelio and me, this would be our final night in Moscow. We invited five Canadian and American friends for dinner. I asked Katyryna to join us for *kvass and vodka* who had a surprise for me that evening. In saying goodbye, she suddenly gave me a big hug and kiss. She was either a good actress or I had misjudged her. But, I concluded that those were real tears. My only consolation was that Adelio was finally successful in getting permission to travel with me to Germany. Naturally, I would have preferred Katyryna.

In accordance with our new schedule, the first stop on our return journey would be the city of Kharkiv, Ukraine, a distance of 743 kilometres. In Western Canada this distance could be covered in less than nine hours, however, in Russia, I knew that it would take considerably longer. Still, we wanted to be in Kharkiv by 2300 hours.

We stopped in Mtensk for lunch in a small roadside truckers' restaurant before continuing our journey to the border that would take us into Soviet Ukraine. The topography resembled rural Alberta and gave it the appearance of being a flood plain; a meeting point of northern fir groves, marshes and typical southern meadow steppe. The region, sometimes agricultural while at other times industrial, stood in the path of Tatar Armies advancing on Moscow. Today, Adelio and I were advancing on a very different kind of journey.

As I peered westward into the late afternoon sun, I could barely contain my excitement.

7.

Ukraine, At Last!

From industrial Kharkiv to the beauty of historical Kyiv

The dream of setting foot on my ancestral homeland had been with me for a long time and even the armed guards and barbed wire could not dampen my spirits. The sun was about to set and the view was panoramic, serene and beautiful. As far back as I could remember, I heard my parents talking about the Old Country. Well, I guess this was it.

Harvesting on the kolhosps was in full swing and garden vegetables were being taken in. As I looked into the distance, I could see why Ukraine was world famous for its wheat. As far as the eye could see there was black earth--the Ukrainian steppes that supply much of the nation's produce. Adelio and I passed several state farms and watched workers load potatoes, cucumbers, and beets for delivery to collection points before distribution to factories and other points within the Soviet Union.

According to statistics, the Soviet Union employs twenty eight million men and women, about twenty five percent of the work force, on state and collective farms and, in accordance with communist doctrine, these worker-partners are responsible for operating the collective farms which are, in essence, cooperatives where each member presumably shares in the profits. Long before we reached the outskirts of Kharkiv, I could see and smell the pollution in the air. When we checked into Hotel Kharkiv and were introduced to our guide, Oksana, a local university student from Melitopol majoring in civil engineering, my first question to her was, *"what happened to Kharkiv during World War II?"*

"Why do you ask," was her rejoinder.

"Well," I explained, *"after the war, a friend of the family married a university student from this city. She still has nightmares about what happened here."*

After a late supper at the restaurant, we spent the remainder of the evening chatting about the history of the local area and particularly about The Great Patriotic Struggle. It was Lydia Kulynych of High Prairie who had earlier told me that the city was heavily damaged during the war, however, it looked as though it was well on the road to recovery, quickly becoming a centre for the manufacturing of machines and turbine engines. Kharkiv is Ukraine's second largest city and, being only 40 kilometres from the Russian border, has been unduly influenced by its northern neighbour, Russia.

The following morning Oksana joined us for breakfast after which she took us across the street, seemingly under the watchful eye of Lenin proudly standing in the midst of it all, to visit the local university. Since our hotel was located next to the town square made it convenient to visit Shevchenko Park and the zoological gardens, which provided a popular place for evening strolls. 'Kharkiv,' explained our guide, 'was founded in the mid-1600s as a Cossack outpost and quickly became a major trading centre.' It was the capital of Soviet Ukraine from 1917 to 1934 and the site of the first wave of repression against Ukrainian nationalists and intelligentsia. And, for this reason, Kharkiv has played a significant role in Ukraine's march to independence.

Our time in Kharkiv was very short, mainly because I wanted to get on the road to Kyiv. As we left the hotel early the next morning, Adelio noticed that the front tire on my Volkswagen was going flat. As luck would have it, we soon came upon an old auto garage. "Excuse me," I asked of an attendant, "is it possible to get a tire fixed?" The request brought out the foreman who told us that his name was Zenoviy and that, yes, he would be able to repair the tire. As he walked to the front end of the Volkswagen, he gave the hood a slap with the palm of a gnarled and grizzled-looking hand asking, "what kind of a machine is this?"

"This," I proudly replied, "is a fine German machine."

First, he looked at me and then Adelio, saying nothing for the moment. Standing tall with his hands on his hips, he took a long look at the Volkswagen. "Are you saying to me that this machine was built in Germany?"

The afternoon was hot and his burly chest was visible as the two top buttons on his blue shirt seemed to be missing. I watched, in horror, as he quickly grabbed the two sides of the top of his shirt and simply ripped it off his chest. I stared at him in disbelief. His chest and stomach were a mess. It looked as though he got in an argument with something very big and came out second best. Maybe a Russian grizzly bear. Towering over me and pounding his clenched fists into his scarred chest, he shouted at me, "...look at this; look at what your people did to me. And now you want me to fix your tire? Take this machine and stick it up your ass. And, while you are doing that get yourself out of here as fast as you can."

I didn't need any encouragement. Adelio and I were out of there like a striped-assed polo pony, in the Volkswagen, of course. When we found another garage further up the road, I told the attendant that I was a Canadian with roots in Western Ukraine and that I was simply trying to get a tire fixed. I made no mention of the make of my car. I got the impression that Ukrainians, particularly in this region, would long remember their treatment by the Nazis.

We left Kharkiv much the wiser for the experience as we set our sights on Kyiv, the capital of Ukraine. We stopped in the city of Poltava for lunch and paid a visit to the towering monument above the city. Perched atop the monument was an eagle displaying its mighty outspread wings holding a golden wreath in its beak. This, I was told, was a symbol of the invincibility of the Russian Army and eternal glory to the heroes of the Battle of Poltava. A Ukrainian guide at the monument told us that the name of Poltava was associated with one of the greatest and most momentous events in the history of the Russian state for it was here that Peter the Great routed the *invincible Swedes* in 1709.

To our surprise, we found Poltava to be a large cultural centre with three institutions of higher learning, research institutes, a musical drama theatre, a children's theatre, a folk art house, clubs, cinemas and three museums. Instead of the one hour we had scheduled for Poltava, we spent nearly five hours in the city. By the time we left, we realized that we would be pressed to make it in time to Kyiv and the 2300 hours check-in time. Sunset found us in Piryatin, still some 155 kilometres out of Kyiv. Since we wanted to arrive in Ukraine's capital city in daylight, we elected to spend the night in my car, on a country road near a kolhosp.

Adelio worried about our safety until I told him about an incident in Minsk. While there, I discovered that the right hand door-closing latch was broken making it impossible to lock the car. I told my guide about the problem who said to me, '*don't worry about your car, Comrade. We have nothing but honest people in the Soviet Union. In fact, you don't even have to lock your car while in the Soviet Union.*' Well, I've taken her advice to heart and stopped worrying about my car and its contents. With that we made ourselves as comfortable as we could and began our catnaps. Not for long, however, because we were awakened by a uniformed officer, "*are you having car trouble Comrade,*" was his question.

Thinking quickly about an excuse, I responded, "*yes, the engine is overheated and I'm a little low on oil. We want to stop here until the engine cools and gets back to normal.*"

"*What is your destination tonight?*"

"*Our destination,*" I told the officer, "*is Kyiv. The Intourist Hotel.*"

After examining our documentation, he seemed to be satisfied with our explanation. Before leaving, he warned us to keep our auto in good running order and to stay away from the state farms. We got an early morning start and by mid-morning we could see the outline of Kyiv in the horizon. Suddenly, I understood why it is said that '*...you cannot say that you have been to Ukraine unless you have visited its capital.*' Kyiv, with a population of 1.5 million, has a well deserved reputation for being one of the most beautiful cities in the world. Reminiscent of Rome, it is a city of magnificent architecture, abundance of greenery, numerous monuments of the past, picturesque environs and the majestic Dnipro River, all of which combine to give the city a special, inimitable colour.

Kyiv is recognized as the Mother City for all Eastern Slavic peoples for it was from the Kyivan Rus that Ukraine, Russia, and Belarus are all descended between the 9th and 11th centuries. Kyivan Rus is also the place of origin of the Russian Orthodox Church and all Eastern Slavic art and architecture. In essence, the city has been ruled from Moscow for over 300 years and it would not be until years later that Kyiv would gain its independence. The older parts of the city stand on wooded hills on the west bank of the Dnipro River while the city proper is blessed with wide boulevards and broad squares; a city that has survived Mongol invasions, devastating fires, unimaginative communist urban planning, and the massive destruction of World War II.

Since our Intourist Hotel was on the extreme outskirts of Kyiv, we were compelled to drive through the heart of the city on Khreshchatyk Boulevard to arrive at our destination. The main thoroughfare was wide, adorned with the greenery of chestnut trees and lindens, and bright patches of flowerbeds. It certainly aroused my admiration. The setting for the Intourist Hotel Dnipro, at the far northern end of Khreshchatyk, was a pleasant surprise. Located in the quiet outskirts of the city on a boulevard lined with evergreens and oak trees, the hotel gave the appearance of a large country home. As we checked in, I was reminded by the manager that we were one day late in arriving. He made it sound as though I had committed a crime. No doubt he took his job seriously and would be filing a report to that effect. However, after further discussion, he did admit that the hotel had been contacted by a military police officer saying that we would be late in arriving.

Our guide, Natalie Andriyskova, was a third year medical student at the University of Kyiv. Her demeanour, voice, and appearance made me think that she could easily have been a student at the University of Alberta. There was little about her to make one believe that she belonged to a specific ethnic group. Over an early dinner, Natalie proudly announced, *"you know, Pan Kashuba, Kyiv is our capital and its people claim more than sixty nationalities from all over this continent."*

"What about your university? Where do your students come from?"

"At my university," she explained, *"you are likely to find Asians with handlebar moustaches and black and white embroidered skullcaps."*

As I looked around the restaurant, I spotted two blue-eyed women, their long black hair braided, wearing colourful head scarves and gold jewellery. It seemed that everyone talked quietly; a characteristic of Ukraine. In another booth was a small group of soldiers, short and husky, perhaps Kazakhs. Like others I had seen, they wore black boots and their tunics were open at the neck. Their tight trousers were held in place by a brown belt with a brass buckle and the ever-present Soviet star.

Taking photographs of military police was strictly forbidden. Kyiv, Ukraine. 1967.

"Even in this café," commented Natalie, *"you will find Gypsy singers, Turks, Lithuanians, Bulgarians, and Russians. You will also notice that for many of them, English is one of the languages they speak."*

Our meal, when it finally came, consisted of meat dumplings, pickled beets, mushrooms, Ukrainian black rye bread, and butter. Of course, no Ukrainian meal would be complete without an appetizer of borsch and deep apple pudding for dessert. Their wine was not from the Mosel Valley in Germany, but it did taste just fine. So did their vodka and their coffee which was extremely heavy-bodied and had to be mixed with a considerable amount of milk. *"Yes,"* I assured Natalie, *"I am going to enjoy my time in Kyiv."*

When we met for breakfast the next morning, I was surprised to notice that Natalie had packed a picnic lunch. When I asked her about the purpose of the lunch, she confirmed my suspicion, saying, *"yes, I want to take you to Shevchenko Park and show you the tall statue of the man half of Ukraine is named after–Taras Shevchenko, the multi-talented 19ᵗʰ century nationalist poet-artist. We can have lunch in the park."*

"Yes, Natalie. Not only is Shevchenko revered in Ukraine, he is also the favourite of many Ukrainian-Canadians," I assured her.

"You may also want to visit the Shevchenko State Museum. It has a collection of over four thousand of his own and his contemporaries' artistic and literary works displayed in a serene setting while at the same time you can listen to classical music. While there, you can listen to his poetry translated into several popular languages."

As the three of us began our tour, Natalie dove right into the history of Kyiv. I could see that she was well primed for providing me with a history lesson. *"In the 16ᵗʰ century, the Slavic prince Kiy fortified a settlement that would become the rich and powerful state of Kyivan Rus. It is the River Dnipro that carried traders and invaders to the Black Sea. Looking at the skyline of Kyiv, you will see the imposing bronze figure of Prince Volodymyr who adopted Christianity in 988."*

"And, just like that, the general population of Kyiv embraced Christianity?"

"Well, not that quickly," responded Natalie. *"The old chronicles tell us that Prince Volodymyr urged it upon his subjects by dunking all the people in the Dnipro."*

Thick green trees were everywhere. Standing out like islands, they made Kyiv beautiful. Like most Ukrainians, Natalie loved to walk, first taking us for a stroll along Taras Shevchenko Boulevard, and then along Kyiv's Khreshchatyk street where numerous shops appeared to be well stocked with goods from all over Europe. Flower beds were everywhere. Vendors stationed at key points along the boulevard served long queues of people waiting for pastries, ice cream, kvass, candy, and yes, coco cola. The sights and sounds of Kyiv made me thirsty.

"Look, Natalie. Let's have some kvass. I can have cola any time."

The kvass in Kyiv, dark brown in colour with just a touch of alcohol, tasted very different from that in Moscow. Served from tank trucks in just about every city in Ukraine I was told, one drink cost ten kopeks. Although the vendors wore long white coats with high white hats, giving it the appearance of cleanliness, I noted that when I finished my drink, the lady rinsed the glass, refilled it, and served the next client. *Not too sanitary after all,* I thought. *"The ingredients,"* commented Natalie, *"are made from fermented rye bran, boiled in water and then strained before being served."* I had to admit, this stuff tasted just fine, thank you.

From downtown Kyiv, we could see the thirteen golden cupolas of the bell tower of the Cathedral of St. Sofia which symbolized Jesus and the Apostles. Now a state museum, the construction of St. Sofia started in 1037 and the unique structure still amazes one by the perfection of architectural forms and the beauty of its frescoes and mosaics. A monument to Bohdan Khmelnytsky, an outstanding Ukrainian general and statesman who led the Ukrainian people in the war of liberation in the middle of the 17th century, stands in the middle of the square adjacent to the cathedral.

Natalie then took us to the remains of the so-called Golden Gate which was once a part of the principal entrance to the city. Always expressing pride in Ukraine's accomplishments, Natalie was quick to point out that the city fathers had given approval to the construction of an underground railway, new bridges to span the Dnipro, new boulevards, streets, squares, palaces of culture, railway terminals, hotels, restaurants, and cinemas. *"Not only that,"* added Natalie as an afterthought, *"but Kyiv is also the home of the Shevchenko Theatre of Opera and Ballet, the Ivan Franko Ukrainian Drama Theatre, a young spectators' theatre, a philharmonic society, a variety theatre, and a circus."*

That afternoon Natalie insisted that we spend some time on the city's riverside beaches. Along the Dnipro and the many shores of its islands, local citizens sun themselves luxuriantly; as many as a half million at any given time on a hot summer's evening. When I looked over the sea of bodies, it

Monument in honour of Ukraine's poet and national hero, Taras Shevchenko (1814-1861). Kyiv, Ukraine, 1967.

seemed to me as though Ukrainian babas took great pride in the size of their girths and not the shape of their physiques. For certain, none was anorexic. A subway ride took us to the Hydropark Station where bikinis were in evidence everywhere. I also noted that chess was a popular game on the beach.

Back at Shevchenko Park Natalie really got sentimental, saying, *"You know, even the grass bends in sorrow as it weeps for our history. The grudge lives on in Kyiv against those medieval people that you call Mongols and we call Tatars. They took everything and gave us nothing in return but their foul speech and disrespect for our women."*

"Why is it," I asked, *"that Kyivans didn't put up a better fight against the Tatars?"*

"Well, it is an established fact that our people occupied themselves with their flocks. They roamed with them and did not possess towns or walls. They were no match for the marauding Tatars."

With Natalie's explanation, I could see how the Golden Curtain descended and progress temporarily stopped on the Russian steppes. Historians point out that the rule of the Tatars was absolute and the glory of Kyiv was buried–at least for the time being. *'Today,'* I thought, *'I am witness to a miracle. It is as though there is a resurgence of the Ukrainian spirit right here in the city of Kyiv.'* And yet, my Intourist guide left me with the impression that Russians living in Kyiv had contempt for Taras Shevchenko, a serf who became a great painter, writer, poet and symbol of Ukraine's struggle for national freedom. The source of this negative attitude had its roots deep in the past where Ukraine was considered to be a province of Russia and that its language, as a dialect, to be inferior. As a consequence, they portrayed the view that its writers were of no consequence and, therefore, unworthy of any serious consideration.

As Adelio and I prepared to leave Kyiv, I looked forward to my very first visit to Western Ukraine and a geographic region known as Galicia, home to my parents. The Nazis attacked Russia in 1941 and by the end of the year controlled virtually all of Ukraine occupying it for two years. It was interesting to note that two major factions of Ukrainian partisans[3] emerged; Soviet partisans which were controlled out of Moscow and the Ukrainian Insurgent Army (UPA) which was concentrated predominantly in the west and fought both the German and Russian troops with the aim of establishing an independent Ukraine. However, this was not to be. The Russian troops re-took Kharkiv and Kyiv by the end of 1943 and then put together an army of 2.3 million men that pushed back the German forces. Ukraine, in the process, was nearly obliterated and an estimated six million Ukrainians died in the process while at the same time leaving all of its cities in ruins.

Most important, after World War II the USSR kept the territory it had taken from Poland in 1939. Because Ukraine had suffered to the extreme during the war, it was given its own seat in the United Nations. But, for many Ukrainians, the suffering did not end there. A Ukrainian army under a government in exile led by Stepan Bandera continued a guerrilla existence into the 1950s while at the same time millions of Ukrainians were sent to Siberia for suspicion of disloyalty to the Soviet Union and its communist regime.

For my extended family living in Poland and Soviet Ukraine, life got just a little bit tougher. Many belonged to the Uniate Church and, as a consequence, Soviet authorities went so far as to suspect several members of collaborating with the Nazis while others were accused of being linked to Polish or Ukrainian nationalism. The Ukrainian Catholic Church was forced to dissolve into a union with the Russian Orthodox Church in 1946. However, most parishioners did not wish to buy into this union because they wanted to preserve their own rituals and customs. As a result, the Ukrainian Catholic Church continued to operate underground.

Our time with Natalie ended on a sad note as she recounted, tears in her eyes, the horrors of wars, famine, and purges which occurred during the first half of the 20th century and which cost the lives of over half of the male and a quarter of the female population. *"Many of those who perished were my*

---

3   Sevirsky, David, Stout Hearts, Dmitry Medvedev, Foreign Languages Publishing House, Moscow, 1948. This book was presented to me by my Intourist Guide in Kyiv in 1967 and depicts the role of Ukrainian partisans during the Nazi occupation of Ukraine.

aunts and uncles." As Adelio and I left Kyiv, I had to confess that Natalie had deep feelings for Ukraine and finally did convince me that she was much more than just another Soviet citizen—she was truly a Ukrainian nationalist. This made me feel very happy.

My Intourist map told us that the distance from Kyiv to Lviv was about 544 kilometres. I felt excited and nervous as I took out a letter addressed to my dad. Carefully, I unfolded the crumpled yellowish and weathered envelope. I could scarcely make out my uncle's return address. As I stared at the name of the village in which he lived, I thought about my dad and his love for his younger brother, Fedjko. *'You know, son,'* he once said, *'I had a bit of a falling out with my dad and with my two brothers. However, Fedjko was not one of them. We were very close and I often talked about bringing him to Canada.'* Although my parents did not encourage me to visit any of their siblings, I knew that Fedjko would be an exception.

With tears in her eyes while giving me a big hug, Natalie assured me that the village in which my uncle lived was on our route to the city of Lviv. Had I known what was in store for me in that village, I would have avoided it like a plague. In fact, in just a few days I would begin to wonder if Natalie was something more than an Intourist guide.

Soviet citizens, especially youngsters, were very interested in meeting a foreign visitor. Kyiv, Ukraine, 1967.

8.

Come With Us, Comrade

Entering a village is strictly forbidden

We left Kyiv with great anticipation yet with a heavy heart. It was the first week of August and the weather was ideal for harvesting as evidenced by the flurry of activity on state farms. As we drove through the countryside, the traffic seemed unusually heavy with vehicles that looked like they belonged in the army. Many, however, were redeployed to peacetime services such as work on kolhosps during the harvesting season. On impulse, we drove into a kolhosp, not for the purpose of meeting any of the workers but for the purpose of creating some bragging rights. We wanted to tell the folks back home that we actually set foot on a state farm.

It was not unusual for one kolhosp to compete with another to see who could produce the best crops and meet state quotas; who would have the grandest entry to their state farm and the most appealing; what message would be posted at the entry to extol the virtues of the working man. We noted that entries varied from ornate metal gates surrounded by flower beds to the strategic placement of large statues of communist leaders under a large banner exhorting the communist way of life. We drove into the main yard of a state farm and discreetly took a few photographs of the buildings which housed a collection of machinery and processing plants. There were several farm workers in the yard but they seemed not to notice us. I practically had to drag a worker away from a combine to engage him in conversation. *"Good day, comrade."*

"Good day to you. Who are you?"

He looked surprised to learn that we were from Canada and seemed reluctant to engage us in any discussion about the state farm. When we noticed a couple of military vehicles pass by on the highway, we thought it best that we leave immediately. At noon we stopped for lunch and refuelling in

Transporting workers to a kolhosp near Zhitomir, Ukraine, 1967.

Left: *A kolhosp near Zhitomir showing an entrance which frequently put a positive spin on communism. Zhitomir, Ukraine, 1967.*

Zhitomir. Service, as usual, was slow and those serving us would not win an award for congeniality. However, once they realized that we were Canadians, they wanted to talk. We wanted to get on the road to our destination.

The road sign pointing the way to the village of Buzk was large and inviting, however, the gravelled road showed signs of wear and tear, full of potholes. Buzk was approximately two kilometres off the main highway and as we wound our way into the village, our vehicle seemed to attract a considerable amount of attention from young and old hanging about in the town square and on their small plots of land. Off to the right we see a soccer field and a group of youngsters engaged in a friendly match. A lazy brook dissected the village and a small wooden bridge took us to what appeared to be the residential section. Not knowing where my uncle Fedjko lived, I stopped an elderly gentleman walking along the side of the road, *"good evening,"* I greeted him.

"Good evening to you," he responded. *"What is your business in Buzk?"*

Now, isn't just like the Soviet Union? Everyone wanted to be a policeman and a stranger in town seemed to be everybody's business. *"Adelio and I are a couple of Canadians. I am looking for my relatives here in Buzk."*

"Well," said the villager, *"I have lived here since 1945."*

"Where did you live before coming here?"

"Many of us who are here in this village were forced to move here from a region that is now a part of Poland."

"And what region was that?" I asked.

"It was from the county of Lubaczow. As for me, I came from a little village by the name of Plazow."

I told him that it was quite a coincidence that the very first person we should meet in Buzk would be from the village of Plazow, as were my parents. When I got out of my vehicle to shake his hand, he pushed it aside and instead gave me a big hug. *"My name is Dmetro, what is yours,"* he asked.

"Kashuba," I told him. *"Stefan Kashuba."*

"That name sounds as though I should know it. What was your mother's name?"

"Eva. Eva Groszko."

"Good Lord, I knew Eva. I knew her when she was a youngster. She is from Plazow. But, she left Plazow when I was a teen. Come, I'll take you to your family."

I asked him to get inside the Volkswagen, but he refused saying that he preferred to walk. By the spring in his step I could see that he could hardly contain his excitement. Even though it had not been my intention to get in touch with my relatives so late in the day, I thought, *what the heck.*

We followed Dmetro along a lane for a few minutes before turning into the front yard of a home. Knocking on the front door, he called out, *"hello, hello."*

I could hear voices inside, *"who is it?"*

"It is your neighbour Dmetro. Come on out. I have a great surprise for you."

Shortly, the lights came on in the house and one figure came out. Then a second and a third. *"I have here a relative of yours,"* explained Dmetro. Each gave me a big hug and kiss. Wearing their nightgowns, they seemed very happy to meet me.

"Where did you say you are from," asked the husband.

"I am from Canada," I proudly responded.

He looked at me with a question in his eyes, *"did you say Canada?"*

"Yes, Canada."

"But, I don't have any relatives in Canada. All of my relatives live in the United States. The same thing goes for my wife's family."

Dmetro was most apologetic and, after some discussion, he got it right, saying, *"yes, now I know where your uncle lives. Follow me."* In short order, Dmetro led us to a home that was presumably that of my uncle. Sure enough, the moment the lady of the house saw me, there was a breathless expression of recognition. She introduced herself as Maria, saying that she was the wife of my uncle Vasyl Groszko who passed away two years earlier. With her were her daughter Olha and her son-in-law, Oleg Abranik. I did not ask, but I suspected that my parents had somehow alerted them that I would be in Ukraine. Otherwise, how was it that Maria acted as though she had expected my arrival? I introduced Adelio, saying that he did not speak Ukrainian. I also explained to them that, *"according to Soviet authorities, we must stay on schedule and be in Lviv before eleven o'clock."*

78

After a brief conversation, I promised my uncle's wife and cousin Olha that we would be back the next afternoon for a visit in exchange for their promise that they would not tell anyone that we had visited them in the village. As Dmetro guided us out of the village I, made him promise that he would keep our visit a secret as well.

Adelio and I arrived in Lviv at eleven-thirty and registered in Hotel Dnister, located on Mateyko Street overlooking the 30-acre Ivan Franko Park. I was impressed with the large Soviet-style hotel which, in many ways, resembled western-style hotels. I wasn't so sure about Adelio, but I immediately felt at home in Lviv. After all, this was the city that bade goodbye to so many emigrants, my parents among them. The search for my roots was finally bearing fruit.

With a population of over one-half million, Lviv, the capital of Western Ukraine, is a Central European city and, until 1939, had never been ruled from Moscow. With its skyline of towers, spires and roofs against a hilly background, the city exuded history. It was a busy industrial and commercial centre with a heavy Russian influence. The narrow cobblestone streets in the downtown core reminded me of other Western European cities and gave it a sense of age and permanence. Place and street names were russified after the war but these would eventually revert back to Ukrainian.

During the war years of 1941 to 1944, Lviv was occupied by German troops during which time, according to Soviet sources, 136,000 people died in the Jewish ghetto and 350,000 in its concentration camps. Soviet troops again occupied most of Galicia, including the city of Lviv in 1946 while at the same time suppressing those Ukrainians who sought independence.

The park-like main street which took us to our Intourist hotel was named Prospekt Svobody *(Freedom Street)* and to the southeast we could see Castle Hill *(Zamkova Hora),* the highest point in Lviv. Our Intourist guide was introduced to us as Svetlana, a history major from the local university. Tall, slim, and relatively dark-skinned, I took her to be from the Black Sea region but no, she said that she was from the Carpathian Mountains. This immediately brought to mind a comment, *"you know, I have always had four images of the Carpathians."*

"Four images? What are those images," asked Svetlana.

"Well, there is the one image of Hutzul dancers while the others have to do with the Boykos, Lemkos and Rusyns."

"Oy, Pan Kashuba," was her response, *"those words are very images with which I grew up! We also studied these in my history lessons."*

"How is that, Svetlana?"

"Well, I was born in the mountain village of Yaremcha. The Hutzuls are a group of Ukrainian highlanders, considered a subgroup of Rusyns. The Hutzuls live in the Carpathian Mountains to the east of the Lemkos and border region with the territory of the Romanians."

"Living in the mountains, how did these groups make a living?"

"Well, the Hutzuls are widely known for their handicraft, wood carving,

brassworks, rug weaving, pottery, and egg decorating. The Lemkos have their own dialect and describe themselves as being Rusyns or Ruthenians."

"What can you tell me about the persecution of the Boykos and Lemkos by Poland? I have heard some very strange rumours about these groups."

"Yes, it is true that the Lemkos were removed by forced resettlement, first to the Soviet Union and later to Poland's newly-acquired western lands. The Boykos inhabit the central and western half of the Carpathians in Ukraine and, once again, some scholars claim that this ethnic group is a part of Rusyns."

"Were the Boykos resettled? Forcibly moved out of their homeland?"

"Yes, much like the Lemkos, most Boykos were removed from their land after the Great Patriotic War. Most as a result of Poland's Operation Wisla in 1946 and 1947."

As we turned back to our late snack of bread, cheese and wine, Svetlana definitely had me convinced that she was a student of local history. Since she was a member of the Communist Party, I could visualize how the parents, the costumes, and the banners would all conspire to indoctrinate young minds and meld them into the shape of communism. Did Svetlana not know how destructive was the communist force to the human spirit? Was Svetlana too blind to see the evil in her Party? Was she not aware of the Party's censorship, destruction of Ukrainian culture and russification? I thought better of asking her about the communist's relentless campaign against all forms of religious worship even though, according to its constitution, the church in the USSR is separated from the state.[4]

The next morning we informed Svetlana that we wanted to spend the rest of the day by ourselves in and around the Intourist hotel. She reluctantly agreed, saying that it was her job to show us the historic sights of the city. Later that morning, and in accordance with the promise we made the previous night, Adelio and I left Lviv for the village of Buzk. Since we had been there the night before, we had little difficulty in retracing our steps to my Uncle, Vasyl Groszko's home. Maria Groszko, Olha and her husband greeted us and invited us indoors. I must confess that I knew very little about my extended family and looked upon this as an occasion to learn more. Not wanting to waste a moment of what I thought would be a pleasant discussion about the history of my family, I unpacked the tape recorder and set it up in the middle of the kitchen table for the interview.

Looking out of the kitchen window, I could see that Maria had a barn, a small chicken coop and a large garden. Beyond were the open fields of a large state farm. All of the garden vegetables and the wheat field looked lush. I could see a number of chickens and domestic geese in the yard and I assumed that the family would have one or two cows in the barn. The family

---

4   Kolasky, John. <u>Two Years in Soviet Ukraine,</u> Peter Martin Associates Ltd., Toronto, Canada, pp. 161 to 173.

home was a modest bungalow and looked clean and well appointed. I could only conclude that the family was relatively well off and led a comfortable existence. A stretch of homes bordered the small brook which flowed through the community and the low-lying area adjacent to the brook was being utilized by the villagers for grazing their cows which were constantly monitored by the babushkas of the village.

After we had established our relationships, Adelio excused himself saying that he wanted to spend some time in the farm yard and the garden. I set up my tape recorder, taped some introductory comments and then asked Maria and Olha to bring greetings to my parents. The introductions went fine but the greetings that my aunt and her daughter formulated for my parents were very emotional and brought them to tears.

"My mom and dad left Ukraine about forty years ago," was my opening statement. *"During that period of time my parents prospered and so did Canada. Much has happened to all of us during those years and to our respective countries. I know what happened in Canada and perhaps I can tell you more about that later. First, I want to find out about your lives here in Ukraine and in Poland."*

"Yes. Since the war I have heard a lot about your family from Eva," said Maria. *"I know that we have exchanged many letters."*

"Yes, this is true. I also heard that your government screened all letters that came from a foreign country and that Soviet citizens could never, ever criticize their government."

From the manner in which Maria looked at me, I could see that she was uneasy with my comments. *"We like it here,"* said Maria in a defensive tone.

"Canada has been very kind to my parents," I continued. *"It is a democratic state and people can speak their mind, worship the way they want to, and vote for the kind of government they want. Now, I understand that your government is repressive, does not allow its citizens a freedom to speak out, and controls all aspects of the economy. Communism is an evil form of government."*

If I did not have their attention previously, I had it now. They all seemed to be upset with my remarks. *"What are you saying about our form of government,"* was Maria's indignant question.

"Are you saying that this Soviet form of government is acceptable to you?"

"Not only am I saying that it is acceptable, I want to tell you the ways in which it is acceptable. It is the best form of government. Look at what we now have," she gestured around the house. *"Think of what we had before the communist government took over. Sure, we were displaced to this location from Plazow which is now a part of Poland. Sure, the Poles stole that land from us. But, in turn, we stole this land from the Poles. Look at the reasons why it happened. We live in Ukraine and no longer have to kiss the feet of Polish aristocracy or cater to Polish land barons. The quality of our life*

has improved ten-fold. We no longer have food shortages. We have a warm house. Our education is free. So is our health care."

I could scarcely believe what I was hearing. I had trouble stopping Maria. She seemed to be on a roll and wanted to hammer home not one point but several of them. *"Don't you have a desire to move freely in the Soviet Union? To travel to another country?"*

"Travel? Travel? Where? What for? I am happy here. I count my blessings each day."

I looked long and hard at Maria and at my cousin. I quite didn't know what to say. Did she really believe what she was saying? Was her house bugged? What was possessing her to say all of these kind things about a repressive government? Had I put her at risk with my line of questioning? I quietly turned off the tape recorder. I could see that this line of questioning was futile. Then, it occurred to me that I was a complete stranger to her. Did she take me to be a spy? A government agent? Did she think that this was a form of entrapment? A setup?

Once I turned off the tape recorder, all three of them seemed to relax. Conversation became much easier and, being a good Ukrainian host, she asked me if I was hungry. She did not wait for a response. I could see that she had an oil burning stove and that a pot of soup was being heated. In short order, each of us was served a large bowl of vegetable soup and dark Russian bread. No sooner had I taken the first bite than I was startled by a loud banging on the door. The visitor, whoever he was, did not wait to be invited. As I looked up from my soup, I was shocked to see two military officers stride into the kitchen. *KGB* was the very first thought that came into my mind. As I looked through the kitchen window into the front yard, I could see a military vehicle at the entry to the yard blocking my Volkswagen and two military police officers nearby. Further up the lane I saw another military vehicle and yet another uniformed military policeman in the rear of the yard. I did not have to be drawn a picture to reach a conclusion. This village was out of bounds for me. Momentarily, I had a vision of what it would be like in Siberia.

The two officers were not in a hurry. They were so calm. I was not. They introduced themselves and asked if they could sit down. My aunt seemed not to be too surprised at their appearance at the door. It was as if she had expected them and promptly set up two chairs at the table for the officers. Their next question caught me off guard. One of the officers asked Maria if he might have a bowl of soup. Maria acted as though this was normal procedure and quickly responded to their request. Both officers were served a hot bowl of soup and bread. They took forever to finish their soup. Small talk, that's all we got from them–about the weather and gardening. When they finished, they casually asked the names of all of those in the house. Of course, they must have known that I was the visitor. On a notepad, the senior officer made careful notes. He then turned his attention to me, *"can you give me your name once again?"*

Entering the village of Buzk, Ukraine, 1967.

The village of Buzk in the background, Ukraine, 1967.

I attempted to hand him my identification. He refused, saying that he preferred to take notes. *"My name is Flight Lieutenant Kashuba,"* I told him. As I gave him this information I reflected upon the merits of establishing a link with the air force while at the same time feeling certain that, if nothing else, they understood the code of conduct in the military.

"Just a moment," said the officer, *"do you mean to tell me that you are a military officer?"*

"Yes sir. I am with the Canadian Air Force stationed in Zweibrucken, Germany."

"Is that a part of The North Atlantic Treaty Organization?"

"Yes sir, it is."

At this point, the officer asked his assistant to get my file from his vehicle. In a moment, his assistant was back. I waited anxiously while the officer reviewed my file. *"Yes,"* he said, *"Here it is. The file says that you are an officer with the Canadian military stationed in Germany. In addition, a note attached to the file by one of our officers states that you are likely to pass yourself off as a civilian. To deny any knowledge about the military. What are you doing away from your planned route and in this village?"*

I thought quickly about my best line of defence, saying, *"Well, yes, I am in the military and these are my relatives. I could not resist visiting them."*

"Are you here on their invitation?"

For me, to say that my relatives had anything to do with my visit would definitely put them at risk. As a consequence, I assured the officer that they had nothing to do with my visit. *"In fact,"* I added, *"my parents, who were born near Lviv, begged me not to visit any of the relatives because it was against the laws of the Soviet Union. But,"* I added lamely, *"I did not listen to my parents. While in Kyiv, I made a decision to drop in on my family here in Buzk."* I then told the officer about my youth in Canada and how I wished that I had at least one relative. *"I had none,"* I added mournfully.

"Did you try to get the permission of Intourist to make this visit?"

"Yes, I did sir."

"And, what did they say?"

"They told me that I could not visit my relatives. That I could not deviate from my planned route on the major highway." For the moment, he seemed satisfied with my answers. However, he suddenly turned his attention to the object on the table. *"What is this?"* His voice was now more demanding; much more authoritarian.

"That, sir, is a tape recorder."

"A tape recorder? What is a tape recorder?"

Much like the officials at the border crossing at Brest, the officer wanted to know the function of a tape recorder. I explained to him that I wanted to surprise my mother by getting a recorded message from her niece and her sister-in-law. While I pleaded my case I recalled my discussion with the Soviet authorities at the border crossing near Brest. I wondered how I would get myself out of this mess. I wanted to crawl under the table. Still, I made an important decision. Not wishing to tell the officer an outright lie, I told him about my trip through Belarus and how lonely it was, saying that I wanted to capture the beauty of Belarus and then Russia on my tape recorder. He seemed impressed with my explanation. At the same time, I hoped that nothing in my dossier would tell him that the *magnetaphone* was sealed at the border with a clear instruction to keep it sealed. To my surprise, he did not confiscate my tape recorder, asking that I put it away until I had left Ukraine, ending with, *"you know full well that having in your possession a magnetaphone in the Soviet Union is forbidden."*

"Yes, sir," I responded. *"I apologize for the oversight but not for the beauty of your nation. And the success of your government."*

There were more questions, many of which I knew could be answered were they to review the contents of my dossier or check with the border guards at Brest. I felt sick when I recalled what recently happened to the American student. I wished him well in Siberia. Who knows, maybe soon I'd be joining him. With this part of the interrogation complete, the officer ordered us out-of-doors saying that he wanted to look around the house without interruption. In a few minutes, the two officers jointed us in the front yard. Their presence must have raised the curiosity of the next-door neighbours who watched from a distance. Two curious youngsters pressed their noses against the fence listening to the proceedings. Adelio knew that something was terribly wrong as he relaxed on a small bench. It seemed as though he was trying to make himself invisible. The two youngsters were asked a few questions and were asked to leave. Reluctantly, they did. I could see that they wanted to stay. After all, what youngster would want to leave just at the moment when things were getting interesting?

The officer then turned his attention to Adelio, asking him one question and then another. No response. I came to his rescue, telling the officer that he did not speak a word of Ukrainian. *"The only language he knows is English."*

"English only, you say? Who is he? Where is he from? Ask him the questions in English and translate them back to me in Ukrainian."

With this, I responded to his initial questions about Adelio's full name, his occupation, his purpose in Russia. Even as I provided the answers to the officers, I could see that the story did not seem to hang together for them. All kinds of thoughts popped into my head. Even *I* wondered about Adelio. I had to ask myself, *'who really is Adelio? What was he doing in Russia?'* Having completed the interrogation, the officer told me that he had no information about Adelio, adding that, *"...your file indicates that you would be traveling alone on this trip."*

"I can assure you sir, it is with the full knowledge of Intourist in Moscow, the Canadian Embassy in Moscow, and the Soviet authorities in Moscow that Adelio d'Amonti is with me. I have their approval to have Adelio accompany me back to Zweibrucken, Germany."

The officers proceeded with their examination of the visas, our passports, vehicle registration, insurance, and Intourist routing. They also examined closely the permission of authorities in Moscow to allow Adelio to travel with me. At long last, they seemed to be satisfied with the documentation but still remained puzzled about Adelio's presence.

"Officer Kashuba," said the official, *"I suggest that you say goodbye to your relatives. We will provide you with a military escort to the city of Lviv and your Intourist hotel. When we get to your hotel, we will have a brief meeting."*

I protested, saying that I really wanted to spend a little more time with

Maria and to visit my uncle Fedjko Kaszuba. I also invited the officer to remain with Adelio and me while we extended our visit. Although he seemed sympathetic to my plea, he would not budge from the official line. *"No,"* he stated emphatically, *"come with us, Comrade Kashuba."*

As Adelio and I drove back to Lviv, my Volkswagen seemed to be sandwiched between the two military vehicles. With the blue lights flashing on their vehicles, I felt very conspicuous and somehow very vulnerable. Those moments of doubt were interspersed with thoughts of how important the KGB officers made me feel. Adelio seemed to be in a space all his own, probably wondering what all of the fuss was about, maybe even second guessing his decision to motor back to Germany with me. Deep in thought, it occurred to me that my Volkswagen might have added to my problems. I felt certain that the military officers would not take too kindly to anything that smacked of being German.

When we arrived at the hotel, the officials took our passports and our visas and asked us to stay put until they had an opportunity to review our case. Of course, there was little else that we could do, especially in that they had our passports. By four in the afternoon we got a call from the front desk asking that we come down for a meeting with the military officials.

"You two gentlemen are under house arrest for the duration of your stay in the Soviet Union. You have not obeyed our laws. You visited your relatives in a prohibited zone. Our authorities will fully review your case before making a decision about your status in the Soviet Union."

I concluded that there would be very little point in being argumentative with the officials and expressed my regrets at not observing more closely the laws of the land and, in so doing, also putting Adelio at risk with my poor decisions. *"At the same time",* I told the official, *"you cannot imagine what a thrill it was for me to visit, for the very first time, my relatives living in Ukraine. In Canada,"* I added, *"our laws do not prohibit a foreigner from visiting anyone he wished, once he was legitimately in the country."* I knew that it would not be useful to criticize their laws. *"Do you have relatives in another country?"* I asked him on impulse. To my surprise, he told me that he had relatives in America but seemed reluctant to talk about it.

Not wishing to drop the matter, I asked the official as to whether or not it would be possible to make some sort of an arrangement to see those relatives living in the village of Buzk and in Kamianka Buzk. His response did not surprise me when he said, *"It is my duty to ensure that foreign tourists, especially those from the West, obey the laws of our land. And, even though you may not have committed a serious crime, you have broken your promise to obey our laws and to stick to your route as planned by Intourist."*

As we sat in silence, it seemed as though he sensed my determination. Consistent with the way in which most of their decisions seemed to be taken, the officer excused himself once again. It appeared as though he wanted to have another discussion with Moscow.

"Since you seem quite sincere about your family in Ukraine, my office

is prepared to consider bringing in those members of your family living in Buzk and Kamianka Buzk into Lviv by auto bus. That is, if they wish to see you. Perhaps we can get in touch with them today and bring them in tomorrow. Meanwhile, I am asking that we meet here tomorrow morning at 0800 hours. Plan to meet briefly with your relatives at about noon."

Trying to relax over dinner, Adelio and I reviewed the events since leaving Moscow. Information was being filtered to the KGB, but by whom? Was it the villager in Buzk who took us to my uncle's home? The family in Buzk that Dmetro thought were my relatives? Could it be my relatives themselves? *Or, was it our sweet, innocent-looking Intourist guide in Kyiv?* That evening, Adelio and I checked our luggage and agreed that someone had gone through our luggage while we were in Buzk.

As I thought about our predicament, I also saw the futility of being placed under house arrest. After all, all of the Soviet Union was a vast prison from which there was no escape. Sleep came slowly—very slowly. I knew that tomorrow would be quite a challenge.

9.

Expelled

From the Soviet Union for twenty-five years

Our meeting with the police authorities commenced at precisely 0800 hours in what appeared to be a board room of the hotel. The three officials were professional, to the point, and left the impression that their decision had been made. Their job, I sensed would be to impress upon us the severity of our misdemeanours. *"Comrades, we now have your files before us which provide us with some information about each one of you. These confirm that you, Officer Kashuba, are from Edmonton, Canada and that you, Comrade d'Amonti are from Sudbury, Canada. It appears that the information you gave our authorities yesterday was accurate. Good, because any false statements would have led to additional and more serious charges."*

At this point, they asked that Adelio leave us so that they might pursue some matters with me in private. It was no surprise to me that our files contained information about our backgrounds, present jobs, and our motivation to come to the Soviet Union. As Adelio left, I wandered what was to come next. I didn't have to wait long. *"Officer Kashuba, our information is that you are a civilian specialist on a Canadian military base. Our authorities want to learn more about your work."*

"A specialist? What kind of a specialist?"

"We have evidence that you have some knowledge about the military installations in Germany and about the nuclear capacity of NATO in Germany. It would also seem that you know of the capability of the inter-continental ballistic missiles located at the Ramstein Air Base near Zweibrucken. Can you tell us more about these? What do you know of these installations?"

"The military? I have very little to do with the military. I was brought to Germany to teach in a high school." Briefly, I explained to the interrogators

my professional education and work experiences and my current role as a school teacher. *"I have no knowledge about the air force other than that which is available to any civilian. I do not have any military secrets and I have never served in the military,"* I explained to them. I then told the authorities about my interest in coming to Europe, not to be a part of the military but to use my work as an opportunity to travel in Europe and to visit the Soviet Union. Without overdoing it, I wanted to present a pro-communist posture by expressing my respect for the accomplishments of Russia in the realm of science and technology as well as in sports. To do otherwise, I concluded, would not help my situation. *"Most of all, I acknowledge the role of the Soviet Union in establishing the borders of present day Ukraine after World War II. Without Russia, I doubt that Ukraine would have survived."* I told the authorities that I was not accustomed to the same laws in Canada and explained to them as to why I had used the tape recorder. At the same time, I assured them that I had not taken any photographs of prohibited objects, installations, or factories.

As had been my experience on other occasions while talking to officials in the Soviet Union, I concluded that they would be pumping me for information about the military and its weapons of war. Since I knew very little about NATO, American bases in Germany, and the strike power of the Canadian Air Force, I could provide them with little information that would be of help to them. As the meeting was drawing to a close, I could see that even though annoyed, they seemed satisfied with my responses to their questions.

The authorities then asked me to wait in the lobby while they brought Adelio in for questioning. As I waited for the interrogation to be completed, I wandered whether or not Adelio was really a civil engineer. What was he doing in Russia? Was he working for some agency? For whom was he working? I recalled telling the officials that I knew virtually nothing about Adelio. Besides, I was in no position to cast aspersions. For all I knew, Adelio could have been an agent or a double agent. When they suggested that Adelio was involved with a left-wing activist group in Canada, I told them that I knew nothing of it.

In due course Adelio came out of the meeting room looking none the worse for wear. It would not be until later that I would find out the questions that they had put before Adelio. In concluding our meeting, an official informed me that my relatives in Buzk had been contacted and that they would be bussed into Lviv for a brief visit with me. *"In this way you will have your opportunity to meet your family while at the same time making it unnecessary for you to break our laws by visiting our villages which are out of bounds for tourists. As for your relatives in Kamianka Buzk, I must tell you that up to this moment we were not able to contact them."* Just as I was getting up to leave, an officer stopped me, *"One more question I would like to ask you, Officer Kashuba, before we close. Do you know a Yuri Molayev in Edmonton?"*

I thought for a moment and concluded that I had never, to my knowledge, heard the name before. Were the officials on some sort of a fishing trip? As suddenly as the questioning had started, it all seemed to come to an end. Once again we were asked to wait in the lobby of the hotel. After another long wait, we were asked to come back into the meeting room. To our surprise, the officials had a tray of carbonated drinks waiting for us. We relaxed over these for a few moments making small talk. Finally, another official came in and his decision was brief. *"Comrades, the decision of the authorities is to expel you both from the Soviet Union. This does mean that the Soviet funds in your possession, gas coupons, pre-paid accommodation, and all pre-paid Intourist service charges for the Soviet Union portion of your journey will be forfeited to officials when you reach the border at Uzhorod. After you have had an opportunity to visit with a few members of your family, we are asking that you leave Lviv at 1300 hours. That will get you in good time to the border before entering Czechoslovakia and your next Intourist stop."*

I thanked the officials for giving us what I thought to be a fair hearing and apologized for any problems that our visit may have caused them. In particular, I expressed my thanks to the officials who provided a bus so that those relatives who wanted to visit me at 1200 hours could do so. I suspected that this courtesy was unusual.

Adelio and I had a couple of hours before the bus was to arrive. I wondered what had happened to our Intourist guide, Svetlana. She was nowhere to be seen. Sure enough, promptly at 1200 hours a nondescript bus pulled up in front of the hotel. I could see that the driver was in military uniform. So was the officer on board who seemed to be in charge of the operation. The bus was met by a couple of officials who had been awaiting the arrival of the bus in the parking compound near the hotel. In total, about sixteen passengers were escorted into the lobby of the hotel at which point I was introduced to what I was told were members of my family. As I looked over the faces of those in attendance, I did recognize Maria, Olha and Oleg, whom we had met previously in the village of Buzk. As for the other members in the party, the stress of the previous twenty-four hours made everything seemed fuzzy. I had a difficult time placing them on the family tree.

From the lobby of the hotel we all retired to a small meeting room where we were served a light lunch. I was not surprised to note that the Soviet officials joined us. To the best of my recollection, in the group were six members of mom's family and four members of my dad's family. Most were from the village of Buzk with the exception of two who, contrary to what an official had said earlier, were picked up in the village of Kamianka-Buzk. I later learned that the latter village was only thirty kilometres from Buzk and was home to my mom's sister Oksana and her family. I met my Uncle Fedjko for the first time from whom I learned that in addition to his daughter Maria, he had two young sons, Yaroslav and Zenoviy. Throughout, our conversations had to do with family, my work in Germany and my trip to the Soviet Union. Having regard for my present predicament, I avoided any reference to or discussion about the Canadian system of government, communism or religion.

A dance troupe from the Soviet Republic of Kazakhstan performing at Moscow's National Economic Achievements Exposition, 1967.

The expanse of Ukrainian agricultural land near Kharkiv, Ukraine, 1967.

Military police brought several family members to meet me in Lviv, L to R are Oleg and Olha Abranik (d. of Vasyl Groszko), Mariann Groszko (d. of Damian Groszko of Liepaja, Latvia), Maria and Fedjko Kaszuba and their daughter Maria. Lviv, 1967.

Bathers and sun worshippers, Dnipro River. Kyiv, Ukraine, 1967.

A common scene depicting women grazing cows near Lviv, Ukraine, 1967.

With the pressures of the interrogation still very fresh in my mind, it didn't take too long for the names of my relatives to recede to the far reaches of my mind. I made an attempt to take a few notes about my relatives. When a Soviet official spotted this, his immediate response was *'nyet'*. His reaction made no sense to me. After all, what were the officials afraid of? Even if I did make a few notes, the information would be of little interest or use to them. For one thing, they were within earshot of our conversations and any future correspondence to my relatives would likely be opened by officials before reaching its destination. Surely, they would be aware of this procedure.

Now gathered in the lobby of the hotel, an official informed me that it was time for us to leave. With this, each member of the family tearfully embraced and wished me a safe journey. Having packed our belongings into our car, we said goodbye to the officials and set our sights on the border city of Uzhorod, a small international city which at one time was known as Ungvar. The route to Uzhorod took us through the Carpathian Mountains which pale in comparison to the grandeur of the Rocky Mountains in Canada. Yet, the Rockies were never as romanticized as were the Carpathians in literature, ballads, songs, and paintings. As we drove through the Carpathians, I could readily see why Ukrainians came to love these mountains; they were beautiful and even the pace of life seemed to slow as if to savour every moment. The people who lived in the Carpathians were *the hill people* who devoted their lives to a peaceful and pastoral co-existence with their neighbours in the mountains and their foreign neighbours, Poland, Czechoslovakia, Hungary, and Romania.

The city of Uzhorod lies in the extreme west of Ukraine on the beautiful banks of the River Uzh *(snake)* in the foothills of the Carpathians. History shows us that this region, known as Transcarpathia, was torn away from the Kyivan Rus in the 11th century. Uzhorod remained for several centuries under the rule of foreign invaders. Following World War II, under a treaty between the USSR and Czechoslovakia, Transcarpathian Ukraine was reunited with the Ukrainian Soviet Socialist Republic. As a result, the city of Uzhorod became the cultural and trading centre of the Transcarpathian region of Ukraine.

The highway to Czechoslovakia took us through a flourishing park-like-city in which we saw not only monuments of the past, but also new schools, cinemas, libraries, and streets lined with modern buildings. We noted that the River Uzh, with its embankments and canals, dams and bridges, blended in with the environs. My Intourist information package, heavily weighted in favour of communism, noted that the city is an important cultural centre of Transcarpathia, housing a university, several technical schools, and scores of secondary schools.

Knowing that we were only a short distance from the border crossing which would take us out of Ukraine, I asked Adelio to reach into the back seat and get my briefcase so that we might ensure ourselves that all of our documentation for our exit would be ready. I could see Adelio fumbling

The beautiful Carpathian Mountains, Ukraine, 1967.

around in the back seat saying, *"Steve, there is no briefcase here."* My heart skipped a beat. I, too, reached behind and groped frantically for my briefcase. Nothing.

Pulling over to the side of the highway, Adelio and I searched everywhere. No luck. I was in a state of shock. Methodically, we retraced all of our steps for those final moments before we left Lviv. We especially went over the procedures we used for packing our luggage and ensuring that these were safely placed into our auto. We knew that the military police had confiscated our passports and our visas in Buzk the previous day. We also knew that the passports and visas were returned to us by the Soviet officials just as we were preparing to go out-of-doors at the Intourist hotel to meet my relatives just three hours earlier. I was very certain that I had placed my visa and my passport in my leather briefcase before I said my last goodbyes to my relatives at the hotel. Adelio and I had just one explanation, the briefcase was either stolen by someone or a Soviet official took the briefcase out of the Volkswagen at the point in time when Adelio and I were saying our goodbyes. One thing was for certain; I was in real difficulty now. To go back to Lviv now would be folly. Since we were near the border, we decided to drive to the border and have the border guards contact the authorities in Lviv about my missing briefcase.

When I explained to the border guards what had happened, we were immediately arrested again and escorted back to downtown Uzhorod and the Intourist Hotel where we were asked to remain in the building. What started out to be a pastoral drive to the exit point at Uzhorod was now quickly turning into a disaster. Having checked with Intourist Central in Moscow, an official looked at me saying, *"We suspect, Lieutenant Kashuba, that this is a deliberate attempt to stay longer in the Soviet Union. You will not be permitted to motor back to Lviv for your credentials. You and Comrade d'Amonti will remain here under custody until we can investigate this matter."*

From Hotel Uzhorod the officials placed a call to the Intourist hotel in Lviv and explained our dilemma. They then placed a call to Soviet authorities in Lviv before placing another call to Hotel Dnister. Throughout those telephone discussions, I was flanked by two military police who listened intently to the conversation with the manager of Hotel Dnister. Handing me the telephone, an official asked me to describe to the manager the colour and size of the briefcase. While all of this was happening, I noticed that one officer was posted at the entrance door to the hotel while another officer stood next to my car. They seemed to be taking no chances with us. The hotel manager said that he would contact police officials in Lviv, undertake a search for the briefcase and have the police call us back with their results.

While having supper, I was called out to the lobby by one of the officers. *"We got a call back from the police in Lviv confirming that your briefcase has been located."* To me, it was like winning the grand prize at a big curling bonspiel! In way of explanation, the official in Lviv indicated that the briefcase was located, officially sealed and that it would be flown to Uzhorod on a regularly-scheduled flight the following day to arrive in Uzhorod at 1100 hours.

I wanted very much to ask the officials if the briefcase could be transported by car that evening and not by an aircraft but thought better of it. As I considered our circumstance, I concluded that characterizing it as being under house arrest was a misnomer. Everyone knew that we could not leave Ukraine without our documents. As a result, we were granted the freedom to wander around the downtown area during the evening. I'm glad we did. Uzhorod turned out to be a city unlike any I had ever seen. It was a very happy city with a strong influence from Hungary, Romania, and Czechoslovakia. It seemed that there was music everywhere. Soulful gypsy music presented on violins at a local market. Hungarian and Ukrainian music and dance. Maybe this was the season for festivals, all of which made me feel out of place. For certain, there was no music in my heart.

True to their word, the Soviet authorities delivered my briefcase to me at Hotel Uzhorod by 1100 hours the next morning. The briefcase was carefully wrapped in brown paper, taped, and sealed with what looked like a wax seal on the front. When I opened the parcel, my leather briefcase was inside. I went through its contents. The two most important items, my passport and visa were there. So were my notes, maps, travel guidelines, gas coupons, telephone numbers, and addresses of various embassies and people that I wanted to visit on my journey. The names of people I had visited or met were also there. Conspicuously missing was my Polish currency, Russian currency, 35mm films, and some of the gas coupons. I immediately asked the authorities about this. Their contention was that nothing had been removed. When I asked them as to where my briefcase was recovered and by whom, they simply shrugged their shoulders. Upon closer examination I was surprised to note that not all of my tape recorder tapes were confiscated. I wondered if the information contained on the two remaining tapes was intact.

At this point the authorities asked us to check out of the hotel before providing us with an escort to the border for final processing out of Ukraine. The border crossing into Czechoslovakia was only a couple kilometres away and I was very anxious to get there quickly and put behind the past three days. When we arrived at the border, security seemed unusually heavy. Without any fanfare, we were asked to pull into a holding compound for automobiles. Adelio and I were then asked to bring our documentation into the border guardhouse.

The opening questions were the standard ones that a tourist to the Soviet Union might expect. These dealt with questions about our identity, the date of entry, the route of travel, expenditures, purchases, and our basic experiences in the Soviet Union. In anticipation of a problem with my exit visa, I thought that I might tell the guards that I spoke no Ukrainian or Russian. There was a moment of silence while the officer referred to his file. *"The information I have,"* he said, *"is that you not only speak Ukrainian fluently but that you can also read and the write the language. Further, my information tells me that you were able to communicate effectively in Russian while in Minsk, Smolensk, and Moscow."*

I immediately saw the futility of trying to gain any advantage by showing any ignorance of the two Slavic languages. I knew that Adelio would not have this problem. The only language he spoke was English. Maybe some Italian. The questioning took about one hour at which point the two officers going through the documentation excused themselves. They were back in a short while and asked me to follow them to another building. Adelio was asked to stay behind. With great apprehension and difficulty I tried to assess my predicament. I wondered how much they knew about my daily activities while in the Soviet Union. I thought about the KGB and how they liked to look upon the children of Ukrainian immigrants living in Canada and the United States as spreading anti-Soviet propaganda; of being strongly anti-communist. I even envisioned their propensity to want to punish these foreigners.

As I was taken to a small room in the interior of the building, I reminded myself that I was a foreign citizen and *not* without *some* safeguards. However, being able to contact a Canadian Consulate or Embassy was not one of them. The interrogation room had a table located in the centre of it and was surrounded by four wooden chairs with a single light protruding out of the ceiling. The two professional-looking officers introduced themselves; a move that was unusual in the Soviet Union. I do not remember their names but they got right to the point. *"We have information, Comrade Kashuba, that you have been involved in activity contrary to the guidelines established for visitors to the Soviet Union. I would like for you to tell us about your time in the Soviet Union and any activities in which you were involved which are contrary to our laws."*

For me, the danger signals were up. To fudge the truth would be folly and I suspected that they had a pretty good idea about any misdemeanours. At the same time, I concluded that it would be unwise to provide them with any more information than was absolutely necessary. While I was being interrogated, the officers also informed me that my Volkswagen would be thoroughly searched. Apparently they wanted some assurance that the story I would be telling them would be consistent with what they found in my car. Likely, they would want to know just what information I was collecting in the Soviet Union and why. They would want to know about any photographs and notes I had taken. And about any tape recorded messages left on my tape recorder. In addition, I knew that they would be very interested in what I did with the consumables that I brought into the Soviet Union. Last, but not least, I suspected that they would want to know why I was leaving the Soviet Union with far fewer clothes than I had upon entry. This meant only one thing; they would want to know as to what happened to the golf shirts, blue jeans, and blue blazer. My mind was in high gear.

For the next thirty minutes I recounted for the interrogators all of my activities in the Soviet Union since leaving Brest. I also spoke about the grandeur of the country and of the sacrifices the brave Soviet soldiers made during World War II and the impact of the monuments I saw in honour of their bravery. I told them of my thrill at visiting the sports palace in Minsk. As I spoke, I noticed that my remarks were being recorded and that one officer was taking copious notes. When I concluded my presentation, I waited for their reaction. The silence hung heavily over me and the two officers seemed deep in thought. Finally, an officer, without looking up from his notes, broke the silence. What he had to say sent tingles down my spine.

"Comrade, we have information that you showed too much interest in our industry. You asked too many questions about our military. You even criticized our form of government. Why all of these questions? Just what is your role with the Royal Canadian Air Force? And what of all of those photographs and notes?"

My first reaction was to disagree with the official. I bit my tongue. The two officers excused themselves and two new officers came in. Unlike the gentle questioning from the first two officials, I was about to get a dose of another type. *"Comrade, you do not have to repeat what you said earlier. We heard your testimony. What we want to know is exactly what you sold on the black market in the Soviet Union, for how much, and what you have done with the money from these illegal sales."*

I thought back to Lviv and my missing briefcase and about the missing currency. My thoughts were broken when the two officers asked me to follow them back to my Volkswagen. What I saw shocked me. My luggage was neatly unpacked and spread out. So was Adelio's. Worse yet, my car had been elevated on car jacks so as to facilitate an under-the-car examination. As I watched, two workers lowered my car to the pavement. What I saw inside the car did not impress me. In several interior locations at the door, the paneling, and in the ceiling the interior lining of the car had been pulled away so that the examining officers might search all of the potential hiding places.

The officers asked me to visually inspect my luggage and to bring into the guard room all of those items that were *illegally* in my possession. I didn't need any prompting. In the metal container I placed such items as the tape recorder, three reel-to-reel tapes, three religious icons, a sizable amount of Polish currency, Czechoslovakian currency, five rolls of undeveloped 35mm film, two bottles of vodka, and from my briefcase, all of those personal notes about the Soviet Union. When these items were placed on the examination table in the interrogation room, even I was surprised that all of these items were in my possession. I had to make an important decision. Knowing that I had been separated from my brief case for a period of one day, I might have contended that some of these items found their way into by possession by some devious and nefarious means. On the other hand, I could claim ownership of all of them. I decided the latter route might serve me better. As a result, it was now up to me to offer up a laudable explanation about each of these.

While explaining how each item came to be in my possession and watching for any reaction from the interrogators, I concluded that the most contentious item was the amount of currency I had in my possession. At the same time, I concluded that some of my American currency had been removed from my briefcase. However, I knew that I would have to provide a reasonable explanation for the Polish zloty and Russian roubles in my possession. I told them about selling some personal items of clothing, pens, pencils, candy, and gum to street vendors in Warsaw, Minsk, and Moscow.

Their questioning techniques seemed to vary from the quick and staccato questions to which they wanted immediate responses to those which were asked slowly and deliberately and which required a considered response. By this time, nearly four hours had elapsed since I was first brought into the interrogation room. My prospects for receiving a clean bill of health seemed to grow dimmer as time went on. While the interrogators came at me in pairs, I had little time to get my thoughts straight between sessions. Then, I found that the approaches used by these two-man investigation teams were quite varied. One pair was gentle and kind while the next came at me like a bull in a china shop. The heat of the afternoon, the close quarters, and the bright lights didn't do much for my level of comfort. The air was heavy and I was certain that the officers had never heard of underarm deodorants.

It seemed that nothing was left out. There was no use in twisting the truth. I knew that they had information about my parents and that no part of my trip was a great secret. The final part of the interrogation had to do with matters military. *'How is it possible to convince them that I know little about the military,'* I thought. The task seemed impossible and they simply refused to let go. We had reached an impasse. However, I soon discovered that they must have been convinced that I wasn't about to provide them with any more information. I could sense that the officers were about to wrap up their questioning when they said to me that my Canadian citizenship was in question and that Soviet Ukraine could well claim my citizenship since I was the first born of a citizen of Ukraine. *"But,"* I protested, *"how can that be. My parents came to Canada carrying a Polish passport."*

"That, comrade," he responded, *"is only a small technicality. Look at your family. Where are they now? Are they not citizens of Soviet Ukraine?"*

I then summarized for the officers all of the items that I had sold or bartered in the Soviet Union. To the best of my knowledge, I told them what I had received for each item. Not wishing to be argumentative, however, I accepted their conclusion that what I had done was wrong, illegal and contrary to the laws of the state. Once again, the two officers excused themselves only to be replaced by the two officers who conducted the first part of the interrogation. Their summary statements, when they returned, were brief and to the point.

"Comrade Kashuba, we clearly have evidence of considerable amount of wrong-doing on your part while you were in the Soviet Union. In particular, you opened the tape recorder which was sealed in Brest. You illegally took photographs. You sold personal items of clothing on the black market. So, we are authorized by state laws, to confiscate all those items illegally obtained and any profit you may have realized from the sale of items. You will be left with sufficient gas coupons and funds for a safe return to your Air Force Base in Germany. In releasing you from this interrogation, we ask two things of you. One, do not talk about your trip to the Soviet Union or our conversations. Two, the Soviet Authorities in Moscow have asked me to relay to you that you are hereby banned from coming back to the Soviet Union for a period of twenty-five years. These are the two conditions of your release which are briefly represented in writing. Please sign this notice of expulsion from the Soviet Union with the two conditions attached."

I read the brief notice duly dated and prepared in the Russian language. *"Can I ask, sir, precisely what does this document say?"*

"It is a brief summary of our investigation, the list of misdemeanours that you have committed against the State, your acknowledgment of all of this, and finally, the fact that you are expelled from the Soviet Union for a period of twenty-five years."

I didn't quite know what to say. While I was in thought, the officer asked me whether or not I had accepted the terms of my release. Without hesitation, I said that I did. I then asked them about Adelio d'Amonti. *"We are not concerned about your friend. He is not associated with the military and he did not enter into the black market. Your file will show that you will not be allowed back into the Soviet Union until the year 1992."*

"Does that guideline apply to my family," I asked.

"Only your immediate family," was his reply.

"Sir," I asked, *"in your view, is this a fair resolution of the matter? I mean, the Soviet authorities will not pursue this matter further in the future, will they?"*

"Well, sir, we have discussed that matter. You see, yours is a petty crime. And, as you can well understand to prosecute you would be a very expensive

undertaking for the Soviet government. It is our decision that circumstances do not warrant such action."

"Then sir," I asked, *"is the matter that I am affiliated with the Royal Canadian Air Force of any importance in your decision?"*

"Perhaps, perhaps," was his noncommittal response.

I had heard about others signing a document which was a confession to all sorts of things that really did not happen. With this in mind, I slowly read the document. Seeing the difficulty that I was experiencing in reading the Russian language, an official promptly assisted me with its contents. Finally, I got the courage to ask him if my signature would put me at further risk.

"No," he replied. *"This will be the end of the matter."*

As Adelio and I packed our belongings, we counted our blessings. Sure, there was some damage to the interior of the car but that was the least of my concern. Those could all be fixed. Of greater concern was the fact that the Soviet authorities confiscated my Polish, German, Russian, and American currency. We were thankful that they had not confiscated Adelio's currency. Under the watchful eyes of security, the authorities waved us to the Czechoslovakian border crossing to a friendly greeting where our passports and visas were checked. As an official was about to wave us through, he suddenly asked, in broken English, *"Vell, comrades, you have good time in Russia, no?"*

"Listen up," I said, *"do you want to buy a pen and pencil set?"*

That brought a guffaw from everyone, including my companion, Adelio.

10.

Return to Germany

And a visit to Check Point Charlie in Berlin

Peering in my rear-view mirror at the receding Czechoslovakian border, I was struck with one thought that bounced around in my head–*it was my parents who made a decision never to return to their beloved homeland.* Would my expulsion from the Soviet Union permit someone else to make a similar decision for me? I had made no such decision. In fact, I had a feeling that my mission to the Soviet Union had not been fulfilled. For the moment, however, it seemed to matter little about my feelings. I had to concede that the KGB and the policies of the Soviet Union had won the first round. I was now a *persona non grata*–an unwelcome guest in a land that lived within my soul. The question was, *would I ever return?*

As I pondered our geographic location, I had to admit that things went terribly wrong. Prior to the debacle in Buzk, it was my intention to seek permission of Soviet authorities to re-enter Poland at the Przemysl border crossing, swing north to the town of Cieszanow and then drive to mom's village of Plazow where I might also make an enquiry about Grohi. The first sign that I might not be able to alter my route occurred in Brest when the Soviets sealed by magnetaphone and indicated that my point of exit would be Uzhorod. This was reaffirmed by the authorities in Lviv. Sadly, a visit to my mother's village would have to wait, perhaps for another twenty-five years.

From eastern Czechoslovakia we crossed into southeastern Poland en route to Krakow. As we drove through the Polish countryside between Krakow and the German border, a strong German influence was evident. The contrast of this region of Poland (*Upper Silesia* or Zielona Gora) to eastern and northern Poland was quite stark, ranging from the style of homes, farm buildings and roads to the mannerisms of its inhabitants. Rumour had it that the roofs of the German farmers and villagers were nearly always constructed of red shale and it was for this reason that the pilots serving in the German Air Force were able to identify which homes and villages were to be bombed. After the war, the Germans living in Silesia were re-located to East Germany and the region re-settled by Poles and Ukrainians.

As we crossed into East Germany at Frankfurt on Oder, we were reminded of the failure of the Allies to agree upon the future disposition of defeated Germany after the war which resulted in the formal division of Germany into Eastern and Western zones. With these historic changes, our only route into Berlin from East Germany would be to motor west into West Germany and then retrace our steps back to Berlin via a highly protected autobahn enclosed by barbed wire (*no man's land*), fully guarded twenty hours a day.

Upon entering Berlin, many of the conditions found on May 4, 1945 when German representatives signed the document of unconditional surrender were still prevalent. Although much of Berlin had been rebuilt, there was evidence of destruction everywhere. The major Soviet offensive against Berlin on April 16, 1945 was composed of 19 armies, 1,600,000 men, 3,827 tanks, 2,344 self-propelled guns, 4,520 anti-tank guns, 15,654 field guns, 3,411 anti-aircraft guns, 6,700 aircraft and 96,000 vehicles. With this kind of firepower, it is little wonder that so much damage was inflicted upon the City. It was also on April 16 that Hitler issued his infamous order, '*He who gives the order to retreat is to be shot on the spot.*'[5]

Since Berlin was completely in the part of Germany controlled by the Soviet Union, the distance from West Germany, controlled by the USA, to the City was about 220 kilometres. The autobahn connecting West Germany to Berlin was constructed in '*no man's land,*' about one hundred meters in width. No vegetation was permitted in this area in order to preserve a better field of fire. Another control strip behind this was about thirty meters wide and was constantly kept sanded so that foot prints would remain visible. The roads inside this five hundred meter strip could be used only for work of economic importance. In all, the prohibited area along this frontier was more than five kilometres in width.

It would not be until 1989 that the Berlin Wall would come down. In 1990 the two parts of Germany would be united as the Federal Republic of Germany following which, in 1999, Berlin would become the capital of Germany in accordance with the unification treaty thereby providing Germans with an opportunity to once again capture from Paris the title of world centre for culture, music, art, and architecture.

Adelio and I realized our mission to Berlin by viewing Check Point Charlie from West Berlin and crossing the border, demarcated by the concrete wall, into East Berlin. Under the watchful eye of border guards with their machine guns trained on us, it was quite an experience. Years later when the wall

---

5   Salmaggi, Cesare and Alfredo Pallavisini. <u>2194 Days of War</u>, Arnoldo Mondadori, Milan, Italy, page 714.

would come down, a private museum would come up about a block away from Check Point Charlie so that artefacts, cards, letters and photographs of those who escaped *(or died trying)* from East Germany might be immortalized.[6]

✖

It is not surprising that the Berlin Wall[7] and all that it stood for wound its way into the hearts and minds of millions of citizens the world over for well over thirty years. Of course, the architects of the wall had but one purpose in mind, but how were they to know that the very idea of the wall would somehow unite people rather than separate them. It seemed as though the concrete barrier stopped time as much as it clocked space. For Adelio and me, a walk between east and west was a study in contrasts. *As I stood staring in awe at the wall that separated a nation, I could not help but think of what it was that separated me from my family in Soviet Ukraine and Poland. I had to conclude that the culprit in both cases was the same; communism.*

Our motor trip from Berlin to the Canadian Forces Base was comparatively short and, in a way, anticlimactic. Security was tight when we arrived at 3-Wing in Zweibrucken. At the entry gate I presented my credentials to security and indicated that Adelio would be my guest at the Base for a couple of days. Since this was mid-August and most of the non-military personnel were on summer recess, I knew that there would be plenty of space in the officers' barracks to provide accommodation for Adelio.

On the following day, and in keeping with my commitment when I first left the Base for the Soviet Union, I checked in with Base Security to set up a time for a de-briefing session. In the meantime, I drove Adelio to the local bus station so that he might get to Frankfurt in time to catch a flight to Canada. As I prepared my notes for the next day's meeting with officials, I had to admit that Adelio and I shared quite an experience; something that would forever be with us.

Having to attend a military de-briefing session was a new experience for me and, unlike the briefing session prior to my departure, I was now facing no less than seven members from various departments of the military base. We indulged in the regular small talk prior to the Chairman calling the session to order. *"Flight Lieutenant Kashuba, it is an expectation that you will provide us with honest and candid answers. We want to monitor, on a continuing basis, the viability of civilian and military personnel traveling to Soviet Bloc countries."* At the outset, I described how I planned for the trip followed by a summary of what happened during each segment of the

---

6   Readers Digest. <u>Condensed from the New York Times Magazine by Paul Goldberger</u>, June, 1995, page 116.

7   Haywood, John. <u>Atlas of World History</u>, Andromeda Oxford Ltd., Etobicoke, Ontario, 1999, pp. 110-111.

103

journey. I ended my summary by saying, *"most of my notes, photographs and tape recordings prior to exiting Soviet Ukraine have been confiscated by Soviet officials."*

There was no shortage of questions from panel members and, as might be expected, most of the questions had to do with my time in Buzk, Lviv and Uzhorod. But, there were many other questions; questions about the Polish family that befriended me and asked me to spend a night with them; questions about my Intourist guides and the KGB officers who joined us from time to time. Their questions were insightful and confirmed that Intelligence of this Base was very knowledgeable and thorough. No detail was too small to pursue.

As can be expected, I did not have all the answers. I could guess, but I did not know who contacted authorities in Lviv about my impending visit to my relatives in Buzk nor did I know who was responsible for the disappearance of my briefcase in Lviv. There was, however, one question that puzzled them and that had to do with my expulsion from the Soviet Union for a period of twenty-five years. Not one member of the panel had heard of anything similar. And, when the Soviet authorities said that they did not wish to prosecute me because of the cost to the Soviet Government, were they sincere or simply posturing?

By noon I had completed my testimony at which point the Chairman indicated that we would have lunch in the Officers' Mess following which we would meet for some summary comments. Before calling me in for the afternoon session, the de-briefing panel met for the purpose of consolidating their comments.

I was impressed with how quickly the Chairman was able to summarize the deliberations of the panel. As might be expected, his comments had to do with legislation in the West as opposed to that in the East and how travelers to Soviet Bloc Countries came under a different set of rules. In the end, he did agree with the Soviet officials who said to me that I had not committed a crime, only that I conducted myself in a way contrary to the principles of communism. *And, just what were those misdemeanours? The first had to do with selling personal items on the black market while the second had to do with my visit to a kolhosp and to a village.* Of course, I was aware that Security was not too happy with the invitation extended to Adelio or the tape recorder caper. Months later I would learn that the Department of National Defense no longer supported travel to Iron Curtain Countries on the part of military personnel. The length of the ban was not made known to me.

The flight back to Trenton, Ontario somehow did not hold the same sense of urgency as did my flight to Marville two years earlier. I picked up a new car in Toronto and took in Expo 67 in Montreal where I visited the Soviet pavilion just to see, first hand, the kind of propaganda the Soviets were advancing. I balanced this visit off with a visit to the American geodesic dome, which was also very popular with Canadians. The talk in Canada was about De Gaulle and his comment of *Vive le Quebec libre* and the demise of my favourite politician, John Diefenbaker. My last major event before arriving in Edmonton was the Pan-American Games in Winnipeg where Canada placed second behind the United States in the number of medals.

When I arrived in Edmonton, I discussed with mom and dad my trip to the Soviet Union. Of course, by this time they had corresponded with Fedjko and Maria of Buzk and were well aware of my troubles in Lviv and Uzhorod. To this day I do not know if the Soviet officials were aware as to the contents of the taped message from Maria Groszko. But, even if they were, I can say with some certainty that the recorded by Maria left no doubt—she left the impression that she was a great supporter of the communist regime; at least that is what is reflected on the tape. Dad was of the opinion that the KGB were not to be trusted and that I was lucky to get out of Soviet Ukraine without penalty. Mom's greatest concern had to do with the manner in which I was interrogated by the KGB in Lviv and Uzhorod. Perhaps my dad said it best with his conclusion, *"You know, son, I fought on the side of the Austrians against the Russians in World War I. There was much more honour within the ranks of the army in those days. Things have changed when the communist regime gained control. From what Fedjko tells me, the KGB cannot be trusted. Yes, a lot has happened since I was a soldier and not always for the best."*

With that, the saga of my trip to the Soviet Union was over. Or, so I thought. At that point I was not aware of how certain elements of the trip would come to visit upon me in the coming days and years. All too soon I'd find out.

Brandenburg Gate, a symbol of national consciousness since it went up in 1791, is the most famous Berlin landmark. When the City was blockaded by the Soviets in 1948, the Gate was the line of demarcation between West and East Berlin, effectively trapping 2.5 million West Berliners without food, supplies or electricity. Constructed in 1961, the Berlin Wall was dismantled in 1990.

Check Point Charlie was one of the crossing points between East and West Berlin for 27 years during the Cold War (1948 to 1985).

PART 2:

WHERE IT ALL BEGAN

11.

The Balkan Front[8]

Andrij reflects on the meaning of war

Sitting in a hastily dug trench, Andrij surveyed the scene around him wondering what in God's name he was doing in Serbia. Being relatively close to the Adriatic Sea, it was not unusual to find his infantry unit shrouded in a dense fog on yet another wet, cold and dreary day. The collision of a warm and moist maritime front with a dry and cold air mass from Hungary could do that. As winter approached, the late fall of 1916 marked the third year of hostilities during World War I, he wasn't exactly looking forward to celebrating his 16th birthday so far removed from home. The image of the trench and all of those infantry soldiers squeezed in around him like sardines in a tin can stayed with him forever.

Just how *did* the war start? Exactly, *what* was it that he was fighting for? Some in his company said that it was the product of large economic forces embodied in the capitalist system which led to the militant imperialism generated by capitalism. Others said that the war came about as a result of old style diplomacy which had bound the countries of Europe into a system of competing alliances leaving little space for compromise. This resulted in an obligation on the part of alliances to be dragged into a dispute; first one nation and then another.

By 1914, Europe was suddenly confronted with a German nation that had grown in population and economic strength. This led to fears, enmities and resentment from its neighbours and seemed especially significant that the nationalistic Balkan states, including Serbia, were patronized by Russia

---

8   Note: PART 2 of this book is written in the third person and reflects the thoughts and feelings of my parents as presented to me in discussions and interviews over the years.

Andrij Kaszuba, passport photo, Lubaczow, Poland, 1927.

thereby threatening the very stability of the Austro-Hungarian Empire. The war was preceded by diplomatic manoeuvres which went awry and one bluff led to another, all ending in diplomatic misjudgements. The end result? Mobilization schemes which quickly swept Europe into self-destruction.

In trying to understand the meaning of war, it was unlikely that Andrij would get any help from the non-commissioned Austrian officer who led the company *was more interested in his machine-gun crew and defending his artillery emplacement in advance of any enemy attack than he was in making small talk.* Pinned down by sniper fire, Andrij knew that his unit's machine-gun battery, as powerful as it might be, was useless against this kind of warfare. To even peer out of the fox hole would risk being picked off like a clay pigeon by a sniper's bullet. But then, the Austrian Officer also knew that most of the Serbs had already retreated and that it would only be a matter of time before the remaining pockets of resistance would be eliminated; forcibly removed, dead or alive. He felt confident that his unit would ultimately triumph. This was confirmed when word spread amongst the troops that the Austrian Army was well entrenched and held the high ground in Serbia. In fact, it was General Erich von Falkenhayn who announced that, *'the Allied troops are largely immobile, constituting the largest internment camp in the world.'*

As a member of the Ukrainian contingent in the Austrian Army, Andrij wondered what went wrong at the outbreak of War in July of 1914. It seemed as though the heads of the Austrian Empire in Vienna and the leaders of the Hungarian Empire in Budapest were reluctant to attack Serbia knowing full well that Russia's tsar would come to the defence of that nation, *even though it was virtually certain that Serbia was behind the assassination of the heir to the Habsburg throne.* In the end, it was the German Kaiser in Berlin who forced the hand of the Austro-Hungarian Empire into armed conflict. This action was tantamount to the Prussian aristocrats and German industrialists declaring war on Russia.[9]

Much of what happened in Andrij's future seemed somehow to have its roots in his service as a soldier in the Austrian Army. World War I began with Austria's punitive expedition against Serbia in August of 1914, nearly two years before Andrij got into the conflict. A determined Serbian Army pushed back the Austrian Army only to be faced with another Austrian offensive in November. Once again, the results were the same. At the same time, a similar fate was experienced by the Austrians at the hands of the Russian Army. It would not be until February of 1915 that a major offensive by the Austro-German Army at Gorlice-Tarnow *(Poland)* would push the Russians out of Galicia in May. However, Serbia continued to be a thorn in the flank of the Central Powers throughout 1915 and plans were drawn up by General von Mackensen,[10] commander of the Eleventh German Army in Galicia, to destroy this irritant. With the help from Bulgarian forces, the Austro-German Army forced the Serbs to retreat westward through the mountains of Albania.

As war broke out, Russia faced the dilemma of opting for an attack on East Prussia in the north or Galicia in the south. It was March of the previous year that Russia launched an attack right in Andrij's back yard and took the Austro-Germans by surprise, breaking their defences in two places and almost destroying the Austrian Army. The Germans counter-attacked and pushed the Russians back after they had reached the foothills of the Carpathians.

As Andrij considered the magnitude of the war, he could not get out of his mind that Ukrainians in his own village longed for a nation of their own. Perhaps they concluded that war was acceptable if it was the road to independence for Galicia. How did the war come about in the first place? Why was he, an ethnic Ukrainian serving in the Austrian Army, aligned against his Slavic cousins, the Russians? What strange quirk in history would bring about this strange circumstance?

There is only one explanation for this. Andrij was born just at the turn of the 20th century with the misfortune of being reared in a geographic region of Galicia that seemed to possess a flexible border; flexible in a sense that over the years a number of nations attempted to lay claim to this region of Europe for its rich and seemingly limitless resources. More specifically, it was Austria, Germany, Poland, Hungary, and Russia that coveted her riches. Being born into a geographic region that would have been a worthy prize for any one of these nations, it is little wonder that the language and customs of

---

9   Clark, Alan. The Eastern Front, 1914 - 1918, The Windrush Press, Gloucestershire, England, 1971, page 11.

10   Prior, Robin & Trevor Wilson, The First World War, Cassell, Wellington House, London, 1999, p. 57.

its inhabitants were constantly buffeted and influenced by her neighbours. It is also understandable that more than one language was spoken in this region and that, over time, it became difficult for the locals to totally embrace one language or another.

This explains why Andrij fluently spoke both languages, Ukrainian and Polish. It is true that both are Slavic languages and to speak one is to at least be able to understand the rudiments of the other. Still, he accepted that the heritage of his family to be Ukrainian. In those days a family had to declare itself for one ethnic group or the other, especially during periods of political upheaval or national conflict, for to do otherwise might leave one as a loner outside both groups, without friend or family. However, this is not to say that some members of Andrij's extended family did not embrace the Polish language.

Although Andrij's family claimed their ethnicity to be Ukrainian, his grandfather, Yushko, liked to tell the story about his roots going back to the Pomeranian region of Poland. He was a good story-teller and took particular joy in telling the youthful Andrij about the tribe which lived in that particular region, developing their own dialect and language. In contrast to most other groups which gradually merged to form one family of Poles, the kaszubians managed to retain their ethnic identity, expressed in their distinctive culture, crafts, architecture and language.[11]

Most lands surrounding the village of Grohi were held by magnates or the crown. However; the Kaszuba family, through their service to the local magnate, did manage to sequester small pieces of land until they became self-sufficient with their own horses and cattle and their own crude farming machinery. Since the Catholic religion commanded its believers not to charge interest, and since the Polish knightly tradition forbade its members from engaging in business of any kind, the handling of money became the accepted responsibility of the Jew.

At the turn of the 20th century, the Kaszuba family was classified as belonging to the peasant class, much like most people in medieval Europe. The local Polish gentry liked to refer to them as *muzhiks*, not exactly slaves, but most belonged to the land, rarely owned their own homes, and had to work a certain number of days for their master, could not migrate to another village without permission, had little or no education, and had little hope of improving their lot in the future. Although through time the Polish peasants did gain certain freedoms, release from ancient impositions came about at a much slower pace for ethnic minorities. And, the Kaszuba clan had two obstacles to overcome. First, they were branded a minority by virtue of their kaszubian heritage and second, the members of the clan intermingled with the Ukrainian community and, as a result, once again fit the category of being relegated to the minority group by the ruling Poles.

---

11   Ellwart, Jarosław. Kaszuby, Przewodnik Turystyczny, Wydawnictwo, Gdynia, 2001.

Despite some of these difficulties, a kind of democracy developed in the province of Galicia under Austrian rule. In fact, this modicum of democracy in a land where fully twelve percent of the population belonged to nobility was much more liberal than was evidenced in Russian Ukraine. In considering the circumstances which brought him into the world war and to Serbia, Andrij had to accept that his family felt quite comfortable with the ruling Habsburgs. However, being under the administration of Polish nobility was quite another matter and this became the reason why not only the Poles but also the ethnic groups willingly elected to go to battle on the side of the Austrians. Each harboured his own reasons for doing so. Yet, in the end, most participants did so with the view of wanting to belong to an independent and free state some time in the future.

This is how Andrij found himself to be following in the footsteps of his father, not only dreaming about a free and independent Ukrainian state but actually doing something about it.

Map of Austro-Hungarian Empire, 1914. Of particular note is the proximity of the village of Plazow (Province of Galicia) to the Russian Empire; a region where West meets East in terms of customs, language and religion.

12.

The Village of Grohi

Home to the Kaszuba clan

Andrij Andriiovych was born on December 15, 1900; the first child of Andriy and Maria Kaszuba. His birth was followed closely by the births of three brothers, Mikhailo, Fedjko, and Dmetro and two sisters, Oksana and Anna. It was not uncommon for a couple to have a large family, the rationale being the relatively high infantile mortality rate, the short life expectancy, and the belief that children would quickly grow up to contribute to the economic well-being of the family. Besides, there was no such thing as welfare for the aged; that became the responsibility of the extended family. Consequently, the larger the family the more likely was it that someone would be around to look after the parents at a time when they were no longer able to provide for themselves.

Grohi was the name of the small village or *selo* into which Andrij was born. It had the attributes of a bedroom community and was, in essence, a satellite community of a larger village by the name of Plazow, both located in the county of Lubaczow in the province of Galicia. At the time of his birth, Galicia was a part of the Austro-Hungarian Empire and was directly under Austrian control. Most residents of the villages of Grohi and Plazow showed their preference for and considered themselves to be proud subjects of Austria. From an historical perspective, Austria acquired Galicia in 1772 after which administrative and judicial districts were created, however, the boundaries of these units never coincided with religious eparchies. For example, the circuit and district courts for Lubaczow, Plazow and Grohi were located in the city of Lviv while the same three villages were administered from the town of Cieszanow. Greek Catholics in Galicia were subordinate to the Galician Metropolitanate in Lviv and the Przemysl eparchy, which

Map of Western Ukraine within the Austro-Hungarian Empire, 1914, showing the province of Galicia. The villages of Grohi, Plazow, Belzec, and Cieszanow are all near the present border between Poland and Ukraine.

encompasses the villages of Cieszanow, Plazow, Lubaczow, and Grohi, was the largest in the region.[12]

Bordered by majestic pine, the village of Grohi was comprised of several extended families, boasted about twenty-seven homes, and a population of less than one hundred souls. At the same time, the village of Plazow had a population of well over three hundred and was the commercial centre for the immediate region. In many ways, the location of Grohi was ideal even though the soil was of only fair to poor quality. After all, the nearby forest provided a good supply of firewood and a small brook which wound its way through the village seemed to be favoured by brook trout as well. Relying on mixed farming and piece-meal work in small industries near the village, the local farmers managed to eke out a meagre living.

During this particular period in history the surrounding forest was a source

12   Himka, John-Paul. <u>Galicia and Bukovina, A Research Handbook About Western Ukraine, Late 19th - 20th Centuries,</u> Occasional Paper No. 20, March 1990, Published by Alberta Culture & Multiculturalism Historical Resources Division, pp. 17 - 23.

of aggravation for the Ukrainians living in the region, especially so since the Polish land barons, who were in the minority, thought that access to the forest should belong only to them. Still, the forest had its redeeming features; it was a source of firewood and lumber and acted as an environmental reserve for the use and enjoyment of local residents. However, to enter the forest without permission from a Polish landlord was forbidden and was punishable under Polish law. Most residents disregarded the law and would frequently wander into the forest to pick wild berries, mushrooms, and firewood.

The topography of Plazow, located 85 kilometres northwest of the city of Lviv, is generally agricultural in nature interspersed with moors, forests, muskegs and lands set aside for forest and lumbering reserves. Controlled by Polish land barons, it was a land where east meets west, a melting pot of various cultures and where the river San is considered by many to be the line of demarcation between three religions--Catholic, Ukrainian Greek Catholic *(Uniate)* and Orthodox. More than any other region of Ukraine or Poland, rival states battled over her riches and its history is littered with sieges, fires, plagues, and ruin. Despite this checkered history, ethnic Ukrainians always banded together to preserve their cultures and customs.

Considerable importance was attached to the first-born in a Ukrainian family, particularly if that child happened to be a boy. Since Andrij was the first child born to Andriy and Maria, he became eligible, by tradition, to a share of the family estate. Of course, this determination was based upon a family's ability to subdivide their plot of land. In exchange, it was an expectation that the first-born would contribute to the common economic goal of the family and take care of aging parents during their *golden years.*

But, even at an early age, Andrij must have known that he was not particularly well suited to this custom of being controlled by another person, even if that person was his father. In a way, he likened his own circumstance within the family structure to that of the ethnic Ukrainians living in the region which formed up a part of the Austrian Monarchy but under the administration of Poland. This sense of wanting to be free from control seemed to take hold early in his life and formed the basis of his feelings about himself, Galicia, Poland, and Ukraine. He found it difficult to carry out, unflinchingly, all of those tasks assigned him by his father and wanted nothing less for himself than he would wish for all Ukrainians; freedom and independence. His resolve and strength of character did not go unnoticed with his family. In particular, his father took careful note of this characteristic and was often heard to say to his wife that his son had a stubborn streak and was hard to control.

Others in the village soon noticed this unusual characteristic; a characteristic that seemed to mirror the personality of his father. As for Andrij, this attribute was both a blessing and a curse; a blessing when it came to starting a task and seeing it to completion while, on the other hand, being sufficiently stubborn and determined so as not to take too kindly to advice. The bigger the challenge, the greater was his resolve and having a mean and

A traditionally-built 1800s Ukrainian home and, according to my dad, looked much like the original Kaszuba residence in Grohi.

stubborn streak did have its advantages. On those occasions when he was disciplined by his father for misbehaving did little to modify his behaviour; it merely reinforced his belief that his father wanted nothing more than to treat him like a chattel, much as was a land baron's control over his grandfather who was not set free until 1858.

The home of the Kaszuba family was typical of those found in the Lubaczow region; built of logs and finished with a whitewash *(lime and water),* and with a straw-thatched roof, it consisted of two spacious rooms, one room was used for cooking and eating and the other for sleeping. In later years, a storage room or *komora* was added to the house. The living area of the house was dominated by the clay oven or *pich* which was always built in the corner of the house facing the door. Furnishings were modest but functional. There was a wooden shelf or cupboard for dishes hung by the oven and the table with benches placed in front of the window. Only a portion of the floor was covered with lumber while the remainder was made of packed clay covered by hand-woven rugs and mats. In some cases, the residents in the region saw the emergence of a large wood-burning stove which provided for the family's heating and cooking needs. Sadly, this latter was not yet the case the Kaszuba household. As might be expected, an outdoor toilet was provided for the family's needs.

Often steeped in religious beliefs, many major tasks of the day had long-standing traditions while other rituals had pagan overtones. For example, when the family constructed the *komora,* Andrij's father chased a rooster inside the house as a symbolic means of bringing good luck to the dwelling before moving in. The following day, bread, salt and a bowl filled with a mixture of wheat, buckwheat and some coins was brought into the house and each of the four corners blessed to ensure a bountiful future. It was normal for every child to learn the importance of religion, ritual, and tradition and it was customary for parents to stress the importance of ritual in everyday life. For those who did not, it was a common belief that God would somehow punish them. A strong sense of community developed and it was not unusual to find one neighbour helping another with important seasonal tasks.

The family's farmyard housed a small barn or shelter for the farm animals, a shed, a water well, and a chicken coop–all surrounded by a willow-wattle fence, a tradition in the region. Not all of the villagers had a threshing barn which was often the largest of the storage buildings used for the storage of unthreshed grain, hay and straw for the animals. It is here that the sheaves were dried and later harvested. Some farmers in the region made a threshing floor of firmly packed clay directly in front of the barn on which the sheaves of grain were spread and beaten with a flail. Andriy and Maria had seven morgs of land *(a morg of land is equal to 2.116 acres)* and was in the process of negotiating for more land from the Polish baron in exchange for services provided at a nearby lumber mill. Not rich by any stretch of the imagination, the family was proud of its accomplishments and felt at home in the village of Grohi.

As a youngster, much of Andrij's time was spent doing the regular chores of feeding the farm animals, milking a cow and keeping the barn neat and tidy. During summer months he took particular joy in teasing the domesticated geese and chickens. This is where he also gained an appreciation for the importance of a root cellar for preserving salted foods and vegetables and a well for suspending milk and cream in a bucket during the hot summer months.

Somehow, even his first recollections of his childhood had to do with a looking beyond. He developed at an early age a curiosity rare for a child so young. It was one of inquisitiveness tempered with a readiness to take some risks, knowing full well that this attitude can have its rewards as well as its punishments. Being an early riser, he found the mornings to be the best part of the day. His mother always rewarded him with potato pancakes or porridge and some freshly-baked dark rye bread and milk. Midday and evening meals often included soup, borsch, mashed potatoes, and other garden vegetables. Occasionally, cured bacon was served on rye bread while meat and poultry were served on special days only. These culinary habits stayed with him for the rest of his life. For supper, he liked cottage cheese and sour cream with his mashed potatoes and never refused another helping of *varenyky, halushky,* or cabbage rolls. Little attention was given to a balanced diet by the villagers. Fruits, to a limited degree, were available during the summer months. So were fresh vegetables. However, during winter months the staple foods consisted of only those vegetables which could be stored in a root cellar for longer periods of time. Although it was true that villagers were fond of sauerkraut, various breads, cereals and tea, nothing seemed to compare with their first love; salted and cured sow-belly (*salo*) which was devoured with gusto and in great quantities!

Vegetables such as potatoes, carrots, cabbage, peas, onions, garlic, sunflowers, poppies, turnips, and beets were grown in the family garden and also available for purchase or barter at the local market in the nearby village of Plazow. Most of the chickens raised were sold to local merchants or at the market. In the fields, fall rye and buckwheat were grown which were always used in the making of bread, pastries, and morning cereals. A family's wealth was often measured by the amount of agricultural land and number of chickens, horses, and cows.

The village of Grohi did not have a school of its own and, as a consequence, Andrij had to walk to the nearest school which was located in Plazow. His first day of school was not without some anxiety, not only because he did not know many of his classmates but also because, to his surprise, the use of Polish was common in the classroom and playground. Although Ukrainian was the language of instruction in elementary grades, he soon learned that those students wishing to pursue higher education would have to do so in Polish.

Polish nobles took their policies toward education from an Austrian statesman who expressed the point of view that '...Ruthenians (*with reference to the Ukrainian minority groups*) may exist at the discretion of the Galician Diet...' This meant that Ukrainians were placed at the mercy of the Poles whose attitude toward Ukrainian national aspirations was naturally negative. This called for discrediting the Ukrainians wherever possible, obstructing their national and social development and enforcing their polonization. As an example, Polish replaced German as the language of instruction in secondary schools, or gymnazia, and by 1914 there were ninety-six Polish and only six Ukrainian gymnazia in Galicia.[13] This discrimination was particularly noticeable in the funding of schools and cultural institutions where the Poles received ten times as much funding as did Ukrainian institutions.

For Andrij, the initial uneasiness associated with those first days of schooling did not last long. Within a couple of weeks he was able to make new friends and conversing in Polish was not a problem. Best of all, attending school, where the curriculum consisted of reading, writing, arithmetic and history, got him away from having to assist with all of those chores at home and looking after his two younger brothers. Providing instruction in Ukrainian was a concession made by the Austro-Hungarian regime to residents living in Galicia. The Polish authorities, who were responsible for the administration of the national programs, including education, would

---

13 Subtelny, Orest. <u>Ukraine, A History</u>, University of Toronto Press, 1988, pp. 315 - 316.

have preferred all instruction to be offered in Polish. Still, they did approve of the policy of offering instruction beyond the elementary grades only in the Polish language even though the majority of the residents in the region were ethnic Ukrainians and would have preferred that instruction were offered in both languages.

The language policy did cause Andrij to reflect on his experiences during those first two years of formal schooling and to ask his parents about it. His father reminded him that as far as he could remember Galicia had been ruled by Polish kings and that most of the local Ukrainians had become accustomed to speaking two languages. Yet, despite this response he came to understand that his parents sided with the local Ukrainian majority in their dislike of this policy. Most villagers were strong advocates of the preservation of their Ukrainian roots and the Ukrainian language. At the same time, it was quite evident that the two groups lived side by side in relative harmony.

At the turn of the century most Galicians derived their income from agriculture while a smaller number were artisans, traders, peddlers, shopkeepers, and estate stewards. In the immediate area there were precious few large scale industries such as railway workshops, tobacco factories, flour mills, lumber, and timber operations. The turn of the century also saw the development of a new and exciting industry in Ukraine; the petroleum industry. As a teenager, Andrij visualized himself as leaving the small village of Grohi to become a shopkeeper or to find work in the oil industry. At other times he appreciated the peace and tranquility of the meadows and forests which surrounded the small village.

Formal education for him began in 1908 at the age of eight and lasted until 1911. For most children living in the larger village of Plazow and the smaller villages nearby, the three-year elementary education program was the norm. And, like so many other youngsters, he would have preferred to go on to gymnazia (secondary school) and maybe on to a university to pursue a career in engineering. In the least, he would have liked to have his father apprentice him to one of the trades available, to a limited degree, in the nearby city of Lviv. But, this was not to be. Only the sons of the well-to-do, particularly the offspring of the Polish land barons, could afford to continue their education. In the end, it would be this very lack of formal education that would force him to challenge his energies and resourcefulness in what would all too often turn out to be a hostile environment.

Life in Austrian-administered Galicia was one of eternal hope. It seemed as though most villagers were subjected to a very low standard of living in a region where the mortality rate was high. Disease was prevalent and access to medical care was difficult, if not impossible. However, despite the many deprivations and hardships, most were optimistic about the future. All but a few of the villagers were dependent upon their own resources for their health care. It was up to the women of the village to know which medicinal herbs should be grown in the garden. Local lore also defined just how these herbs should be picked, dried, and stored to ensure the best curative properties.

Should a broken bone need to be reset, it was up to the village bonesetter to look after these bodily injuries. On rare occasions it was up to the newspapers and enlightenment societies such as Chytalny and Prosvita to inform villagers of their rights as Austrian citizens and to affirm their independence from the attitudes of the hitherto dominant Polish nobility.

Ninety-five percent of the Galician population was involved in agriculture while only one percent in industry. Although the majority was Ukrainian, most of the officials were of Polish descent. In 1914, the Poles had over 300 high government officials in Galicia while Ukrainians had only 25. As a consequence of these inequities, far too many Ukrainians borrowed excessive amounts of money out of desperation. In turn, this resulted in alcohol abuse and increasing debt loads on the part of those least able to repay loans, most of which were established at over 100 percent interest per annum. In many cases, whatever land was held by peasants, was all too often auctioned off.[14] Little wonder that the life expectancy of the average Western Ukrainian was fully thirteen years less than that of an Englishman living during the same period!

Andrij's earliest recollection of matters political occurred when his father would often remark that the political changes in Galicia came about as a result of its geographic location. His father believed that the Russian influence seemed to lessen as time went on while Ukrainians became more and more nationalistic in the views they embraced. The number of Ukrainian members in the Seim in Lviv and the parliament in Vienna was steadily growing. In 1907, the new electoral laws based on universal and equal franchise were applied for the first time. Thirty Ukrainian deputies entered the parliament in Vienna and formed an important political group. By 1914, following another understanding with the Poles, Ukrainians obtained 62 seats in the Galician Seim, more than one-third of the total. This political climate made it easier for Ukrainians to develop a network of sport and gymnastic organizations. Economic cooperation was encouraged and Ukrainians in Galicia became more self-reliant. The Uniate *(Ukrainian Greek Catholic)* clergy became more nationalistic and along with the intelligentsia began to play a more active role in developing new political thought.

Six state high schools and fifteen private secondary schools came into existence in Galicia before the outbreak of World War I. Numerous volumes of Ukrainian history, ethnography, and folklore were published. The national Ukrainian museum in Lviv was founded in 1913 and the most outstanding author of the time, Ivan Franko, published his works, many of which are housed in that very museum today.

Villagers were often heard to say that in the new money economy the taxes imposed by the state, church, and landlord of upwards to fifty percent

---

14 Magocsi, Paul Robert. A History of Ukraine, University of Toronto Press, Toronto, Canada, 1996, pp. 418 to 435.

were too burdensome and often exploited the poor. In fact, rumour had it that other countries and even other provinces had a rate of taxation as low as three percent and where the state had previously controlled common property, such as pastureland and woodland, it was now leased to villagers at exorbitant rates. Worse yet, common access to pasture land for cattle and woodland for firewood was lost. Prices on farm products were low while prices on purchases of manufactured goods were extremely high. In cases where credit was advanced, interest rates were also very high. Having experienced the inequities of the availability of formal education, Andrij vowed that his children would not suffer the same consequences.

Andrij always looked upon his father as being the disciplinarian in the family and, as a consequence, it was not unusual to find him in the company of his *Dido (Yushko)* with whom he developed a close relationship. *Dido* delighted in telling his grandson stories about life in the village when he was a youngster; a life much more rigorous and demanding than was the case with the younger generation. In fact, he was often heard to say that today's young people were very spoiled, showed a lack of respect for their parents, and did not appreciate the importance of hard work. Although there was some discontent with the Austrian monarchy, *Dido* was not among that group. He believed that the monarchy had served the people of Galicia in a most democratic manner, often referring to an earlier time during the middle of the 19th century when, as a child, he was a serf indentured to the land and the positive changes that took place since. And even though it would have been unusual to find a person who would want to go back to those days of serfdom, *Dido* would also point out that living in a democratic state can bring too many freedoms to its inhabitants and that in the old days at least a man knew his place in life. Change, in his view, was not easy and not always for the good because democracy had its privileges while at the same time an individual was now forced to look after himself and his family as opposed to being a chattel of the landlord who had to look after his basic needs and that of the indentured family.

According to *Dido,* the village of Grohi was first established some forty years before the turn of the century and, under the leadership of a Ukrainian Greek Catholic priest by the name of Father Aleksandr Dukhnovych[15] the first school textbooks appeared in the Ukrainian language. As Andrij began to assimilate the brief history of Galicia, he was struck at how young, politically, was this aspiring region. After all, it was just a few years earlier that the peasants were emancipated from serfdom, thereby bringing about many changes and, more recently, *Austria allowed the ethnic Ukrainians to have their own military formations which gave many members in its midst hope that one day they might have an independent nation of their own.*

---

15 Magocsi 415 - 416.

Fieldwork for the family had a certain rhythm to its performance and followed a calendar of its own with cycles and seasons, each regulated by folk customs and traditional practices. In some instances the neighbours worked on a particular task together in the fields, threshing grain or husking corn. The villagers would begin work in the field with the preparation of the soil and the seeding of spring crops. It was the custom to begin the new agricultural season after the Feast of the Annunciation which is the date of the biblical announcement of the angel Gabriel to the Virgin Mary of the incarnation of Christ. Each year a festival was celebrated in memory of this event on March 25 and any work on the soil undertaken prior to this date was considered to be a sin. The land was fertilized and ploughed and the grain sown by hand in a broadcast motion. Upon completion of the seeding, a harrow was dragged over the field to cover the grain. Although much of the farm work was done manually, changes were in the offing and it seemed just a matter of time that some of the repetitive tasks would soon be mechanized. The completion of a major task was often celebrated in the village.

By 1900, fully three-quarters of the land holdings in Galicia were five hectares or less in size and comprised nearly one-third of the total arable land. Aristocrats and churches accumulated major tracts of land amounting to over one-quarter of the total area. Many priests became prosperous farmers; a situation which made it more difficult for the peasant to gain access to land. To add to these problems, the leaders within the community soon realized that a lack of formal education on the part of a large number of Ukrainians left them with a low level of self esteem and an image that the peasants were ignorant, servile, crude, and often superstitious. Yet statistics show that over a period of years before World War I, the illiteracy rate had decreased from sixty-seven percent to about fifty percent. And, as a result of military service, many young Ukrainians quickly learned to speak a second or third language such as Polish, German and Russian.

In those days, daily newspapers were unheard of nor were weekly magazines available. It would be years before the radio and television would come into common use. How then did information of great importance find its way to the intended target? The common practice was to post official notices in the village or town square. However, since a considerable amount of information was exchanged verbally, too often there was no way of verifying a rumour. Even in cases where important information, called *ukaze,* was posted on a village notice board, there was no guarantee that a posted notice was, in fact, official. There appeared to be few avenues through which a young person could get accurate and up-to-date information or, for that matter, continue his formal education where accurate information is presented in the more formal setting of the classroom.

During those times when Andrij was not required to assist his parents with chores or the modest farming operation, he liked to wander into the nearby forest to take in the sights and sounds of nature. The forest provided shelter for a wide variety of upland game, squirrels, frogs, and birds. The walk took him into Plazow and to his cousin Ivan Tychanewycz's home where the talk often turned to the species of local birds and mushrooms found in the region. Neither of them seemed to know much about the topic and decided to look into the possibility of joining the Prosvita Reading Society. Founded in Lviv in 1868, its main purpose was the promotion of culture and education to adults, the establishment of village reading rooms, and the publication of textbooks and works in Ukrainian literature and history.[16] As world events suddenly took on a darker tone by the fall of 1913, Andrij realized the importance of the Prosvita reading group. Along with Ivan, they were able to rub shoulders with the intelligentsia while feeling at home with the peasantry and soon gained knowledge about how the Austrian government functioned while at the same time learning about other European countries.

Although Ukrainians recognized the importance of education in the future development of Western Ukraine, they were also made aware of the difficulties. Of the 32 gymnazia in Galicia, only two offered its programs in Ukrainian while the other 30 offered their programs only in Polish which reflected the significance of the changes since 1854 when the two were equal. A similar situation was evident in Lviv University where only eight of eighty professors were of Ukrainian heritage. Despite these humble beginnings, by 1913 Western Ukraine boasted 80 periodicals in Galicia, Bukovyna and Transcarpathia. It would be from one of these periodicals supported by a session at a reading room that Andrij first heard about a country named Canada.

However, his interest in Canada was pre-empted by news from Lviv for on June 28, 1914, as a group of sharpshooters was performing drills and gymnastic exercises before a large crowd, the proceedings were interrupted by a messenger.

The announcement, given over a loudspeaker, was not good.

16   Subtelny 307 - 330.

13.

World War I Breaks Out

But, just who is the enemy?

Those attending the nationalistic rally in Lviv would long remember the date. It would be June 28, 1914 that would ever ring a bell in the minds of many. The message that was announced over the loudspeaker was unmistakable in its importance; Archduke Franz Ferdinand, the heir to the Habsburg Monarchy, was assassinated by a Bosnian nationalist in Sarajevo, then a part of the Austro-Hungarian Empire. *(At the time, Bosnia was in the southeast corner of the Austrian Empire and some people there wanted to set up an independent state.)* This, in turn, unleashed a series of events. In trying to understand the events of the day, the finger of suspicion pointed towards Berlin for it would be the Kaiser's government that would cause Vienna to draw up an ultimatum which would be unacceptable to Belgrade, intended not as an act of diplomacy but as a prelude to invasion.

Germany's decision to enhance its powerful economy and military power since the turn of the century played a key role. And, even though many forces might have acted against any resort to war, this did not in itself deter a compulsion on the part of nations to move towards violence. Even prior to the assassination of the Archduke, Austria-Hungary and Russia seemed to edge towards a war footing by imposing harsh alternatives on each other by either submitting tamely to drastic humiliation or of resorting to mobilization followed by armed resistance. After all, the European countries knew that in the event that Serbia was attacked, Russia would come to their aid.

As for Andrij, the outbreak of hostilities could not have come at a worse time. His parents were convinced that life for ethnic Ukrainians in Galicia under Austrian rule was better than it was for Ukrainians living in what was Eastern Ukraine under the Tsarist rule. It was also true that Russia insisted that Ukraine *was* an age-old Russian land and that Ukrainians were of the same cloth as the Russian Orthodox people. Because of this belief, Russia continued to treat Ukraine as a colony and exploited her rich natural resources. At the same time, it was a generally accepted belief that Ukraine contributed over one-quarter of the Russian treasury but received only a small part in return. It would be this kind of inequity that would stir those deep feelings of independence for Ukraine amongst many of those members attending the Prosvita associations and extend to the very heart of the village of Grohi.

Russia continued with its policy of keeping the Ukrainian masses in ignorance, prohibiting the distribution of Ukrainian literature, eliminating the use of the Ukrainian language in the church, and sending hordes of teachers, priests, and officials from Russia to Ukraine as part of the russification process. This policy of the russification of Ukraine was obvious, not so much in the villages of Grohi and Plazow, but especially in communities to the east which compelled the local villagers to conclude that living in Galicia under Austrian rule was not all bad. Still, the ethnic Ukrainians had their share of what they perceived to be their enemies. For some it was Poland. For others it was Russia or Germany. There were few, if any, that believed Austria to be the enemy of ethnic Ukrainians; a belief that had a very direct impact upon whose side the Ukrainians would take up arms in the province of Galicia.

As the news of the fate of Archduke Ferdinand spread from household to household in Grohi, the villagers began to realize the seriousness of the situation, which caused Andrij's father to conclude that the dark clouds of an all-out war were gaining momentum. Although it was true that the village was relatively isolated, the residents knew that world events would not spare their involvement. A feeling was shared that the villagers should prepare for conflict, but how? Some said that a good place to start would be to ensure that the root cellars were well stocked with vegetables. Others wanted to polish their old rifles and make certain that these were in working order. For sure, it was not a good time for idle or careless talk. Important decisions would soon have to be made. After all, if war came, who would they be called upon to defend? Would it be the Austrian monarchy or Russia? One thing was certain–it would not be Ukraine or Poland. Neither, in reality, existed!

As might be expected, the residents of Grohi were saddened with the news. After all, they had a lot of respect for the Habsburgs and knew that the Archduke Franz Ferdinand was heir to the throne of Austro-Hungary. Austria secured the support of Germany and promptly sent an ultimatum to Serbia. Serbia, on the other hand, was not too anxious to cooperate. The reaction was swift and the consequences would prove to be catastrophic. On July 28, 1914 Austria declared war on Serbia. In turn, Russia pledged its support for Serbia.

Galicia, cradled between two belligerent powers, Germany and Russia, would soon find itself enmeshed in World War I. In some ways, the war would have a silver lining. It would provide all of those Ukrainians living in the villages of Grohi and Plazow with a prospect for national liberation and the re-establishment of independent statehood. Perhaps the local Poles felt much the same. After all, it was over 100 years since Poland existed as a nation and many within its ranks were agitating for nationhood as well.

The Central Powers of Austria-Hungary and Germany, through a series of binding alliances, aligned themselves against the Allies of France, Britain, and Russia *(a number of other nations would enter the world conflict later)*. The Eastern Front in late fall of 1914 came perilously close to the village of Grohi and one would not have to travel far to the Chelm region to find a sizable German settlement or to Rava Ruska which had many Russian sympathizers. And Grohi, in turn, was located just 35 kilometres from the Przemysl fortress, the site of two major battles yet to come. Little wonder that both the Poles and Ukrainians in this region felt vulnerable and very much exposed to the forces of war. At the same time, this explains, in part, why this period of the history of Ukraine was extremely complex, yet very interesting; complex because of the number of significant events that took place not only in the province of Galicia but in all of what is present-day Ukraine.

With the outbreak of the war, hundreds of thousands of Ukrainian conscripts ended up in the Austrian or Russian armies simply because they happened to reside in a region so close to competing powers. On the first of August in 1914, the local Galician leaders declared their loyalty to Austria and issued an appeal for a united stand against the Russian Empire. In all, about 28,000 responded. In contrast, those young Ukrainians living in eastern Galicia were either recruited or elected to enlist in the Russian army. This phenomenon highlights the difficulty that Ukrainian leaders experienced in rallying all Ukrainians to any common cause. In the final analysis, it mattered very much as to the exact location of an individual's village. The closer was a person's village to Poland and within the sphere of influence of the Austrian Empire the more likely was a young man to support the cause of Poland or Austria as opposed to Russia.

The outbreak of the war found Andrij to be too young to be conscripted into the Austrian army. For the moment, the hostilities left him with no alternative but to provide assistance to the family in its efforts at economic survival. His father had already been conscripted into the Austrian army and would soon find himself on the Italian Front. In the meantime, the Austrian Army found itself fighting on two fronts; one against the Russians and the other against Serbia. When Italy joined the Entente Powers in May of 1915 and aligned itself against Austria and Germany, Andrij's father found himself on the third front in Italy. As for the village of Grohi, it would not be long before the locals would be witness to several great battles right at their doorstep between the Austrian and the Russian armies.

During the early stages of the war, the Habsburg forces occupied Belgrade only to be counter-attacked by the Serbian Army. On the Carpathian front, the Austrians found themselves to be outnumbered by the Russians, suffering heavy casualties of over 300,000 and another 100,000 taken prisoner. In East Prussia *(now Northern Poland)*, the Russian Army suffered its heaviest losses in the Masurian Lakes region and surrendered to Germany thereby ending any occupation of German territory for the remainder of the war.

During these first crucial months of the war, Andrij watched the Russian Army march through the nearby villages before taking the fortress at Przemysl. Since many ethnic Ukrainians in the region saw themselves as belonging to one of three branches of the East Slavs; the Great Russians (*velikorossy*), Belorussians (*belorossy*), or Little Russians (*malorossy*), the invading army was not without some support. On the other hand, most Ukrainians in the immediate area saw themselves as belonging to a distinct Ukrainian nationality. They did not take too kindly to this invasion.

Those living in Grohi wondered why there were so many splinter groups in their midst. They must have concluded that it would have been much better if the groups could unite and speak with one voice rather than having one group leading the young people in one direction while another group wanted to take the group in another direction; one group being influenced by Austria while another group was being influenced by Russia. Much of the local Ukrainian support for the Austrians came about as a result of the fear that they had for the privileged Poles living in the region. At the same time, the Supreme Ukrainian Council (*Holovna Ukrainska Rada*) issued a manifesto on August 1, 1914 requesting that all Ukrainians band together to destroy the common enemy, Russia.

Even as this manifesto was being posted in the village square, locals did not forget that the issuance of such manifestos was commonplace. It was not unusual to receive two or more conflicting statements of a political position or requests for action from two or more competing groups vying for control of a region. Although the Ukrainian leaders resented and feared the privileged position of the Poles in Galicia and were indignant at Vienna's repeated duplicity towards them, they saw the advantages of close links with the Habsburg Monarchy. This contrasted sharply with the feelings of many Ukrainians living in Eastern Ukraine who had developed an allegiance to Russia. Having developed an appreciation for the democratic policies of Austria, Ukrainians living in the province of Galicia regarded Russia as the greater enemy of the Ukrainian nation than did those living in Eastern Ukraine.

As a wave of patriotism swept Galicia, Ukrainian volunteer military units, known as the *Sichovi Striltsi* came into being. These units were initially composed of youths and males not eligible for conscription. Their purpose was broader than simply serving Austria. One of their objectives was self-preservation in the face of renewed Polish hostility. As Andrij busied himself with membership in the Sich Sharpshooters, Russia occupied Galicia and, in their words, reunited it with *Mother Russia*. They argued that the newly acquired territory was really ancient Russian land. Ukrainian cultural institutions, cooperatives, and periodicals were shut down and limits placed on the use of the Ukrainian language. At the same time, efforts were made to introduce Russian into the educational system. The Greek Catholic Church

A youthful Andrij Kaszuba was attracted by the uniforms worn by Austrian officers in 1915.

Austrian soldiers providing assistance to the wounded during World War I.

was attacked and hundreds of its priests were exiled to Russia and Siberia. An attempt was made to convert West Ukrainians to the Orthodox faith. During those first two years of the war, most villagers in Grohi wanted to keep a low profile since, in their view, it was the best way to escape the horrors of the war or conscription into the Russian, Austrian, or Polish armies.

Before all of the Russian plans could be implemented, the Austrians counter-attacked and by mid-1915 recovered most of Eastern Galicia. Many Ukrainian cooperatives, bookstores, scholarly societies, and newspapers began to function again. The retreating Russian army, along with the local Russophile, persuaded more than 25,000 Galicians to flee eastward for resettlement around Rostov. Unfortunately, Ukrainian leaders who had not already fled westward before the tsarist army's advance were arrested and deported to Russia and Siberia. By mid-June of 1915 the Austro-Hungarian army, with the help of Germany, drove the Russian forces completely out of Galicia. Once again Ukrainians were punished, only this time by Austria. Those suspected of having cooperated with the tsarist forces were arrested and deported to an internment camp.

As circumstances would have it, the Kaszuba clan had earlier declared itself for Austria. This decision likely saved the family from catastrophe because at the outbreak of the war Austria put out a call for an all-Ukrainian military unit in order to form up the Ukrainski Sichovi Striltsi. These volunteers served on the Habsburg side and were routinely inducted into regular Austrian units. Andrij informed Austrian authorities that his father was already serving in the Austrian army and was able to convince Austrian authorities that he was mature enough at fifteen to join the Striltsi. His wish to serve in the Austrian army was awakened earlier[17] when he heard that the Austrian Crown Prince had visited the Austrian troops in a nearby centre. He was subsequently able to catch glimpse of a unit wearing their pike-grey greatcoats with pointed collar-patches (*Paroli*) in the facing-colour with the soft pike-grey kepi and brown leather equipment. It was this kind of characterization of the soldiers which intrigued him and compelled him to dream of one day serving in the Austrian army.

As the Russian Army retreated through Plazow, Andrij could hear the Austrian siege-howitzers banging away in Przemysl and Rava Ruska. On one occasion he caught a glimpse of one of the gunners wearing a greatcoat with an *over-the-shoe gaiter* and a soft cloth *kepi* with a *front-flap* fastened with two buttons. With the addition of the goggles, the officer struck an imposing appearance, almost looking invincible. On another occasion, he was able to examine several small abandoned rifle-pits in the direction of Przemysl and, rather than acting as a deterrent to his entry into the war, these images acted as a catalyst, ever beckoning him.

Perhaps it was because Andrij had already spent some time with the local contingent of the Sichovi Striltsi that his acceptance into the Austrian army was relatively easy. His cousin Ivan Tychanewycz joined the army on the same day. In short order, both were out of the Sichovi Striltsi and into the regular Austrian Army training camp. Coming from a family where hard work and discipline were the norm made it easy for Andrij to function as an obedient soldier. Having a cousin at his side made it even easier.

However, nothing in the training camp could have prepared a teenager looking forward to his sixteenth birthday in December for front line duty. And, in the fall of 1916 that is precisely what happened. To make matters worse, the front line duty was not in Galicia, it was in Serbia—a country that seemed to be a million miles away from his village of Grohi. And, trying to understand the purpose of it all was even more difficult. There was that perplexing question as to just who was the enemy? True, the enemy was presumably Russia. But, weren't the Russians his Slav cousins? For a Ukrainian living in a land under Austrian rule, coveted by Poland and eyed by Russia it was not difficult to understand why one would want to liberate Ukraine—a country that existed only in the imagination of so many.

In the middle of all of these ambivalent feelings, fortune did seem to smile upon Andrij for in many ways the timing of his arrival in Serbia was impeccable. Why? Because the campaign by the Austrians was earlier joined by Germany against the Russians and had already taken place in the Carpathians in January of 1915. By the end of March, they had inflicted over 400,000 casualties against the Russians while losing a similar number of its soldiers. By June 3, 1915 the fortress at Przemysl was retaken by the Germans

---

17   Haythornthwaite, Philip J. A Photo History of World War One, Arms and Armour Press, London, England, 1994, plate number 64.

and by June 20 the Russians ordered a general withdrawal from Galicia. *All of this meant that by the time Andrij entered the conflict, the Carpathians and Galicia were under the control of Germany.*

So, on the one hand he would not be involved in any major battles while on the other hand he had difficulty in putting aside important political questions. For him it became easier to accept the commonly held belief that Russia was the common enemy of Ukraine and even as he was holed up in a hastily dug trench, he could not put to rest the rumour that a new group in Russia had embraced the ideals of Lenin and Marx. The word in his unit was that these Russians called themselves Bolsheviks. Bolshevism was not a pleasant thought. Neither were their sinister and evil policies. This belief made it easier to fight on the side of Austria not only against Russia but against Bolshevism as well.

When the Russian Army first overran Galicia in 1915, some suggested that Brusilov's earlier victory was made all the easier due to mass desertions on the part of a number of Slav units who may have been sympathetic towards their Russian cousins. As a result, the Commanders at the Galician front expressed some concern about the composition and commitment of the new troops arriving from Galicia. However, General Mackensen,[18] a young German officer who had developed a reputation for leadership, had few, if any, reservations about the replacements. Besides, it would now be his German Army joining the Austrian Army that would counter-attack Brusilov. By the time Andrij's unit joined the fray, the Russian Army had been pushed out of Galicia. Instead of being a part of this major offensive, Andrij's unit would now play a diminished role of holding positions already taken in Serbia while conducting cleanup operations.

In the distance Andrij caught a glimpse of the Serbian artillery entrained for the front line. He could barely see that their soldiers wore greenish-grey service uniforms. But, he also saw soldiers wearing old and bedraggled uniforms. In fact, some soldiers wore nothing more than civilian clothing. All of these sights and sounds led him to believe that one should never equate the willingness of a soldier to defend his country by the looks or the quality of his uniform. You would have to look into his head and into his heart. It seemed that the Serbians were quite ready to defend their sovereignty. It was Andrij's fervent hope that one day Ukrainians would have a nation to defend.

At first Andrij's thoughts had been with his personal safety and his ultimate survival but of greater concern to all was the challenge of providing sufficient armament for the unit's offensive. The German railheads, pushed forward by the exertions of the railway troops, nevertheless lagged far behind the front. Supplies had to be manhandled the remaining distance and the troops were becoming exhausted, the artillery was wearing out, ammunition was running short and fresh water was all too often hard to come by. There

---

18   Clark 71 - 84.

seemed to be no lack of things to do even though some of them seemed a little bit fruitless. There were trenches to be dug and armaments to be put into place. And, throughout it all, there seemed to be a considerable amount of confusion as to the short and long term goals of the unit.

In November of 1916, Austria and Germany announced their decision to create a Polish nation from lands they captured from the Russian Empire. Although Galicia was not included in the re-alignment of lands, the province was assured more autonomy and, on the death of Franz Joseph on November 21, 1916 and the ascension of the new emperor, Charles I, who reigned from 1916 to 1918, promised that Ukrainian demands would be settled favourably after the war. Local residents had a lot of faith in Austria and felt certain that changes were in the offing. However, as one looked into the future, momentous events would intervene and make it virtually impossible to grant Galicia more control over its own destiny. Effective political change was not in the cards for Western Ukraine.

With the dawning of 1917, the war had been blazing for over 28 months with the resulting carnage of unimagined proportions and with neither the Allies nor the Central Powers in a position of dominance. It seemed that as soon as one side got a bit of an advantage, this would quickly be negated by subsequent events. The Russian Revolution of 1917 not only removed Russia from the Allied war effort but also overturned one of Europe's oldest monarchies. As a result, the balance of power suddenly changed. In 1917, the United States entered the war on the side of the Allies and even though it would be months before the American military would be deployed in substantial numbers, the boost to the prospects of the Allies was instantaneous. Just as suddenly, the devastation of war took a turn for the worse. Heavy bombers attacked civilian and industrial targets and armoured vehicles were introduced into massed attacks. Taken in the context of all of these new developments, the shortages of materiel for Andrij's unit took on less significance.

In November of 1917 the Bolsheviks under Lenin and Trotsky seized power and began to negotiate peace with Germany. This led to the signing of a Treaty in Brest Litovsk on December 15, 1917 and ended all hostilities on the Eastern Front. The Central Powers could now concentrate their efforts on the Western Front.

Both Andrij and his father felt lucky *not* to be a casualty of war. Mercifully, as the year came to a close, so did most hostilities on the Serbian and Italian Fronts. It seemed that all of the fire power was now being concentrated on the Western Front. With the entry of the Americans, the huge German offensive in the spring of 1918 which was intended to defeat the French and British, soon turned the tide against the weakened Central Powers which collapsed on all fronts. In addition, Germany itself was shaken by internal unrest and mutiny.

With the Armistice of November 11, 1918, all hostilities ground to a halt.

14.

Postwar Dilemmas

As two Ukrainian republics are proclaimed

Neither Russia nor the Austro-Hungarian Empire looked kindly upon Ukrainian aspirations of *national unity* or *autonomy*. Austria arrested and interned thousands of known and suspected Russian sympathizers and with the defeat of the Austrian armies and the impending Russian invasion of Galicia, thousands of Ukrainians were slaughtered. The cruelties imposed upon Ukrainians seemed to be without limit. When in 1915 the Russian Army was forced to retreat in its campaign in Galicia, it attempted to evacuate nearly four million ethnic Ukrainians to Eastern Ukraine saying that they were *Russian sympathizers*. Since the final tally was only about 100,000 reluctant refugees, the answer seemed clear; most did not want to leave Galicia. This action tended only to increase the resolve of many Ukrainians to seek total independence. For, in the end, could *any* Ukrainian rely upon another nation for its safety and security?

As hostilities wound down and official information was made available, Galicians were appalled at the destructiveness of the war. In all, 34 countries participated in the conflict mobilizing over 65 million soldiers. Of these, 10 million died while over 20 million were wounded.[19] Andrij and his father felt blessed to come out of the war alive. Casualties in Galicia reflected the numerous foreign invasions, foreign and internal interventions, and the civil and social eruptions. The Bolsheviks, White Russians, Germans and Poles tried to establish their authority over the land and, in the end, learned that a foreign nation may be able to occupy Ukraine but conquering the Ukrainian

---

19 Keegan, John. <u>The First World War,</u> Vintage Canada Edition, A Division of Random House of Canada Limited, Toronto, Canada, 2000, pp. 420 - 423.

lands was another matter. Ultimately, it made Andrij yearn for peace, order, and prosperity and *for a real country that he could call his own.*

Facts confirmed that some of the biggest and bloodiest battles fought on the Eastern front took place in Galicia. The seemingly impregnable Austrian fortress of Przemysl fell to the Russians in 1915 only to have the German offensive break through the Russian front line just three months later. In total, about 3.5 million Ukrainian soldiers served in the Russian Army and an additional 0.75 million in the Austrian forces. To conclude that Ukrainian soldiers should be expected to or, alternatively, elect to serve on opposing sides of the war was incomprehensible.

Even before the culmination of World War I, the revolutionary era which was to transform Ukraine and Poland began to unfold. In 1915 a number of political leaders and intellectuals fled to Vienna and founded the *General Ukrainian Council* calling for a free and independent Ukrainian state. However, to their dismay in November of 1916 Germany and Austria proclaimed an independent Poland, perhaps as a buffer against Russia. This declaration included lands taken from Russia and with them a large Ukrainian population. Ukrainian members of the Austrian parliament publicly announced that the Ukrainian people would never recognize the placing of Eastern Galicia under Polish rule or give up their fight for Ukrainian lands in Austria. The new Austrian emperor, Charles I, assured the Ukrainians that after the war the matter would be settled favourably. This assurance caused Ukrainians throughout the land to push for a legal status of the Ukrainian language, the creation of Ukrainian schools, military units, and even the independence of Ukraine. With the collapse of the Russian front in July of 1917, Lenin called for an immediate peace with Germany during peace talks in Brest-Litovsk while at the same time Ukrainian soldiers in the Russian Army began to organize and held their first all-Ukrainian military congress in Kyiv in May of 1917. *Their demand was clear; national autonomy for Ukraine.*

Although Central Rada's intent *was* democratic, it unfortunately found itself sorely lacking in leadership and without an army it quickly became impotent. Its void was soon filled by Lenin and the Bolsheviks. By mid-1917 the Bolshevik ranks in Russia had swelled to 350,000 while at the same time it is estimated that 4 million Ukrainian soldiers served in Russian armies. Defections from Central Rada increased and as more and more Ukrainians aided the Russians in wresting lands from private individuals, the last vestiges of democracy were being shorn from Ukrainians.

The Soviets, being Russian and Bolshevik-dominated, considered Ukrainian autonomist aspirations contrary to the spirit and intent of international proletarian solidarity and thus treasonable to the revolution itself. Most Ukrainian leaders would have preferred a meaningful federation with Russia rather than independence. However, Russian distrust of Ukrainians gave rise to an adversarial relationship which pushed Ukrainian leadership along the road to separatism. Continued agitation in parts of Galicia

Wladimir Lenin, 1870-1924, leader of the October Revolution in 1917 and the first head of the Soviet Union, pointing to an uncertain future.

and Bukovyna led to the introduction of the Ukrainian language into public administration, the courts, schools, and churches and the restoration of civil and cultural rights. Meanwhile, Russia's provisional government rejected, in July of 1917, Central Rada's demands for autonomy on the grounds that no fundamental change could be effected in the nature of the Russian state.

As these complex political events were being sorted out and consolidated, a great event unfolded on November 17, 1917. Led by Vladimir Lenin and Leon Trotsky, the ruthless Bolshevik Party overthrew the Russian provisional government. Their aim was to destroy the capitalist system and centralize the control of production and consumption. This revolution, with its proclamation of political freedom, unshackled the Ukrainian political organizations from the underground where they had been compelled to operate as a result of Tsarist oppression.

Following the victory of the Entente Powers, the Ukrainian intelligentsia in Eastern Ukraine pledged its loyalty to the Russian throne and disassociated itself from the Austrian-based voices of Ukrainian separatism. Clearly, most Ukrainians were federalists who saw the future of the Ukrainian nation bound tightly with the destiny of the Russian Empire. This association was regrettable because the Russians were only interested in their own aspirations and not those of Ukrainians and considered Ukraine to be vital in its ideological journey for world domination. As a first step towards this goal, Soviet Russia invaded Ukraine on December 25, 1917.

With no shortage of political intrigue, on January 22, 1918, the Ukrainian Central Rada, representing Dnieper Ukraine, proclaimed the *Ukrainian National Republic* to be a sovereign country. Not to be outdone, the Bolsheviks in Kharkiv formed up the *Soviet Ukrainian* government, marched on Kyiv and precipitated the struggle for Dnieper Ukraine. But, the declaration of the Ukrainian National Republic mattered little for on February 9, 1918 the Red Army under the Bolshevik banner over-ran Kyiv. In all, fourteen months had elapsed between February 1917, the first phase of the Ukrainian revolutionary era and capitulation.

All in all, Central Rada's most important achievement was the re-establishment of a Ukrainian state for Ukraine which was recognized as an independent state in 1918. Its major failure was its inability to consolidate its governmental authority over the country. Rada's anti-militarism and the squabbles with the Russian provisional government eventually led to its downfall. Within days of signing the Brest Litovsk Treaty, the Germans and Austrians divided Ukraine into spheres of influence thereby ending Central Rada's national movement.

Strangely, a similar situation was unfolding in Galicia during the same time frame.

In October of 1918 political and religious leaders in Western Ukraine (*Ukrainska Narodna Rada*) proclaimed the existence of the *West Ukrainian National Republic (also known as the West Ukrainian People's Republic)* and stated their goal to be one of uniting those lands under the former Austro-Hungary into one autonomous state. However, by the spring of 1919 the very existence of the *West Ukrainian National Republic* was becoming increasingly threatened. Poland refused to recognize the new state and claimed Eastern Galicia as an integral part of the new Polish state. In fact, it was in June of 1919 that the Entente's Council of Ambassadors acknowledged Poland's right to occupy all of Eastern Galicia thereby protecting the civilian population from the threat of Bolshevik bands.

These conflicts led to the Polish-Ukrainian war. On July 16, 1919 with the Polish artillery hammering at their backs, the Galician army and thousands of Ukrainian civilians crossed the Zbruch River into Eastern Ukraine. In the process, Poland laid claim to Eastern Galicia, including the villages of Grohi and Plazow and lands as far east as the city of Lviv.

Suddenly, the military struggle for Eastern Galicia was over. However, the cost was dear; 15,000 Ukrainians and 10,000 Poles perished in the conflict.

The situation in Ukraine during this period of time was most confusing. To the north there was the menace of Soviet Russian-Bolshevik aggression. In the south there was a threat of intervention by the armies of the Entente and in the southwest, on the Dniester River, the Romanian forces occupied Bessarabia and Bukovyna. Still, the biggest threat came from the Polish and Soviet Russian fronts. By 1919, total chaos seemed to engulf Ukraine. Within its territories operated Bolshevik, White, Entente, Polish, and Ukrainian armies. And, as the neighbouring nations soon discovered, Ukraine was a land easy to conquer but almost impossible to rule.

Even though the *Ukrainian National Republic* (January 22, 1919) declared Galicia and Bukovyna to be one autonomous province in the newly-created republic, the practical aspects of the union were never implemented when Poland invaded from the west and Russia invaded from the east. To make matters worse, Josef Stalin was earlier given command of the anti-Ukrainian front in 1918 and began directing military operations against the Directory without formally declaring war. A Galician army of 85,000 attempted to liberate Ukraine from Soviet Russian occupation while at the same time the counter-revolutionary White Russian armies were advancing against Kyiv. Considering Poland to be their chief enemy, Galician politicians were inclined to cooperate with the White Russians hoping that this move would make it possible to free Galicia from Polish occupation. However, the West Ukrainian government under General Petliura favoured an alliance with Poland.

On April 22, 1920, the Polish Republic under General Josef Pilsudski and General Symon Petliura of the *West Ukrainian People's Republic* signed a treaty in Warsaw directed against Soviet Russia. In a dramatic campaign, the forces of Pilsudski and Petliura captured lands all the way to Kyiv only to be counter-attacked by the Red Army which moved their forces back all the way to the outskirts of Warsaw where Poland was saved by what is commonly referred to as the *Miracle on the Vistula*.

In Warsaw, Ukrainians bargained from a position of weakness. Reluctantly, Petliura renounced the *Ukrainian National Republic's* claims to Western Ukraine, causing a political crisis in the Directory and leaving a bitter legacy of a sell-out of Galicia. The Warsaw Treaty was signed on April 22, 1920 and the Ukrainian-Polish border was designated as the Zbruch River continuing north along the Old Russian border. Since the treaty gave large Polish landowners special status in Galicia, it had an enormous impact on all those living in the villages of Grohi and Plazow.

All of these events finally led to an armistice with Soviet Russia. The Polish government broke off relations with the Directory and, by the Treaty of Riga on March 18, 1921, recognized the *Ukrainian Socialist Soviet Republic*. Petliura continued to wage a desperate military struggle. The last major Ukrainian thrust into soviet territory was in the winter of 1921. The campaign failed and the remainder of the Ukrainian army was interned in Poland which had become a temporary home of Petliura's government-in-exile.

Petliura was assassinated by a Bolshevik agent on May 25, 1926.

He was loved and hated; praised and vilified; respected and feared. His controversial role in the history of Ukrainian national liberation continues to generate conflicting passions.

15.

A Romance Begins

As sovereignty over Eastern Galicia is handed over to Poland

The Galician question was considered an international problem to be settled by the Paris Conference. Since France was obsessed with the fear of a revived Germany and was committed to the creation of a powerful Polish state, the Allied Supreme Council sanctioned the presence of Poland in Galicia and on June 15, 1919 empowered Poland to establish a civil administration in the region. This decision had a profound effect upon those living in Grohi and Plazow where mixed marriages were common. This resulted in mixed emotions when the villagers learned that Poland would establish a civil administration in the region and many would soon have to take sides—continue to support those who were seeking a free and independent Ukrainian state or accept that this region was now a part of the Polish state.

Elsewhere, the Romanian army occupied Chernivtsi and Bukovyna on November 18, 1918, which terminated any Ukrainian aspirations in that province. The future of Bukovyna was formally sealed on September 10, 1919, when Austria signed the Treaty of St. Germain and ceded Bukovyna to Romania and Carpathian Rus was united with Czechoslovakia as an autonomous region. By the summer of 1919 Andrij came to realize that the three Ukrainian territories in the former Austro-Hungarian Empire, Eastern Galicia, Bukovyna, and Transcarpathia found themselves, respectively, in Poland, Romania, and Czechoslovakia. These political decisions along with the establishment of Bolshevik rule in Dnieper Ukraine put to rest any aspirations that Ukrainians living in Grohi might have had.

Those revolutionary years of 1917 to 1920 brought little else but failure to nationalistic Ukrainians and the reasons were many. There was the matter of political inexperience and in-fighting, lack of effective leadership, and especially the break-down of any cooperation between Galicia and Dnieper

Fedjko Kaszuba, Polish Army, 1924.   *Mikhailo Kaszuba (right), Polish Army, 1924.*

Ukraine. And, most destructive of all, was the tendency of Ukrainians to join destructive bands and splinter minorities. It is little wonder that Ukrainians experienced difficulty in establishing a national identity!

Yet, despite these failures, any hostilities associated with World War I did die down. Andrij, now being nineteen years of age, was ready for the next challenge. But, what would that challenge be? Staying at home on the small family farm was not a reasonable alternative. Would the next challenge come from industry? Would it be in the city of Rzeszow?

Despite these uncertainties, Andrij was glad that the war was over. It was an opportune time to spend some time with family and friends and to go to church to give thanks to the Lord for bringing him home safely. The meaning of all of this hit home when he learned that many of his friends and neighbours were not as lucky. For certain, the population of the villages of Grohi and Plazow seemed somewhat depleted as a result of the war. Many of those who sympathized with the Russians and enrolled in the Red Army were missing in action while others were languishing in a work camp somewhere in Siberia, banished by the Soviet Regime.

The end of World War I found Andrij attaching a new meaning to faith and the importance of religion. One of the first promises that he made to himself at the Serbian front was that of attending Sunday Mass upon his return, a promise he intended to keep. This would be his way of expressing his thanks to God for seeing him through the war. Dressed in his Austrian uniform and with his cousin Ivan Tychanewycz in tow they struck up quite a sight at the Dormition of the Blessed Virgin Mary Greek Catholic Church. If it was their intention to attract attention, it seems that they had accomplished their goal. The priest, too, seemed thankful that the war was over and expressed this view in his sermon. They both felt good about themselves, especially so since neither sustained injury during the war.

After Sunday Mass, the two soldiers exchanged pleasantries with parishioners, friends, and family. As might be expected, the topic of conversation was not of religion but of the war. Have you heard of what happened to this neighbour? Did you hear that this person or that person joined the Red Army and has disappeared? No, there was no shortage of gossip and of rumour. Everyone seemed to have a story to tell or an opinion to express about the Germans, Poles or Russians. Just about every family had a tale of sorrow to relate while at the same time wondering about the future in a new Poland. It was without a doubt that each member of the congregation carried the scars of the war in one way or another.

But, for the moment, that was history to Andrij and Ivan. Both seemed to be much more interested in the present than they were in the past and wanted very much to enjoy the moment and the beauty of the surroundings. The splendour of the church seemed to be enhanced by two large oak trees. It was nice to be home again. Little had changed in Plazow during the war. It seemed that the armies gave wide birth to the nearby forest, perhaps feeling that the tall pine trees afforded too much protection for the snipers and partisans. The Polish land barons still controlled the forest and the amount of arable land remained constant. The beauty of the surroundings in the church yard reminded Andrij of the family home in Grohi.

It is said that in the spring a young man's heart often turns to thoughts of love. It would be in this seemingly idyllic setting that Andrij would make an enquiry about a girl who attended Mass; an attractive girl wearing a white and yellow dress. To his surprise, he discovered that her name was Eva Groszko. And, yes, after giving it some thought he concluded that, in fact, he had met her before. He recalled that particular Sunday three years earlier when he had first met her. However, at that time she was simply a gangly youngster of twelve. She looked so different now. So mature. It took all of the courage he could muster to approach her parents who were engaged in a conversation with their neighbours. Of course, Eva remembered meeting Andrij shortly before he joined the Austrian army. Although their conversation was short, the meeting was to leave a long-lasting impression upon both of them; a moment that would be recalled on numerous occasions in the coming months and years.

Although the Polish-Ukrainian war raged in eastern Galicia in 1918 and 1919, most of the villagers elected to stay out of the conflict and refused to join Ievhen Petrushevych's West Ukrainian People's Army. However, Petrushevych's Army was defeated by the Polish Army and its remnants joined Symon Petliura's Ukrainian National Republic's Army operating out of

Kyiv. Since Petliura favoured an alliance with Poland as a means of repelling the Bolshevik and White Russian advances from the east, Andrij elected to join this newly-constituted army. So, just as was the case three years earlier in 1916, and the chance meeting with Eva, he once again vanished as if into thin air. Eva would not see Andrij again until 1923. In the meantime, any romantic intentions that Andrij might have had were put on hold. Having little freedom and without any effective means of transportation from the army's headquarters in Przemysl, it was difficult if not impossible to pursue the friendship. Besides, he had heard that Eva's father and mother had already selected a young man as an eligible husband for her. Not only that, but Andrij's parents had also had it in their minds that he should marry a neighbour's daughter; a sort of arranged marriage selected by virtue of a discussion with the community's *starosty* or marriage match-makers.

When Galicia renounced its claim to its lands in favour of Poland on April 21, 1920, many Galician soldiers joined the Poles in an attack on the Bolsheviks. For so many of those young Ukrainian lads who had earlier served in the Austrian army, finding a comfortable place in the new nation of Poland after the war was not easy, even though it was much better than it might have been for those who joined the Red Army. Having become accustomed to the democratic way of life portrayed earlier by the Austrian Monarchy, they felt compelled to take up arms against the Bolsheviks. Rumour had it that the Bolsheviks were anything but democratic in the manner in which they approached their dominance and rule over their subjects. While some of the most dedicated soldiers sought refuge in Poland, other troops joined various partisan units behind the Bolshevik lines. As a consequence, remnants of the two Ukrainian governments and their armies often found themselves in the camps of each other's enemies.

Although the immediate future was uncertain for Andrij, the same could not be said for Galicia. Important events were quickly unfolding. It would be on April 22, 1920 that the Polish Republic and the Ukrainian People's Republic, whose heads of state, Josef Pilsudski and Symon Petliura, respectively, signed in Warsaw a treaty of alliance, directed against Soviet Russia. It would be this campaign that Andrij would join. It was but a brief moment in history that the Poles and Ukrainians were allies and comrades-in-arms when a decision was taken to join forces in a war against the Bolsheviks. In short order, the advance became a full-fledged Polish-Soviet war. Their combined forces attempted to drive the Red Army from Ukrainian lands only to be rebuffed and pushed all the way to the outskirts of Warsaw in March of 1921. *The end result was that the two powers, Poland and Russia, divided Ukraine. Poland retained Eastern Galicia and Volhynia and most of the remaining Ukrainian lands became a part of the Ukrainian Soviet Socialist Republic under Moscow's domination.*

This constituted the third and final phase of the Ukrainian revolution for independence. Had the outcome been different, Petliura might have been held in a more kindly light. However, this was not to be, which left Andrij with a lot of uncertainty as to the future and reflected the mind-set of most Ukrainians who longed for a stable government, peace, and tranquility.

Now a resident of Poland, Andrij took the momentous decision to remain with General Pilsudski's Polish troops with the knowledge that General Petliura's troops were disbanded. He believed that Pilsudski's policy was to maintain an independent Ukraine as a barrier against Russia. However, in the final analysis, Pilsudski's conquest of Eastern Galicia had effectively destroyed any chances of Ukrainian independence.

Although the Bolshevik movement in Ukraine was never totally unified in its purpose, one thing remained clear; the movers and shakers of the movement wanted a close relationship with Russia. The Ukrainian Communist Party succeeded the Bolshevik movement and took the position that it wanted an independent and sovereign Ukrainian Soviet State friendly to Russia yet independent of Russia. This dogma became an essential prerequisite to national independence of the Ukrainian Soviet State. Although Russia was undecided as to whether Ukraine should remain a separate Soviet republic in a federation of Russia or as an integral part of Russia, it was recognized as an independent republic on December 20, 1920.

Andrij was caught on the horns of a dilemma. It seemed that he had but two choices: an orientation toward a Warsaw of landowners and capitalists or toward proletarian Moscow. Living in Grohi, to stay neutral was not a choice that he could entertain. By 1923, he need not have worried. On March 14, 1923, the Council of Ambassadors in Paris, acting for the Allied Powers, awarded sovereignty over Eastern Galicia to Poland and, as events unfolded, it was noted that Poland, which had stubbornly denied Western Ukrainian lands to a free Ukraine, was in the end forced to hand them over to the Soviet Union and even Poland itself fell under Russian domination. Thus, the inability of the Poles and the Ukrainians to resolve their differences amicably had already twice caused the destruction of Ukraine and Poland and paved the way for Russia's triumph.

Andrij served in the Polish Home Army for a period of two years at which point he decided to retire his Polish military uniform forever. In his mind, the thought of a free and independent Ukraine was finally put to rest. The spring of 1923 found Andrij to be no more than an everyday civilian, and, on paper, a Polish one at that!

The Bolsheviks had a vision of what Russia might look like in the future. Their vision of the future included Western Ukraine. Following their invasion of Galicia in 1920, the next seven years brought war and civil strife. In their wake the Bolsheviks left plenty of destruction, leaving the former Russian Empire as well as Western Ukraine in shambles. Hundreds of thousands abandoned the cities for the villages due to a lack of food, heating materials, and employment. Although Lenin died in 1924, the Bolsheviks continued in their debates as how best to create a communist society.

Despite a multitude of hardships, Ukrainians living in Western Ukraine experienced a surprising resurgence of self-confidence and began to prosper under Soviet rule during the 1920s. New policies came out under the heading of War Communism and included the nationalization of large estates and industry, the forced mobilization of labour, the rationing of food and goods, and the expropriation of grain from peasant farmers. However, Eastern Ukraine drastically decreased the production of grain in 1921 which led to a famine in 1921 and 1922 during which time hundreds of thousands of people simply starved to death. This caused Lenin to back off from some of his policies and to permit peasants to keep a greater percentage of their grain so that they might have sufficient grain for their own purposes as well as to sell privately.

To alleviate some of these problems, Lenin proposed that states such as Russia, Ukraine, and Belarus form republics that would become a *union of equals*. With this theory in place, the Ukrainian Soviet government would have jurisdiction in its republic over agriculture, internal affairs, justice, education, health, and social welfare and share authority with the all-union government in matters relating to food, labour, finance, and the national economy. As for the residents of Grohi, these policies had little, if any, impact upon them. Being a part of the nation of Poland, they would now have to look to Warsaw for their government policies.

Soviet Ukraine officially became a member of the Union of Soviet Socialist Republics (USSR) on December 30, 1922 and on January 31, 1924 the Soviet Union, comprised of Ukraine, Belarus, Transcaucasian Federation, and Russia was formed. From 1923 to 1933, it became the policy of the Soviet Union to convert the Soviet Ukrainian state into a truly Ukrainian entity. In this regard, it is interesting to note that Josef Stalin became the commissar for the nationalities in 1917 and the unchallenged dictator of the Soviet Union in 1933. The Russian republic became the largest land mass in the USSR while Ukraine became the second largest encompassing 450,000 square kilometres and a population of 26 million.

Ethnic Ukrainians living in the Lubaczow region of Poland speculated as to why the centralized government in Moscow would allow Ukraine to co-exist as a state. Most were skeptical of the belief that it was the intent of the Supreme Soviet to permit Ukraine to co-exist harmoniously and develop freely. In all of this, the boundaries of Ukraine became well defined and the territory possessed its own administrative centre and apparatus in the newly selected capital of Kharkiv. For the moment, Ukrainians living in Eastern Ukraine had their own territorial and administrative framework that reflected their identity.

A period of the *ukrainianization* of Soviet Ukraine followed. Moscow made an endeavour to conduct its governmental affairs in Soviet Ukraine using the Ukrainian language. In 1922, only twenty percent of government business was conducted in Ukrainian. By 1927, this figure rose to seventy percent. A similar situation arose in the political establishment. In 1923, only one-third of the government employees were Ukrainian. By 1927, this figure had risen to over fifty percent. Even more dramatic, according to Soviet sources, was the effort in decreasing the level of illiteracy in urban centres from sixty to thirty percent during the decade of the 1920s and eighty-five to fifty percent in rural areas. At the same time, Ukrainian was being taught to an increasing number of students in Ukrainian schools; ninety-seven percent in elementary grades, eighty percent in general education school and thirty percent in post-secondary institutions. When considering that Ukrainian schools were almost non-existent prior to the revolution, it is easy to conclude that many good things can be said about progress made under communism in Ukraine during this particular decade.

By 1928 Ukraine was well on its way, under Soviet rule, to industrialization and collectivization. This process caused many agrarian peasants to move to larger urban centres such as Kyiv, Kharkiv, and Zaporizhzhia. At the same time, the Ukrainian language was becoming the primary means of communication and expression of a newly emerging society.

Although the 1920s appeared to be a very good decade for Western Ukraine, Andrij must have had an uneasy feeling about the future. Perhaps he felt that the death of Lenin in 1924 would lead to a power struggle among the Bolshevik elite in Moscow. In actual fact the outcome was less party discipline which allowed the various factions and ideological currents to develop. Unfortunately, this period of liberalism and pluralism would soon end even though the death of Lenin gave rise to a new kind of hope. In many ways Andrij was saddened with the thought of not being a part of this new nation of Soviet Ukraine. For the moment he had to be content with being an ethnic Ukrainian living in Poland satisfied with a dream that perhaps one day things would change.

Andrij's father, in particular, saw the emergence of a new hope with the death of Lenin in 1924. After all, was he not the architect of the Bolshevik Revolution? A vision of a new world order? A tyrant of immense proportions? To commemorate his passing, the father and son discussed the undertaking of some special event to mark the occasion. They talked about attending Sunday Mass in Plazow followed by the laying of a wreath at the local Ukrainian Greek Catholic Cemetery. Other parishioners joined in the small and informal commemoration, first in Church then at the cemetery. But, the most important gesture would not take place until several families reached their homes in the village of Grohi. *For, it would be here, with the family and villagers looking on, that Andrij and his father, recognized as veterans of World War I, would plant two small apple trees in the front yard of the family home in Grohi.* Everyone in attendance seemed to agree that this was a most appropriate way to mark the end of World War 1 and the passing of Lenin with the belief that the world would be a better place without him.

It would not be until seven decades later that these two apple trees would take on a very special meaning.

16.

The Groszko Family

With strong roots in two ethnic communities

The Groszko family had lived in the village of Plazow for a very long time. Ivan Groszko was born in 1861, just about the time that Austrian serfs were being emancipated. Prior to this date, peasants were often indentured to the land and did not have freedom of movement. His handlebar moustache gave him the outward appearance of sophistication in a small village sort of way. Taking great pride in being able to make small talk, he was extremely well suited to life in a small community. It would have been difficult to find someone in the village of Plazow who would have had an unkind word for him. As was the case with many others in the region, he was fluent in both languages, Ukrainian and Polish. Although he was not born into aristocracy or into Polish nobility, he had the respect of those who were elevated to these positions through birthright or as a result of seniority. Although he was a part of the Polish community through intermarriage, the local ethnic Ukrainians looked upon him as being one of their own.

At the relatively young age of twenty and with the support of his parents and the village *starosty,* he took a local Polish girl, Anna Jakubiec, to be his bride in 1881. This, in many ways, was an example of the spirit of cooperation in the community of Plazow between the two ethnic groups. Naturally, there were those who frowned upon the marriage. Some said that he should have married a Ukrainian girl while others said that he should not have married a girl of Polish heritage. Still, if there were any serious feelings of ill will between the two ethnic groups, they did not seem to be very serious. In fact, it would not be until years later that political events of the day would bring varying degrees of friction between the larger Ukrainian community and the smaller Polish community. The creation of this mistrust did not necessarily come from within the community. In many cases it was brought to the village

Highway leading into Plazow, Poland, 1997.

from the outside or as a result of national or international conflict. It was at times like this that one group or the other would try to establish its control or sovereignty over the other group. Ultimately, this led to open conflict.

Ivan's wife, Anna, gave birth to a daughter named Maria in 1882. The very next year, in 1883, she gave birth to a set of twins, one of whom died during childbirth. The surviving son was named Michal. Anna recovered sufficiently from the loss of one son to give birth to a second daughter, Katarzyna, in 1885. As fate would have it, Anna fell ill and without access to proper medical attention, died that same year at the tender age of 24. Some said that she died of pneumonia. Others were more philosophical and said that it was the will of God and that Ivan should not have married a Polish girl in the first place. Ranging in age from two months to three years, the three children were all that Ivan could handle. Were it not for the assistance of his neighbours and relatives, the challenges might have been too much for him.

The Klymus family lived nearby and it would be this family that would, in particular, help Ivan with the care and upbringing of Maria, Katarzyna and Michal. And, as fate would have it, the Klymus' had a teenaged daughter named Tetyana who took great joy in assisting her mother with the care of the youngsters. In a very short period of time, a very close bond developed between the children and Tetyana Klymus; a bond that seemed to spill over into a casual and easy-going relationship with Ivan Groszko as well, even though he was 14 years her senior. Dmetro Klymus, Tetyana's father, took note of this very special relationship and remarked that it was a pity that his daughter was so young. He felt that she would make a very good wife for Ivan.

The remark, although made in a casual way, stayed with Ivan Groszko. In fact, the more he thought about Dmetro's remark the more he was intrigued by it. It would be several weeks later that he would have occasion to find himself alone with Dmetro at a community work-bee in the local Ukrainian

Greek Catholic Church. With great effort he worked up enough courage to ask Dmetro if he was serious about the possibility of his taking Tetyana's hand in marriage. Ivan was silent for the longest time. Finally, he assured Ivan that he would not interfere with any relationship that might develop between the two. To no one's surprise, the rumour started to circulate in the community and found its way to Tetyana. She was both surprised and shocked to hear that her father would even consider such a proposal.

However, time went on and the bond between the children and Tetyana continued to grow, all of which compelled Ivan to approach her directly with a proposal for marriage. Not knowing how best to refuse without hurting his feelings, Tetyana told Ivan that she was not worthy of a man like him. Still, the proposal of marriage would not go away. Conversations bantered back and forth and Tetyana said she would respond in due course if her parents consented to the marriage. In the end, it would be her father that suggested to his daughter that she may never again find a gentleman as fine as Ivan. Fearing that disobeying her father may lead to other problems, she finally consented to marrying Ivan. The marriage took place in 1886 and the couple quickly settled down to a regular routine. Ivan, as time went on, felt quite fortunate to have so young a bride. As might be expected, by the end of the year Tetyana was pregnant with her first child.

Still a teenager herself who just turned 15, Tetyana gave birth in late 1888 to a daughter and named her Anna, perhaps in memory of Ivan's first wife. A second daughter, Parania, was born in 1890 followed by a son, Vasyl, in 1895, Stefan in 1897, Eva in 1903, Damian in 1909, and Oksana in 1911. From the two marriages, Ivan would have his hands full looking after the needs of ten children; three from the first marriage and seven from the second marriage. And, of the children born to Ivan Groszko, it would be Eva who would play a pivotal role in this story.

During her formative years, Eva found that she was just another member of a large family who had the good fortune of having several siblings around her to look after her best interests. Most of the household and farming chores were left to her older sisters and brothers. Since the province of Galicia was under Austrian rule, Eva came into the world as a citizen of Austria. However, as was the practice of the time, her Austrian certificate of birth did reflect her Ukrainian heritage while the children of Ivan's first marriage reflected a Polish heritage.

As Eva began to understand her surroundings at a relatively young age, she realized that she had two half-sisters and a half-brother and, in reality, was a member of an extended or blended family that embraced two ethnic groups, Ukrainian and Polish. But, this circumstance in itself was not unusual. Many of the residents in the community found themselves in a similar situation. For the present, Ivan conceded that his wife was of Ukrainian heritage and the family also decided to embrace the Ukrainian Greek Catholic faith. Although this change from the Polish Roman Catholic Church to the Ukrainian Greek Catholic did not seem to bother the children, there were other issues in the community having to do with language, civic government, and independence for ethnic Ukrainians that simply would not go away.

At the time of Eva's birth, her oldest sister, Maria, was twenty-one years of age, Michal was twenty, and Katarzyna was eighteen. All of this made it very easy for Eva's mother, Tetyana, to look upon Maria and Katarzyna not only as helpers but as companions as well. Ivan and Tetyana were both very proud of Maria and gave considerable thought as to who might be the most eligible young man to take her hand in marriage. After all, matchmaking was a shared responsibility of the village *starosty* and the parents of the young people. Eventually, with the support of the village starosty, Maria married a strapping Polish lad by the name of Mariusz Mazurkiewycz, a son of a parishioner in the Polish Roman Catholic Church in the nearby town of Cieszanow. Mariusz would go on to play the organ in this very church for over forty years at the end of which time he would receive a citation from the Pope for his dedication and work. In addition, two of Mariusz' sons entered the Catholic priesthood, one of whom currently resides in Lublin.

The Austrian province of Galicia was an underdeveloped agrarian region and its raw materials were exploited by the more industrialized provinces in the Habsburg Monarchy. Most of the residents were engaged in agricultural pursuits. Even though Eva's grandfather was legally freed from bondage in 1848, the children and grandchildren suddenly became economic serfs. The peasants living in Plazow now had to pay for the use of the gentry-owned woods and pastures because their use was revoked at the time of emancipation. The only source of income for the Groszko family was piece-meal employment in the region and the small plot of land which they owned adjacent to the village. All too often the family had to borrow money and staying away from chronic indebtedness was a challenge in itself. Many peasants in the region sought relief from poverty by emigrating to North America or Brazil. The out-migration of people became so severe at the turn of the century that the Austrian authorities feared a complete de-population of much of Galicia and, as a result, attempted to control the exodus.

For those not involved in agriculture, railroad construction provided a number of job opportunities. In addition, Galicia had a sudden spurt of industrial growth in 1902. A number of new plants began to spring up which employed hundreds of food, lumber and wood processors, clothes manufacturers, mineral extractors, machine-builders, and metal workers. Most of the Poles living in the Lubaczow region were, much like their Ukrainian cousins, peasants. However, there was one major difference; on a percentage basis more Poles were engaged in industry, trade and transport, administration, and the professions than were Ukrainians. Sometimes, it seemed an impossible burden for the family just to eke out a meagre living. For another, World War I broke out just about the time that Eva entered the most important of years, the teenage years. It is little wonder that Eva had ambivalent feelings about her childhood.

Originally constructed in the late 1800s, the Groszko family home has undergone several upgrades. When members of the Groszko family were deported to Soviet Ukraine in 1945, a Polish family, relocated to Plazow from Soviet Ukraine, took possession of the home.
Photo taken in 1998.

When Eva reflects upon her earliest memories, she was heard to say that she did not really get to know her father until he came back from the United States in 1908. As events unfolded, Katarzyna, along with a small group of other young people from the Lubaczow region, emigrated to New York in 1905 via Triest, Austria. Ivan decided to journey to New York in 1906 in search of short-term employment and for an opportunity to spend some time with Katarzyna. In 1907, Ivan and Katarzyna were joined in New York by Michal and by Anna. Michal negotiated passage to America via Hamburg while Anna sought passage via Rotterdam.

When Ivan arrived in New York, twenty-one year old Katarzyna was employed as a *domestic* while at the same time taking advantage of her employer's generosity to enrol in night school. Not only would Ivan's trip provide him with an opportunity to see Katarzyna but it also provided him with employment while he awaited the arrival of Anna and Michal. In this way, he concluded that a nucleus of their family could start a new life in America. This idea was not Ivan's alone. He had heard tell of others in nearby villages that had followed a similar plan. In fact, a small network had developed. For a small fee, arrangements could be made with a local agent who worked closely with an American contact to assist families with the required paperwork to get passage to the United States as well as a work permit. Besides, there seemed to be an insatiable appetite in New York for domestic employees and getting an entry visa was relatively easy and inexpensive. To make the proposal even more palatable, Ivan was assured of short-term employment in a mining community in the nearby State of Pennsylvania.

Ivan's arrival in New York was a joyous one; particularly so since he was able to see his daughter Katarzyna once again. There was much to see in New York and many employment opportunities beckoned. Following the advice of friends, he took a train to a coal mining district in the State of Pennsylvania.[20]

20   Subtelny 13 - 21.

Employment seemed easy to come by, the pay was excellent and he dreamed of one day bringing his the whole family to America. Life in Pennsylvania was good and by the end of 1906 he had put together sufficient funds to bring Michal and Anna to New York the ensuing year.

The spring of 1907 came too early and Ivan made the trip to Ellis Island to collect Michal and Anna. Although it was only two years since he had last seen them, he could not get over how much they had matured since he last saw them. Perhaps it was because they were rather smartly dressed compared to that which he was accustomed. It would now be the turn of Katarzyna to take Anna under her wing and help her make the transition from Poland to America. In the meantime, he took Michal with him to the coal mines of Pennsylvania. If nothing else, he was comforted by the fact that he now had three members of his family in America where he felt certain that they would find economic success and personal freedom. Upon returning to New York from Pennsylvania, Ivan was pleased to see that the younger Anna had taken Katarzyna's domestic job while she found a full time job in a garment factory. Both continued their evening classes, saying that they were very happy to be in America. All too soon, it was time for Ivan to return to Galicia.

In parting, Ivan made Katarzyna, Anna, and Michal a solemn promise saying that he would soon return and perhaps bring Parania to New York with him. Meanwhile, he was secure with the knowledge that his faith in God would see all of them through these troubled and emotional times. When his three children saw him off on the ocean liner bound for Amsterdam, they had trouble holding back their tears. Ivan didn't know whether he should smile or cry. He did both.

On the trip back to Galicia, Ivan had plenty of time to think about the city of New York and the mining industry in Pennsylvania. He thought about employment opportunities and about his social life, both of which were quite different from that which he experienced in Plazow. In particular, Ivan struggled with his feelings of guilt and wondered whether his daughters had suspected that he had dated a young woman in Pennsylvania. Was he making the right decision to go back to Galicia? He had to admit that he had courted the notion of taking up permanent residency in America. As Ivan looked out over the ocean, the moonbeams glistened and bounced off the calm waters. Even the moon smiled and seemed happy. In all of this, he was suddenly struck with the realization that the young lady in Pennsylvania was truly in love with him. As he pondered his fate, the answers were not forthcoming. He knew that sooner or later he would have to reconcile his ambivalent feelings with Tetyana.

When Eva saw her father in the fall of 1908, it was difficult for her to really understand the true meaning of the word father. To her, this man was a complete and utter stranger. After all, she had not seen him since she was two years of age and had only the slightest recollection of him. It took a lot of coaxing and some New York sweets to finally get any kind of a welcome from his newest offspring. Looking around, Ivan was surprised how his family had grown since he left for America over two years earlier. Parania was now eighteen years of age, Vasyl was thirteen and Stefan eleven. He could see that Tetyana had plenty of help around the house and garden in his absence. It didn't take him long to get caught up on the latest news in Plazow. In spite of mixed emotions about his personal life, Ivan was glad to be home.

As the autumn days got shorter and the nights longer, the world was right with Ivan except for one thing; he had this yearning in his stomach to be back in New York. Worse yet, not only did he miss Katarzyna, Anna and Michal, but he especially missed the company of Nikolasha, the young black-haired Yugoslavian woman he had met in Pennsylvania. Yes, this was his home but he was already looking forward to his next journey to New York. Throughout this period of self-examination interspersed with feelings of guilt, he felt relieved that Tetyana did not pursue the matter. In that way, he knew that he would not have to tell a lie about a liaison with another woman. Besides, it appeared as though Tetyana suspected that something was wrong but made a decision to avoid a confrontation. After all, she was glad to have Ivan back in Plazow.

Time passed quickly and the spring run-off from the melting of snow and the chirping of birds signalled the coming of spring. The unusual warm westerlies brought an early spring to Plazow and Ivan soon had the spring crops and garden planted. His thoughts turned to New York and his second journey to America. This time, it would be the turn of nineteen-year old Parania to accompany him to the land of milk and honey. He visualized the dock yard in Ellis Island and the techniques that immigration authorities used to process thousands of immigrants each day. In itself, Ellis Island now signified something very precious to Ivan. It was here, on this island which was only about 27 acres in size, that something symbolic took place over and over again. This little island, located in Upper New York Bay, was the leading immigration centre between 1892 and 1943 and would soon become a part of the Statue of Liberty National Monument. This is where countless immigrants in search of a new life first touched American soil.

But, as the curtain fell on 1909, Ivan began to have doubts about his next journey to New York. The two years of work in the coal mines seemed to have taken their toll. Besides, he was now nearly fifty years of age and lacked the energy and ambition he had just two years earlier. As a result, he made a decision to use the money he had accumulated in Pennsylvania to purchase the passage for Parania to New York. Tetyana, in particular, was happy with his decision.

Parania would leave the village of Plazow in the spring of 1910 via Hamburg, Germany, and join her two sisters in New York. In due course, Parania settled in with her sisters in New York while Michal continued to work in the coal mines in Pennsylvania. With that, Ivan closed the book on his romance with America. By 1909 Tetyana was once again pregnant, giving birth to Damian that same year and to Oksana in 1911.

In the meantime, Eva had long since put behind those memories of her father being in the United States. This was a period of bonding with her father and helping her mother with the household chores. Tetyana, in particular, was happy to have Eva at home. She had lots of friends and could always rely on her two brothers, Vasyl and Stefan for companionship and support. All seemed so normal, yet little did Eva know or understand the pain and suffering that her mother was enduring with the loss of her two precious little daughters just so that they might seek a better life in America.

During the ensuing months, the best of times were those when a letter or parcel would come from New York. Sometimes it would be a small present for the children while at other times it would be American money which could be exchanged for Austrian valiuta *(Austrian currency known as waluta austriacka in Polish)*, Polish zloty, or Kreuzer coins. Sometimes the funds would come from their daughters in New York. At other times the funds would come from their son Michal. Eva began to take a real interest in events as they affected the family and her community. Even as she prepared to enter the elementary school, she already knew a lot about Galicia and its people and developed a vision of just how New York and Pennsylvania might look. And, like so many others before her, she would soon begin to learn a little more about Western Ukraine and its role in the Austrian Monarchy and how government policies legislated in Vienna were being implemented in Poland.

The commercial centres of Cieszanow, Narol, Belzec and Lubaczow were all within fifteen kilometres of Plazow. For Ukrainian Catholics living in Plazow, the Greek Catholic Eparchy was located in Przemysl and the regional seat of the Church in Cieszanow. Since the village of Plazow was located in the administrative district of Cieszanow, it would be here that all family records would be maintained, to be re-located to the town of Lubaczow at a later date. Belzec,[21] *(the location of a Jewish Death camp during World War 2 where 601,500 Jews were put to death)* to the northeast and Lubaczow to the southwest served Plazow with an excellent railroad transportation system. These trading centres, in turn, were within eighty-five kilometres of the city of Lviv, a bustling trading centre.

For so many emigrants who left Galicia for a better life, they would always recall their childhood by the presence or absence of the community church. For many, it was central to their lives. For Eva, childhood was chock-full of memories of Sundays in church and of helping the family with farm chores and hoeing and weeding the garden, collecting eggs from the chicken coop, herding cows, making bread and, the most common of all tasks, peeling those potatoes. It seemed that potatoes were used in the preparation of just about every meal!

---

21   Hogan, David J. Editor in Chief, <u>The Holocaust Chronicle</u>, Publications International Ltd., Lincolnwood, Illinois, United States, 2001, page 699.

In most respects, Plazow was a typical rural village. Even the Groszko village home was typical of the region: a couple of partitioned rooms, an earthen with a section covered with rough-hewn lumber, scattered rugs, a thatched straw roof, plastered and whitewashed walls, and a well in the front yard. Next to the house was the family garden, which contributed much to the self-sufficiency of the family, and nearby were six morgs of land set aside for crops.

The Greek Catholic Church was less than a hundred metres from the family residence which facilitated attendance at Sunday Mass and socialization after each religious celebration. Religion played an important role in the life of villagers. In fact, the cultural development in Galicia can be expressed in religious context. The Uniate Church was western-oriented with its own hierarchy headed by the Metropolitan of Kyiv. On the other hand, the Orthodox Church continued to be the dominant religious body in Russian-dominated Eastern Ukraine. Some of the religious practices had their origins in pre-Christian pagan rituals while others had their origins in the doctrine of the church.

In the village of Plazow and in villages throughout Galicia, the church was so pervasive as to touch every aspect of a person's life. The church served two roles, one which dealt with a person's beliefs and the worship of God while the other had to do with the world of work and how the community organized itself. In Galicia, the distinction between the church and the state was not that clear. Tasks undertaken in the garden, in the fields, in industry and in the marketplace all seemed to call on the power of God so that the fruits of one's labour would result in a bountiful harvest. Prayer was commonplace and was expected by the clergy of its followers.

The local church had faithfully served parishioners for over one hundred and fifty years and the Groszko family recognized its proud history and took great pleasure in attending Sunday Mass. When it was first founded, it formed up a part of the Uniate Eparchy. It was not until 1774 that the Uniate Church, on the urging of the Empress of Maria Theresa, began to take on the new name of Ukrainian Greek Catholic Church. However, no matter which label it embraced, one thing appeared certain; its preservation was assured by the Austrians because of the Habsburg's desires to use the church as a means of strengthening the barrier against Russian expansionism in Galicia and as a counterbalance to Polish attempts at regaining control of Lubaczow. The Poles, on the other hand, never wavered from their belief that this region belonged to them even though it was currently under foreign rule.

Nowhere was the Uniate Church as entrenched as it was in the Eparchy of Przemysl while at the same time being so exposed to Polish Roman Catholic influence. The church played an important role in the education of youngsters and the local elementary school was operated by the parish sexton *(diak)*. Perhaps as a counterbalance to the power and control of the church, the Prosvita reading society was created during the latter part of the 19th century. During this period in Ukraine's history, it also became evident that the russified Orthodox Church supported the reactionary forces in the tsarist government while the Greek Catholic Church, particularly in Galicia, became the bearer and defender of Ukrainian identity.

Eva, as a young girl, escaped much of the controversy swirling around religion. Like most Ukrainian children, she was satisfied that most of her friends attended the Ukrainian Catholic Church and that they were somewhat distinct from the Poles who attended the Roman Catholic Church. It did puzzle her, however, that these distinctions continued to be made while at the same time she had a small number of Polish friends who were very nice and seemed to be no different from the Ukrainian Catholics.

As a budding teenager, Eva felt good about herself. Unusually confident during those times of political upheavals, she learned quickly the value of patience and perseverance, the two qualities that would forever stand her in good stead, confound her closest friends, and delight the members of her immediate family. Eva's family believed that a strong religious upbringing had much to do with how young people felt about themselves and those around them. This seemed particularly true of Eva. When the war broke out, tsarist Russia mounted an attack on the Greek Catholic Church in Galicia; yet it was the only national institution, headed by Metropolitan Andrei Sheptytskyi, that remained intact after the crackdown. Unfortunately, as a result of a sermon delivered in 1914 at the Dormition Church in Lviv, Sheptytskyi was arrested and deported to Kursk. He did not return until 1917 at which time he continued in his efforts to establish Greek Catholic parishes in Western Ukraine.

The prestige of the Polish language continued to increase throughout Galicia. In fact, many young Greek Catholic seminarians fell increasingly under the influence of the Polish culture. Despite these difficulties, a small number of intellectual leaders, many of whom were clergy, continued in their efforts to raise the status of the Ukrainian language among Ukrainians in Eastern Galicia. In nearby Przemysl, Ukrainian schools were being organized and promoted and elementary textbooks began to be published. It would be the Greek Catholic Church that would establish a special relationship with its parishioners and play an important role in the national movement. The village priests became the conduits for national sentiment among the common people. It was the priests who taught young people in the village schools and established a communications link with parishioners of all ages through the medium of Church Slavonic. They impressed upon the faithful that they belonged culturally to the Eastern Rus World. What made them so effective in their ability to communicate, frequently in contrast to their Polish counterparts who were Roman Catholics and thereby celibate, was that church doctrine allowed them to marry, have children, and pass on their patriotic fervour to their wives and children.

Many of the efforts of the Greek Catholic Church were consolidated by the leadership of Andrei Sheptytskyi as Metropolitan who reigned from 1900 to 1944, even though his tenure was severely interrupted, from time to time, by important political events. His influence was most notable in the realms of the church and in the political cause of Ukrainians who saw in him the ability to restore the historic bond between religion and nationality.

For Eva, one of the most pleasant of childhood memories had to do with religious celebrations in a simple home which included those common items of a kerosene lamp, holy pictures, embroideries, tapestries, and potted plants on the windowsills. For, it would be during this time of the holy festival that twelve special food dishes would be served on Christmas Eve, January 6. During the celebration of Christmas and the birth of Christ, it was customary to dress the dining room table with a fine embroidered tablecloth and decorate it with three round and braided loaves of specialty bread called *kolach*, placed one on top of another. A lighted candle was placed inside the *kolach* and another lighted candle was placed in the window to extend an invitation to neighbours who wished to join in the celebration. Who could forget the taste of *kutya*, a specialty dish of boiled wheat and poppy seeds smothered in honey and the custom of the head of the family raising the first spoonful then invoking God's blessing. The bowl would then be passed around to the other members of the family so that everyone might share in the meaning and joy of a Christian Christmas.

As far back as the Groszko family could remember, they had special decorations during the winter time holidays. Many of these are associated with the special supper on Christmas Eve, *Sviata Vechera*. Of special significance was the placement of the *didukh*, made of the best wheat of the field, which commemorated the family's ancestors. On Christmas Eve as the family awaited the arrival of the first star in the sky, the commencement of the meal always began with the customary ritual opening. This was done by the head of the household who brought the *didukh*, a symbol of the gathering of the clan, and greeted his family with traditional salutations expressing joy that God has bestowed upon the family with good health and general well-being.

The twelve dishes which followed represented the twelve apostles. These dishes were always meatless and were made without the use of milk or cheese as ingredients. Included were marinated herrings, dumplings or *varenyky*, mushrooms, beets, sauerkraut, stewed fruit, buns, and a variety of pastry. Little wonder that Eva associated this feast with her love for Christ.

Eva realized just how few occupational choices were available to the young people of Plazow. This short list included blacksmithing, tanning, beekeeping, basket weaving and plait work, grease work, gathering peat moss, cart and wheel-making, cooperage, quarrying, fishing, cobbling, and candle-making; few of which survived the passage of time. There was always someone in the village that had some expertise in at least one of these occupations and it was not unusual for one of these villagers to pass on a trade to one of the children in the family or to other members of the community.

As a teenager, Eva discovered that a woman's work was never done. Work included planting and tending the vegetable garden, harvesting, preserving food for the winter, cooking, washing the dishes, cultivating and working the flax and hemp, spinning, weaving and sewing clothes, tending the cattle, poultry and pigs, washing and mending clothes, keeping the house, acting as a caregiver to children, and just plain helping with the raising of the family. She particularly cherished the markets which were a central part of the economic and social life in Galicia. These were colourful, crowded, teeming with activity and full of new and wonderful things to be seen and enjoyed. The markets were held on a regular basis in larger centres throughout the region.

Eva began her formal education in 1911 at the age of seven. To her surprise, two languages were spoken in the school, Polish and Ukrainian. Even at a very young age, she was reminded by her mother that Plazow was a part of the Austrian Empire where, in accordance with democratic principles, the use of Ukrainian and Polish in the same village was not discouraged. She also learned that Poland wanted very much to claim this soil as her own. For the first time, she heard the words national identity and that Ukrainians in the village cared very much about this concept. Most villagers were of Ukrainian descent and continued to preserve their rich customs and heritage. Meanwhile, the Poles, who were in the minority, seemed not to mind the ethnic mix.

The school program in elementary grades concerned itself with the basics only; reading, writing and calculation. Textual material was scarce as were library materials. Every child was taught in Ukrainian but Polish was the second language that each child was also required to learn. This unique arrangement, during the years that Eva attended school between the years of 1911 and 1914 seemed to work rather well. The Austrian government encouraged all schools in Western Ukraine to teach children how to read and write in their mother tongue first followed by Polish and then German. This latter guideline was particularly emphasized in gymnasia, the equivalent to high school in Canada, where German was a popular language.

Eva's educational program was interrupted by world events. In fact, had not the dark clouds of world conflict presented themselves in 1911, it is almost certain that Eva would have been the next daughter to be whisked away to New York to join the other members of the family. However, the outbreak of World War 1 pre-empted any possibility of Eva pursuing further education. Still, in later years, Eva regretted that she was unable to continue her education, especially so in that she was an outstanding student. However, it is perhaps this one circumstance which would become the catalyst for the direction that her future would take.

Customs were an important part of a villager's life. It was not uncommon for Ukrainians to reaffirm their faith in God when an important calamity was about to occur. Such seems to be the case in 1914 when everyone in the village seemed to acknowledge that war was inevitable. Eva's family attended the Dormition of the Blessed Virgin Mary Catholic Church with a special prayer in their hearts. However, for Eva, the prayers of the heart were suddenly interrupted. It was here, at the age of eleven, that Eva first made eye contact with a strapping young lad by the name of Andrij. For the moment, Andrij did not register on her consciousness nor did Eva register on Andrij's mind. After all, it is rare that a fourteen-year-old boy would take notice of a girl who was three years his junior. Yet, long term relationships often have their beginnings in those fleeting moments.

It was not the best of years for the youthful Eva as she turned thirteen in 1916. War seemed to be raging everywhere. However, this did not deter her from dreaming about falling in love. At least it was a good year for dreaming of a prince charming who might take her away from all of this to a place just a little more cosmopolitan—a place like New York. When she shared her dreams with her mother, she discovered that her mother had similar dreams when she was a teenager. It seemed natural to dream of better things, even at a time when the war raged on. Still, Tetyana did not find it in her heart to tell her daughter about her own dreams when she was a teenager and how those dreams came crashing down to earth when her father encouraged her to marry at the tender age of fifteen. At the same time, Tetyana hoped that Eva would eventually meet some decent young man in the Lubaczow region who would add to the family's economic security. In fact, she already had a boy in mind.

Eva was well used to her mother lecturing her about boys and marriage and already knew the game plan when she overheard her parents discussing the matter. It was the expectation that parents wanted to play the role of matchmaker. Yet, it seemed as though these plans would be derailed when Eva met Andrij for the second time in 1916. Although it was true that the stench of the war seemed everywhere and the sound of the big guns in Rava Ruska, Jaroslaw, and Przemysl was unmistakable, Andrij would not be deterred from formulating a plan to join the Austrian army. There was just enough time for the two youngsters to exchange a few pleasantries and for Andrij to declare his intention of joining the Austrian army.

Although Eva's parents objected to any romance between their daughter and Andrij, they seemed to know little about psychology. Tell a girl that you don't like a particular boy and she will surely spend a lot of time and energy trying to prove them wrong. Maybe it is an expression of independence or an indication of the process of maturation. Whatever the case, Tetyana realized that her fears may have been premature. After all, Eva, who had just entered her teenage years, was several years away from any real serious romance and marriage. Besides, the question of any kind of romantic involvement with Andrij became moot because he was suddenly accepted into the Austrian army and disappeared.

She would not see him again until his return from the Serbian front, two years later.

17

Andrij Exchanges his Uniform for a Bride

And launches a plan to leave Poland

Arriving in Grohi from military duty with the Polish Home Army in 1923, Andrij tried to comprehend the politics of his earlier military service with Commander-in-Chief Symon Petliura. He now realized that Ukraine had its best chance at independence in 1919 when the two Ukrainian states, the Ukrainian People's Republic *(central-eastern Ukraine)* and the Western Ukrainian People's Republic *(eastern Galicia)* had proclaimed a union on January 22, 1919. However, with the Polish invasion during the same year, the Ukrainian Army was not able to push back the Russian Red Army or Denikin's White Army.[22]

In retrospect, it was not so much the invasion from Russia that would seal Ukraine's fate, as the Polish-Ukrainian war of 1918-19 during which time Andrij briefly served under Petliura. When the treaty in Warsaw was signed between Petliura and Pilsudski,[23] he concluded that he had no other alternative but to join Marshal Pilsudski's Polish Army to help protect the sovereignty of the nation to which Galicia had earlier been ceded. Now being 23 years of age, he reflected on his two years of service in the Austrian Army, one year in the Ukrainian Army, and most recently three years in the Polish Army. He had to conclude that he was left with very little to show for his six years of military service.

Upon reaching home, his first thought was of a warm bed and some home cooking. As was the case three years earlier, his homecoming would

---

22 Magocsi 512 - 520.

23 Potichnyj, Peter J. <u>Poland and Ukraine, Past and Present,</u> The Canadian Institute of Ukrainian Studies, The University of Alberta, 1997, pp. 19 - 28.

not be complete without spending some quality time with his friends and especially Ivan Tychanewycz. Dressed in his army uniform, with boots and buttons highly polished, Sunday found him attending Mass with Ivan. To his surprise, Eva Groszko was also in attendance. As he listened intently to the sermon, he thought about the day he last saw her, admitting that he was witness to quite a transformation; she was no longer a teenager but every bit a young lady who seemed mesmerized by his stately appearance.

Eva's mother, Tetyana, must have sensed, without speaking, that her nineteen-year-old daughter did not hear a word of the sermon. It seemed as though she was in a trance, now looking at Andrij as though he were the centre of the universe. Tetyana must have felt as though she were herself on another planet, completely out of touch with her daughter. As she took in the scene right before her eyes, she realized that her dream of bringing Eva together with boy she had selected for her was now just that: a dream. At the same time, she must have thought about the custom of matchmaking which was a favourite Ukrainian tradition known as *svatannia*, visualizing how the matchmakers, called the *starosty,* would carry out their role and ask the father of the bride, on behalf of the groom, for the hand of the daughter in marriage. She even saw the image of her husband Ivan greeting them at the door and the *starosty* and groom entering as though on the pretense that they were hunters from a distant land in search of a particular animal; searching out a king for their queen. The ecstasy of a positive reply followed by the sharing of some bread, food, and a shot of the finest brandy in the land was very real.

Alas, this was just a daydream. All too soon Tetyana was back to reality. She recalled her own youth and how headstrong she envisioned herself as being when she dreamed of selecting a mate. At the same time, she knew full well that her dream never did come to fruition. She recalled how her father had, in many ways, persuaded her to marry Ivan Groszko. She knew that it would be useless to try to intervene or dissuade her daughter from making the final decision. After all, why should she force on her daughter that which was really forced upon her? Besides, it seemed that the young people of today more and more wanted to select their own husband from two or three alternatives acceptable to the parents. In the end, Tetyana had to admit that the road to a long-term commitment was very different from fleeting infatuation.

In the coming days, Andrij took every opportunity to be in the company of Eva. In fact, the more interested he became in her, the more desirable she became to other bachelors in Plazow. In later years Eva would recall how, on one particular occasion she was invited to a social in the community centre and, in turn, invited Andrij. Well, as the story goes, Andrij barely escaped with his skin. It appears as though another young man was also seeking her hand in a long-term relationship. As might two stallions, the two lads wanted to challenge for the hand of Eva right on the spot. Of course, Andrij always maintained that he was more than capable of handling himself. Obviously,

Eva was not about to take any chances, saying that '...*I rescued the love of my young life.*' If nothing else, the incident accelerated the romance and, in order to solidify his feelings, Andrij proposed marriage. In keeping with tradition, Eva withheld her response saying that the road to her heart was through her mother and father.

The romance blossomed and Andrij finally got enough courage to approach Eva's parents. He knew that his proposal may meet a considerable amount of resistance even though they were aware of the seriousness of the romance. To his surprise, the Groszkos accepted the inevitable and gave their consent. However, his own parents resisted to the end saying that the girl they had picked for him would come with a greater dowry.

It would be just one year after hanging up his army uniform that the date for the wedding would be set for June 17, 1924. Even though the time was short to prepare for the wedding, the days seemed to drag forever. Well in advance of her wedding day and in keeping with custom, Eva and her bridesmaids went from door to door in the village to invite the guests while at the same time leaving behind at each home a specially-prepared small loaf of bread called the *korowy*. They even sang their invitations. All too soon, the wedding day was just around the corner and the young couple knew that they would have to embrace and participate in a number of customs and pre-nuptial celebrations. Before the arrival of the wedding day, formal approvals were sought from the parents of the bride. This was a very special and joyous occasion because it was a form of betrothal known as the *zaruchennia* or the joining of hands between Eva and Andrij where the hands of the two were tied together with an embroidered cloth and blessed with bread. Gifts were exchanged between the couple and songs were sung wishing fertility in their marriage. The couple was escorted to the seat of honour, which in this case was Eva's dowry or hope chest, while the guests sang *posad,* a traditional wedding song.

Being committed to each other, they reflected upon the role of the church in their lives and how regular attendance can become one's reputation as a villager. They found it hard to envision life without the participation of the church in the baptism of children, wedding ceremonies and certain funeral rites and rituals. Special ceremonies and village processions, the marking of anniversaries, the beginning of the harvest season were all organized and led from the church. In fact, that very morning Andrij paused at the sight of a small shrine at the outskirts of Plazow to offer up a prayer. Those roadside crosses and chapels were often placed at intersections of roads, on routes leading to hospitals or in front of churches as symbols of divine protection. As a war veteran, he was comforted by their presence on sites of former battles, in front of cemeteries and at crime scenes. He was convinced that these shrines contributed to the salvation of the dead and to the protection of those living in the region.

The day before the wedding, Andrij and his friends went out into the nearby forest to find a small sapling branch called the *hiltse*. This they decorated while at the same time singing wedding songs as they transported it to the home of the Groszkos. Perhaps it was a good thing that the songs they sang were sung in the forest. After all, some folks would have said that the lyrics of these songs bordered on being ribald! Finally, the time arrived for the young couple to take the wedding vows in the local church. Only then would the wedding celebration begin.

Early on the day of the wedding, the Kaszubas arrived at the home of Ivan Groszko so that the respective families might observe a traditional leave-taking ceremony. Seated around the kitchen table, the parents of the bride and groom placed a small ceremonial loaf of bread on their laps. On cue, the bride bowed three times to each while kissing each loaf of bread. In turn, the parents gave an emotional blessing to the bride. Following this pre-nuptial ceremony, the bride and groom were joined by the wedding party composed of two bridesmaids and two groomsmen for the short walk to the church. The talk was light and charged with anticipation.

The wedding, in most respects, was a typical Ukrainian celebration which consisted of the formal church ceremony and the less formal civil registry. Eva's wedding attire consisted of a simple white blouse, contrasting vest and skirt all embroidered by her mother to reflect the art of the region as well as an ecclesiastical motif. The attire of the bridesmaids was similar to that of the bride and was also embroidered by their mothers. This folk art, much like the shrines in the region which were first inspired by faith in the power of protective symbols, was embodied in embroidery. Being able to take a photograph of a wedding in those days was rare unless one belonged to the landed gentry. *'Too bad,'* Eva was heard to say years later, *'I would love to have had a photo of our wedding. The way we looked. How young we were!'* The Dormition of the Blessed Virgin Mary Greek Catholic Church where the wedding vows were taken was very special to them; it was originally built in 1728 and was later to be re-built in 1936. The entrance to the church was festooned with a *zaruchennia* or dove to bring the young couple peace and happiness and the evergreen in the front yard was decorated with written wishes of good luck from friends and neighbours and hung on the branches. The tree, in reality, took on a life of its own as a symbol of the union of two people.

The wedding ceremony was a solemn affair and reflected the importance and gravity of the occasion, especially for Eva. After all, in a Ukrainian girl's life, perhaps the most important and memorable event in her life is her wedding day. On the Friday prior to the wedding ceremony the bride's wreath was made by the two bridesmaids. Although the wedding ceremony may have been a solemn affair, the celebration which followed was anything but. It lasted for a full three days. Musicians played and there was plenty of dancing and singing by the young people of the neighbourhood. A number of guests that attended were of Polish heritage and it would have been difficult to find any indication of discord between the two ethnic groups. The church in which the vows were taken was a part of the Eparchy of Przemysl and a member of the Greek Catholic Rite. Because the church had a long and proud history, it would forever be remembered by Andrij and Eva as having played a pivotal role in their lives.

As might be expected, Andrij and Eva thought that the ceremony was far too long and did not adequately reflect the happiness they felt in their hearts. Still, they were thankful that the distance from the church to the Groszko residence was very short. After all, they were aware that massive amounts of food and drink awaited them. Although the outdoor reception included a variety of fish and meat dishes not available in their daily lives, it soon became obvious that the guests preferred, above all else, those dishes most dear to their hearts. Yes, great quantities of *holopchy* and *pyrohy* were consumed! These were washed down with the finest home-made brews. But, the wedding reception did not end that evening. It continued right through Sunday and into Monday. After all, not only were the invited guests expected to partake of the festivities but so were friends, local residents and all those who helped with the wedding—wagon drivers, cooks, brew-makers, and musicians.

Each guest at the wedding reception was given a piece of the *korowy*. In sharing this sacred bread, it was believed that the marriage would be a happy one. After this sharing of the bread, the bride and groom danced the *khorovid* around the table and then moved outside. At the end of the evening, the bride was covered with a kerchief to indicate her transition from a maiden to a wife. During the *pokrevennia*, the couple received gifts which included linen, clothing, furniture and other practical items for the new home. Also, the bride brought gifts for the groom's family and the groom brought gifts for the bride's family.

The official part of the wedding was finally over when the bottom crust of *korowy* of the wedding cake was taken by the musicians. The *korowy* is a sacred wedding bread prepared by seven women with water from seven different wells, wheat from seven different fields, eggs from seven different hens, and salt from seven different salt blocks. Decorated with doves for fertility, flowers for beauty, and *barvinok* vine for a long and healthy life, it seemed to have special significance for all of those in attendance. Consistent with the Ukrainian custom, the wedding did not end in Plazow. Many of those from the village of Grohi continued with their celebration in their village on Sunday and on Monday. As for the newlyweds, they joined in both celebrations.

And, no, there was no honeymoon. Just a short walk through the meadow and stately pines of the 'polski las' in advance of taking up residence with the Kaszuba family in Grohi.

Being accustomed to the strict hierarchical structure within the military setting, the transition from being single to marriage seemed easier for Andrij than for Eva who suddenly gave up the life of a carefree teenager. Those first days of marriage gave them an opportunity to reflect upon their childhood and how their educational and work experiences might have prepared them for a life together. In the end, they had to conclude that there would be no shortage of challenges in the future because their work experiences and formal education left a lot to be desired. In a search for meaningful work, Andrij, in particular, wished that he possessed more knowledge about apprenticeship trades and industry in Galicia.

Thinking about what might have been did not put food on the table for Andrij who began to look for work in the lumber industry. Perhaps his service in the Polish army did help because he managed to find work in the lumber mill that required him to work six days a week with Sunday off to be with Eva. His employment in the mill would continue for over a year during which time the newlyweds resided in the Kaszuba home in Grohi. However, as might be expected, all did not go well with this arrangement. Sibling jealousies, in particular, set in and it was just a matter of time before Eva would be accused of this misdeed or that infraction; of being lazy and not contributing sufficiently to housekeeping duties.

By the middle of 1926 the situation had deteriorated to the point where Eva wanted Andrij to seek alternative accommodation; perhaps with her brother Stefan who had recently started the construction of his own home in Plazow. Eva even advanced the idea of joining two other women in the hopes of finding work in France. However, Andrij would have none of it, suggesting that whatever they do, they do it as a team. When he approached his parents with Eva's concerns, the unexpected happened; his father immediately told him that if he was unhappy living in the family home, the exit door was always open. Being veterans of the war made it difficult for either to back down. Andrij was not about to be browbeaten and immediately took the decision to move out, knowing full well that he would have to forego any possibility of inheriting a portion of his dad's land holdings.

From that moment on, Andrij and Eva changed their focus from one where they would remain in the county of Lubaczow to one where they would now actively look for long-range possibilities outside the village. Andrij recalled that just prior to the outbreak of the war the Russian border was near Rava Ruska where he met a Polish land baron who seemed sympathetic to the cause of Ukrainians. On impulse, he left the lumber mill early that Saturday for a meeting with the landowner. Fortune must have been smiling because the Polish family did need a couple of farm labourers and the owner was prepared to employ them both in exchange for a reasonable salary and accommodation. It would be here that they would spend the better part of 1926 and 1927, during which time they put aside most of what they had earned while considering their future. In particular, it gave Andrij time to put some distance between himself and his family and to draw upon what he had learned from his attendance at the Prosvita Reading Society meetings.

Being a fan of Taras Shevchenko, whose works brought about a national consciousness, he found himself thinking about what it meant to be a citizen of Poland. Countless Ukrainians used Shevchenko's words as they searched for a measure of self-fulfillment while at the same time trying to understand

162

their situation. This is why Shevchenko's words, penned in 1849, resonated with him;

Rather than grieve my fellow men and trouble folks at all, I'll follow where my eyes may lead, and let what will, befall! If I have luck, I'll take a wife; if not, I'll drown myself; But will not rent my services, or sell myself for pelf.

And so I went where eyes might lead, but luck eluded me, And good folk would not strike a deal that gave me liberty; They haggled not but cast me out to exile far away– A weed so poisonous they scorned to have among their hay.

The poem reinforced his self-image and dream of independence.

Despite these difficulties, love endured and the reward, on November 15, 1926 was the first-born child to be named Maria after Andrij's mother and Eva's older half-sister. This indeed was a time for celebration for the proud parents, even though Andrij was heard to say that he would have preferred a son. Still, looking at the big smile on the face of his robust daughter, these thoughts were quickly put aside. In no time at all Maria was about to celebrate her first birthday. The realization was soon reinforced that the temporary work quarters they occupied were simply too small to accommodate even a family of three. Since Eva's brother Stefan had now completed the construction of his new home, they accepted his invitation to move into his home for the time being.

Now a family man, Andrij could not help but worry about what awaited his daughter in Poland. Would she be denied an education in her mother tongue, a privilege that was won in World War I under the Austro-Hungarian regime? Even as he thought about this question, Poland began to systematically change the language of instruction from Ukrainian to Polish. This precipitated a widespread resistance to these measures which too often took the form of sabotage and terrorism. Having served in the Polish military, Andrij knew that any resistance to government policies as related to language rights was unthinkable. To make matters worse, he heard that the Polish military government of Marshal Pilsudski would soon initiate a program to pacify ethnic Ukrainians living in Poland.

These thoughts led him to discuss the matter with Ivan Tychanewycz at which time they concluded that the time was right to look for better opportunities where they could acquire some land, have religious freedom, and escape from Polish government policies. Concluding that it would be premature to share their concerns with others, they set out to garner as much information as was possible about the successes or failures of other emigrants who ended up in France, Brazil, Argentina, Canada or the United States.

Finding reliable sources of information upon which they could base their decision was difficult. Newspapers were not readily available and those individuals who knew a lot about foreign lands often had a reason to speak of these destinations in glowing terms. After all, many of them were agents for local and foreign governments or for steamship lines where there was a price on the head of every person who took the decision to travel abroad.

While these thoughts reverberated in his head, the region was inundated with rumours of Canada which seemed to be magnified in the village. These softly spoken rumours kept cropping up from time to time as if carried by gentle breezes coming from afar, ever beckoning to him. Some said that they first heard about it in Przemysl while others said that they had read about it in a newspaper. Still others said that they had seen posted notices of this kind of information in town squares in Bukovyna. In all of this, the two magic words were *free land*. Rumours had it that this land was offered in a country that embraced democracy and where economic stability was a reward for diligence and hard work. Little wonder that these words fell like soft petals upon the ears of Andrij. When he shared his thoughts with Eva, she recalled how her father had traveled to New York to facilitate the beginning of new opportunities for three of his children. Andrij thought about fate and about his own chances for success in a new land.

What made it easier to think about emigrating was the realization that taking up residence in Grohi was no longer possible for it certainly looked as though he was being squeezed out by his own father. Eva, too, felt that they could not reside with her brother indefinitely—particularly if another child should come along. As the first flowers of spring filled their senses, Andrij was moved by the splendour of the evening, finding it hard to put his thoughts into words. Eva seemed to sense this. As they listened to the girgling of the spring in the centre of the village, Andrij finally managed to put words to his feelings saying that he was thankful that the rumours were of Canada and not the United States. He preferred to talk of *free land* and farming as opposed to life in a large metropolitan centre such as New York.

There was little need to say much more. Once in Canada, they knew that they would have to learn a new language. In the meantime, Andrij felt confident that his knowledge of Polish, Ukrainian and some German would help him to learn English. However, for the moment, the real challenge was to develop a plan that would generate sufficient funds for the long journey into the unknown. They concluded their evening's walk with a hug and a kiss to seal their decision. Tomorrow, their plan of action would be put into motion.

Andrij slept like the proverbial log for the very first time in weeks. Lying beside him, Eva must have felt the same way. As usual, Andrij was up early the next morning. He wanted very much to visit Ivan Tychanewycz to tell him of his plans. It was a clear, crisp morning as he took a circuitous route to Ivan's home and noticed, as if for the very first time, the ageless beauty of the countryside and the majestic forest. It was as if the stately fir trees stood at attention as he passed. *Funny,* he thought, *how the senses become so much more acute when great events are about to unfold.* Looking back, he could not understand why he was so reluctant to share his thoughts with Eva, who also felt the same frustrations. She received the news as though she had expected it, leading Andrij to conclude that he had made the right choice for a companion.

When he told Ivan about his plan, Ivan reacted as though he already knew. He, too, felt that Canada promised a better future than did France or Brazil. They spent the better part of the day discussing their political circumstance and the lack of opportunity in what was now a part of Poland. They both wanted a strong and independent Ukraine but also accepted, for the moment, that it was not likely to happen. The most urgent discussions, however, had to do with matters financial. How much would the trip to Canada cost? How would these funds be raised?

As they were about to part, Ivan asked Andrij to consider an alternative plan. The alternative plan would require that Ivan precede Andrij to Canada thus giving Ivan an opportunity to report back to Andrij about any job opportunities in Western Canada. It did not take Andrij long to appreciate the merits of such a plan. In accepting Ivan's proposal, Andrij decided to delay his own departure until such time that funds were in place for his passage.

Later that evening, Andrij shared these discussions with Eva. Reluctantly, she agreed to the plan. The most difficult part of the decision was the matter of leaving Eva and Maria behind until he was settled in Canada. Other emigrants had followed a similar plan, never to be heard from again. In some cases, an emigrant would find a new mate in Canada while in other cases it was the spouse that had taken up with someone else in the Old Country. Breaking the news to Eva's family was difficult even with the knowledge that Eva would remain behind for a short period of time. After the shock of the announcement had worn off, both Stefan and Damian promised to provide financial help.

However, the attitude of the Kaszuba clan to the news of their leaving Galicia was in sharp contrast to that of the Groszkos. They seemed relieved by the news. In fact, Andrij's father went so far as to say that, *"You'll never make it in Canada. I have heard nothing but bad news about their climate."* In the days and years to come, especially when the going got tough, Andrij would recall those words. No other thoughts would motivate him more.

Now that Andrij and Ivan had determined that their destination would be Canada, they made a trip to the nearest railroad station at Belzec to confirm that Canada, in fact, would welcome new immigrants from Poland. To their relief, the town square did have a posted notice with an invitation from the Government of Canada along with assurances that a local railway agent was ready to provide them with the necessary information about passage to Canada. Having confirmed all of this, they could now concentrate their efforts on putting together the best possible information about the new land. They knew that Canada was a very large country and that it would not be possible to determine a final destination without first receiving some first-hand information from locals who had earlier immigrated to Canada. It was now time to start raising funds for the journey.

Andrij found that the best source of information about Canada continued to be the Prosvita Reading Society which confirmed that many peasants were leaving Galicia in search of a better life. It was in 1923 that Canada first made a concerted effort to attract farmers from Eastern Europe, even though their preference might have been from the more industrialized nations of Western Europe. And, it was the federal government in cooperation with banks, Canadian railway companies, and overseas shipping lines that played the leading role in promoting settlement in Canada.

Ivan's steamship agent told him that he would need the equivalent of at least one hundred and fifty Canadian dollars to pay for his passage to Winnipeg, Manitoba, but seemed reluctant to provide any additional information. After all, these agents knew that even the smallest of negative reports would dissuade a Ukrainian from taking the journey and thereby lose for them the opportunity to earn an agent's fee. Additional information came from families in the area who had recently heard from a relative in Canada. Ivan was convinced that he had the best information possible and was reassured as to the appropriateness of his decision when he read a letter that a neighbour recently received from a family member now living in Canada.

Andrij reflected upon his decision to emigrate to Canada and, in particular, the timing of it. The din of the guns of the war had died down and here he was preparing to leave his beloved homeland forever. What then, was the meaning of war? Was conflict a natural phenomenon amongst men or was it as a result of the lack of effective leadership? Did great nations feel it necessary to go to war to secure their boundaries? The thought of having risked his life for the Austrian Monarchy seemed to have little meaning. After all, just what did it do for Ukraine? It did not seem to matter that the family lived here for many years because political circumstances suddenly altered those feelings of belonging.

Being born at the turn of the century meant that it was most opportunistic to be a part of a malleable society; a melting pot of peoples emerging from feudalism striving for a better way of life. However, even when Andrij served in the Austrian Army to defend against the onslaught of the evil Russians, he found himself fighting Ukrainians from Eastern Ukraine. Not only that, but it bothered him that his roots were just as deeply imbedded in Poland as in Ukraine. This bizarre circumstance left an indelible imprint on Andrij's mind and forever shaped his feelings about international conflict. *Maybe the border was in the wrong place, but at least Poland had one. And, it was the very thought of any kind of a political border that separates a people that eventually propelled him to take the decision to emigrate to Canada.*

18.

The Attraction of Canada

Spurred on by promises of free land

As the twentieth century dawned, Canada, the United States and Brazil opened their doors to immigrants from Eastern Europe and it was now up to Galicians to determine the most desirable destination. Getting accurate and up-to-date information about any of these countries was not easy. Western Ukraine and Eastern Poland were being inundated with information from steamship companies, immigration agents, foreign governments, and unscrupulous entrepreneurs passing themselves off as agents. In addition, an assortment of other facilitators wanted to get in on the gravy train. However, Ukrainians soon learned that conditions in Brazil were not overly desirable. As a consequence, the United States and Canada became the destination of choice for most emigrants.

It was in 1897 that Sir Clifford Sifton[24] became Canada's Interior Minister under Prime Minister Sir Wilfrid Laurier and developed an aggressive immigration policy which was intended to woo Ukrainian immigrants to Western Canada by defining it as the *World's Bread Basket*. It was his choice of words that immediately attracted Ukrainians to the message. After all, was not Ukraine a bread basket to Eastern Europe? In retrospect, immigrants who landed in Winnipeg noted that Sifton omitted to say anything about the weather. Even as early as 1882, a settlers' guide to the Canadian Northwest published in New York told prospective pioneers that the climate of Manitoba consisted of *seven months of arctic winter and five months of cold weather*. It was a good thing that prospective immigrants did not have access to this

---

24   Makowski, William, <u>The Polish People In Canada, A Visual History,</u> Tundra Books, Montreal, Quebec, 1987, pp. 44 - 45.

kind of negative publicity. For certain, the agents who placed a price on each immigrant's head would have been unlikely to create any negative impressions about Canada. If they had, the final destination for so many would not have been Winnipeg.

In particular, the federal government's program for the settlement of Western Canada called for new sources of manpower. Offers of free land, political and religious liberties, and especially freedom from compulsory military service attracted the attention of many. In fact, the news spread to Bukovyna in printed form on posters before 1900 and even though there was some criticism in Canada about those *foul-smelling sheepskin-wearing immigrants* did not deter them from coming. However, World War I interrupted the flow of emigrants to Canada and it would not be until after the war that the news would be of interest to Andrij.

Some said that good news travels fast. Well, not everyone in Eastern Poland looked upon this information as being good news. Many did not wish to leave their homeland even if there was an ounce of truth to the rumour. Others wanted to stay in what was once Galicia in the hopes that the political circumstances would change for the better in the near future. Some wanted to stay and continue in their quest for full-fledged nationhood for ethnic Ukrainians while only a handful were prepared to be polonized. Since the conditions for staying in Poland were not acceptable, Andrij concluded that the circumstances were ripe for emigration and, even though Sir Clifford Sifton left public life in 1905, his policies to build *a nation of good farmers* once again took hold in the 1920s.[25]

The Government of Canada had a *kicker* to the offer of land; a free homestead of 160 acres with an option on the adjoining quarter section of land. As Andrij thought about all of this free land, he was not aware that government officials offered a bonus for each new person they recruited to Canada. In fact, many agents went directly to villages in Eastern Poland in an effort to recruit emigrants to Canada. However, the *war was* responsible for leaving the impression in the minds of many that Ukrainian-Canadians were aligned with the Central Powers and, as a result, un-Canadian, thereby putting a damper upon the welcome mat to Ukrainians. It took many years to dispel these false impressions. In fact, hundreds of Ukrainians who had immigrated to Canada prior to the war were interned as alien Canadians sympathetic to the Central Powers. Now that the war was over, Sifton's policies were once again pursued and were given a boost when a government report concluded that Ukrainian immigrants placed a high priority on cleanliness and hard work.

With continued pressures from various lobby groups in Canada, the Canadian government in 1925 lifted the restrictions placed on immigrants

---

25 Berton, Pierre. <u>The Promised Land, Settling the West 1894 - 1914</u>, Pierre Berton Enterprises Ltd., Anchor Canada edition, 2002, pp. 13 - 19.

from *non-preferred* countries such as Ukraine (or *Ruthenia* as it was referred to prior to 1921). As a result of the invitation from the government of Canada, the seven million ethnic Ukrainians living under Polish rule after World War I found it easier to consider Canada as a destination of choice. Despite some reservations from Anglo-Canadians, between the years of 1925 and 1930 about 55,000 Ukrainians settled in Canada. The peak year for this immigration was 1928.

As Andrij prepared for his journey to Canada, he noted a curious twist of fate in history. Canada became a nation in 1867, the very same year that the Austro-Hungarian Compromise was signed and the year that Austria was defeated in a war with Prussia. As a consequence, the Habsburgs were forced to make concessions and about one-half of the Austrian Empire, including Transcarpathia, was placed under Hungarian rule, eventually leading to the birth of the Austro-Hungarian Empire. When Poland pledged its support for the Habsburgs, it got in return a promise that the Austro-Hungarian Empire would not interfere in the Polish conduct of Galicia's affairs. As a result, in 1867 the province of Galicia became a *Polish state within a state* leading to a great deal of disenchantment on the part of Ukrainians. Since the Ukrainians feared further intrusions on the part of the Poles, many turned to Russia for closer ties, especially those living in Eastern Ukraine. Some went so far as to say that Ukrainians living under Polish rule developed an inferiority complex and this was why it became fashionable and popular for many to identify with the mighty Tsar and the flourishing Russian culture.

Sufficient funds for Ivan's passage to Canada were raised by the fall of 1927 making it possible for him to apply for his visa and passage on a steamship liner. The fateful day finally came on April 19, 1928, and the goodbyes at the railway station in Belzec were emotional and tearful; a scene that would be repeated over and over again with other emigrants and eventually with Andrij and Eva. The first stage of Ivan's journey took him to Lviv where he completed his emigration documents before continuing to Rotterdam and, by a smaller passenger ship, to Liverpool, England. In all, the journey to Winnipeg would take Ivan three weeks.

Postmarked *Winnipeg, Canada* and displaying a two-cent stamp, it would not be until late May that Andrij would receive a letter from Ivan. The news was encouraging; *yes,* land was available in Western Canada to settlers from Poland and Ukraine. However, much of the good land was already picked over by earlier settlers and by immigrants coming to Canada before World War I. 'It appears,' stated Ivan in his letter, '*that most of the fertile land along the railway network in Manitoba went to settlers from preferred nations. Sad to say, Poland is not on that list. I will be looking for work on the railroad. If that does not work out, it will be in the lumbering industry...*' There was no shortage of bad news when Ivan, in another letter, described the amount of discrimination towards non-English speaking immigrants, going so far as to say that the Winnipeg Telegram seemed to take joy in describing the *strange looking Ukrainians* as being *stupid, dishonest and uncooperative.*

As the time for departure drew closer, Andrij admitted that the realization of being separated from his two sisters, Oksana and Anna, was stressful. As for his three brothers, well, he definitely had mixed feelings. Perhaps it was sibling rivalry. Maybe it was because he had a falling out with his father which also affected his relationship with his brothers. Sure, he did love them as brothers but not quite in the same way as he loved his two sisters. *In some ways*, he concluded, *the friendships developed in times of war are all as close as those developed amongst siblings.* Yet, as important as were these relationships, none compared with his bond with Eva. He recalled how, on New Year's Eve, he had taken a stroll with her on a cool, moonlit evening, marvelling at the beauty of the village nestled in the stately pine. *Would this be the last time that he would breathe the soft moist air of his home town? Would he ever see his friends again?* As these thoughts crowded his mind, he found it difficult to come to grips with the realization that he had no intention of ever returning. *What would Christmas be like in a new land? Would it have the same religious significance?*

As Andrij checked off in his mind the things that he had to do before embarking on the journey, he suddenly realized just how deeply entrenched he had become in the community. Making certain that Eva and his daughter Maria would be comfortable in his absence occupied much of his thoughts. He felt blessed to have a caring brother-in-law, Stefan, who he knew would make certain that the best interests of Eva and Maria would be served. Although uneasy about the possibility of Polish persecution in the coming days, Andrij knew that, to some extent, many of the Ukrainian residents of Plazow were already polonized. As a result, he felt confident that nothing catastrophic would occur while he was in Canada, even though Poland did take great pleasure in treating Ukrainians as second-class citizens. However, there was also reluctance on the part of Polish leaders to impose too many restrictions on Ukrainians; after all, they were ever aware that Russia looked upon Ukrainians as their ancestral cousins. To be overly zealous and discriminatory against Ukrainians could very quickly bring the wrath of the big Russian bear pressing up against the Polish nation.

With the funds received from Ivan and the proceeds of his own labour, Andrij soon had sufficient funds for his passage to Canada. After all of the planning and decision-making, he was glad that the day of departure was fast approaching. However, when he told his dad that he had purchased passage to Canada, his father seemed more interested in the disposition of his land holdings than he was in Andrij's future plans. Since the laws of succession in Poland were such that Andrij was automatically assured a portion of his father's holdings, the conversation quickly turned to the procedure that they would have to follow to disinherit Andrij. To accomplish this, Andrij signed a waiver in the District Court in Lubaczow and appeared with his father before a judge in the Circuit Court of the Supreme Crownland in Lviv. On the train ride to Lviv, the silence was deafening. Each must have been hurt by the attitude of the other, yet neither was prepared to give in. With that,

Mikhailo, Andrij's younger brother became eligible to inherit a portion of the Kaszuba estate. As for Andrij, this seemed to be the last and most important task to be undertaken before departing.

Andrij left Plazow on July 23, 1928. Saying goodbye to all that he had come to know and love was an unforgettable experience. It was heart wrenching. Knowing that perhaps millions of others before him had the same experience did not lessen the enormity of the moment, made all the more difficult by the realization that the promises made in good faith by many husbands to their spouses as they left them behind, often with one or more children, did not come to fruition. *Could this possibly happen to him? Could all of those promises of the moment evaporate? Is it possible that some intervening event would rob him of seeing his wife and daughter again? Would he survive the hardships in a new land which would surely challenge and sap his strength?*

As the village of Plazow receded in the distance, Andrij thought about how all of this seemed so unreal and even anti-climactic. As the three wagon loads of family and friends made their way to Belzec, there was plenty of time to reminisce about the past and what the future might hold for both families. It was hard not to have mixed emotions. On the one hand, relief that the plan to emigrate was finally being implemented while on the other hand a deep sense of loss. As the group neared the train station in Belzec, Andrij looked around at family and friends concluding that it would have been much easier had he come to the train station alone. He reflected upon the route that would take him to Canada and was thankful that Ivan explained in his letters what he might expect. There was no turning back now. With a heavy heart, a few tears, and embraces for all family and friends, his wooden trunk was loaded onto the train. Planting a kiss on his daughter's head, he promised Eva that he would write just as soon as he got to Canada. As he boarded the train, he asked for God's blessing so that his family might remain healthy and strong. In turn, everyone wished him a healthy and safe journey to Canada.

With a shriek of the train whistle amidst billows of black smoke, the train slowly pulled out of Belzec. Andrij felt a sense of relief as he waved frantically to his friends and family. Dozens of others waved back, perhaps to another loved one on the train headed for Canada. Suddenly, he was full of anticipation of what the trip held in store for him. The names of cities such as Lviv, Warsaw, Amsterdam, and Liverpool danced in his head. Andrij pinched himself to make sure that all of this was not a dream. The clickity-clack of the steel wheels passing over the steel rails confirmed that this was no dream.

Despite all of the heartaches, there was something magical about boarding a train. At a time like this it was difficult not to think about his rifle unit in the Austrian army and his train journey to Serbia. For the moment, this helped him to take his mind off the gravity of his present circumstance. From his window he could see the last images of his family and friends. In less than two hours the train pulled into Lviv. From the hustle and bustle, Andrij knew that he would not be making the trip to Warsaw alone. He was amazed as to the number of young people who were boarding. For certain, it would not be an overnight trip for them unless, that is, each of them wanted to take a couple of large trunks with them for a weekend trip! Clearly, they too were leaving their beloved homeland behind. The stop in Lviv would not be long, just long enough to process his exit papers at the Department of Emigration.

Towards the evening Andrij was informed that the train had reached the historical city of Lublin, Poland. Train officials made a thorough check of documentation carried by passengers at which point one was heard to say that he was surprised at the number of exit visas, to which another official retorted, *'good riddance; after all, most of them are Ukrainians.'* As the train wound its way to Warsaw, the attitude of the Polish officials confirmed that Poland truly coveted the land that once was Galicia. *'Too bad,'* thought Andrij, *'that I shall not be here to defend her.'*

The cost of the passage to Canada was one hundred and sixty-six dollars, sufficient to pay for the fare, *head charge* to a Canadian agent and a fee to a Polish agent in Lubaczow. Although quite a large sum in those days, it was a small price to pay for those things that are priceless; a chance to own real property in a democratic state that had unlimited possibilities.

The train's arrival in Warsaw interrupted his daydream of what might have been. During his two days in the city, Andrij discovered just how close in character were the customs of Ukraine and Poland, inextricably bound together in architecture, art, history, and literature. For one thing, he noted that Shevchenko and Franko were published in the Ukrainian language in Central Poland even at a time when there was considerable animosity between the two nations. For another, he discovered that this ill will, common amongst the power structure, was not evident among the working class of Poles. In this metropolis, there seemed to be a condemnation of the Polish policy of not encouraging the assimilation of the Ukrainian minority into the main stream of life, the harassment of the Uniate Church, and the scaling down and closing of Ukrainian schools and Ukrainian language classes. Some Poles criticized the intolerance of Catholic priests toward Uniate Ukrainians while others thought that Poland should present information about Ukraine in a more truthful way so that old hatreds could be diffused.

The next leg of his journey took Andrij to Berlin, the cultural and political heart of Germany; a city of museums, churches and wide boulevards. Lying at the geographical heart of the European continent, its reputation as an intellectual, cabaret, and boulevard life centre of Europe was well deserved. As the train pulled out of Berlin, there was little to indicate that soon it would become the staging ground for Hitler's ill-fated scheme for world domination. German towns came and went and with each stop a new mix of passengers would board the train. It was all refreshingly new for Andrij. And, perhaps that was the best way for him to describe Amsterdam, a city of museums, water, canals, and bridges. Needless to say, many of those in his group took special note of the *red light district,* in operation since the 17th century.

Disembarking in Liverpool on August 5, 1928, Andrij soon found himself on an ocean liner named *Montroyal.* Built for the Canadian Pacific, the Montroyal was the first of the Atlantic Empresses and sister ship to the ill-fated Empress of Ireland which sank in the St. Lawrence River after a collision with a Norwegian freighter on May 29, 1914 with a loss of 1,000 lives. The Empress of Britain was 570 feet long, 68 feet wide and had a top speed of 19 knots. The ship had its maiden voyage in 1906 and was re-named the Montroyal in 1924. In all, the ship made a total of 190 round voyages on the North Atlantic with the final run in 1929 following which she was sold and scrapped. However, its beautiful woodwork lives on in a hotel as the Montroyal Ballroom. Being able to carry 1,580 passengers, it was a full-service ocean liner operated by the Canadian Pacific, offering three classes of service, a luxurious dining room, a small movie theatre and impromptu entertainment in the form of national music and dance put on from time to time by the passengers themselves.

In later years, Andrij was heard to say that he enjoyed watching two movies, the ever-popular Mickey Mouse and Steamboat Willie en route to Canada. Much of the excitement about the impending journey to Canada was lost in Andrij's fascination of watching the hustle and bustle of new passengers coming on board. The day was overcast and a light drizzle enshrouded the ocean liner. Right on schedule, a couple of tugboats towed the ocean liner away from the pier in Liverpool and with a blast of the ship's foghorn the Montroyal set a course for Canada.

It took the *Montroyal,* on relatively calm seas, six days to traverse the Atlantic Ocean. Still, as the ocean liner picked up the movement of waves, gently rocking back and forth and side to side, a number of passengers began to get queasy. The never-ending drone of the engines and the constant vibrations of the ship did not help. As might be expected, a feeling of esprit de corps quickly developed among the passengers. Many spoke a Slavic language which made it much easier for Andrij to effectively communicate with other passengers. He found that learning a few words of English did not present any problems and soon enabled him to have a rudimentary discussion with English-speaking passengers. While at sea, he made every effort to add three or four new English words to his vocabulary each day. To his surprise, those around him appreciated his initiative and provided him with all of the help he needed, including an English phrase book.

The most welcome words that the weary immigrant can hear is *land ahoy.* Those two words were like music to Andrij's ears for off to the north was the rugged shore of Newfoundland. However, it would be one more day before the *Montroyal* traversed the southern tip of Newfoundland and reached the Gulf of St. Lawrence on August 13, 1928. As he looked at the far-off shores of the St. Lawrence River, Andrij was most impressed with the expansiveness of the new land. Late on the evening of August 14, the ship tied up at the Port of Quebec and most of the passengers elected to stay on board until the early hours of August 15 at which time Andrij presented his passport and visa to immigration authorities and got his visa stamped with the words *Dominion*

Group of immigrants, Liverpool, England. Andrij Kaszuba appears in the third row from the bottom, fourth person from the left, wearing a hat, 1928.

THE CANADIAN PACIFIC LINER EMPRESS OF BRITAIN

Postcard depicting the passenger ship, Montroyal, 1928.

Map of Canada showing rail route from Quebec City to High Prairie, 1928.

Government, Quebec, Aug 15, 1928, Immigration Office. On the reverse side of the visa, in twelve languages, was the directive, *This card should be kept carefully. It should be shown to government officials whenever required.*

The train ride from the City of Quebec to Winnipeg was unlike anything he had experienced. A ribbon of rails carried him through the Northern Ontario country that had been hitherto a wilderness untrodden by the foot of any human being. As the train worked its way through the Precambrian cliffs, a conductor informed the passengers that the amount of explosives used to blast a rail-bed was staggering as was the cost for dynamite, nitro-glycerine, and black powder.

As the rails hugged the shores of Lake Superior, Andrij experienced the grandeur of the Great Lakes. Noting Andrij's interest in his surroundings, a fellow passenger declared that '*...much of the track was laid in winter months in 1883 when temperatures dropped to forty or fifty below and the blasting of the Shield was accomplished at great loss of life.*' He spoke of the railroad

175

bunkhouses which housed sixty to eighty workers and how these workers slept in verminous blankets on beds made of straw or hay in double-decker bunks. During the hot summer days the air in those bunks was oppressive and the only source of light was through the small windows. Worse yet, the hotter the days the more bothersome were the mosquitoes. It was not unusual to fill the air with smoke to drive off those maddening clouds of mosquitoes and black flies. It was often said that the rails were no place for a man who enjoyed the occasional bath and laundered clothes.

But, the expanse of land was not without a special beauty. The late summer days seemed to be tinted with accents of rose, buttercups, and lily. Small lakes abounded everywhere. The beauty was especially Canadian. 'The scenery,' wrote Andrij in his letter to Eva, 'is truly magnificent. It is grand. Surely, this is God's work!' The train's progress was frequently interrupted by ravines and streams, an everlasting monument to all who ventured through this region. As the train clicketty-clacked its way through Ontario, Andrij pulled out a photograph of Eva. 'Good Lord, I wish she were here. She would enjoy this scenery.'

The only thing that seemed to cheer Andrij about railroading stories was the thought of the food served to the workers—freshly baked bread, salt pork and corned beef, molasses, beans, and potatoes, and a breakfast of oatmeal and tea. Wages for a labourer at the time of construction were $1.75 to $2.00 per day. Board, in many cases, was free or minimal in cost and deducted from a worker's wages. As one day stretched into another, the province of Ontario suddenly gave way to the province of Manitoba and the city of Winnipeg.

North Winnipeg, the staging place for railroad work gangs, impressed Andrij as an area of the city where Slavs tended to congregate in their little *tar paper* shacks made of boards and strapped with tar paper topped off with tent-like roofs of old tobacco tins or made of slabs of that same useful but unsightly tar paper. And, like so many immigrants before him, all that Andrij wanted was some bed space on the floor because a homemade bunk which lined the walls came with a higher price tag. As he assessed the economic conditions in Winnipeg, he discovered that hundreds of immigrants looking for work would line up at the Immigration Hall for a bowl of porridge in the morning and a bowl of soup in the afternoon. For those wanting to catch a train ride to another location, the situation was even worse. The rail yards were patrolled by police and guard dogs so as to discourage this practice. Andrij's stay in Winnipeg, a city known as the Empress of the Prairies and a staging area for the push into the wilderness where homesteads awaited hardy pioneers, was relatively brief.

Being in a democratic country, he kept attuned to the latest political news, be it provincial or national in content. Perhaps the first bit of Canadian news that was of any interest to him was that Ottawa, in recent months, had taken the position that a shift in policy was necessary in order to stop European immigrants from coming to Canada only to take up residence in a city rather than in the country where manpower was needed to break new land.

The federal government concluded that the ranks of the unemployed were being swelled by this internal migration of new Canadians to urban centres in search of employment and a higher wage. This new government policy, however, suited him just fine. He had no intention of taking up residence in any city.

Other pieces of new government legislation caught his attention. He noted that senior citizens over the age of seventy were now eligible for an old age pension; however, they had to be British subjects and residents of Canada for at least twenty years with an annual income of less than one hundred and twenty-five dollars. Although the question of favourable legislation for non-British subjects could have been raised, there was no reason to despair. With this kind of favourable legislation, many new immigrants felt confident that, over time, all Canadians would benefit and saw no reason why his confidence in Canada's future should be dampened.

In this expansive land, Andrij could not help but take notice that what was important news in Winnipeg may carry little interest in Montreal. It seemed that everyone in Montreal was talking about some strange game called professional ice hockey and that the Montreal Maroons were beaten in mid-April three games to two by the New York Rangers to lose the Stanley Cup. *'Strange game, this hockey,'* wrote Andrij to Eva, *'and yet it certainly has those Quebecers in an uproar!'*

As time went on, Andrij began to accept the pervasiveness of a new phenomenon in the vastness of Canada; a phenomenon that seemed to have little to do with the world of work, religion, or politics. It was an endeavour called professional sports. Thinking back to the hustle and bustle of Amsterdam, he suddenly realized that the Olympic Games had been scheduled for mid-August and that Canadians were now being inundated with information about Canada's athletes. Athletes like Ethel Catherwood of Toronto in the running high jump and the Edmonton Commercial Grads who won the world championship in basketball.

Even his new-found Ukrainian friends in Winnipeg seemed to take an interest in professional sport saying that they were influenced by the print media. At least it gave Canadians something to talk about other than the weather and the sagging economy. All of this is not to say that good news was not being printed. Recognizing the malaise that had enveloped the economy, the Canadian government decided to give Canadians an early Christmas present by restoring the *penny postage* for letters sent within the British Empire as opposed to the postage of two cents required on regular letters.

The news about employment opportunities in Winnipeg was not good and the news about employment in the surrounding rural areas was even worse. It was common knowledge that the relative isolation and the attendant lack of any medical care made the immigrants especially vulnerable. And, immigrants quickly learned about two other formidable enemies: the mosquito and the cold Canadian winters where knee-deep snow disheartened many new arrivals. Finally, Andrij would be able to validate for himself the news out of New York directed at prospective immigrants, which spoke of the hardships presented by mosquitoes and cold winters.

Even if the news was sometimes bad, Andrij knew that it was too late to do anything about it. Physically fit as a fiddle and in the prime of his life at twenty-eight, he knew he could withstand minor difficulties. However, not all of his Ukrainian friends were so agreeable. One went so far as to quote the last two verses of Symon Palamariuk's 1903 poem entitled Song of Canada;

Here, our people thought, that they would be lords, But here they all go to work, carrying bags.

Oh Canada, dear Canada, how unpleasant you are,One can only hope, dear Canada, that no one will dream of you.

Despite these criticisms and reservations, Andrij was not worried. He knew that his military training and his resolve to make a go of it in Canada would see him through. Looking around, he questioned the dedication of some of the immigrants. It seemed as though they *were* looking for a handout! His first task in Winnipeg was to check into the Immigration Hall and get any kind of official information which would help him decide as to whether he should stay in Manitoba and seek free homestead land nearby or travel farther west where it was thought that more opportunities would present themselves. An Immigration official, who spoke Ukrainian, informed Andrij that much of the desirable land in Manitoba had already been taken by earlier settlers. As a result, recent arrivals were forced to consider homesteads on marginal farmland where the soil was often of inferior quality.

It was only natural that many of the immigrants quickly became homesick and looked for all of the reasons why they should not have come to Canada. To Andrij, this reflected a lot of wasted energy. He wanted instead to look for success stories and to build upon the positive features of his newly adopted country. Many immigrants coming to Winnipeg looked for work on the Hudson Bay Line. Any thoughts of working on this railway line, which reached over 800 kilometres north to Churchill, were dashed when he learned that the railway, much of it over muskeg and permafrost, would be completed in three or four months and no later than the spring of 1929. Despite this disappointment, he did hear one message coming though over and over again: *go west young man, go west!*

Being the latter part of August, Andrij was struck by just how much Western Canada looked like his homeland of Galicia. Even more revealing was the official word as to just how much land was already under cultivation throughout Manitoba, Saskatchewan, and Alberta. However, to a large degree, this phenomenon was somewhat deceiving. Most settlers looked upon land adjoining the railway as offering the most important of ingredients; transportation. With the long warm days and the gentle nights, it didn't take Andrij long to gain a deep and abiding appreciation for the greatness of his new country. Couple this with the ease with which new friends could be made in a democratic nation and you have the formula for a lasting love affair.

While in Winnipeg, Andrij's thoughts turned to his cousin Ivan

Tychanewycz whom he had not seen since the first week of May. A check with the Immigration Hall did show that Ivan had checked in on May 28, almost three months earlier. As might be expected, a forwarding address was not left with the authorities. Perhaps this was due to the realization on the part of Ivan that he would not have a permanent address until such time that he gained permanent employment. To track Ivan would be difficult, if not impossible, without first getting the information, by letter, from his family in Plazow. Since the turn-around time for this process would be no less than two or three months, Andrij concluded that he would not be able to establish Ivan's location for many months to come.

Franek Shewchuk, a new acquaintance, marvelled at all the new inventions which made life for the pioneer more palatable. Mail was being delivered to outlying areas of Canada by plane and new electrical plants in remote locations were being built. Gold fields and coalfields were being developed and a Canadian was even taking credit for discovering pork and beans which appeared in small tin cans on the shelves of general stores throughout the land. On a more serious note, Andrij and Franek continued to assimilate the latest information about jobs and homesteading opportunities, soon discovering that the very process of disseminating information by Canadian authorities was not an exact science. Much of the news was circulated by word of mouth and for every door that seemed opened to opportunity, they soon discovered that someone else beat them to the punch. They could only conclude that the opportunities for economic success in Winnipeg were pretty well exhausted for the time being. In short order, both made a decision to leave Winnipeg for points west.

Packing their meagre belongings, Andrij joined Franek and took the only means of transportation available to them, a railroad boxcar. The price was right and besides they learned a new word, *hobo*. But, getting onto a freight car was not easy because the railway cops seemed to be everywhere and they looked unusually vicious. So did their guard dogs. On the other hand, Winnipeg's politicians asked the same cops to go easy on the new immigrants. They said that the best place for them during this period of high unemployment was anywhere outside of Winnipeg. Looking around in the freight car, Andrij counted twenty other hobos, most of whom, he presumed, were recent immigrants to Canada, all heading to Saskatchewan and Alberta.

Perhaps the idea of an Edmonton destination first came from Franek who pulled out a copy of a newspaper article written in an Edmonton newspaper which talked about the first Ukrainian pioneers who settled near the city in 1891. The final leg of *their* journey was by train and, the article went on to say, they had become successful farmers over a short period of time. In selecting Edmonton as their destination, Franek and Andrij felt that at least they would be amongst some earlier pioneers who had immigrated from the Austrian provinces of Galicia and Bukovyna in search of a new life.

With a population of seven hundred, Edmonton was incorporated as a town in 1892 and quickly became a supply post for the Klondike Gold Rush and a service centre for the north. Being connected by waterways to the Mackenzie River, it was not uncommon to see dozens of prospectors piling off trains in Edmonton to join the gold rush.

Upon arriving in Edmonton, Andrij was rudely awakened to the realities of the situation. Despite the comradery that was so quickly established, the first priority was finding work; any kind of work. Luckily, that proved to be relatively easy in the autumn of 1928. His first job, near Bruderheim, was that of stooking; a process of placing about six bundles of cut grain into a pyramidal-shaped stack to allow the harvested grain to cure while at the same time protecting them from excessive damage from rain, snow, or frost. Although the pay was meagre, even by standards in 1928, it was an opportunity to learn more about farming, about Canada, and especially about the rudiments of the English language. Somehow, Andrij knew that his first exposure to life in Canada would provide him with a bridge to the future.

In some ways, the fact that Andrij found temporary work in Bruderheim was no accident. For it was here in 1891 that the forerunners of the Ukrainian migration, Ivan Pylypiw and Vasyl Eleniak came to look over the possibilities of settling in Canada. And, it was in 1892 that several of their compatriots filed for homesteads in the valley of Beaverhill Creek. *They were the first of thousands of their kin to arrive in this region to subdue the soil and above all, taste freedom.*

19.

Blue Sky Country

"But, let me tell you, you'll never make it in Canada"

As Andrij landed in Canada, his mission was clear—to set down family roots in a country that embraced democratic principles. And, as he thought about the circumstances that led to his decision to come to Canada, he suddenly realized that the words of his father, *'go ahead, go to Canada but let me tell you this, you'll never make it,'* did nothing more than act as a catalyst. For a strapping young war veteran, these were fighting words; an invitation to take up the challenge.

Looking at a cloudless Alberta sky, Andrij was struck with just how much the plains of Alberta reminded him of the county of Lubaczow where the villagers liked to refer to a cloudless day as having a *high sky,* much as they did in Alberta. *'On a clear day,'* Andrij wrote Eva, *'you could see forever.'* As the afternoon waned, a few scattered clouds rolled in. It didn't take much for Andrij to journey to his own little dream world. He had to pinch himself to break away from this feeling of extreme sentimentality and loneliness knowing full well that this was not the time to become overwhelmed with thoughts of family. He knew what lay ahead and any show of weakness could quickly defeat his resolve; his promise to himself to make good. *'In the end I'll show my father just how wrong he was.'*

As he assessed the kind of people who lived in Alberta, he was struck with the lack of conformity in every walk of life. As someone else phrased it, *'...why, there are men who are well dressed and those that are commonly dressed. Some are awfully dressed while others are shabbily dressed...'* And, their personal habits often reflected the nature of their dress. Most men were sober but then there were those gadding about *'...half drunk, nearly drunk, quite drunk, frightfully drunk, howling drunk or dead drunk...'* It seemed that the larger Alberta communities had some things in common. One was always able to find a poker game, a billiard hall, and a whiskey dive or two. 'Odd,' concluded Andrij, '*that the English should refer to us as the foul-smelling, sheepskin-wearing Ruthenians.*' Looking around, he concluded that the criticism was misplaced.

As darkness fell over the prairies, Andrij noticed another phenomenon that piqued his curiosity--the northern lights. He had heard about them from other pioneers but had never witnessed them before this particular evening. In fact, it was just the previous night that John Schmolsky, a local railroad foreman, told him that they were peculiar to this part of the hemisphere. Andrij marvelled at this luminous phenomenon that consisted of arches of light in the sky, reminding him of the Cossacks of Ukraine—swift, silent and mysterious, forever dancing. Schmolsky said that they had their origin in Indian mythology, portraying the freedom of a young Indian maiden's coming of age dance and, if you listened carefully, you could hear the *zinging* sound made by those northern lights.

Work for Andrij had a special meaning. But, in the end, work simply meant that: work. And, work often meant constraining your conscious world to the surroundings immediately around you. Within that space there was time to think, to plan, and to daydream, even though the conversations were difficult with English-speaking co-workers. At times like this a man could wait until he found someone who would listen to him in his own language, or take the opportunity to build upon the English language. Being gainfully employed in Bruderheim, Andrij now had the occasion to think about the expansiveness of his newly adopted country. Another day of stooking was completed and he was now ready for a good night's rest. Looking around the bunkhouse, *the only possessions he had were in the wooden suitcase--personal possessions that every immigrant brought with him--a change of clothing, personal papers, a passport, a small amount of money, and a lot of dreams.*

This was the first real opportunity that Andrij had to relax since arriving in Canada. Two other workers shared the bunkhouse with him; a bunkhouse that had all of the comforts of home. It had an old Franklin heater with sufficient space upon which to heat water for tea or coffee, room to make a basic meal, or to provide comfort against the coolness of the evening. Getting accustomed to life in Canada was not all that bad. It was those simple things that began to change his life around. In the Old Country, it was a custom to drink water or tea when thirsty. Here, it seemed that these guys could not get started at their tasks without first drinking a cup of coffee. Sleep did not come easily for Andrij. Finally, he concluded that it was this darned coffee that upset his routine. But, even coffee could not push back the sandman for long. Comforted by the thoughts of a good day's work and the assurance of having made one dollar, he was in slumber land.

Morning came soon enough and Andrij did not need an alarm clock to tell him when to get up. For him, everything was governed by the sun; up at sunrise and to bed at sunset--that was the rule of thumb. As for his two co-workers, Helmut and Hans, they too seemed to set their biological clocks by

Farmer cutting stand of wheat in 1916. Source: Provincial Archives, Edmonton, Alberta.

the sun, were soon awake and had the old Franklin stove pumping out heat and the coffee perking. In short order, they had a breakfast of bacon, eggs, fresh bread, and coffee, in the words of his co-workers, '...*fit for a king.*' Unlike relationships in the Poland, the lines of demarcation between the landowner and the workers were almost indistinguishable where everyone was a part of the team. The object was to complete a particular task as quickly as possible because the unpredictable Canadian weather controlled everything on the farm.

Having finished all of the stooking in six days, it was now time for him to look for other work. The word from Hans and Helmut, both of German ancestry, was that work was available in central Alberta in the town of Ponoka. Although the arrangement was to pay Andrij one dollar for each day's work, the landowner was so pleased with the amount of work accomplished by the stooking team that he paid Andrij eight dollars in cash rather than the promised six dollars. He knew that Andrij would need the money to survive the coming winter months.

Their employer took the three stookers to the train station in Fort Saskatchewan where they were able to catch a freight train to Edmonton. Although Andrij's time Edmonton was short, it did provide him with sufficient time to see first hand just how pervasive was the depression. There were unemployed immigrants everywhere and he realized just how fortunate he was to find work at all. It would be here that they would catch another freight train headed for Calgary and disembark in Ponoka. In assessing his first week in Alberta, Andrij was rather pleased with himself; free room and board and a free ride from Bruderheim to Ponoka. When a man made one or two dollars per day, that was the take-home pay. There were no taxes to pay

Hitching a train ride. Source: Glenbow Archives, Calgary, Alberta. NC-6-12955i.

and no other expenses. And for ten dollars a man could buy a lot of groceries! *'Life ain't so bad after all,'* concluded Andrij.

Unlike so many places elsewhere, a man's word in Alberta was his bond. If an Albertan said that he would pay you one dollar for each day's work, that was precisely what you earned. If he extended a verbal contract, it was done with little fanfare. A man did not need a formal written contract. Andrij liked this because it reminded him of the Old Country where a man's word meant a lot to its owner and to everyone else in the community. Lose that and you lose your honour and, perhaps, your soul. Finding work in Ponoka was not easy. It seemed that the crops were marginal and he was in competition for work with many other immigrants and unemployed Canadians. Once again luck was on his side when a local farmer offered Andrij some harvesting work for a short period of time and, once the stooking was completed, he joined a threshing crew as a *field pitcher* on the nearby Holt farm, concentrating his efforts at helping the other teams load their hayracks with sheaves of grain before delivery to the threshing machine operated by a Rumley steam engine. A spirit of cooperation developed among the farmers and it was not unusual to find one farmer helping another with harvesting operations. When you finished one task, you did not sit around on your hands admiring your work. *'There just isn't time for that kind of an attitude,'* smiled his employer, *'for today the weather may be great but tomorrow? Who knows? You have to make hay while the sun shines.'*

By the next morning, Andrij knew exactly what Ben was talking about. The heavens opened up and the rains came to Ponoka. Here it was, early September and it felt like winter. It rained off and on for ten days. During this time Andrij had occasion to drive the farm wagon into Ponoka for supplies.

The local grocer seemed to know everyone in the community and extending credit was not a problem where a running outstanding balance was entered into a log book. Communication with the clerk was not a problem either. It seemed that most everyone in the community knew a few words of one foreign language or another.

From the general store, Andrij drove the team of horses to the meat market where the meat cutter was a middle-aged ethnic Ukrainian. Upon discovering that Andrij knew a considerable amount about slaughtering a pig or a cow, he was offered part-time employment during those days when harvesting was not possible. In a sense, the part-time position was akin to enrolment in an apprenticeship program--an opportunity to let others teach you about the marketing of meat products. His new role helped him realize that World War I hastened the racier lifestyle of those aspiring to the middle class. There was talk of refrigerators for the home along with vacuum cleaners, electricity and running water. Women, too, were now able to earn money and to drink, smoke, and even drive that most favourite of all horseless carriages, the Model T Ford. By this time, Canada had over 75 thousand kilometres of paved road which gave quite a boost to the automobile industry and a new meaning to horse power. Suddenly, Albertans embraced the horseless carriage.

Women, too, were beginning to assert their equality in dress and deed. The days of the corset were going the way of the dodo bird. *'Yeah,'* said the owner of the meat market, *'the women of today bind their breasts and belt their lips. Why, their silhouette is now like that of her brother. I long for those frilly white collars and full skirts with all of those underclothes and the fancy pompadours and God-given eyebrows.'*

'Tak, tak,' responded Andrij, *'strange, these Canadian women. Hard to understand them. I like a woman the way God created her. The way she should be, at home with the children. While there, she can wear what she wants.'* Even though he disapproved of many of these changes, he had to admit that there was something exhilarating about these new mores.

In late October, the harvest season was finally over. Enough good weather was squeezed out of the weatherman to allow the local farmers to take off all of his crops. Andrij felt that the inclement weather had worked to his advantage. He not only completed his work at the Schwartz farm, but he now had an offer for continued work in the local butcher shop. But, even while working in the butcher shop, he saw the importance of the railway system. Everywhere in Alberta, groups or individuals followed the railway which was extended from Calgary to Edmonton.

Late October saw the end of an unusually warm fall which locals liked to call *Indian summer*. This gave the local farmers sufficient time to harvest their crops. The only exceptions seemed to be the cases where a farmer's thresher broke down and could not be repaired in time for the late harvest. Halloween was an unusual experience for Andrij for it was an opportunity to let off some steam and to learn a little bit more about some of those crazy Canadian customs. The winter months passed quickly and work at the butcher shop provided plenty of opportunities to learn about Canada and the English language and to write Eva about Ponoka, to put a human face on his experiences. He took great pride in telling her about how quickly close friendships can be developed in an otherwise harsh land. Contrary to what he had heard from others about how badly the *smelly sheepskin-wearing immigrants* were treated, he saw very little of it himself. It seemed that most everyone was prepared to help him with his English and make him feel comfortable about himself and his surroundings. '*Yes, Eva,*' he concluded one letter, '*I feel confident that you'll love this new land.*'

Although Andrij survived the winter months without too much difficulty, he had to admit that others were not so lucky. In mid-February, a group of five hundred unemployed men marched on the province's Parliament Buildings in Edmonton. Under the watchful eye of the police, the anticipated violence did not break out. However, the march did highlight the unemployment problem, not only in Alberta, but in all of Canada for that matter. The feeling in Ponoka was that the short-term solutions such as the provision of bed and meal tickets were woefully inadequate. Politicians were being urged to develop long-term solutions to a problem which could quickly get out of hand.

As unemployment rose in the province, the residents in Ponoka were unable to spend as much money at the butcher shop as they wanted to or as they had during earlier boom times. In short order, Andrij became a casualty and a statistic; he was now unemployed. Once again luck was with him when he found work on a local cattle ranch; work that offered free room and board and an opportunity to learn about cattle, mixed farming, and the latest techniques in crop rotation and cultivation. With the worsening employment picture, he realized that the best he could do was to find piece-meal work; scrimping and saving throughout. It was now a case of survival until better times came along.

By this time Andrij heard all kinds of rumours about the unpredictability of Alberta's seasons. Still, there was nothing unusual about the weather in Ponoka. The cold spells didn't last that long and these were often tempered by warmer westerlies which came to be recognized as *chinooks*. Unlike his experiences in Galicia, the cattle roamed the range during winter months and seemed none the worse for it in the spring. It would be here that he would learn more about Canada's Dominion Lands Act which was passed in 1872 and provided for free homesteads of 160 acres or a quarter section of land for settlers. In 1928 a homesteader had to pay a ten dollar filing fee, live on the land for three years, and clear no less than fifteen acres of land before he became eligible for a clear title to the land. Only one problem existed; good arable land was hard to find in central Alberta. It seemed that most of the arable land near every transportation link, be it the main highway or a railway, had already been gobbled up.

There seemed to be no shortage of stories and rumours about the Indians of Alberta nor about the *half-breeds*, or more correctly, the Metis. Originally, the word was applied to a man of mixed Indian and French-Canadian ancestry but more recently to any offspring of a white man who married a full-blooded Indian girl. For it was these two distinct groups of peoples who helped the first white settlers navigate the rivers of Canada; rivers that were used as a means of transporting goods and services to new frontiers. In fact, the waterways were crucial to the development of the west where the upper terminus of a line of steamboat communication started in Winnipeg and ended in Fort Saskatchewan.

Andrij liked to read older copies of newspapers such as the Edmonton Bulletin. He did not mind if the newspaper was two or three weeks old. It would be an article in one of these newspapers that he would first learn about the success of growing wheat, barley, and oats in Northern Alberta. To him, good news often withstood the test of time, as it were, and it did provide him with many opportunities to improve his command of the English language at his own pace and without political filtration.

As times got tougher, survival often depended upon a man's ability to exchange his labour for food. Even the cattle being raised in Central Alberta were not immune from the trials and tribulations of survival on the open range in extreme temperatures. Cattle were first introduced to Alberta from Montana nearly one-hundred years earlier and it was during one of these expeditions that a cattleman found seams of good coal north of Edmonton. These events triggered the cattle, coal, and lumbering industries in Northern Alberta; all of which would soon become very important to Alberta's future as well as to that of Andrij.

Having lived in Canada for less than one year, Andrij felt that he was being indoctrinated into the Canadian way of life. Although it was true that many new immigrants wore their Ukrainian ethnicity on their sleeve, he decided that it would be to his advantage to befriend workers from other ethnic groups. Besides, he wanted very much to become a *good Canadian*. He saw how the white man had elbowed aside the Indians and how the settlements had sprung up all over the horizon. He couldn't help but marvel at the richness of the soil and the promise of a bright future. This explained why Canada had gained an international reputation for the quality of its wheat. But then, as the days went by during the summer of 1929, Andrij realized that the long sunny days had much to do with the quality of the crops. Despite these many successes, catastrophe was just around the corner; a catastrophe that touched every Canadian. On October 29, the prices on the Montreal and Toronto Stock Exchanges plunged in the worst collapse ever witnessed in Canadian financial history. Panic also gripped Wall Street in New York.

The only good news in Ponoka, it seemed, was the excellence of the weather. Locals assured Andrij that this was the finest summer and the warmest fall in their memory. As predicted by some of the Indians in Southern Alberta, the good weather continued well into the fall. Then, it even got better. In fact, the winter of 1929-30 turned out to be, perhaps, the warmest on record and, in most of Alberta, the winter turned out to be completely free of snow. The weather in central Alberta was so favourable that January became noted for its brush fires in the village of Rocky Mountain House.

As the 1920s came to a close in Alberta, the ranks of the unemployed continued to swell as the economy worsened. Cots were being set up in offices to provide overnight accommodation for the homeless. The only beds available to some were the park benches; on Alberta farms it often turned out to be the barn or even the haystack. Alberta, hard hit by the depression and drought, received shipments of relief food from Ontario. Where the good news should have been that Alberta gained control of its natural resources on October 1, the impact of the depression took centre stage and it was now a matter of survival and not of development.

The onslaught of the Great Depression had a sudden and direct impact upon Andrij's plans to bring Eva and Maria from Poland to Canada. It was hard enough to feed one person. To feed three would be a herculean task. At the same time, it was difficult not to recall the words of his father which kept reverberating in his ears, '...*you'll never make it in that hostile environment called Canada...*' Despite the hard times, he remained optimistic.

The devastation of the depression touched everyone and especially those Ukrainian settlers who came to Western Canada and settled in the Lamont region. Someone once said that they came empty-handed to an empty land. Despite these seemingly insurmountable obstacles, the homesteaders had reason to be optimistic. By this time in the development of the west, Canada had built a reputation for producing the finest wheat in the world. This success likely came about by accident when a Scottish farmer by the name of David Fife wrote a letter to a friend in Europe in 1842 asking him for a handful of wheat. The European friend found out that a merchant ship had just arrived from Danzig, Germany, with a load of wheat and was anchored in the port of Glasgow. Fife selected a few hard kernels and planted these in the spring. The results were very encouraging. So much so that Fife wanted to know the source of the wheat. To his surprise, he discovered that the wheat originally came from Galicia, Western Ukraine. Little wonder that Ukrainian pioneers looked upon suffering as being a prelude to better times.

Ivan Schmolsky was of the opinion that his Red Fife wheat had conquered all of North America as no other wheat had. It would be Dr. Sanders of Ottawa who would cross Red Fife with other strains of wheat over the years and produce new assortments of wheat for which he gained national and international fame.

In the midst of the depression, Andrij dreamed of the day that he would be able to start up his own farming operation and try his hand at planting some of this Red Fife.

20.

Rails and Trails

Lifeline to settlers in the Peace River Country

Although the great depression gripped nearly all of Canada by 1929, Andrij felt optimistic that good times would follow. In listening to the conversations and the wisdom of local workers, he developed the impression that Alberta was headed for new prosperity. Despite the onslaught of the depression, there was considerable discussion about the wealth of Alberta's resources; of forests and fields that stretched as far as the eye could see. Mines were quickly opening up and there was plenty of talk about oil and natural gas and the farmers near the town of Ponoka wanted to experience the thrill of harnessing electricity.

Many small towns in Alberta had their own electric-generating plants as Calgary Power set about to buy up many of these small and often poorly-run power plants and connect them into a much larger system. The importance of this thrust could not be underestimated since townspeople could now rely on a continuous supply of electricity rather than a service offered only during daylight hours. As Andrij watched the direct competition between Calgary Power and Canadian Utilities, he was able to grasp the true meaning of a market economy in a democratic state. But, what *really* began to captivate his imagination was the railroad industry in Alberta; an industry that was attracting an increasing number of Ukrainian immigrants. In Northern Alberta, new railways and steamboats were pushing back the frontier. And, even though farmers complained about their rate of return on investment, each person seemed to aspire to the same goals of economic independence, good health, and happiness.

To help Andrij celebrate a successful year in Canada, his boss broke out a bottle of homemade wine made of rhubarb, while at the same time bragging that red beets, carrots, wild raspberries, high bush cranberries, or wild strawberries could also be used. While enjoying the wine and listening to some western music on Ivan's majestic gramophone, Andrij set out to demonstrate to his hosts how to dance the *Ukrainian hopak*. In a letter to Eva, he said that it might have been the music that caused him to miss a dance manoeuvre. Or, maybe the wine. Whatever the reason, there was no shortage of laughter when he landed flat on his fanny.

Everywhere the talk was of the number of miles of track being laid in Alberta. The Canadian National Railway built a line north of the North Saskatchewan River, right through the Ukrainian settlement of Smoky Lake and the sand hills east of the community, all the way to Father Lacombe's St. Paul des Metis. Embracing free enterprise, the Canadian Pacific Railway wasn't going to be outdone by the Canadian National. They built a railway along the South Victoria Trail south of the Saskatchewan River to Ukrainian communities such as Andrew, Two Hills, and Lloydminster. The railroad had always been important to Canada and Canadians; important because Canada is the second largest country in the world and its population is relatively small and scattered. The Fathers of Confederation placed considerable faith in the ability of the railroad to serve the pioneers. In fact, it was the dream of a continental railway that convinced British Columbia about the merits of membership in the Dominion of Canada.

The Confederation of Canada in 1867 spurred railway construction and the Canadian Pacific Railway soon spanned the nation from coast to coast.[26] The first locomotives ran on public roads. However, this proved to be less than adequate and man's inventiveness soon had the locomotives on iron rails. The two prime purposes for the construction of railroads was the movement of freight and passengers. Initially, third-class passengers did not have seats. But then, who would want to sit through a bumpy ride! A man could wear out a pair of pants in short order when sitting on a vibrating seat.

Once the route for the transcontinental railway was established by survey crews, teams of railroad workers prepared a rail bed using ploughs and scrapers. The locomotive was then able to steam to the end of the line with a supply of ties, rails, and spikes. Horse-drawn wagons hauled the ties along the graded section following which the locomotives were able to move up again. To a large degree, the manpower shortage was somewhat alleviated by Chinese workers from the Chinese province of Kwantung. The transcontinental railway was completed in 1885 and the first truly transcontinental passenger train made its initial run in 1886. Soon, colonist cars were bringing thousands of immigrants to fill the vast expanse of western Canada. Harvest specials were providing special-rate trips for field workers coming out west to help with the prairie harvesting. In addition, the railways had the important task of sorting and delivering mail to each town along the way.

26 Berton, Pierre. <u>The Last Spike,</u> McClelland and Stewart Limited, Toronto, 1983, pp. 328 - 337.

By 1914 and the outbreak of World War I, railways provided troop trains to take soldiers to ports of embarkation for Europe. In due course, the trains were again used for bringing back the wounded and the veterans. Following the war, trains gained considerable notoriety when thousands of unemployed men took free rides on empty boxcars in a desperate search for employment. Even today, those Canadians old enough to remember *the good old days,* tend to romanticize *riding the rails* and look back upon those days with considerable nostalgia.

Before long, the federal government made a decision to build a northern railway running through Edmonton and the Yellowhead route through the Rockies to Prince Rupert, British Columbia. Although easier to construct than was the CPR through the Rogers Pass, it still presented numerous difficulties, many of which were overcome with the thirty-nine tunnels. Delays were caused by a shortage of rails, funds, and labourers, especially at harvest time when many workers turned to harvesting. The railway bought land at strategic locations along the way and established town sites. The last spike on the northern route was driven on April 7, 1914 at Finmore, British Columbia. The first transcontinental train reached Prince Rupert on April 8, 1914. Unlike the CPR which was mainly built by Irish and Chinese labour, the Canadian Northern and the Grand Trunk Pacific railways were built mainly by Eastern and Southern European workers. These *blanketstiffs,* as they were called, filled most of the unskilled jobs at minimum wages while paying handsomely for goods purchased at the company-controlled store.

Yet, it was not possible for one *northern* transcontinental railway system to serve the needs of all of those settlers northwest of Edmonton, particularly in the Peace River Country. It would be from this identified need that an important branch line would spring up to connect with the river boats at Peace River and for points down the Mackenzie River. Although the Northern Alberta Railways Company was not incorporated by an Act of Federal Parliament until 1929, the construction of the lines which form up the company started several years earlier. In fact, it would be between 1912 and 1930 that a standard gauge railway would be built by E.D. & B.C. Railway between Edmonton and Dawson Creek, British Columbia. However, the owners of this particular railway system ran into financial difficulties and the provincial government was forced to intercede. In 1928, the two major railway systems, the Canadian Pacific and the Canadian National Railways, jointly purchased the troubled E. D. & B. C. Railway and created the Northern Alberta Railway. With its starting point in Edmonton, the railroad would connect dozens of communities before reaching High Prairie, the Aggie Settlement, and terminate in Dawson Creek, which later became Mile Zero on the Alaska Highway.

The most significant impact of the Northern Alberta Railway was on people. Its construction over a contracted period of time provided hundreds of full-time and part-time jobs. Most of the workers were unskilled and poorly paid and all too often the company's treatment of its workers was high-handed and unfeeling. During summer months the workers laboured long hours on work that was often hard and dangerous, putting up with mosquitoes and blackflies in a scorching sun. Little wonder that many settlers preferred to combine two endeavours to make extra cash: harvesting near Edmonton and railroading during the cold winter months.

After much searching, work *did* become available to Andrij with one of Canada's most stable employers, the Northern Alberta Railway. In reality, this opportunity came about by accident when he was undertaking a search for Ivan Tychanewycz and visited the offices of the Canadian National Railway in Edmonton. *No,* the officials had never heard of Ivan; however, on a hunch he made an inquiry about job opportunities with the railway company. *No,* they did not have any openings. However, he was told that the single track railway with light steel was not adequate for the traffic being handled and new lines were being laid west of High Prairie to provide heavier steel to take care of the increasing traffic with heavier locomotives and larger capacity cars. *As a result,* explained the official, *the region is a beehive of activity, quickly attracting new settlers.* Although not in the prairie region, he was assured that the area showed considerable promise for agriculture and mixed farming.

Hitching a ride on a freight, car he headed northwest through what seemed to be endless forests and the villages of Westlock, Smith, and Slave Lake before setting a course for the village of High Prairie. It was difficult for Andrij to comprehend the vast difference in the topography of this region to that of Ponoka. Where Ponoka portrayed a considerable amount of open space and fertile land, the region between Athabasca and Grouard was a never-ending forest broken only by muskegs, swampland, and lakes. Surprisingly, the High Prairie agricultural belt reflected a considerable amount of cultivated land, bordered, as it were, by the East and West Prairie Rivers. Staying overnight in a local rooming house in High Prairie, he was able to glean some information about job opportunities with the railway company. The best he could do was to take the advice of the station agent who said to him, *"...why don't you grab a train tomorrow morning and head on west of here about eight miles to Aggie. There you will find the field crews working on the Northern Alberta Railway."*

Early the next morning, Andrij left his belongings at the rooming house and headed west to the whistle stop of Aggie which turned out to be a large water storage tank used by steam locomotives to take on water for their steam engines. As luck would have it, the railroad section foreman turned out to be a Ukrainian by the name of Steve Blonski, who promptly impressed Andrij with the importance of the railway system to the region and the extra manpower needed to install new water supplies, new sidings and related facilities, coaling plants, wyes, and renewing old and inadequate sidings for the sixteen locomotives which operated by-weekly between Edmonton and Dawson Creek. It was not unusual for Blonski to recruit the best possible workers and, to him, the best were those who were willing to work hard and

A 1920s railroad work crew. Source: Provincial Archives, Edmonton, Alberta.

Wagon stuck on a muddy wagon trail. Source: Glenbow Archives, Calgary, Alberta. NA 488-4.

ask few questions. Not only did Blonski put Andrij on the railroad's payroll, but he would play a pivotal role in the ability of Andrij to set down roots in this very region of Alberta.

Initially, the work consisted of *dressing* railroad ties by hand and hauling these to the railroad. And dressing ties was a lot easier said than done. Using a crosscut or Swedish saw, fallen spruce and pine were cut to length and dressed using a broadaxe *(adze)*. The ties were then skidded by horse to a collection point adjacent to the railroad. Another crew would load these onto a flatbed railway car for use in constructing a new section of railroad bed or for repairing an existing section of the railway. Although the work was not easy, Andrij saw the merits of setting down his roots at this location. To do so, he would have to expend a considerable sum of money to purchase a couple of horses to be used for skidding railroad ties. In this way, he would be paid for both, dressing and skidding railroad ties.

As the spring days of 1930 got longer and warmer, Andrij discovered that the High Prairie region was home to a number of Ukrainian immigrants, making it easier to entertain the idea of purchasing a homestead in the region. To the immediate north of Aggie, three *quarters* had already been spoken for and even though very little of the land had been cleared by the *squatters* who were likely awaiting an opportune time to register their interests in the land, he felt that the location would be more than acceptable. In searching for the most appropriate location, he considered the availability of arable land, trees for the construction of buildings and for use as firewood, availability of water, the distance from the village of High Prairie, access to roads, the possibility of future growth, and the distance from the Northern Alberta Railway, which would be his place of work. Having made a decision, he filed an application with the Regional Provincial Lands and Forests Department in Peace River for a homestead.

The Canadian Land Act, passed in 1872, was similar in many respects to that passed ten years earlier in the United States. For a fee of ten dollars, a settler would be given a quarter section of land to which he could gain title after living on the property for three years, clearing 30 acres of land, and building a house. This policy was put into place to ensure that settlers would develop the land and not congregate in a village. At the same time, settlers often complained about the policy which resulted in homesteaders living in loneliness and isolation. In addition, there was further dispersion due to land within each township being withheld from settlement until the railway company got the best land and a further two sections being set aside in every township for school revenue. Finally, the odd-numbered sections were reserved as public lands to be sold by public auction at a later date.

The provision of part-time work for Andrij and other Eastern European settlers came at a very opportune time and took place during a time when the rest of the world was experiencing a Depression. Andrij worked on the *extra-gang* during those first two critical years since arriving in Aggie, thereby providing him with flex time in which to carry out improvements to

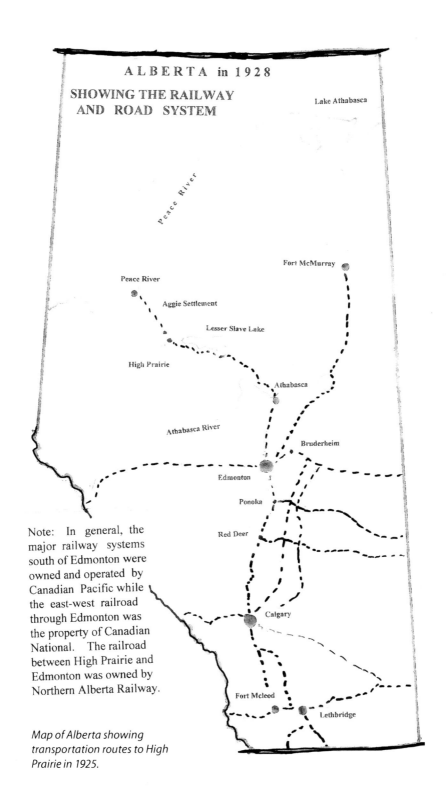

ALBERTA in 1928

SHOWING THE RAILWAY
AND ROAD SYSTEM

Lake Athabasca

Peace River

Fort McMurray

Peace River

Aggie Settlement

Lesser Slave Lake

High Prairie

Athabasca

Athabasca River

Bruderheim

Edmonton

Ponoka

Red Deer

Note: In general, the
major railway systems
south of Edmonton were
owned and operated by
Canadian Pacific while
the east-west railroad
through Edmonton was
the property of Canadian
National. The railroad
between High Prairie and
Edmonton was owned by
Northern Alberta Railway.

Calgary

*Map of Alberta showing
transportation routes to High
Prairie in 1925.*

Fort Mcleod

Lethbridge

195

his homestead. Without this extra income from the railroad and the harvest work for the larger farm operations, first in the Edmonton region and later in the *Peace Country,* a settler would not have the ready cash to buy seed grain, the essential farming tools, and the basic household staples such as flour, sugar, salt, eggs, bacon, and cereal necessary for survival.

The approval of Andrij's application for his first homestead came very quickly. This reflected the government's anxiety in ensuring that the region was settled as soon as possible with ambitious immigrants. The Government of the Province of Alberta had a Department of Lands and Mines regional office in Peace River and, in making application through a representative in High Prairie, Andrij could not help but think back to the public notice posted in the railway station in the village of Belzec; *Free Land in Canada.* Yes, these words were like magic to a young war veteran looking for economic stability and unlimited opportunity. Finally, the dream was coming true!

Since the quarter section had a small creek meandering through one corner of it, he concluded that this would be an ideal location for a cabin, a garden, and some farm buildings and a ready supply of water for household purposes, as well as for the farm animals. Not only that, but the wagon trail on the adjacent road allowance provided an access to the homesteads to the north as well as to the village of High Prairie. The legal description for the quarter section was listed as NE quarter of Section 2 in Township 75, Range 18, West of the 5th Meridian.

For certain, the Aggie Settlement was no paradise; its location left a lot to be desired, the pay on the railway was low and the contract work making railway ties was piecemeal. But, Andrij was his own boss. He could work as hard as he wanted to and concentrate more of his efforts on clearing land. Being the architect of his own destiny, he soon learned that the strong exploited the weak. In his mind, the exploitation of his physical prowess was a temporary sacrifice for a long-range goal even though there was no doubt in his mind that the pioneers living in Northern Alberta were, in fact, being exploited by the Eastern Canada oligarchy that called all of the shots and collected most of the financial rewards. This came in the form of exploitation of natural resources and the financial penalty of high freight rates attached to all items transported from Eastern Canada to Alberta.

Andrij found the Section Foreman, Steve Blonski, to be an excellent source of information, not only about the railway, but also about natural resources, farming, politics, and the church. According to Blonski, the drought in Southern Alberta led to hardships and an influx of new settlers to Northern Alberta in search of jobs. Many found work building new roads, while others found employment with the railway, which was being extended into the Peace Country. Most of all, it seemed that people wanted freedom and were finding it in the north. Bumper crops were in evidence everywhere in the province. Each cultivated acre, on the average, produced 28 bushels for a total of 145 million bushels. The organization known as the United Farmers of Alberta built community halls throughout Alberta.

Earlier, at the UFA convention in Calgary in 1913, the framework was laid for the formation of the Alberta Farmers' Co-operative Elevator Company. By the fall of 1914, the company had fifty grain elevators in operation. Meanwhile, the price of wheat fluctuated between $0.77 to $1.50 per bushel. This uncertainty in the price for wheat led to the creation of a marketing system to be known as the Alberta Wheat Pool. Its impact on the agricultural industry in Alberta could not be underestimated. Having stabilized the price of wheat somewhat by 1925 at about $1.19 per bushel, the trend to farm mechanization was in full swing as several self-propelled combines made their initial runs in the wheat fields of Alberta along with over eleven thousand tractors. With the religious freedoms available in Alberta, the province soon became a haven for non-conformists. Religious sects seemed to spring up everywhere. One such evangelist was a school principal named William Aberhart. His radio broadcasts over radio station CFCN in Calgary became so appealing that he was moved to a two-hour slot on Sunday.

Despite the promises of riches in tilling Alberta's rich soil, many farmers soon realized a harsh reality; good times cannot last forever. Following several years of drought, thousands of farmers abandoned their land in Southern Alberta by 1927 for greener pastures in central and northern Alberta. Instead of getting better, things got worse. It's as if the smiles of the gods turned to frowns and directed them at the farmers. In retrospect, many pioneers suddenly realized that perhaps the land in southern Alberta should have been left unploughed. The hardy native grasses could no longer protect the freshly cultivated soil. In locations where the per acre yield was previously upwards to thirty bushels per acre now fell to as low as fourteen and fifteen. Worse yet, the price of grain did not necessarily reflect the decrease in yield because other areas of North America were not struck with the same climatic conditions. Besides, during the onslaught of a world depression, who could afford high prices for grain?

When Andrij first landed in the Edmonton region in 1928, he found a flurry of farming activity. And not all of it was attributable to landed immigrants. He soon discovered that many established farmers from Southern Alberta loaded all of their chattels into one or two wagons and headed for the wetter woodlands of Northern Alberta and the Peace River Country. A number of them found new homesteads north of the North Saskatchewan River. When cultivatable land became scarce near the North Saskatchewan River, hundreds of the pioneers continued right on to the *Land of the Mighty Peace, a reference to the Peace River.*

During the decade, the area of cultivated land in the province increased from 29 million acres in 1921 to 35 million acres in 1929. At the same time, the province boasted 95,000 farmers, many of whom owned a car or a light delivery truck. Mechanization was in full swing, as witnessed by the fact that 3,000 of these farmers had a combine for threshing their grain directly in the fields. Everything seemed to be progressing in the farming and business communities, as if ordained by the Almighty. Andrij's philosophy of independence was in keeping with what he observed. All he wanted was some land surrounded by a good stand of timber for lumber and trees for firewood. As he set out to clear land for cultivation and for a garden plot, he felt secure that his wishes were coming true. The work was hard and the progress was slow. At times he felt that he had over-simplified the enormity of his undertaking

By 1931 the population of Alberta had grown to over 730,000. Power lines were springing up everywhere and larger towns were being connected by roads in addition to the already existing railroads. Refrigerators were just a few dollars away and radios were now being operated by electricity rather than the weighty batteries. Not only did High Prairie come into existence, but so did many other hamlets. Traversing the province's roads and highways in the summertime was no great problem during ideal weather conditions. However, any amount of rain and the situation changed quickly on any road that was not gravelled or paved. In low-lying areas, a road could quickly become a quagmire. Potholes would develop in short order and travel often became difficult, at best. In winter, most roads were passable only by horse and sleigh. Frozen muskegs, streams, and rivers suddenly became navigable by horse-drawn sleigh. In spring, many settlers prayed against an early break-up of frozen rivers, which often provided a shortcut to a town or village.

This also became a time when railroad transportation came into its own. Over nine hundred depots and whistle stops in Alberta became connected to the outside world. Suddenly, even the water stop at Aggie was no longer isolated. Since the steam-engine-driven train had to stop frequently for about five minutes to take on water in the first place, the engineer could drop off a passenger or two, perhaps some groceries, mail, or any other staple for that matter.

With the constant pressure to make a success of himself, Andrij would attack each day with renewed vigour. His days were totally occupied with the work on the railroad and the work on his newly-acquired homestead. He now saw this as providing him with a stable environment, no longer having to rely on someone else for his livelihood. This was a nice feeling to have particularly so at a time when the shock waves of a financial calamity reverberated all the way to Aggie. Although it was true that Aggie did not escape completely from the effects of the depression, the impact was not nearly as great as it was in Toronto, New York, or London. For most people, the gravy train of prosperity was suddenly and unceremoniously derailed.

To pioneers, talk about politics seemed to be as important as talk about prevailing weather conditions, and politicians loved to lay the blame for the economic hardships on the depression. The electorate, in turn, took great pleasure in turfing out politicians. For certain, this was the case with Canada's Prime Minister William Lyon Mackenzie King's Liberals. As was the case with many leaders the world over, King lost his job in 1930 when the voters thought that the first Conservative leader, Richard Bedford Bennett, a Calgarian, would do a better job. As a consequence, King became a casualty of the Great Depression which had swept Canada and the world. The continuing lack of jobs motivated many voters to heed Bennett's promises of *a better future for Canadians.*

In Alberta, the leading politicians felt the sting of the depression one year earlier. In 1930, Premier Brownlee's United Farmers of Alberta suddenly faced a debt incurred by the Alberta Wheat Pool when it anticipated higher prices for wheat. Unfortunately, grain growers were paid in advance of sales by the Alberta Wheat Pool. As prices fell, the Board found itself with an increasing debt load. Brownlee rescued the Wheat Pool and called another election in June of 1930. Although the government was returned to power, the message for politicians was clear; never spend more money than you can raise!

The depression accelerated a number of changes in Alberta. The Royal Canadian Mounted Police began to police the province rather than the Alberta Provincial Police. It was in 1873 that Sir John A. MacDonald introduced a Bill into Parliament which sought to bring order to the frontier, encourage settlement and establish Canadian authority in the North West Territories. With its passage, the North West Mounted Police came into existence. First stationed in Fort Dufferin, Manitoba, the force totalled 275 officers and men and soon established a post in what was to become Saskatchewan and one at Fort Edmonton.

In 1904, King Edward VII bestowed the pre-fix *"Royal"* upon the North West Mounted Police in recognition of their service during the South African War of 1899 - 1902. In 1920, the Royal North West Mounted Police became the Royal Canadian Mounted Police and the headquarters were moved from Regina to Ottawa. Police services were extended throughout Canada and the Force took on the responsibility for intelligence and security duties in addition to its normal police and crime prevention work. Over the years, the RCMP had built an international reputation as one of the most effective police forces in the world.

The fact that the province's natural resources were returned to the province, did not help to save the government of the day. As events unfolded during the Great Depression, Premier Brownlee's United Farmers of Alberta found itself facing considerable debt and depression, that spawned skepticism and voter unrest. And, seemingly right out of the prairie dust storm came the evangelical voice of William Aberhart. He wondered *why, in a province that owned its own resources, nobody could exploit them? Why, with rich soil which could grow unlimited wheat, forests which could produce enough lumber to house every Canadian family, the present system of government could not find a way to put them to work?*

Fuel shortages were evident everywhere. This caused many a farmer to revert to the use of horses. As for Andrij, he did not have to revert to the use of horses for, in the first instance, he had not progressed to the use of a farm tractor. Out of ten million Canadians, one and one-half million were on relief. Prices had fallen, crops had failed, and merchants suffered. Banks and loan companies called in their loans. Throughout all of this, Andrij felt sheltered. None of these problems touched him to any great extent; after all, what did he have to lose? A savings account? An investment portfolio? No, none of these maladies touched him. Besides, he knew where to keep his money and it sure wasn't in the local bank.

Living in High Prairie during the depression had its advantages. For one thing, it certainly was not a collecting point for the unemployed. Most of those looking for work congregated in bigger centres such as Edmonton, Calgary, and Winnipeg. For Andrij, his work with the Northern Alberta Railways was secure. There simply were not the hordes of the unemployed looking for seasonal or part-time work in an out-of-the-way location.

A similar situation was evident with Andrij's homesteading operation. A single man could survive for a long period of time on very little ready cash. Besides, money was quickly becoming a scarce commodity. Values on the stock markets had slumped nearly out of sight. In cities such as Edmonton, men walked the streets looking for work or lined up at unemployment offices. Soup kitchens fed many of the unemployed. By 1931, Edmonton had a population of over seventy-nine thousand. Of this number, over fourteen thousand were on direct relief.

The first to feel the pinch of the depression were the casual workers followed by the semi-skilled. Even the skilled carpenters and bricklayers began losing their jobs. Despite the hardships, the settlers in High Prairie and the surrounding area had one thing in common; they were a hardy bunch who hated to go on the dole. They came to Canada to make it on their own and even a major calamity such as the depression did little to deter them. Besides, most of them established the habit of saving for the future. As a result, many of them had already put away sufficient cash for the *rainy* day. Still, the rainy day seemed to stretch forever and touched everyone in the Land of the Mighty Peace. Yet, despite hard times, Canadians found a reason to celebrate Thanksgiving Day. Most settlers in the Peace Country witnessed an excellent garden and the crops were not all that bad. Indeed, there was reason to be optimistic about the future. To help celebrate the special day, Steve Blonski invited Andrij to a Sunday dinner. In addition to traditional Ukrainian cuisine, Tekla Blonski served pumpkin pie.

Andrij was so impressed with the meal, especially the pumpkin pie, that he promptly announced to all within earshot that he was bringing Eva home.

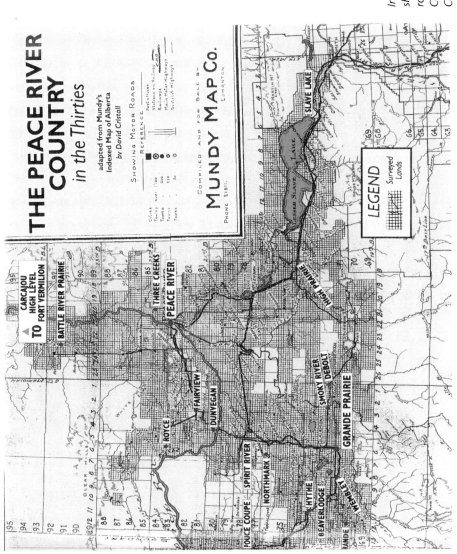

Indexed Map of Alberta showing surveyed lands and roads in the 1920s in the Peace Country. Source: Mundy Map Company.

ALBERTA

Plan of Township 75, Range 18, West of the Fifth Meridian

FIRST EDITION

SCALE 40 CHAINS TO AN INCH

The Aggie Settlement, Plan of Township 75, Range 18, West of the Fifth Meridian. Schematic shows the names of the first title holders. Andrij Kaszuba's first homestead was in Section 11 but abandoned in favour of a homestead in Section 13. Source: Department of the Interior, Ottawa, Canada.

21.

Bringing Eva Home

Right in the middle of a world-wide depression

There was great joy in the Stefan Groszko household when Eva received the first of many letters from Andrij; letters that described his work experiences and his plans for the future. In fact, the letters were sufficiently detailed so as to make Eva feel as though she were right there with him. Although the contacts between Eva and her in-laws were few and far between, the letters *were* read by family members in both villages. It was no surprise to Eva that Andrij's parents took joy in putting a particular spin on the letters to make it look as though he was barely surviving. Somehow, they found it difficult to accept that Andrij may be doing fine. Still, his parents were not entirely wrong. There was a severe depression in Canada and some villagers were well aware of this. As Eva re-traced Andrij's journey to Canada on a map, she was confident that she would soon make the same trip.

As the 1920s drew to a close, the political climate in Eastern Poland (*the former Galicia*) began to change as authorities initiated a policy of *polonizaiton*. The same held true for the Ukrainian Soviet Socialist Republic (*Eastern Ukraine*) where the organizational superiority of the Russians allowed them to monopolize the various political and economic thrusts which ultimately reflected their own aspirations and not those of the subjugated nationalities. Yet, according to Russian historians, prior to 1920, fully eighty percent of the population was illiterate and by 1929 this figure had dropped to thirty percent. Great changes in the publishing industry were also taking place as 373 of 426 newspapers were published in the Ukrainian language leading to a boon in performing arts, theatre, music, opera, and cinema. *Regrettably, this did little for ethnic minorities living under Polish rule where, despite their dislike of communism, many longed to be an integral part of Ukraine.*

Josef Stalin, 1879-1953, born as Iosif Visserionovich Dzhagashvili in Gori, Georgia, took the pseudonym of Stalin (Man of Steel) in 1910. Secretary General of USSR from 1922 to 1953.

This period in the history of Ukraine also saw economic growth and greater urbanization as new arrivals from villages caused the balance of Ukrainians to Russians to shift from 38 percent to 50 percent in metropolitan centres. Unfortunately, Stalin, who in 1929 assumed complete control over the communist party and the state, drastically changed his personal vision of the direction in which communism would move. He had a vision of a centralized totalitarian society where rapid industrialization would require the utilization of all possible economic and human resources and the total centralization of management. Stalin created a series of Five Year Plans and ruthlessly began to impose them on Ukraine. However, the Ukrainian peasantry opposed collectivization by all means possible, including hiding grain and slaughtering livestock. This led to penalties where it is estimated that 70,000 Ukrainians were deported to Siberia, imprisoned or killed between 1930 and 1933.

Yet, in due course, Ukrainians would learn that this policy of mass deportations on the part of Josef Stalin paled in comparison to the artificial famine of 1932-33. It was a man-made famine that raged through Ukraine that resulted in the death of about seven million people. The main goal of this artificial famine was to break the spirit of Ukrainian peasants and to force them into collectivization. The famine was also used as an effective tool to break the renaissance of Ukrainian culture that was occurring under approval of the communist government in Ukraine. To restrict any internal movement of Ukrainians, an internal passport system was implemented. Grain was stored in elevators and guarded by military units while Ukrainians starved in the immediate area. In effect, the actions of this Moscow instigated action was a deliberate act of genocide against the Ukrainian peasant.

These political events seemed to have little impact on Eva, even though the Poles did not miss the opportunity to listen and watch what was happening next door to their nation. *Could it be that the Russian Bear was looking southward to sweeten the pot? Was it possible that the Ukrainians living in their midst would one day become the source of political unrest?* The Polish rulers living in Warsaw felt secure in their belief that Galicia ceded to them in 1919 really belonged to them; however, they wondered if this sentiment was shared by the communists in Moscow. Eva was ever suspicious that one day even Plazow would come under Soviet rule; and it is one of many reasons why she yearned to be on her way to Canada.

Just about the time that the Groszko family was making preparations for the 1931 Christmas holiday season, a very important letter did arrive. It could not have been a better Christmas present for Eva as she read the words, '...*I want you to make the final arrangements to come to Canada.'* Of course, Andrij had written the letter much earlier, just after the Thanksgiving Day weekend, but ocean liners did not make the trans-Atlantic sailings as frequently during the late fall and winter months as they did in the spring and summer months. As a consequence, it took the letter over two months to reach Eva. Still, Andrij's words of invitation were like music to her ears and the funds from him and Ivan Tychanewycz were more than sufficient for the journey. Andrij concluded his letter by saying, '*I shall send you the necessary documentation and your train ticket from the city of Quebec to High Prairie. Meanwhile, you should purchase your trans-Atlantic ticket from our agent in Lubaczow.'*

The happiness of Christmas was now being replaced by thoughts of Canada. *What will the journey be like? Will Maria, as a four-year old, survive the trip?* Time seemed to drag and there was plenty of time to think about her relationship with the Groszkos and the Kaszubas. Suddenly, her in-laws who had treated her as though she was in everyone's way and, in essence, forced her to move in with her brother Stefan in Plazow, must have been struck with the realization that Eva would soon be leaving. Each, in their own way, tried to make amends. In particular, her mother-in-law Maria Kaszuba made several awkward overtures to undo the hurts that she had inflicted upon Eva. Even Andrij's father began to treat her more kindly.

Mercifully, the day of her departure finally arrived. Although June 22, 1931, turned out to be a clear and sunny day, it did not reflect the sadness in her heart. Yet, it would be a day that she would forever remember as being filled with joy, yet tinged with a considerable amount of sorrow and sadness. It would now be the turn of the Groszko family to say goodbye to one of their own. The wagon ride from Plazow to Belzec took three hours during which time every attempt was made to keep the conversations light and happy. At the train station, the Groszkos were joined by another wagon-load of well-wishers from Plazow. Eva knew that her leaving was not a joy ride to a local market; it would be forever. The realization of this circumstance made the moment all the more poignant and the biggest hugs and kisses were reserved for her parents Ivan and Tetyana Groszko and her four siblings, Stefan, Vasyl, Damian and Oksana.

From Belzec, it would be the same mode of transportation that took Andrij away from her that would bring them together again. With the last frantic goodbyes while clutching four-year-old Maria's hand, Eva boarded the train to the shouts of the conductor, *all aboard for Lviv*. Since Eva had rarely ventured far from Plazow, the train ride to Lviv proved to be most interesting. After a brief stop in Lviv for the purpose of processing exit visas, the train struck a course for Warsaw. Ever deep in thought, Eva found that having a young daughter with her provided an easy way to break the ice and enter into a conversation with other passengers. It seemed that everyone gravitated to four-year-old Maria.

Eva's joyful thoughts were frequently interspersed with feelings of doubt about the future. Polish cities came and went and after a stop-over in Warsaw, the next leg of the journey took them through northern Germany to Amsterdam, the breeding ground for some of Europe's most outstanding art masters. Space in the city was at a premium. In fact, the houses were so crowded that tiny hooks had to be built into the roof gables to lift furniture into the narrow, crowded homes. There seemed to be flowers and bicycles everywhere. Following a short ride to the seaport to board a small ship, it took them less than twelve hours to reach Liverpool.

The *Duchess of Richmond*, a relatively new ocean-liner, was built in 1929 for the Canadian Pacific Railways. Consisting of four decks and numerous amenities for passengers, the ship was powered by six steam turbines which developed a horsepower rating of 3,748, had electric lights, refrigeration machinery, a submarine signalling device and a direction finder. With a rating of 20,000 tons, a length of 581 feet and width of 75 feet, it was similar in many respects to the *Montroyal*, the ocean-liner that carried Andrij to Canada in 1928. However, unlike the smooth passage that Andrij had across the Atlantic, Eva's passage was anything but. In fact, it bordered on disaster. The weather was cold and rainy and the Atlantic was very rough—quite a contrast to that experienced three years earlier by Andrij. It seemed that the bug was contagious as everyone got seasick. To make matters worse, eating while sick was impossible. Mercifully, after six days of this kind of torture on the open seas, Eva smiled wanly to the shouts of *land ahoy!* It would be another full day before The *Duchess of Richmond* reached the port of Quebec City on July 10, 1931.

From an historical perspective, Ukrainian immigrants came to Canada in three waves; the first one taking place during the 1891 to 1914 time frame, the second during the years 1923 to 1931, and the third, after World War II between the years of 1945 to 1961. During the first wave, of the 300,000 emigrants that left Galicia, over 170,000 Ukrainians came to Canada, mostly from the provinces of Galicia and Bukovyna. During this same period of time, nearly one-half of the population of the Ukrainian province of Transcarpathia left their homeland. Since the annual income of peasants during this period in history was the equivalent of fifteen Canadian dollars, it is no wonder that so many left Galicia[27] where most of the land was owned by rich landlords, leaving little for the excessively taxed peasants.

Upon arrival in Quebec, Eva discovered that French and English were spoken; the two official languages of Canada. After disembarking and checking into the immigration office to get their documents processed, it was a matter of seeking reliable information about the next part of the journey from the city of Quebec to Edmonton. When in doubt about train schedules, boarding procedures, baggage transfers, and the provision of meals; information was readily available from fellow passengers, many of whom were also headed to Western Canada.

The week-long journey by rail across Canada was quite a learning experience about the topography and history of Canada where the teachers were train officials and fellow passengers. There was talk of the process that new immigrants used to access homestead land and how these same newcomers were being duped by steamship companies and government officials. Add to this the problems that Canada was experiencing with the native Indians and you have the ingredients for a considerable amount of deceit which often led to a lot of suffering on the part of new arrivals. Even the Peace Treaties that the Canadian Government signed with the Indians to help with any mediation process did not guarantee that future conflicts would be avoided.

From Quebec City, the train took Eva through the province of Quebec and into Ontario and even though she was still feeling the effects of seasickness, it didn't take her long to warm to the expansiveness of Canada. Ontario's northern landscapes presented a spectacular view the likes of which she had never seen before. The forests seemed to stretch forever, broken only by the spectacular scenery of the many lakes of western Ontario. The trip from Quebec City through Ontario took over three days by which time both felt rejuvenated and fully recovered from the journey across the Atlantic. However, as the train wound its way into the prairies near Winnipeg, there were distressing stories about unemployment in Canada and about suffering and destitution. Even more disturbing were the stories of hundreds of horses starving to death in Saskatchewan. Knowing the importance of horses to the farming community, Eva felt a special sorrow about this bit of sad news.

Even the recent experience of seeing the first native Indians seemed to be lost in the devastation of the drought on the prairies. A train conductor seemed to know a lot about prevailing conditions in Western Canada, saying that the hot dry winds in Saskatchewan were blowing away the topsoil and the black blizzards were so bad as to make it unsafe for children to venture to school. There were even some accounts of tumble weeds being blown against

---

27   Potrebenko, Helen, <u>No Streets of Gold, A Social History of Ukrainians in Alberta,</u> New Star Books, Vancouver, British Columbia, 1977, pp. 23 - 24.

fences creating a collection point for dirt packs over which cattle could wander at will.

As though the farmers on the prairies were not having enough problems with the drought, the news from the government of the day was even worse. The government of Saskatchewan was foreclosing on farms in an attempt to make good on outstanding loans. Properties were being sold to cover tax arrears. While Eva hoped that this bad news did not extend all the way to High Prairie, she wondered why Andrij hadn't told her anything of this bad news. Was it because he feared that she would change her mind about joining him in Canada? Or was it because the village of High Prairie was so isolated that news of world events were slow in reaching him?

Arriving in Winnipeg, Eva saw first-hand just what the drought was doing to the prairies. Dust storms deposited thousands of tons of silt on the city. The topsoil blew in from the drought-stricken farms of southern and central Saskatchewan and even from as far away as the Dakotas in the United States. When the wind had shifted to northeast, much of the silt was blown back out of the city. But, even with the devastation of the dust storms, she noticed something new and refreshing. Everywhere that the train took her, there was evidence of the spirit of cooperation amongst Canadians. Western wheat was being doled out to relieve the hungry. The Red Cross announced that 150,000 residents in Saskatchewan were in need of food, clothes, and fuel. It seemed as though everyone was trying to help out. So desperate was the government of Saskatchewan that it lifted the ban on the illegal Indian rain dance and allowed its revival as a last-ditch effort to bring rain. Even this did not help.

The two-day journey across the prairies from Winnipeg to Edmonton was another history lesson. Even Maria recognized the sight of the cattle near the railway to resemble those in the old country. However, the first sight of buffalo, which possessed a peculiar shape and were much larger than cattle, caused some consternation. As the train approached Edmonton, the drought did not seem to have the same strangle-hold. The crops were maturing and seemed much like the fields in Lubaczow. Several of the passengers spoke Ukrainian or Polish thereby facilitating conversation. A new excitement gripped Eva for she knew that in a very short time she would be re-united with Andrij.

Upon arrival in Edmonton, Eva was advised that she would have to check into the local Immigration Hall for processing, a recent change from Winnipeg. A new two-storey building located near the railway station, it would soon become the *Ellis Island of Alberta* for new immigrants. In fact, those newcomers that did not have family to receive them or a job upon arrival could stay at the hall for a short period of time. Over the period of its operation and until its closure in 1960, the Hall would welcome in excess of 144,000 immigrants to the province of Alberta.

Having cleared the Immigration Hall in Edmonton, Eva changed trains to the Northern Alberta Railway to begin the final leg of her journey to High Prairie. The abrupt change in the topography surprised Eva. Where the

Eva Kaszuba and daughter, Maria. Passport photograph, Lubaczow, Poland, 1927.

countryside throughout the journey from the Ontario border to Edmonton reflected a considerable amount of cultivated land, this would not be the case between Edmonton and High Prairie. The beauty of the Athabasca River valley was overwhelming as was the view of Lesser Slave Lake. She had never experienced such an expanse of forests, lakes, muskegs, swamps, and rivers. Other than a number of small whistle stops, the region seemed devoid of human habitation. Pulling into High Prairie was a lot like coming out of the darkness into sunlight. The crops were ripening and there was no evidence of the drought that she had witnessed earlier. Just as these thoughts were going through her head, she spotted Andrij peering at her passenger car.

"Look Maria, there is daddy!" There was no mistaking his friendly smile and husky build. He looked tanned and considerably slimmer than she remembered him. Suddenly, all of the doubts that she had about coming to Canada and what lay in wait for her were washed away with the tears of joy.

"Welcome to your new home town, Eva. Welcome to High Prairie. Thank God for your safe arrival. And, who is this little girl hiding behind your skirt? Is that my precious little girl?"

Even as Eva embraced Andrij, Maria would not let go, perhaps fearing being separated from her mother. But, Andrij was wise to the ways of little girls. From inside of his shirt he pulled out a beautiful rag doll. In a moment, Maria was in her father's arms for the first time since she was two. Eva couldn't help but reflect upon her own experience when she was three years old and greeted her father upon his return from New York.

A brief blast of the train whistle signalled that they were off for the Aggie Settlement, the final destination for the newly-reunited family. For two years Eva had been conjuring up images of what this place Aggie would look like. To her surprise, not one of those images even came close to resembling what

Railway station in High Prairie, 1920. Source: Provincial Archives, Edmonton, Alberta.

Northern Alberta Railways' water tank. Source: Provincial Archives, Edmonton, Alberta.

Andrij Kaszuba's log cabin, Aggie Settlement, constructed in 1930, photographed in 1962.

she was about to see. Aggie turned out to be no more than a railroad water tank, a section of a secondary rail for passing another train, and two small buildings; one for the storage of railroad equipment and a second one for the use of the section foreman. This small enclave was totally surrounded by a dense forest of spruce, poplar, tamarack, and muskeg. Surveying the landscape to the north which would take them to the homestead, Eva noted that the railroad ran through a low-lying area of swamp, entered another forest, and swung to the west. There was no evidence of a road leading north and if there was any agricultural land in that vicinity, it certainly was not readily visible to her.

As they disembarked, Eva noticed that a wagon trail *did* lead to the water tank from the south but no wagon trail was visible to the north which would take a settler from the water tank to the Aggie Settlement. Knowing that Eva was curious about her surroundings, Andrij explained that it would not be possible to get to the whistle stop from the Aggie Settlement by horse and wagon during summer months. There was no road to connect the two points which were separated by a creek, muskeg, a stretch of wetland, and forest. *"However,"* explained Andrij*, "during winter months when the creek is frozen over, it is possible to use the railroad right-of-way to get from the Aggie Settlement to High Prairie, thereby shortening the distance by over three kilometres."*

With Eva's two modest suitcases in hand, the three of them set off on foot to the homestead. The first one-half mile was along the railway while the last portion was via a wagon trail cleared by the local homesteaders. Emerging from the forested walk, Eva was happy to finally set her eyes on the small log cabin in a clearing near the bank of a small creek. The log cabin had one large room, one door, one window, and a cellar in one corner used for the storage of vegetables. Staples such as salt, flour, oatmeal, sugar, coffee, tea, and homogenized milk were kept in a small shelf next to a small flat-topped heater which also served as a stove. Next to the log cabin, a small enclosure constructed of slab boards housed a small flock of chickens. Noticing Eva looking at the chicks, Andrij remarked that he started with twenty-four, except that the coyotes must have dined on a few of them.

Finally in Canada as a family, it was time to take stock and make some plans for the future. A homestead with three acres of cleared land, a garden plot, a log house, a plough, some household utensils, a few chicks, and a couple of horses and that's it. As Eva looked around the interior of the house, she noticed only one large bunk bed and a straw mattress. The quilt was made of goose down and the pillow casings from white flour sacks. In the middle of the room was a rocker-cradle constructed for Maria, however, looking at her size, he could see that a small bed would be required. In the meantime, she would have to make-do with this invention.

Besides, he must have felt confident that they would soon make good use of the small cradle.

22.

The Aggie Settlement

Adjusting to life in an isolated settlement

With the arrival of Eva in the Aggie Settlement, there was much to talk about. Talk about family and particularly of what Canada was all about. Perhaps for the first time Eva realized that even in a democratic country with unlimited possibilities, there were problems. Over-riding most other considerations was the matter of Canada finding itself in the midst of a worldwide depression which made it doubly difficult for Andrij to gain an economic toe-hold. The cost of the two horses was ninety dollars, basic farming implements over a hundred dollars, and the cost of bringing Eva and Maria to High Prairie was two hundred dollars. Of course, there were other expenses such as the cost of constructing a log cabin and daily living expenses. Since coming to Canada, Andrij had two sources of revenue; farm labour and railroading. As a farm labourer, the take-home pay was in the neighbourhood of one dollar per day while the NAR paid only eight cents for each *dressed* railroad tie, two cents per tie for skidding these to the railway line and two cents each for loading these onto a flatbed railroad car. To generate this amount of cash, one would have to hew and load an awful lot of railroad ties!

In the face of so many demands, the bloom of the reunion was quickly displaced with having to deal with reality. Fall was quickly approaching and the hot, sunny August days quickly advanced the harvesting season. Knowing that crops would be ripening earlier in central Alberta, Andrij decided to hitch a train ride to the Edmonton region and join a harvesting crew so as to supplement his depleted savings. However, before leaving, there was much work to be done to ensure that Eva would be able to carry on in his absence. Since he did not have a binder of his own, he borrowed one from his neighbour, cut, bound and stooked his three acres of wheat before making a trip to

Farmer's Trading Company in High Prairie in order to stock up on staples such as flour, cured bacon, eggs, lard and vegetables. Owned and operated by Nick Chodzicki, it was truly a general store that carried household goods and an assortment of hardware supplies. Best of all, once you established your credit with the store, you did not have to pay for your purchases until such time that the harvesting season was over. This convenient one-stop shopping centre not only sold the necessities required by a settler but Chodzicki also purchased much of the store's supply of vegetables, milk, cream, butter, eggs, and meat from local farmers.

Andrij arrived in Edmonton to a harvest that was in full swing and soon found work near Leduc. Although the crops were of poorer quality than the farmers could remember, they were much better than those in southern Alberta, Saskatchewan, or Manitoba. And, with the dry weather, the crops had matured much earlier than was the norm. All of this enabled the farmers to complete the threshing operations by mid-September. To Eva's pleasant surprise, Andrij was back home by the last week of September, just in time to take in the hay and the garden. But, other challenges arose. The well had gone dry as did the nearby creek. This left Eva with but one alternative and that was to carry the water needed for domestic needs from a creek near the Aggie water tank. Although the distance was only one kilometre, carrying two pails of water made the distance seem much longer. Without any mitts or gloves, she was forced to wrap the pail handles with rags so as to minimize any potential damage to her hands.

None of the homesteaders in the Aggie Settlement had a threshing machine of their own. As a consequence, Andrij was obliged to transport the sheaves of wheat about three miles to Triangle to have them threshed. The yield was poor; less than twenty-five bushels per acre for a total of seventy-five bushels. Some of the wheat was set aside for use as seed grain in the ensuing year while the remainder was milled for use as flour and morning cereal. Whatever was left over was fed to the chickens and pigs. The garden, as well, was a bit of a failure producing only a small amount of potatoes, carrots, beets, and turnips. Once harvested, these would be stored in the cellar of the log cabin during the winter months.

Earlier, Andrij had started the construction of a log fence around the perimeter of the property but, in view of the poor crop yield, he was struck with the futility of the exercise. Somehow, he must have known that he would be making the decision to abandon the present location. The thought made him sad because he had just completed the construction of a crude chicken house made of spruce slabs along with a small log barn for the two horses, heifer, and sow. To provide for the heating needs for the cabin, he set about sawing, splitting and stacking sufficient firewood for what surely would be a cold winter.

That winter, as Andrij alternated his time as a labourer on the railroad's *extra gang* and as an independent contractor making railroad ties, he considered his options for the coming spring concluding that staying put on a homestead that exhibited marginal soil and no water was not an option. Having spent only one year at this homestead site, he would now be looking for another homestead in the new year. With all of the trials and tribulations that went with the preparation of meals on a meagre budget and fewer staples and supplies, Eva had little time to dwell upon the past and the beloved homeland she had so recently left behind. She did concede, however, that the timing for her trip to Canada was not the best.

The year went by quickly and by the end of 1932, Andrij had taken off his second crop of wheat on the homestead. As was the case the previous year, he retained all of the wheat for domestic needs. The price of No. 1 wheat plummeted to 38 cents a bushel in Winnipeg. This meant that a homesteader in the Aggie Settlement would get about 18 cents a bushel delivered to the elevator in High Prairie. Little wonder that the homesteaders elected not to sell their wheat. But, in all of this there was a silver lining. He did not own a tractor or a truck–either would have been problematic since fuel was expensive and hard to come by. He would have to make do with two horses, a couple of basic farm implements, a wagon and a sleigh.

During the same summer, the garden was expanded to include peas, beans, and cabbage. But, with the decision to move to another location, the reasons for continuing to make *any* improvements to the first homestead were removed. It made him sad to think that he selected this particular land for the right reasons but that the quality of the soil and the obvious lack of water would force him to consider an alternative. Although he liked the wooded area in that it provided for his firewood and building needs and the nearby low-lying meadows provided a supply of hay, the one thing that he did not anticipate was that the fifteen-foot-deep well, which he dug with by hand, would go dry.

Within one year of Eva's arrival in Canada, the expected happened. Eva became pregnant and on the morning of April 21, 1932 she assured Andrij that the labour pains were sufficiently regular as to convince her that the birth of another child was imminent. Andrij hurried over to the nearest neighbour's homestead for assistance. Early that evening, Eva, with assistance of the neighbour's wife, gave birth to a second daughter, Anne. Naturally, Andrij hoped for a boy and showed his disappointment. Maria, on the other hand, now seven years of age, thought that having a sister was just fine.

With a nucleus of a family in place, Eva and Andrij would sit late into the night, digest the latest news from Galicia and discuss their plans for the coming days. On some evenings they would invite a couple of the nearby settlers for a game of cards. One thing struck Andrij as being a bit unusual. Up until now he had made all of those important decisions. Big decisions such as marriage and coming to Canada. However, in the most recent discussion with Eva, he sensed that she was trying to exercise more control over his actions. Perhaps she now wanted to test the democratic principles underpinning society in Canada.

Survival in the Aggie Settlement depended very much on cooperation and teamwork. To do otherwise would be to court disaster. As homesteaders, the belief that things would get better kept them both working very hard every day. Despite the hardships, Andrij and Eva concluded that in Canada the skies seemed just a little bit bluer, the days more gentle, and the neighbours just a bit more congenial. They could now control as much land as they could cultivate, worship in any manner that they wished, and associate with any one they liked. However, they knew that the next real challenge would be to find a school for Maria to give her the advantage of education that they never had. The nearest school was located in High Prairie; a school not too readily accessible by foot. Access by horseback, although possible, did not seem practical.

However, Andrij was reluctant to discuss the matter of Maria's education. The depression was still in full force and this was no time to consider anything that would add to the financial burden of the family. The difficulties experienced in the Aggie Settlement were not unique; they simply mirrored what was happening nationally. Even the federal civil servants were forced to take a ten percent pay cut. There seemed to be very few things to cheer a homesteader. The only event that really caught the imagination of the settlers had to do with one of the longest manhunts in northern history. It was the case of Albert Johnson of the Yukon Territory, commonly known as the Mad Trapper of Rat River, who was chased over distances exceeding 240 kilometres. He was a resourceful and inventive fugitive from the law. The RCMP finally brought him down in a hail of bullets. However, the pioneers admired his resilience and spirit of survival and, at times, themselves felt like Albert Johnson.

As the new day dawned, Andrij thought long and hard about the previous night's conversation which had to do with education and religion. On the one hand he conceded that Eva wanted too much too quickly while on the other hand he knew that without effort and commitment, progress would not come easily. But, where to start with limited resources? What steps could one take now to start on the path of success? That Sunday, Eva and Andrij packed up the family and made the wagon trip to High Prairie to attend Mass at the Roman Catholic Church. Delivered in English, they understood very little of the priest's sermon. But, that did not seem to matter. After all, the celebration of the Eucharist is the same, no matter the language in which the message is delivered. Besides, a Ukrainian Catholic Church was nowhere to be found.

When the family got back to the Aggie Settlement, there was a sense of relief that somehow a communications link to the Almighty had been established. Eva realized that it was difficult for the homesteaders to practice their own religion; any religion for that matter. With all of the other problems confronting a pioneer, religion was often the last item on the menu. Still, with agitation from other homesteaders, the word was out that there was sufficient interest in the provision of the occasional church service in the Ukrainian language. It was at times like this that Eva recalled the proverb which said, *'Trust in the Lord with all your heart, and He will make your paths straight.'*

In due course, a small Ukrainian Catholic church was constructed some five miles southwest of High Prairie. This made it possible for the family to attend the Roman Catholic Church in High Prairie or the Ukrainian Catholic Church in Gilwood. Unfortunately, the services provided at Gilwood were sporadic, at best.

As 1933 rolled in, Andrij tried to keep abreast of the latest developments on the political and economic fronts of Canada and abroad. This particular year would bring a madman onto the scene the likes of which the world heretofore had not seen. On January 30, Adolf Hitler became the Chancellor of Germany. It would turn out to be the same year that police would raid the western headquarters of the pro-Hitler, anti-Jewish Canadian Fascist Party in Toronto. The federal government seemed to be very keen on upholding the 1919 section of the Criminal Code which permitted police to round up suspected Communist sympathizers. As Andrij reflected on the nature of politics in Alberta, he was pleased that he had settled in a region of Alberta which seemed to be devoid of communistic sympathizers. He was well aware of what the Russian Bolsheviks had done in Ukraine. Above all else, he was strongly anti-communist.

The significance of this attitude would not be lost when they received letters from their respective families which described how the Russian government was sending starving Ukrainians to Siberia and how Ukrainian farmers were withholding grain from Russian authorities. The letters went on to say that many of the discontented were shot or put in jail and tortured. In one such letter, Ivan Groszko stated that '*Ukrainians in Eastern Ukraine have nothing to eat. Not even a goat or a cow, let alone a dog or cat. Those poor children are starving. We are told that thousands have already died and many more are starving to death...*' Andrij and Eva admitted that perhaps being under Polish rule in Galicia was better than being under Russian rule in Eastern Ukraine. It appeared as though Josef Stalin was turning out to be some sort of a devil sent from hell. For certain, his five-year economic development plans sounded a bit crazy. They hoped that Adolf Hitler would not turn out to be another Josef Stalin.

In the midst of these tragic events, Andrij's wish was granted when on July 20, 1933 a son was born to them. After much deliberation, Andrij caved in to Eva's wishes and named him after her brother Vasyl. Now that he had a son, Andrij dreamed of the day that Vasyl would be able to help with an expanding farming operation. Still, making the decision to abandon the first homestead was not easy even though he realized that he was not the only homesteader that was forced to abandon a piece of property. In fact, and contrary to advanced advertising, the Homestead Act *did not* turn out to be a generous piece of legislation. With a ten dollar filing fee, the land was not free, neither were the implements to clear and break the land. To add to the problems, there were no roads in the Aggie Settlement while at the same time there was no shortage of bush, swamp, and mosquitoes. Little wonder that so many gave up the struggle after the first unsuccessful try. Still, the dream did not die.

Once the decision was made, Andrij did not waste any time in making application for his second homestead by paying a ten dollar fee. He wasn't surprised to hear from the Government of the Province of Alberta, Department of Lands and Mines that he would have to abandon his quest for title to his first homestead before being granted approval for the second application. Of course, he was fully aware that he had not made the necessary improvements to qualify for title. The decision to abandon his first homestead did not bother him because he knew that he would continue to cultivate the five acres he had cleared without fear that someone else would want to apply for title. After all, the Provincial Land Office noted that '...*when this land is disposed of, the improvements, if any, will be valued, and the amount of such valuation will be collected from the party securing the land...*' The improvements to the property, as listed by the Government of the Province of Alberta, Department of Lands and Mines, totalled $260. This, of course, meant that if another homesteader wanted to lay claim to this particular piece of property, he would have to pay this amount for the improvements.

While making his second application for a homestead, Andrij heard the disturbing news in High Prairie. Ottawa was becoming increasingly concerned about the Red menace in Canada. For the first time, Andrij realized that political freedom, could, as a result of the Red menace, be circumscribed in Canada. Somehow, the rumour of a communist threat from Russia simply would not go away and the Canadian Government wanted to put limits on political affiliation and, in a way, on free speech. In a way, this was good news for Andrij. He disliked the very concept of communism and now saw the threat of fascism with the appearance of Adolf Hitler on the scene.

Although the dark clouds of international conflict seemed to be gathering, Andrij felt that the planned move to a new homestead adjacent to three other settlers would provide for farming support as well as for any socialization. Light by which to read an old issue of The Winnipeg Free Press, The Ukrainian Voice, a letter from home, or the well-worn bible came from a coal oil lamp. In fact, the days were so long during the summer months, that it was rare that the lamp would have to be used. In most instances, Andrij and Eva were too exhausted after a long day's work to do anything else but reminisce about their life in the old country and plan their activities for the next day. As time went on, Eva was convinced that her vision of the future was quite different from that of her spouse. Her vision of the future included a full range of educational opportunities and improved living conditions while Andrij's planning seemed to include little beyond the roots he was now setting down in the Aggie Settlement.

After filing a notice of abandonment on the first homestead in the spring of 1933, Andrij set out to find an appropriate location for farm buildings on the new homestead. His first structure, a large log granary to be used for seed grains, chop for hogs and hay for the cows and horses was completed in the fall of 1934. To him, it was important to accommodate the farm animals before thinking about constructing a house for the family. That fall, a rather meagre harvest was in full swing in central Alberta as a *black blizzard* swept across the prairies, leaving farmers in trouble and city dwellers covered with dust. Starting in the Rocky Mountains and sweeping across the prairie provinces all the way to the Great Lakes, this was the third storm of the season. To the south of Edmonton, the dust storm packed winds up to sixty-five kilometres per hour and blocked out the sun. Along with the top soil went the crops in southern Alberta. To make matters worse, those crops that did survive were hit with upwards to ten centimetres of hail. Luckily for Andrij, the crops in the High Prairie region were relatively unaffected by the dry spells and winds encountered in the southern regions.

As the fall days wore on, Andrij tried as best he could to keep abreast of the latest developments on the world stage while Eva was once again expecting a child. Naturally, Andrij wanted another boy. At the same time, he acknowledged that with the ever-increasing size of the family, economics may well become a factor. Perhaps the politicians in Ottawa were cognizant of this challenge facing Canadians when Prime Minister Richard Bennett made a strong case for bringing legislation out of the *'horse and buggy days'* dealing with social policy and health in order to *'reduce the evils of double taxation and provide a more logical allocation of sources of revenue.'* This change in policy was good news for all Canadians.

Life had its lighter moments and pioneers liked to talk about matters of the heart as well as the pocketbook. There was talk of the quintuplets born to Dionnes in Ontario, overshadowed by news that Adolf Hitler, now the Chancellor and President of Germany, who declared that in less than two years he had attained total political dominance over Germany. His party had earlier seized control over trade unions, outlawed the Social Democratic and Communist Parties, and introduced a plan for the *'purification of the Aryan race.'* Suddenly, Hitler became so powerful as to begin to unabashedly talk of a 1,000-year Reich. Even more frightening for those living in the Aggie Settlement was the thought that no country was powerful enough in Europe to stop him.

But, for the Kaszuba family, the news was not all bad. As Eva prepared Ukrainian delicacies for the upcoming Christmas celebration, a great event was about to take place. Shortly after Christmas and just about the time that Ukrainians would be ringing in a new year, another son would be born to Andrij and Eva.

PART 3

FROM DREAMS TO REALITY

23.

Translation Troubles[28]

The challenge of getting it right

There is no better proof of the struggle my parents had with the Canadian culture than is reflected on my certificate of First Communion and school records. It all started on the day that I was born and manifested itself at various stages throughout my life. As the head of the household, my dad was required to complete various forms and documents for the provincial and federal governments. Since his knowledge of the English language was limited, it was necessary for him to seek the assistance of someone who was fluent in Ukrainian *and* English. This, unfortunately, created a problem because it was not always the same person who completed those forms. Consequently, the information provided lacked consistency, frequently leaving government officials in a quandary; just *what was* the correct information?

Take, for example, my registered name, Slawko; a name that is common in Ukraine and Poland. On my birth certificate the name does appear as Slawko but on my Christening Certificate it is entered as Yaroslav. Now, for most Ukrainians, this variance in the two names would not create a problem. After all, they *would* know that Slawko is a derivative of Yaroslav. However, would an official in Canada know that?

Historically, the name *Yaroslav* has an important religious and political significance and reflects the reverence my parents had for religion and history. It was in 1019 that *Yaroslav the Wise* first established his rule over Kyiv with the view of improving relations with the rest of Europe, especially the Byzantine Empire. His brother, Vladimir, chose Eastern Christianity as

---

28   Note: PARTS 3 and 4 of this book are written in the first person and are based on my personal experiences, interviews, and research.

Ukrainian Catholic Church, Gilwood, First Communion, 1941, front row, 3rd from left, Carson Kashuba (holding certificate); far right, front row, Bill Kashuba (holding certificate); third row, centre of row is Anne Kashuba (holding certificate).
Source: *High Prairie, The Trails We Blazed Together*.

Gilwood Ukrainian Catholic Church, High Prairie, Alberta, built in about 1940 and photographed in 1962.

the religion for all Kyivan Rus; a decision that had long-ranging political, cultural, and religious consequences. Maybe my parents had history in mind when they chose the name Yaroslav. However, dad once said that, *'our son does not seem to have any of Yaroslav's wisdom.'*

There are other abbreviations for Yaroslav *(Jaroslaw in Polish)* such as Slavko, Slavic, Yars, and Jars—depending upon whether one wanted to stress a Polish or Ukrainian heritage. Since my parents came from Poland, those registering births in Alberta would invoke the Polish spelling where the *"v"* sound is derived from *"w"*. Case closed. My birth certificate shows Slawko. As for my First Communion, which is a special ceremony to bring a child into the Christian faith, my name is entered as Yaroslav. In this case, I can only conclude that it was the intention of my parents to reflect *their* Ukrainian heritage.

In translating from one language to another, mistakes *can* be made. Some mistakes are of a minor nature and have a short shelf life. Others, however, are far more serious and have a very long shelf life. To illustrate some of these difficulties, I would have to go back to the date of my birth. The weather statistics for the winter of 1935 confirm that the month of January was unusually cold; record setting, bone chilling, frigid temperatures throughout Alberta and I am told that a homesteader had to be sure that there was a good supply of firewood next to the house during those cold days. And, the wearing of long flannel underwear was the order of the day. In retrospect, it is no wonder that there was some confusion in the minds of my parents as to whether I was born on the 7th or the 15th of January. After all, why would a man want to hitch up his horse-drawn sleigh for a trip to High Prairie just for the purpose of registering a newborn in January when you could wait until the arrival of warmer temperatures?

That, perhaps, is the reason why dad did not register my birth until several weeks after the event. Maybe the cold weather had something to do with this temporary lapse of memory. Whatever the explanation, the fact remains that by the middle of February he must have felt a twinge of conscience for he did make that journey to visit the local Justice of the Peace in High Prairie to register my birth as January 15; a statistic which would be transmitted to the Provincial Department of Vital Statistics in Edmonton. For most, this would be the end of the story. Not so in my case. My mother insisted that I was born on January 7. Maybe she wanted to attach a special meaning to the date of my birth. After all, according to the Julian calendar, January 7 *is* Christmas day; a day of religious celebration. Maybe she took this to be a strategic cost-saving strategy. The family could now celebrate Christmas and my birthday on the same day thereby saving a considerable amount of money over the years. On school registration day my dad must have bought into the plan because he registered my birthday as falling on January 7, *even though he had already registered my birth with Vital Statistics as January 15.*

I do not believe that my dad really thought about the trail of confusion that he was about to unleash. Of course, he kept records--of sorts. I recall how he kept all of his important documents tied together in a bundle with a piece of binder twine. As a teenager, I would never have a reason to question what was in that bundle. In turn, my parents saw no reason to share any sensitive information. Since I did not have access to my birth certificate until many years later, I had always *assumed* that I was born on January 7. In a Ukrainian family you always knew your place. You would never ask your parents for any important documents or for *any* important information for that matter. In fact, I did not find out about the actual date of my birth until a long time later; at a time when I required proof of date of birth. The incident very nearly scuttled a career decision.

In researching the records at the Provincial Archives, there is one other significant example of the language obstacles experienced by my dad. When dad made application for his second homestead municipally described as *SW quarter, section 13, township 75, range 18, W of the 5th meridian*, it appears that a John Stromstedt cancelled an application on this same homestead on July 17, 1929, saying that it had *too much bush*. The Declaration of Abandonment indicated that the property had no residence and that no improvements had been made. On July 25, 1931, and after the required two-year waiting period, the Dominion Lands Office in Peace River confirmed the abandonment and on August 1, 1931, the land was posted as being available for registration. The next entry upon this land was made by William Labiuk of Two Hills who, in turn, made application for this same homestead on September 15, 1931. This was followed by a Cancellation Notice on November 11, 1932. Once again, there were no improvements on the land. No reason was given for the abandonment.

On July 18, 1933, my dad, whose name on the application form appears as *Andrew Kirshuba* and his wife, *E. Kirshuba* made application for a homestead on this property for a fee of ten dollars. At the same time, my dad abandoned his first homestead located one mile south on *NE quarter, section 2, township 75, range 18, W of the 5th meridian* on July 18, 1933, because the land was *non-productive*.

The first indication of a problem with dad's application appears on August 29, 1933, when D. H. Boles, Director of Lands in Peace River, indicated that this particular piece of property was to be set aside as *'reservation for timber'* thereby seeking cancellation of the request. On September 5, 1933, a letter from an agent by the name of J. J. E. Clarke acknowledged the error saying that *'Mr. Kirshuba was inadvertently granted entry, which is very much regretted'* but that he should not be put through the expense of making another application for yet another homestead. The appeal was granted by D. H. Boles on September 14, 1933, with a copy to the Department of Lands and Mines in Edmonton.

Improvements were made to the homestead between 1933 and 1939 and on December 11, 1939, my dad was given 30 days in which *'to give in detail all of the residence and improvements you have performed on the above described land since your date of entry, July 18th, 1933...'* In response, my dad indicated that he had lived on the land since 1933 and that the house was worth $300, the barn $300, the granary $150, and the fence $50. Of particular interest is the statement that *'The biggest hold back is the road which is impassable for any kind of big machinery, threshing can only be done in the winter and marketing grain as well, is done at an enormous cost..'* This information was transcribed in typewritten form on a second document which indicated that the house was completed in 1934. On January 15, 1940, a letter from the Director of Lands in Peace River confirmed that my dad had complied with the necessary improvements and that an inspector would examine the lands.

The next problem arose when, on November 13, 1940, my dad took out an Application for Patent for the homestead and filed a sworn statement to that effect. However, his name was now spelled as *Andrew Koshuba*. Suddenly, a red flag must have gone up with the officials because they raised the question as to whether *Andrew Kirshuba* and *Andrew Koshuba* were one and the same person. To further complicate matters, Andrij's name on his passport was spelled as Kaszuba and on his first and second homesteads as Kirshuba. Suddenly, it was spelled as Koshuba. In order to claim title to the homestead, he had to make a declaration, pursuant to the Canada Evidence Act, that the three last names belonged to one and the same person!

More hurdles appeared when, on January 3, 1941, it was required that dad provide a Naturalization Certificate before laying claim to the homestead. Once again, a letter from the Agent of Provincial Lands in Peace River indicated that *'...there does not appear to be any regulation preventing you from making application for naturalization and, in view of the fact that you have now held homestead entry for more than seven years, it is expected that you will inform this office within the next ninety days that you have made application for naturalization'* and, the document goes on to say, *'... I note that when obtaining homestead entry for this quarter section you gave your name as Andrew Kirshuba and also note that in your application for patent your name has been given as Andrew Koshuba and Andriew (Androw) Koshuba. It will, therefore, be necessary that you complete this enclosed form No. 59 before a J. P. or Commissioner and return same to this office giving therein a statement of your full, true and correct name.'*

Documents show that it would not be until May 31, 1941, that my dad would receive a letter from the Agent of Provincial Lands in Peace River asking him to appear in Court on October 24, 1941, in connection with his request for a Naturalization Certificate. Meanwhile, the officials indicated that his application for title to the homestead would be held in abeyance until November 15, 1941, for a decision of the Judge. Further correspondence does show that my dad was successful in his quest of a Naturalization Certificate by January 4, 1943. It would not be until July 31, 1943, that he would be asked to *'...solemnly declare that Andrew Kashuba, as given in my Certificate of Naturalization Certificate, and Andrew Koshuba, as given in the declaration previously completed by myself, both refer to me. I further declare that my full, true and correct name is Andrew Kashuba.'*

On July 31, 1943, the confirmation of his Requisition No. 23407 was received from the Department of Lands and Mines in Edmonton and the good news came on August 17, 1943 which read, *'The South West quarter of Section Thirteen (13) of the said Township, as shown upon a map or plan of survey of the said Township approved and confirmed at Ottawa on the Eighteenth (18) day of November, Nineteen Hundred and Twelve (1912), by Edouard Deville, Surveyor General of Dominion Lands, and on file in the Department of Lands and Mines in Edmonton; The land herein described containing by measurement One Hundred and Sixty (160) acres, more or less.'*

The Notification for Issue of Certificate of Title was completed on August 27, 1943, in the name of Andrew Kashuba and issued on August 30, 1943. Finally, it seemed as though the name game had ended and after this date, the spelling of the family name, in Canada, would be Kashuba. However, this correction in the spelling of the family name took place in 1943, one year *after* dad had registered his children in West Prairie School under the family name of Koshuba. In due course, this, too, had to be corrected.

There was one other problem which did arise but which was successfully mediated. It seems that the previous applicant for the homestead failed to read with care the application form which, in part, said, *'...any person who is desirous of making entry must visit the land personally before making his application, and satisfy himself that there is no one in resident, as he will require to swear when making application that the land is unoccupied, and that there is not more than 100,000 feet (board measure) of spruce, jackpine, or tamarack, suitable for sawlogs, railway ties, telegraph poles or building timber on the land...'* Obviously, he declared that the marketable amount of timber on the quarter section of land fell outside of these parameters. At that point, and even though the Lands Inspector determined in 1943, that the land did have more than 100,000 board feet of potential lumber, he chose to wave the restriction feeling that the error was the responsibility of his office. In the end, my dad must have accepted that the land became even more valuable with the timber on it than it would have been had the land been strictly agricultural in nature.

Even at the age of three, I marvelled at how my dad would hone and stack those huge logs to form the outside walls of our new home; memories of how the each member of the family would tumble into the wagon for the short trip to the new homestead. I particularly remember dad splitting his own shingles for the roof and then climbing the ladder to apply these. Memories of how my sister Anne and my brother Bill, despite their youth, helped dad with the construction of the home by hand-sawing to length the pine logs to be split by hand. But, the memories are not just of the wonder of moving to a new home. The talk of the day in the Aggie Settlement had to do with international affairs and of war. I heard dad talk about a war that took place a long time ago in the Old Country and, here it was, twenty-five years later and a similar situation was developing. Even the combatants seemed to be the same.

By late fall of 1937, the construction of the new home was complete, as was the granary and a water well–all necessary improvements before dad could make application for ownership of the homestead. Perhaps the biggest challenge for dad came from the necessity of making enough money to finance the construction of the new home. I recall how, after the move to the new location, dad continued to clear more land even after the first snows came in October.

The settlers in Aggie either celebrated Christmas on December 25 or January 7. Ordinarily, the family would have attended midnight Mass on January 6. However, that luxury simply was not available to residents in the remote settlement. Instead, my parents accepted an invitation from the Wasylchuks, who lived on an adjacent homestead to the north. Before leaving on what would turn out to be the coldest night of the season, my dad left clear instructions with Maria as to how she might keep the fire burning in the heater throughout the night. '*The damper,*' I recall him saying, '*has to be set just right to control the burn.*'

At the Wasylchuks, the talk was of a new trade agreement with the United States and of the recent *Crystal Night* in Germany where anti-Semitism raged in full fury through the streets of Berlin. They might have even touched on Prime Minister Mackenzie King's praise of British Prime Minister Neville Chamberlain's cable which said, '*...your achievements in the past month alone will assure you an abiding and illustrious place among the great councillors...*' The Wasylchuks turned out to be generous hosts, ensuring that their guests got plenty of the finest Christmas food washed down with homemade wine. By midnight, my parents embraced their hosts, wished them a Blessed Christmas and a Happy New Year and set off for a short walk to their home. What awaited them shocked them to the bone.

Maria recalls how earlier that evening she felt proud to be left alone with her sister Anne and her three brothers. She knew that her parents would not leave her alone with the children unless they were confident that she would carry out the responsibility. '*Don't worry, mom,*' she said as she got a hug from mom and dad before they left for the evening, '*I will make sure that the fire does not go out. We'll all cuddle up in your bed before you get home.*' The instructions left with Maria were clear; look after the kids and keep the fire burning. During the early evening we sat around the pot-bellied stove and by about eleven o'clock we were all asleep, snuggled up in our parents' bed. Maria had a good fire going, making sure that there was just the right amount of cured and raw wood to maintain a slow burn. Before falling asleep, Maria observed the braided string of onions and garlic hung near the stove-pipe so that these might cure before being used for cooking and perhaps for medicinal purposes. All was quiet and peaceful except for the lonesome howl of the wolves. It sounded as though they were in the very next room. '*What a frightening sound,'* commented Maria. *'Are they trying to say something to me?'* Just at that moment Maria took another sniff of the air. *'What's that I smell?'* she asked. As she opened her eyes to look at the heater, she suddenly leapt out of bed, mesmerized; frozen to a spot on the floor. What met her eyes needed no explanation. It seemed as though the whole house was on fire. *'Oh my God,'* yelled Maria, *'the house is on fire! Quick, get your clothes on, all of you. Wrap that quilt around you. Everyone. Outside!'*

The heat from the burning floor next to the heater was intense. *'What will my parents say?'* she asked as shooed us out-of-doors into the freezing night air. For a moment, the front door resisted. With considerable force, Maria opened the door. The blast of cold night air laced with fresh oxygen seemed to lend encouragement to the fire. Despite the extreme cold, the area next to the front door felt warm. Maria, having ensured that all four of us were accounted for, went into action as though guided by divine providence. At first, she yelled at us to gather as much snow as quickly as possible and throw it onto the fire. In the meantime, she quickly organized a bucket brigade, drawing water from the nearby well and passing each pail-full to Anne who would scurry into the house and throw the water onto the flames. Snow, water, and a wet blanket slowed the advance of the fire.

By this time, the weight of the melting snow and water on the heater caused it to drop through the floor into the cellar. This seemed to take care of *that* portion of the fire. As Maria watched the fire slowly eating its way through the attic and into the roof, she suddenly changed her strategy. She grabbed a ladder, re-positioned it next to the location of the stove pipe which protruded through the roof and, using a dipper, began to attack the flames from the top. Slowly, the plan seemed to have the desired affect.

Weather records confirm that the outside temperature on that night was about -30 degrees Celsius, perhaps helping to slow the progress of the fire. Within a short time, the fire seemed to be under control. Maria felt certain that the punishment she was about to receive from dad would far exceed the pain of putting out the fire. Barehanded, she dragged the heater from the cellar onto the living room floor. She seemed oblivious to the pain.

My parents could smell that something was wrong long before they came within view of the house. Running as quickly as they could, they were now able to smell the acrid smoke and knew that something terrible had happened. It seemed like an eternity before they were at the front of the house. The damage done to the interior was not immediately visible. Maria, expecting an immediate attack by her stern father, was shocked to see him break out in tears and give her a big hug. She did not expect it. Suddenly, it seemed that everyone was crying.

Without a fire to heat the house, my dad knew that the family would soon perish from the extreme cold. Despite the smoke, everyone went back into the house. Mom lit the coal oil lamp and dad extinguished any smouldering embers before undertaking the task of shoring up the gaping hole in the ceiling and roof. Once he had the planks over the holes in the floor and ceiling, he

Forest road between High Prairie and McLennan. Source: Glenbow Archives, Calgary, Alberta, 1920. ND 3-5319.

Homesteader's wife with cream cans, reminiscent of family homestead in the Aggie Settlement. Source: Glenbow Archives, Calgary, Alberta, NA 4172-6

As an election campaign promise, Premier William Aberhart planned to distribute 25 dollar Prosperity Certificates to Albertans in 1935. Source: Glenbow Archives, Calgary, Alberta. NA-2377-1.

secured the heater and re-connected the stove pipe. Finally, he announced that the heater was ready to be re-lit. It seemed odd that we had struggled so hard to put the fire out only to have dad struggle to re-light it.

Even after several weeks of scrubbing and cleaning, mom could not rid the house of the smell of smoke and roasted onions and garlic. Not wanting to discard either, mom did her level best to salvage the best of the burnt onions and garlic for use as garnishment in boiled potatoes and soup for the next couple of weeks. To this day, I have mixed feelings about the smell of fried onions. As for Maria, she has never been able to explain how she accomplished the impossible. Maybe her guardian angel was at her side. Perhaps it was luck that the heater fell through the burnt-out floor into the cellar and the rapid advance of the fire could be halted. Maybe the biggest factor was that the area between the big bed and the heater was open and the fire was spotted by Maria in its early stages. Perhaps the spread of the fire was slowed because the logs used in the construction of the walls were green and were slow to burn. Without ready access to the snow and water, it is doubtful that the home could have been saved.

Mom experienced great difficulty in putting the near-tragedy out of her mind. Being of a suspicious mind, she thought that this was God's way of getting a message to her. She shared this feeling with dad. As expected, dad immediately said that it was a lot of nonsense. He resisted any suggestion of moving out of the Aggie Settlement. His dream was to build a large farming operation right there while mom's plan was to ensure that the children prepared themselves for a better life. As far as she could determine, the best route to success was through education.

It would be that summer that my dad would look at the growing family and wonder whether things were getting out of hand. The pursuit of economic stability was one thing; however, a more serious problem was evident. Maria was now ten years of age and provincial legislation required that she attend school regularly. My parents had little choice but to look at different means through which Maria could get to school. While working on the railroad, dad mentioned his dilemma to Steve Blonski. *'You know,'* he responded, *'we live just two miles out of High Prairie and I have two kids attending school. Why don't you board her at our home?'*

My dad did not need much coaxing even though he knew that he would be losing a willing worker. This arrangement was made all the more palatable in that Maria could use the railway shortcut to get to the Blonskis rather than the more circuitous road through Triangle Corner to get to the school in High Prairie. In exchange, my dad paid Blonski a small monthly stipend and, from time to time, provided his family with eggs, poultry, and beef.

Although Maria did not begin her formal schooling until all of the land under cultivation and garden duties were completed in the fall, she was a willing and attentive student. With the assistance of the Blonski children, who helped in the translation from English to Ukrainian, Maria quickly caught up to the rest of the pupils in grade one. However, this arrangement was particularly hard on mom. She not only lost a good little worker around the kitchen and a baby sitter, but she also lost the one person with whom she could always make small talk. This made her more determined than ever to make the family's stay at the Aggie Settlement as short as possible. With all the activity, my dad was not aware that mom was already planning the family's next move.

Meanwhile, the national news from the rest of Canada was not good. Over 500,000 potential workers were suddenly unemployed. Even Prime Minister Richard Bennett's new Employment and Social Insurance Act seemed to do little to stem the flow of the unemployed. It was also a time that workers in the west organized an *On-To-Ottawa* trek. The government branded the trekkers as communists who wanted to overthrow the government. A riot broke out in Regina, a policeman was killed and dozens of civilians injured. Trek leaders were taken off the train and arrested.

On the political front in August of 1935 William Aberhart, the leader of the Social Credit Party in Alberta, scored an overwhelming victory in Alberta by capturing 56 of 63 seats in the provincial legislature. The United Farmers of Alberta who had been in power since 1920 failed to win a single seat. This victory came, in part, as a result of Aberhart's promise of a $25 dividend per person per month. Aberhart, himself a respected school principal and a gifted preacher, was not a giant in the fields of economics and politics. Despite his shortcomings, he did raise the expectations of the people who wanted low interest rates, full employment, and a respectable standard of living. In October of the same year, Prime Minister Richard B. Bennett's Conservative party was annihilated in a federal election. The Liberals under William Lyon Mackenzie King came into power with a vast majority. Given that Canada was in its sixth year of economic chaos, the voters thought it was time to throw out the Conservatives in favour of the Liberals.

This was not a good time for politicians, be it provincial or federal. It seemed that they were being blamed for all of society's ills. The winter of 1935-36 was the coldest on record and the summer of 1936 seemed to be the hottest ever on the prairies. In southern Alberta and Saskatchewan, the Canadian Pacific Railways used snowplows to clear the tracks of soil drifts as high as ten feet as the dust bowl extended all the way to Texas. And, as the drought continued, it would become the year that saw a seven percent increase in the number of farmers. Many urban dwellers were moved off the welfare list and forced to seek subsistence on farms-- often stealing grain in order to survive; while in Calgary, many women turned to prostitution. The police dealt brutally with demonstrators and many were arrested and locked up in jails. However, in rural districts it was not uncommon to find the RCMP helping with the administration of relief.

In Edmonton, the Ukrainian Workers Home provided a place for conferences, meetings, and rehearsals in support of unemployed Ukrainians. This did not stop several hundred unemployed from marching on the Legislature in Edmonton demanding the closing of soup kitchens saying that they preferred a cash or voucher system. As usual, these types of marches were quickly dispersed but held out some hope with the election of the Social Credit Party even though the promised $25 never did appear. However, in the summer of 1936 some public workers were paid in the new scrip and most merchants accepted it as money. In all, about $360,000 of these prosperity certificates were issued before the funny money was declared illegal. Throughout, Premier Aberhart blamed the federal government for all of the ills of Alberta. During this terrible period in the history in western Canada, the Peace River Country remained somewhat isolated from overwhelming cold, heat, grasshopper infestation, grain rust, sawflies, early frost and political upheaval.

To control the masses during the hungry 30s, police often beat on demonstrators, strikers, farmers, freight riders, transients, foreigners and the unemployed and it was up to the media to help lessen the impact of this malaise and despair. The talking and moving pictures produced in Hollywood helped many escape reality; a reality where public attention was often focussed antagonistically upon aliens. In other words, racism was acceptable during this period of Canada's history and there was much talk about a Jewish conspiracy to take over the world. Others were led to believe that Ukrainian immigrants were Communists because many subscribed to the Ukrainian Labour News, a Communist-based newspaper. Yet, despite the many hardships for the twenty percent who were unemployed or poor, many in the middle and upper classes had decent jobs at a time when a small amount of money could buy a large amount of goods and they could occupy their spare time at the movies, playing softball, bowling, or curling.

But, these were not the best of times for the farmer and the politicians were well aware of this. The government of the day was paying Alberta farmers $5 a month if they agreed to keep a hired hand through the winter and another $5 for the hired hand. This policy did help and prevented many families from committing serious crimes as a means of getting by. At the same time, assaults on women were rarely reported, rape of domestic labourers was common, and wife-beating due to the hopeless economic situation went unreported. Despite these societal problems with Canada mired in a deep depression, dad felt that he was overcoming some of the obstacles to the accumulation of wealth. The demand for grain was high and the prices that these commanded in the marketplace would once again make farming a lucrative occupation. A sense of camaraderie developed in the Aggie settlement. Neighbours could rely on one another when it came to sharing farm implements and they could call on one another at any time. The doors to their homes were never locked. During those times of the year when farm work was not possible and dad was not working on the railway or making railroad ties, inter-visitations among the homesteaders were commonplace. It was a time to catch up on the latest news which often travelled at a snail's pace. Some of the homesteaders subscribed to an English language newspaper while dad subscribed to a Ukrainian language newspaper published in Winnipeg. Amongst them, they shared the news of the day as well as their newspapers. But then, these were times of peace. News, although interesting, was relatively unimportant.

Or, so thought my dad.

However, things began to change. Ollie Olafson, a Scandinavian neighbour to the east, had the only radio in the settlement and the news on this particular day was not good. When the opportunity arose, dad would visit with him to catch the latest news on radio station CFGP, the *Voice of the Mighty Peace* as the station liked to call itself. There was troubling news out of Germany. Adolf Hitler was getting more and more militant. It seemed that he was quite serious when earlier he had said that he was building a new 1,000 year Reich. Were these the rantings of a madman? World tensions continued to increase as Japan announced that it had signed the Anti-Comintern Pact which extended the year-old alliance between Italy and Germany; an alliance particularly disturbing because it reflected their militant actions. Germany occupied the previously demilitarized Rhineland and other European countries were re-arming. Even Canada increased its defence budget.

When Cordell Hull, the Secretary of State in the United States, spoke to Canada's prime minister, he went so far as to say that *war was inevitable in Europe*. He believed that dictators Hitler and Mussolini would one day go too far and another international conflict would be the result. The German Olympics of 1936, held in Berlin, did little to allay the fears of western democracies. On the local front in Western Canada, many of the unemployed continued to agitate against the seeming inaction of the provincial and federal governments. All the while dad busied himself on the homestead. To him, all of these political events seemed to be *so* far away.

For my parents, a visit to Chodzicki's Farmer's Trading Company general store in High Prairie became more and more frequent and gave them a chance to leave the kids in the care of Maria. These were joyous occasions. Shopping for staples was but one reason for such trips and, as might be expected, the list of necessities was not very long. The scarcity of funds would not allow a longer list. Most vegetables needed for sustenance were grown on the homestead but dad would reward himself with a can of *Dominion* tobacco. When he ran out of commercial tobacco, he improvised by crushing dry leaves and rolling these into a cigarette. Mom sewed, by hand, all the clothes for the children. It would be another couple of years before dad could afford a foot-operated sewing machine.

Credit at Chodzicki's Store was available to most every pioneer. They could be trusted to make good their debts as funds became available to them. While shopping for food stuffs or farm implements, settlers liked to talk about education and schooling, methods of farming and farming machinery; who was buying and who was selling. The seeds for long-range planning were often sown in those Saturday night outings. Sunday was set aside as a day of worship. Earlier, the fall work was completed just in time for Eva to get through her final semester of pregnancy. On November 15, which happened to be Maria's birthday, mom gave birth to the third boy in a row. Dad decided it was time to preserve his heritage and named him *Andrew*. Maria was now in the second grade and was promoted to grade three by mid-term. By 1937, dad, with the help of the family, cleared another ten acres of land for a total of thirty acres.

With the first trans-Atlantic and trans-Canada flights offered by Trans-Canada Airlines, it looked as though Canada was finally clawing its way out of the depression. The minimum wage was now 33.3 cents per hour or $15 per week for men with more than one year's experience in the work in which they were currently engaged and the visit of the King and Queen solidified Canada's position in international affairs.

Yes, things were looking up for Canada and mom was about to make sure that her children were included in that vision of a bright future. In her mind, with children came added responsibilities and dad was about to get a dose of reality.

24.

Hitler Attacks Poland

As Andrij reflects on World War I

Throughout the first months of 1939, dad seemed to be pre-occupied with thoughts of an earlier era as thousands of Canadians were labelled as *"enemy aliens,"* herded into Canadian concentration camps, forced into heavy labour, had their assets confiscated, disenfranchised and subjected to various other state-sanctioned censures. When, in March of 1939 the news came crackling over Olafson's radio that Prime Minister King joined other western democratic states in condemning the German seizure of Czechoslovakia, he must have had an uneasy feeling as to the impact of the next war on his family, not only in Canada but in Poland as well.

Like so many people throughout the western world, dad continued to keep his ear closely tuned to the latest developments in Germany. He was fully aware that Hitler was flexing his muscles and knew that these developments would have dire consequences for the members of his family in Europe as well as for all Canadians. Worse yet, by this time my parents had become staunch Canadians and did not look forward to any confrontation with their European cousins. With the political uncertainty in Europe, it was not uncommon for settlers to reflect upon the horrors of war and what happened to immigrants from Central and Eastern Europe at the outbreak of World War I; reflections about how the Canadian government invoked the War Measures Act and through an Order-in-Council required that tens of thousands of *enemy aliens* register with officials. As a result, over 8,000 were interned of which nearly 6,000 were from the Austro-Hungarian territories, mostly ethnic Ukrainians.

World events caused my dad to move quickly to harness at least one frontier from the long list of evolving technologies. He decided that he would soon have to purchase a radio and install a long outdoor antennae so that he might be able to get the latest news in his own home. In the meantime, he would continue to listen to the news at Olafson's as often as he could. In August, Prime Minister King appealed to Adolf Hitler and Polish leader Ignacy Moscicki to seek a *just and equitable settlement* of the problems that existed between the two nations. King could see the storm clouds gather and decided to ask Italy's Mussolini to intervene and preserve peace between Germany and Poland.

On September 1, 1939, the federal government assumed wartime powers and, even though war had not been declared, Canadian officials engaged in a flurry of meetings. Early that day, a cabinet order was presented to the Governor General proclaiming the War Measures Act. In a prepared statement, King declared '...*it is now apparent that the efforts which have been made to preserve the peace of Europe are likely to be of no avail.*' Canada stood at the ready to help Britain. War production had already begun in parts of the country. High explosive artillery shells were being produced in Ontario and the Ottawa Car Company began building heavy bombers. On September 3, Prime Minister Neville Chamberlain of Great Britain told his nation that '... *a state of war now exists with Germany,*' further stating that '*German Chancellor Adolf Hitler can only be stopped by force, and we and France are today, in fulfilment of our obligations.*'

One can only imagine the shock waves the world over when on September 1, 1939, Hitler's bombers and panzer columns over-ran Poland. Two days later Britain was at war with Germany following which Prime Minister King called a special session of Parliament to vote on the question of Canada's participation, and the country was once again at war on September 10. In short order over 58,000 Canadians signed up, due in part to the offer of a coat, new boots, three meals and $1.50 a day. If nothing else, these volunteers decreased the ranks of the unemployed.

The most up-to-date news of the war was slow to filter to the settlers in Aggie. A daily newspaper was not available and most did not have a radio. Still, it was very hard to shut out the horrors and tragedies of the war. Poland was laid to waste in short order by Hitler's blitzkrieg. In France and in Belgium, the opposing armies watched each other in suspended animation as if frozen in time and reluctant to make the first and irreversible move. Canada's Prime Minister Mackenzie King seemed uncertain as to what role Canada might play in the conflict. On May 10, 1940 the news crackled out of Grande Prairie, '...*Hitler's armies crashed into Belgium and Holland today.*' The fate of Britain was turned over to Winston Churchill.

By June 14, Hitler had laid claim to Paris and all of France was soon neutered. As the war escalated, my dad's level of anxiety rose with each passing day. Although he was not eligible for conscription into the armed services, a number of young sons of pioneers from the High Prairie area either volunteered or conscripted after the *conscription go-ahead* was given by Parliament on April 27, 1942. "*Well, Eva,*" he was heard to remark, "*there goes our plan to escape from war, hunger, and oppression.*"

Ukrainian Canadians interned as foreign aliens in the Castle Mountain Internment Camp in 1915. Photograph titled "Leaving the Compound." Source: Jessie Carothers Collection, Glenbow Museum, Calgary, Alberta. NA 3959-2.

Benito Mussolini and Adolf Hitler in a reviewing stand during a visit to occupied Yugoslavia, 1941.

Winston Churchill, Time Magazine's Man of the Year, 1940 and 1949.

The federal government was well aware that within the ranks of Ukrainian immigrants were Fascist sympathizers as well as anti-Communists. For purposes of security, the government wanted to exercise control over them and, in consultation with the Department of External Affairs, formed up, in November of 1940, the Ukrainian Canadian Committee (KYK) which represented over ninety percent of Ukrainian Canadians of Greek Catholic and Orthodox faiths. In 1942, Ukrainian News of Edmonton reported that *'...the major aim of KYK is to help Canada and Britain win the war, to help Ukrainians in Europe in their demands for an independent Ukraine, and to represent Ukrainian Canadians to the government.'*

In the spring of 1940, at five years of age, I would frequently accompany my dad on his early morning visits to Olafson's to catch the eight o'clock morning news. I was not able to understand the full meaning of war, but I did know that something terrible was happening to people in a faraway land. Despite my dad's preoccupation with what was happening in Europe, he had an important message for Vasyl and me, *"...you boys are big enough and old enough to help with some of the smaller tasks around the farm yard. Maybe you can help your mother with the feeding of the chicks. Maybe even the hogs. Soon, perhaps soon, you will be able to help me with picking roots."*

"Sure, dad, I'd like to help," I responded.

At first, helping with those small chores seemed like fun. Learning to pick roots, however, was another matter. It was no picnic. Even during those short periods of time that we assisted dad, the amount of help that we could offer was limited. Dad would chop and pull the roots out of newly-broken soil and Vasyl and I would drag these to a pile to be burned at a later time. The sun always seemed too hot and the roots bigger and tougher with each passing moment. It was as if the roots wanted to engage us in some sort of a contest. At the end of the day our hands were blistered and our feet were sore. *"That's it,"* Vasyl would say, *"let's go in."* By early afternoon on those hot days, he'd had enough of it. And, like an obedient little brother, I showed very little resistance to his suggestion. Of course, dad was never too pleased to see us leave early.

By mid-summer the root-picking was completed and dad turned to clearing more land. We helped by dragging underbrush and deadwood onto a pile. By mid-August the crops were beginning to ripen and dad once again hitched a train ride to Edmonton in search of job during the harvesting season. Vasyl and I were thankful that dad would be away for awhile. We knew that we would not have to work as hard in his absence. Someone once said that too much free time for young boys was just plain no good; that idle hands can sometimes get into trouble. Not having much to do on a sunny day in late August, Vasyl and I wandered over to our neighbour's homestead. Steve Badan was servicing his binder when we entered his yard, saying to us, *"...boys, my wheat is ready to be cut and tomorrow I'll be hitching up my three horses to begin the cutting and the stooking."*

"Can we help?" asked Vasyl.

"Do you think you can stook?"

"Sure, if you'd let us!"

"No, I was just kidding, boys. Come back in a couple of years and we'll talk."

After leaving Badan's homestead, Vasyl turned to me, *"...hey, I think he likes our company. Why don't we come back tomorrow and watch him harvest his wheat?"*

When we returned the next day, we could see from the adjacent road allowance that Badan was ready to begin cutting his wheat. We tested the ripeness of the wheat by eating a handful. Yes, it was very chewable; very ripe. Since Badan did not want our help, Vasyl stumbled upon another idea. *"Why don't we surprise him?"*

"Surprise him? How?" I asked.

"Come with me and I'll show you." Vasyl promptly led me to a location along Badan's property line where he had piled a large number of tree stumps after clearing his land two or three years earlier. *"Come here and help me,"* insisted Vasyl.

I didn't know what Vasyl was up to but it looked like a lot of fun. We huffed and puffed as we rolled a partially burned-out stump into Steve Badan's wheat field to a distance of about twenty-five feet from the fence. As we covered our tracks, we made sure that the stump was fully camouflaged. We then hid in the trees nearby and waited. Badan made one circle around the field cutting and binding the wheat into sheaves with his horse-drawn binder. He made a second circle. *"Aha,"* said Vasyl, *"one more circle and he is in for a surprise!"* On the next circle, the binder, the horses, and Badan came to a sudden and abrupt halt. True, we had heard foul language from dad, but the blue streak coming out of Badan was enough to make our hair stand on end. For a moment, it sounded as though he was mortally wounded. As we scrambled in the direction of our home, Vasyl was heard to say, *"the man should be ashamed of himself using that kind of language!"*

The next day we decided that we should not go to the Badan homestead for some time. After all, he knew that there were no other kids in the immediate vicinity. Surely, he would be able to put two and two together and conclude that we were the guilty rascals. *"Today,"* ventured Vasyl, *"we will visit our other neighbour, Mr. Sawchuk. I heard dad say that he would also be going to Edmonton to do some harvesting. He will not be at home."*

"Why, then, do we want to go to his home?"

"You'll see."

Alex Sawchuk's homestead was one kilometre south of our home and, much like Badan, he had an excellent crop of oats. But, what really got Vasyl's attention was Sawchuk's garden. The carrots and peas were all as large as the ones in mom's garden. For certain, they looked scrumptious. *"You know Slawko, it is better that we eat Mr. Sawchuk's peas and carrots than mother's. That way we will not get into trouble."* We had quite a feed of Sawchuk's carrots that afternoon. Pulling a few at a time, we would take them over to the well, draw up a pail of water, wash them, and devour them. We didn't spare the peas either. By mid-afternoon we had our fill of peas and carrots. *"It's time to have a look at his potatoes,"* suggested Vasyl.

"You mean we are going to dig up some potatoes and cook them?"

"No, silly. I have something else in mind."

After digging up one plant, we attempted to eat a couple raw potatoes. *"Yuch,"* somehow, they did not taste as good as the carrots. *"Maybe,"* said Vasyl, *"we should drop a few of them into the well. Hey, that's quite a sound the potato makes when it hits the water a way down there!"* We dug up a few more carrots and threw those in the well. To finish the job, we took a pee in the well. In leaving the Sawchuk homestead, we gave little thought to any possible consequences.

All too soon, dad was back from the harvest work in Bruderheim, saying to mom that he had to get on with cutting his own crop fields which were about two weeks behind those in Bruderheim in maturing. He also said that he had earlier made an arrangement to borrow Steve Badan's binder to take in his crops. With this explanation, he suddenly left for Badan's to determine a day on which he might be able to get use of his binder. When dad got home from a visit to Badan's homestead, Vasyl and I thought that the war had broken out right there in the Aggie Settlement. Dad didn't even have the courtesy of asking us if we were responsible for rolling the tree stump into Badan's prized wheat field. Quickly and efficiently, he set about administering the appropriate punishment. *"Not only did you boys cause considerable damage to Badan's binder, but you delayed his harvest by a couple of days. In turn, that will delay my harvest. Worse yet, maybe he won't even lend me his binder."*

Because Vasyl was older, he was told to lower his trousers to his knees and lay down over a chair. Hearing Vasyl scream and yell for mercy suddenly made me wish that I was elsewhere. I even wished that I would be the first to be punished rather than having to listen to the groans and moans emanating from my brother. Finally, I could see why my dad wore a belt. Up until that time, I thought that it was to keep his pants up. After the spanking, I was not so sure. Perhaps it was a belt that served a dual purpose. We got the message loud and clear and vowed never to repeat the offence.

Just two days later Alex Sawchuk approached our house. He did not seem too steady on his feet. Vasyl and I immediately concluded that his strange and unsteady walk might have something to do with our visit to his house earlier that week. Hiding in the cellar of the house, we could hear the conversation between Sawchuk and dad. The news was not good. Alex, almost in a delirium, explained to dad how he got home the day before, thirsty and hungry, almost dying for a drink of cold water out of his well. *"Now,"* he said, *"I feel that I am about to die because I drank that awful water."*

"What happened to your water?"

"It seems," he said in a strange voice that we could barely hear, *"that*

somebody got into my garden. Not only did they make a mess of my carrots and my peas, but they threw my potatoes into the well. What a mess."

"How come you drank it if it was such a mess?"

"I don't know. At first I thought that it was my mind playing tricks on me. My well water always tasted so good. Why should it have been any different. Besides, I got home at dusk. How could I tell what was in that water?"

We had never heard dad bellow so loud. "Vasyl. Slawko. Hustle your ass up here. Come here this minute."

Not to obey, we knew, would make matters even worse. In retrospect, we should have held out longer. Maybe dad's anger would have subsided after a cooling off period. My butt was still tender from the spanking of two days earlier. In fact, Vasyl and I had some difficulty sitting for a few days. The only saving grace from the incident was that dad had an opportunity to take his mind off the war which was now raging in Europe. Besides, Vasyl and I were very thankful that Mr. Sawchuk was not aware that we had also peed in his well. Otherwise, God only knows what the punishment might have been!

Now that dad was back at the Aggie Settlement, Vasyl and I were once again assigned various tasks around the house, yard, and garden. However, Vasyl must have experienced great difficulty in forgetting about the Badan and Sawchuk incidents. He particularly disliked the punishment that dad meted out. This must have bothered him a lot because right out of the blue he said to me, "let's run away from home."

"Run away from home? Why?"

"Well, we're getting all these lickings from dad just for trying to have a little bit of fun. Now he has taken all the fun out of staying at home."

How was I to know that running away from home had a special meaning? Vasyl was older and I must have felt that he should know all about running away from home. It appeared as though he took this decision without any kind of planning. The idea of running away must have popped into his head at that moment and he was bound and determined to carry out his little plan. Without a backward glance, we left home about noon. The destination was unknown. We did not file a flight plan with our parents.

As we wandered around our homestead eating wild strawberries, saskatoons, blueberries, gooseberries, and raspberries, Vasyl tried to explain to me his reasons for running away. "Work, work, work--that is our daily routine. Picking those roots. That's hard work. And what of cleaning the barn and the chicken coop? Bringing in the firewood? Even looking after the cows." Listening to Vasyl, I didn't know what to say.

Having had our fill of wild berries, we headed for an abandoned house on a homestead just to the west. The domestic raspberry bushes seemed to embrace the log structure. Shortly, we were off once again to the Wasylchuk homestead, just to the north. The long shadows of the late afternoon made me feel uneasy. When we arrived at the Wasylchuk home, we found it to be unlocked, so we walked right in. However, after just a few minutes, Vasyl suggested that we start on our way back home. As we walked along the wagon trail, we spotted a small haystack in a meadow. *"Vasyl, I am getting tired. Can we take a nap?"* I asked.

Vasyl thought it was a good idea. He said he, too, felt a little tired. With that, we curled up in the haystack and took an afternoon nap. When we awoke, it was late afternoon and the sun was beginning its descent into the tall pines. We could hear the rustle of the leaves as a light evening breeze blew in from the west. *"Maybe,"* said Vasyl, *"we should head back to a location closer to home."*

"Yes, let's go home. I'm getting hungry. And thirsty."

With that, we started our leisurely walk back home. *"What's your hurry Slawko. We'll only have to do more chores if we get home early."*

It seemed that Vasyl was bound and determined to exercise his individuality and decision-making ability. He either thought it was too painful to think about the consequences of his actions or he failed to think about anything. In a short while we were back at our homestead where Vasyl suggested that we crawl under the granary. Since the granary was constructed on top of large logs, there was sufficient space under which we could crawl. As darkness fell, the stars and moon came out. We could hear dad, mom, and Maria calling out our names while Anne rang a cow bell in an effort to attract our attention. More shouts of *"Vasyl. Slawko. Where are you? Come home."*

"Don't give away our location," admonished Vasyl.

The shouts became more desperate. Mom was now banging the lid of a pot so that we might know the location of the homestead. I recalled how she would use this technique to frighten away any wild animals on those occasions when we walked at night. Even dad once said that wild animals disliked noise and would do anything to avoid the racket. By this time, dad had built a large bonfire in the yard. *"Why the boys?"* he asked of no one in particular. *"What will I now do without their help?"* Maria disappeared to Badan's in an effort to find out if we were at his house.

In the absence of any other means of communication, dad hoped that the large bonfire would help us find our way home in the event that we were lost in the forest surrounding the homestead. Aside from Badan, my parents had no one else they could alert regarding our plight. Even though most of the homesteaders were away harvesting, a small search party was organized. Under the granary, I was ready to capitulate. Vasyl would have none of it. In the meantime, the banging continued as did the shouts of *"Vasyl. Slawko."* By this time, we were getting very cold. Vasyl suggested that we get go to the hayloft in the barn where we made a bed for ourselves and promptly fell asleep. Occasionally, we were awakened by the shouts from the yard. The night seemed to pass quickly and we were awakened by the mooing of the two milk cows. We then heard mom milking the cows. Cold and hungry, we jockeyed for more space in the hayloft.

"No, Slawko, you move over," was Vasyl's response to me when I asked him to move over.

241

"No, Vasyl, you are the one hogging all the space. You move over," was my response.

Mom must have been listening for any unusual sounds as she milked Bossy. She thought she heard something and yelled out *"who's up there?"* The next thing we knew, mom's head appeared right there in front of us. We were rendered speechless. So was mom. No one said a thing for the longest time. Then mom yelled out, *"Andrij, Andrij, come quickly."* At that moment, we knew that our adventure was over and that we would be punished. However, we were not prepared for what was to come next. Hugging us, mom broke into tears. When dad arrived, he just stared at us. He seemed genuinely glad to see us. For whatever reason, neither mom or dad asked us any questions.

That morning mom served the best breakfast ever. Hot cakes, bacon, and eggs and fresh milk. This was quite a contrast to our typical breakfast of hot porridge and milk. Yes, we did run away from home. Yet, as strange as it may seem, no one ever said very much about it. From that moment on, it seemed as though dad's attitude towards us changed. Although he continued to be very strict, he did cut us a little more slack when dealing with our behaviour. Perhaps in us he saw a little bit of himself. It is difficult to say whether or not this event had an impact on mom's pregnancy. However, years later dad was heard to remark that the events of early fall may have caused mom to give birth to another child a little earlier than expected.

Alice was born on September 28, 1941.

25.

War Ends and Schooling Begins

The decision to leave the Aggie Settlement

The snows of winter came early making the fall of 1941 seem much shorter than usual. The days were filled with anticipation because the radio news out of Grande Prairie was much easier to receive. Radio waves prefer to travel over frozen ground and forests devoid of leaves and foliage and the latest news about World War II seemed always to take centre stage. On the morning of December 7, the news seemed to be especially bad for the United States. Japan attacked Pearl Harbour and forced the Americans into the conflict. News reports about Canada's role in the war were not very encouraging either. The first real action that Canadians saw in the war was a disaster at Dieppe, France on August 19, 1942. Over six thousand soldiers took part in the assault of the fortifications of which nine hundred were killed and nearly two thousand captured. The shock waves quickly permeated the farthest reaches of Canada when the casualty list was published.

Shortly after the outbreak of the war, thousands of citizens of German and Italian heritage were stripped of their Canadian citizenship because it was felt that they would sympathize with Mussolini and Hitler. Only those who could convince the Registrar-General that they had been and would continue to be loyal subjects would be granted an exemption certificate. At the same time, thousands of German prisoners of war were being transferred from Europe to Canada for internment. The question of Canada's position on conscription went to a national plebiscite on April 27, 1942 and over sixty-three percent voted in favour; however, the province of Quebec strongly rejected conscription. Not only did Alberta send its finest young men to war but its women as well. At first, many women replaced men in munitions factories; however, they soon took a more active role near the war front where they played a significant role in liberating the free world while at the same time fighting to liberate themselves. When on July 15, 1940, those men who were not married were declared to be single for purposes of recruitment, there was a sudden and unusual rush to the pulpit.

The impact of the war on Edmonton was instantaneous; the air traffic from the United States increased 100-fold, making it necessary to build a satellite airfield in Namao. With 7,000 foot runways, it became the largest airport on the continent and was able to ferry lend-lease aircraft to Russia. Even more significant was the decision by the Americans to build a highway to Alaska with Mile Zero starting in Dawson Creek. In all, 10,000 troops, 7,000 pieces of equipment, over 50 contractors, and 17,000 civilians worked on the project. By the end of the first summer in 1942, over 850 miles of highway were in place and in a scant nine months, 1,523 miles of highway were ready for use. What is even more amazing was that the highway traversed some of the most difficult terrain in the world. The Alaska Highway truly made Edmonton the gateway to the north.

The supply of energy to American troops was critical, triggering a search for oil in Northern Alberta. In short order the Norman Wells oilfield would serve Alaska via a 500-mile long pipeline connected to an oil refinery in Whitehorse. Freight destined for transport via the Alaska Highway was delivered by rail to the Peace River country which quickly became overburdened. With all of this activity, it was only natural that World War II had quite an impact on the homesteaders in Aggie. Many of them worked on a railroad section gang and as private contractors making railroad ties. These major developments drove prices upward for railroad ties as well as for labour and helped to ensure that homesteaders would be able to supplement their meagre farm income through work on the Northern Alberta Railway.

Although the war may have been uppermost in the minds of my parents, it became increasingly evident that continuing to live on the homestead would jeopardize the children's education. After all, Anne was now ten, Vasyl eight, and I was six. Soon, Andy and Alice would be of school age as well. I am sure that at times like these mom wished that school authorities would pay a visit to the settlement and compel my dad to send the children to school just as soon as they reached school age. At the moment, the only member of the family that was attending school was Maria. While mom agitated for education, dad portrayed a lack of commitment to the cause, saying that he was quite content living in the Aggie Settlement.

Listening to my parents, I realized just how much they missed the good times of the Old Country; the opportunity to get together with other young people in the village and to attend a play or improvised theatre. There were times when dad went so far as to say that he missed the comradery of military service in Poland. As homesteaders, they tried to put their cares aside from time to time and enjoy life in Canada. Good times meant getting together for an evening of cards with a neighbour or for dad to smoke a cigarette made from Dominion tobacco. As for mom, learning to sew an item of clothing for the children using a new pattern borrowed from a neighbour seemed to be a priority. Since the cost of commercially-prepared beer was relatively expensive, most homesteaders preferred to drink homemade wine. Several pioneers became proficient at making wine from wild berries and vegetables while others went so far as to perfect a method of making a powerful alcoholic drink they called *white lightning.*

Prior to 1941, mom had not accompanied dad on one of his harvesting trips; however, this year was different. There seemed to be plenty of harvest work in the High Prairie region making it unnecessary for dad to journey to Edmonton. On this particular weekend, dad invited mom to make a Saturday trip into High Prairie to do some grocery shopping while he served on the McCue threshing crew nearby. In many ways, my parents could not have picked a better farmer as an example of what the future held in farming. Mac McCue took over the family farm and embraced new technologies with fervour. Not only did my dad learn of the modern methods of harvesting, but he also took note that Mac owned one of the first Model T Fords in the area. He would also be among the first to purchase a combine which would eventually replace the threshing machine. As it turned out, dad had another surprise awaiting him.

It appears as though dad had earlier heard of a small farm that was for sale five miles southwest of High Prairie and within two miles of Gilwood School. However, knowing that mom would show immediate interest in the farm, he was heard to say, *'The last thing I want to do is tell Eva about this farm because the next thing she would be doing is agitating for a move. She'd be talking once again about putting the kids in school.'* Meanwhile, as mom sat at the kitchen table with Estella McCue, she was not about to let a language barrier stop her from pursuing some very important questions. Immediately, a kindred spirit developed between the two women when mom learned that Estella had mastered the skills of knitting, crocheting, cooking, baking and gardening. Knowing but a few words of English, mom made an inquiry about a farm near Gilwood School. *'Yes,'* Mrs. McCue said, *'I have heard of a farm for sale southwest of High Prairie. I believe that the owner wants 650 dollars for the farm.'* That evening while shopping at the Chodzicki's general store, mom confronted dad with this information. Not only was dad taken aback with mom's question, he was also surprised that mom was able to get this information from Estella McCue. Shamefacedly, he could do little else but confess that he knew about the property. *"After all, Eva, there's a war on and it is only now that we are getting our feet under us."*

"Yes, I know Andrij. But what of the children? When you wrote me in Plazow, you promised that we would be providing schooling for the children. We can't have them all stay at the Blonskis. They cannot walk to the school in High Prairie. I will not hear of it."

Now, there is one thing mom seemed to understand. If you approach a man with a good plan that makes a lot of sense in mixed company, it is unlikely that he would attack you for trying your best for the children. It would not be the right thing to reveal to your friends or associates that you were so unfeeling as to attack your wife in public. Mom did not have a degree in psychology but she knew how to advance an argument. *"Besides, Andrij, you know that this province has a law. The children are of school age and they belong in a school. Look at Vasyl. He is now eight years of age. He should be in school."*

Dad must have felt a little guilty about withholding this valuable information about the farm in the first place and, as a result, seemed more conciliatory and prone to listen to mom. On the way home that evening, he promised that they would have a look at the property next day. True to his word, early the next day my parents attended church services in High Prairie and detoured to the prospective property. Although some of the farm soil appeared to be marginal in quality, the southern portion of the quarter-section was under cultivation and looked fine. There were a couple of farm buildings on the property and the adjacent homesteads were occupied by settlers. Even better, the distance to Gilwood School was only two miles.

That fall dad took the decision to sell the Aggie homestead and purchase the Gilwood farm for $650, thereby adding fifty acres of cultivated land to the existing thirty-four acres. Considering that all of the farm work was being done by horses, dad felt that this was about all he could handle. By this time Maria had completed her sixth grade and was no longer required to attend school. This made it convenient for my parents to continue the homesteading operation in the Aggie Settlement while at the same time making the old house on the new farm sufficiently habitable so that we could reside in it until the operations would be wrapped up in the Aggie Settlement, some time in the new year.

Operating two households was not easy and my parents wondered if they had made the right decision. There was the matter of ensuring that the new home was stocked with groceries, firewood, beds and bedding, and clothing for the children. As difficult as was the move, mom felt comfortable with the knowledge that the children would soon be in school.

My first day of school in late October was unforgettable and even today I have mixed emotions about events surrounding the registration. The year was 1942 and World War II had been raging for three years. As a seven-year-old, I had heard a lot about the war by listening to my dad in conversation with other settlers and especially through my visits with him to the home of Ollie Olafson. My dad said very little about the war. In fact, insofar as his children were concerned, he was not very much of a conversationalist. In those days, you did not discuss matters with your parents. You listened very carefully and spoke only when spoken to and then only in the proper way. You never addressed your parents or a person in a position of responsibility by using the familiar second person pronoun *tu (short u)*. Instead, it was drilled into every child that you show respect by using the plural form of the personal pronoun, *vu (short u)*. When it came my dad's turn to register his children, the first question from the teacher, Miss Melnyk was, *"...are these three youngsters your children?"*

"Yes, yes," replied my dad, cap in hand. After all, it was always my dad's belief that one should never wear a cap or hat indoors. To do so would show disrespect. In fact, my dad was always very fussy when it came to head wear. He always insisted that there was a particular way to hold your cap; you never ever placed it up-side-down on a hanger or on a shelf. I was at a loss as to whether this was military-learned behaviour or a tradition. Maybe it had something to do with religious beliefs.

"And, the oldest daughter, what is her name?"

"Her name is Hanya. Anna in English, I think," answered my dad.

"What is her middle name?"

"Middle name? She has no middle name."

Well, it was a good thing that the teacher's mother tongue was also Ukrainian. Whenever my dad experienced difficulty in understanding English, she would address him in Ukrainian, just to make certain that he understood. *'Good for her,'* I thought, *'at least now I will be able to understand some of their conversation.'* Dad proceeded to enrol Anne, Vasyl, and me by providing the teacher with our names, ages, and dates of birth. Registering Anne was not a problem. Her name, in Ukrainian or in English, was always Anne. With my brother, Vasyl, I noted that the teacher and my dad agreed that the translation of his name would be Bill. Then, it was my turn to be registered. After a long pause, *"Slawko."*

"But, Mr. Kashuba," asked the teacher, *"what is Slawko's English name?"*

"Can't I register him as Slawko?"

"I suppose you could if you really insisted. But, the School District has asked me to make every effort to register all pupils using their English names."

"Then, I really do not know the English translation," responded my dad. More discussion followed as other parents waited anxiously to register their children. I recall my dad saying that a family had a son by the name of Yaroslav and that he believed the English translation was Carson. Since Slawko was one of the short forms for the name Yaroslav, he must have deduced that Carson would be a reasonable translation. So, at the end of the discussion, it was agreed that I would be registered by the name of Carson. The next bit of information my dad provided the teacher was my date of birth. *"Yes,"* he said, *"he was born on January 7, 1935."* On this day of registration, Anne was twelve, Bill nine, and I was seven coming on eight. Maria, now sixteen years of age, was not required to attend school.

As difficult as was the school registration process for dad, it was even more awkward for the three of us. After all, English was totally foreign to us. And, this is why we had quite a surprise awaiting us. Immediately after registration, just as my dad was taking his seat on the wagon for the return trip to the farm, he called us over to the side of the wagon and said, in Ukrainian of course, "від тепер говоріть по англійському в школі," which means from now on you shall speak only English in school. *"And at home,"* he added, *"you will speak only in Ukrainian."* No questions. No discussion. That's the way it was. There was rarely any discussion on any topic. In a Ukrainian home it was a given that a child never questioned the authority of a parent. Parents gave the orders and the children carried them out. I have often thought about that moment and asked myself, how was it that my father suddenly wanted us to use English *only* in the classroom? Wasn't he aware that most Ukrainian pioneers wanted to preserve their mother tongue and encourage their children to use the Ukrainian language as often as possible? What motivated him to insist that we use only the English language in the classroom? Did school policy support his actions or was it a shared experience of other Ukrainian pioneers? These were perplexing questions.

Looking back, I can only conclude that my dad made that particular decision based upon his own experiences. Unlike so many other immigrants who came to Canada with the hopes of preserving all of the customs and traditions of their homeland, dad wanted us to become proud Canadians. That, however, is not to say that he allowed English to be spoken at the home or church. In those cases, he insisted that the language of communication be Ukrainian. To underscore the importance of the Ukrainian language, three years later mom enrolled us in a church-operated Ukrainian language summer camp. In the meantime, my parents wanted what was best for us in a new land while at the same time doing everything in their power to ensure the preservation of the Ukrainian language and customs in the home, church, and within *the Ukrainian community*. I was able to make one other interesting observation. My parents must have suspected that children of Ukrainian heritage were often held up to abuse and ridicule. Being proud parents, they did not wish this to happen to their children and, as a result, supported the concept of integration.

In part, I do believe that my dad formulated his position on the subject of languages when he worked in Bruderheim. Apparently, a co-worker told him that nearby school districts, which experienced a high enrolment of Ukrainian children, decided to put into place a strict language policy—*no Ukrainian was to be spoken in the classroom*. Not even on the school grounds. For one thing, this was one way of ensuring that the teacher knew what was being said. For another, it was one way of providing at least one English-language environment for the student who might otherwise be exposed to Ukrainian only. My dad did not want his children to be punished and humiliated for speaking their own language or to end up with the belief that there was something undesirable and unworthy about one's mother tongue.

If nothing else, the manner in which my parents handled the question of language piqued my interest. In fact, it would be from situations such as this that I would develop a curiosity about the place of birth of my parents and the circumstances that shaped their lives and attitudes. They often talked about the Old Country and a faraway place called Ukraine. I recall asking myself the question, *just where is this place called the Old Country? Halychyna? Ukraine?* Their love for their homeland never diminished, for it was here that their attitudes must have been shaped. I hoped that one day I would have the opportunity to learn more about the source of their unusually strong beliefs. In the meantime, I knew better than to ask any questions about their childhood, their heritage, or the rationale for their decisions.

True, I often heard my parents speak proudly of their Ukrainian heritage but rarely, if ever, about their Polish heritage. Yet, I did know that they were fluent in both languages. In fact, it would not be until years later that I would discover that my parents came to Canada with Polish passports. *How then*, I asked myself, *is it that they continually claimed Ukrainian ethnicity without any explanation about Poland, the country from which they emigrated?* Some of this information came to me years later when I reviewed my parents' responses in their application for Canadian Citizenship as well as from documents *they* completed when they applied for an exit visa from Poland--information they never shared with their children. Perhaps they thought it was none of our business. Maybe they wanted a new start in Canada and did not want to saddle their children with the memories and the hurts of the Old Country. Up until that time I simply assumed that my parents *did* come from Ukraine. It would not be until many years later that I would begin to fully understand the life and times of my parents.

Even living in faraway Canada, my parents were wary of the long tentacles of the Soviet Regime and preferred to say as little as possible about the political situation in the Old Country. In fact, my parents have often said that the simple act of sending a letter to Poland or to Soviet Ukraine after World War II was not without risk. For instance, if they were to send a letter to a relative criticizing *their* government and the letter were to be opened by authorities, it was unlikely that my parents would be punished, however, that is not to say that the recipient of that letter would not be earmarked for surveillance and punishment.

Also of interest is the protocol used by authorities in Eastern Bloc countries in processing passports for its citizens. An individual was required to first list their ethnicity followed by the country of residence. As an example, if your mother tongue was Hungarian and you lived in Austro-Hungary, you would list Hungarian as your language followed by the country of residence. However, the policy of the Polish government during the inter-war period was quite at odds with this policy. Polish authorities, after World War I, made it a policy to encourage its residents to learn Polish *and* to list Polish as *their* language. One thing was clear; the exit documents for my parents show *Poland* to be their country of origin and *Ukrainian Greek Catholic as their religion.*

This explains why the first Ukrainians who came to Canada in 1891 with fresh and painful memories of the impediments to the development of their national identity in their oppressed homeland experienced a similar difficulty in a new land. For many of them, the question was, *'from what country did I come?'* If they came from the Austro-Hungarian Empire, they might have listed Austria or Hungary on their documents. But, their ethnicity would likely have been shown as Ruthenian, Polish, Russian or German.

Further, it should be noted that the use of the word *Ukrainian* did not come into common usage until after World War I. As a result, from a Canadian statistical point of view, it is only after World War I that a person's ethnicity would have been shown as Ukrainian. To further complicate the question, if an immigrant came from Poland after World War I, it is unlikely that their ethnicity would have been listed anything *other than Polish!* As for the Ukrainian Soviet Socialist Republic, political events of the day made it nearly impossible to emigrate to any country between the years of 1945 to 1991. The only exception appears to be the small number of refugees from German or Austrian camps who found their way to Canada after World War II.

But, all of this is history. It was not the custom of my parents to dwell upon the past, riddled with painful memories. They grew up under very different circumstances where loose talk could lead to dire consequences. It was an expectation that a person living during those bygone times in a region ripe with political upheavals would cultivate the skills of listening and not speaking. It was much safer to keep one's thoughts to oneself. For many of those who did not, they suddenly disappeared from the face of the earth.

With the influx of a large number of settlers to the west and south of the village of High Prairie in the late 1920s and early 1930s, a need for a local school was evident. As a result, several residents agitated for their own school. Unlike modern day school divisions and larger urban school districts, during those early pioneer days it was the policy of Alberta's Department of Education to first establish the need for a school before creating a school district and building a school. As was the case with so many other settlements throughout Alberta, the school had to be within walking distance of most of the children. With this in mind, the West Prairie School District No. 4465 was created. Located just seven miles southwest of High Prairie, it would serve its first class of pupils in the 1931-32 school year. As was typical, all those who enrolled in the school for the first time during the first year of its operation started in grade one, no matter whether the child was six years of age, ten, or twelve. Promotion during and after the first year was not only based upon performance but on the age of the pupil as well.

Built of logs by the pioneers, West Prairie School would serve the settlers for four years. During those initial years of operation, instruction was provided by one teacher, Hermie Martin. By 1935 the school boasted an enrolment of twenty pupils in grades one to six. For those wanting to continue their education beyond grade six, or after they surpassed the compulsory school attendance age, they would have to do so in a junior or senior high school in the village of High Prairie. The life of this very first school in the Gilwood district was sadly interrupted in 1935 when it burned down. It was soon replaced by another log structure in 1936 and continued to operate as a one-room, multi-grade elementary school until after World War II.

Building a school was one matter but recruiting a qualified school teacher was quite another. Good teachers were hard to recruit in new settlements and keeping one on staff for any length of time was quite a challenge. For many of Alberta's schools, the provision of qualified instruction was once again interrupted with the outbreak of the war in 1939. To make matters worse, any young male teacher who wanted to launch a teaching career might suddenly find himself in the Canadian military. In fact, over the next six years, this seemed to be the fate of several teachers recruited by the West Prairie School District.

Following registration, Miss Olga Melnyk prepared a seating list for the pupils. This was done with regard for grade and age. *"Bill and Carson,"* she stated, *"you will be joined at this desk by George Belyan."* The desk assigned to the three of us had two parts; a lower bench seat and the upper table-like writing area. The writing portion was hinged and sloped towards the bench seat and by lifting it we could store our school books and lunch pails. When dad earlier said that I would have to use English in school, I wanted to practice a couple of words. Turning to Bill, I said, *"Hello, my name is Carson."* With that, my formal education began.

My first day of school ran the gamut of emotions. First of all, seeing so many strangers in one large room was stressful. Everything about the school was new; everything from hearing English being spoken to having to share a desk with two other pupils. To ease my discomfort, it seemed that only a small number of pupils claimed their mother tongue to be English. As the day wore on, I began to feel more comfortable with not being able to speak English; I was not the only pupil in that predicament. Other than two or three pupils, it appeared as though the mother tongue of the majority was Slavic. Imagine, twenty-four pupils enrolled in a one-room school in grades one to six where a large percentage of the pupils did not know English! If that wasn't challenging enough, consider being a teacher and having to structure an educational program for so diverse a group. The youthful teacher was like a football coach calling out orders, making sure that each pupil was busy. To facilitate learning, she did not discourage quiet discussion among the pupils during the first few weeks of school or using Ukrainian where necessary or desirable.

However, Miss Melnyk soon discovered that she would need assistance if she were to deliver a quality educational program to so diverse a group. Slowly, she began to develop a unique system for delivering a program to suit a full range of individual needs by getting the assistance of pupils in grade six. Older students helping younger students with their alphabet, enunciation, pronunciation and reading skills. In particular, the teacher found it useful to structure a *buddy-system* wherein an older student would be paired off with a grade one pupil who needed assistance. There were very few learning materials in the school and most were well worn. At long last, additional learning materials were brought in from an elementary school in High Prairie. However, pupils were required to bring their own scribblers and pencils. For some, even this expenditure was a hardship, especially in cases where a family suddenly found itself sending two or three children to school where previously none had attended.

Whatever the three of us learned in school was reinforced on the walk home. And, without any interruption from a radio or television, there was little competition for our time at home. Immediate reinforcement and the belief that mistakes could be made without retribution hastened the learning process. In short order, there we were, chattering away in English and learning to read and write those simple words that were composed of one syllable. I loved those first days of school, in part because I was required to do fewer farm chores. Schooling became very important to us. Why? Because mom told us over and over again that it was. I suppose she saw in her children the realization of a dream that she had for herself in Plazow. Dreams that never came true due to prevailing economic conditions and political circumstances.

Those first days of school, however, will forever be remembered not so much for their educational content but for what was happening on the world's stage. At least three of the students in the school reported that their older brothers were serving Canada in the army. As a result, the war took centre stage while schooling was too often put on the back burner. In fact, it was not uncommon for the teacher to introduce a topic to the grade six students which did not appear on the curriculum but which brought in some aspect of the war. Even the children in grade one, who spoke very little English, were soon able to assimilate a lot of information that was very new and interesting.

As the Christmas season approached, the winter days really got cold. Suddenly, the two-mile walk to school was no longer a stroll in the park. Since we took a shortcut through two adjacent homesteads, the walk was considerably shorter than the two miles by road. Unlike today's modern school buildings, this particular one-room school was heated by a large potbellied wood-burning heater. Naturally, the teacher did not want to be the one to light the fire in the morning; this was left to one of the pupils enrolled in grade six. In most instances, the volunteer was a student who lived relatively close to the school. Living two miles away from the school had some advantages; this was one of them.

Maria was now the *chief cook and bottle washer,* but as might be expected, she was not an accomplished cook. We soon discovered that things simply were not the same without mom, who could take a pot of potatoes, serve them up with sour cream and cottage cheese and make them taste heavenly. Although Maria tried her level best, she could not master this particular art or that of making *pyrohy* and *holuptsi.* And most certainly she should not have baked that bread at such a high temperature, burnt on the outside yet virtually raw on the inside. The lunches, too, left much to be desired. The menu was very limited; bacon sandwiches interspersed with baloney and beef. And, yes, I do recall how my parents insisted on the redeeming qualities of *salo;* cured pork belly served on home-made bread. Thank goodness for mustard, otherwise there is some doubt as to whether or not we would have eaten them at all. Maybe my sister was trying to get the message out to us; she simply did not want to succeed at her new role. However, with each passing week, her cooking did improve. By the Christmas break I would have to give her a passing grade.

Just about the time that the school broke for the Christmas holidays, mom and dad closed down the home at Aggie and joined the rest of the family at the Gilwood location. Instead of the four of us, we now had seven family members in a relatively small house. It took us quite some time to get accustomed to the cramped quarters. In fact, the large home-made bunk bed with straw to serve as a mattress was now made to accommodate Bill, Andy and me. But, that wasn't so bad after all, especially on those cold winter nights.

That year, Christmas turned out to be very different. Up until that time the family had always celebrated Christmas Eve on January 6 in accordance with the Julian calendar and the Eastern Orthodox Church. The West Prairie School District made it a policy that Christmas would be celebrated on December 25. Not only that, but I learned that it was a common practice for parents to buy their children Christmas presents. That had never happened before in our family where Christmas had always been celebrated to honour the birth of Christ. Still, I liked this new idea. I liked it because we exchanged names in the school. The plan was that each pupil would be required to buy one gift for the person they drew from a box. I noted that senior students got into the habit of exchanging names with others in the class until they ended up with the name of a friend. That, to them, would make the buying and exchanging of a Christmas gift more meaningful. I was happy with the name I drew. At least it was not a girl.

All too soon, the Christmas holidays were over and it was back to school. The only problem was, no one could find the teacher; it seemed as though she had disappeared as if into thin air. The days came and the days went and still no teacher. Finally, after three weeks of this, the word came down from the school district office that Miss Melnyk had taken herself a husband over the Christmas holidays. She was now trying her best to prevent her husband from going off to war. It would not be until early February that she would be replaced with another teacher. However, even Miss Berta Martin, the new teacher who was a recent graduate of a Normal School, could not guarantee the district that she would be able to complete the school year. After all, Canada's effort to win the war might well have an impact upon her career plans.

Anne was promoted to grade two by the time Christmas holidays arrived while Bill and I would not be promoted until March. In those days, it seemed that a pupil did not have to wait until the end of the year to be promoted; promotion was based on scholastic performance and age. I guess I qualified in both categories. The first year of school taught me much more than that which was contained in the school's curriculum. When you were a member of a family, it became an expectation that you would look after your brothers and sisters. Even more important, you learned that you had to look after yourself first. Since no one in the community had a telephone, it was not good enough to simply do your own thing. It was a custom to join the neighbours' kids along the route to school where we learned to rely on one another for safety and for companionship. Most of all, we developed a very close bond with the knowledge that we could count on one another in times of need.

Except for the underclothes, the clothing that we wore to school was sewn by mom. She finally got her wish; a new Singer sewing machine. True, it was manually operated deriving its power from a foot pedal but it certainly beat the alternative of stitching the material by hand. In most cases, mom did not require a commercially-produced pattern to sew the various items of clothing. In cases where one was required, she found that some other pioneer woman in the Gilwood farming community had a desirable pattern. If the size was wrong, she knew just how to adjust it for a perfect fit. Unfortunately, the three of us often ended up wearing the same coloured shirts and pants. This did lead to some good-natured teasing. Having mastered the art of sewing, mom turned to knitting wool sweaters.

A small number of the students would occasionally come to school on horseback or by a specially-made horse-drawn sleigh called a *cutter*. However, this became a bit of a problem since the horses, secured to an out-of-doors hitching post, had to be covered with a horse blanket on cold days. On rare occasions dad would take us to school on a horse-drawn sleigh. On days when the temperature plummeted to minus thirty Celsius, we dressed in our long woolen underwear and felt boots and walked to school. The brisk walk kept us warmer.

During the days of spring breakup, walking to school was another matter. Unlike the high-grade or elevated highways of today, the road leading to the school was constructed at ground level. Any amount of melting snow and you would get the formation of puddles and even large pools of water, some of which would stretch for quite a distance. In many cases, it was not possible to detour around all of the puddles. As a consequence, it was not uncommon for us to get thoroughly soaked by the time we arrived in school. Just about the time we got dried out, it was time to head back home. On other occasions, one of us would wear dad's knee-high rubber boots and, in turn, carry one sibling, then another over the puddles. Sometimes, we used the excuse that the puddles were so bad that the only way to get across them was on horseback. On those occasions, dad would allow us to ride a workhorse to school.

There was much to be learned in the great out-of-doors. It was no secret that the senior students in the school wanted to control the younger kids. These were not gangs by any stretch of the imagination but *small clicky* groups formed around this or that pupil whose aim it was to develop control over another group. The basis for the formation would often be along ethnic, religious, or geographic lines. If you lived west of Prairie River School, you belonged to the Shadow Creek gang. If you came from the area east of the school, you belonged to the West Prairie River gang. It would not be until upper elementary that belonging to one of these groups became important as a means of avoiding physical confrontations with other groups. Of course, if you came from a relatively large family you had much less to fear than did the student who had the misfortune of having no brothers or sisters.

The federal government was in the process of enacting legislation that would provide for compulsory training for those in the appropriate age bracket and in good health. It was during one of these discussions that Maria confided in mom and dad that a couple of the young bachelors in High Prairie hastened to get married as soon as possible just to escape active duty. She said that in some cases a young man could be excused from military duty if his services were very important to the family. Mom asked Maria if she had it in her mind to save some young man from military duty. She seemed not to hear the question.

Many of the settlers supplemented their diet with wild game such as moose, upland birds, deer, or rabbit. However, unlike some of the other settlers, dad and mom preferred the consumption of grains, poultry, pork, beef, and vegetables; items that were readily available to a mixed farmer. Even at that, any neighbour who shot a moose or a deer would often share their good fortune with others. Mom and dad did not like the taste of wild game even though some of the settlers believed that wild rabbit tasted much like chicken. Besides, for Bill and me, rabbits were a source of spending money. Their hides were worth five cents each.

By the spring of 1943, the farming operation moved to Gilwood; however, dad continued to cultivate the homestead in Aggie for another two years. Since the farming operation was becoming increasingly profitable, he also decreased the number of hours worked on the NAR. When the family got its first radio, the family dynamics seemed to change drastically. Saturday nights were reserved for Foster Hewitt and Hockey Night in Canada and everyone's favourite team became the Toronto Maple Leafs; to pull for any other team seemed somehow un-Canadian. Bill and I seemed to get interested in the game at a very young age, in part because so many others fell in love with the sport. As was the case with some other kids, we knew the names of most every player in the National Hockey League.

And, every day right after school we would all hurry home to listen to those radio programs such as The Farmer and his talking parrot Jo-Jo, The Whistler, The Shadow Knows, and The Lone Ranger Rides Again. These were the programs that quickly captured the imagination of all children. On the other hand, dad was a news hound. Every night at six and eight found him intently listening to the news out of Grande Prairie. He wanted to hear the latest news about the war. It was not unusual for him to become very animated about a particular news item. When the Royal Canadian Navy sank a German sub off the west coast of Portugal, he was heard to yell *yes* as he punched the air with his fists.

The summer of 1943 turned out to be a very dry summer, especially in the Gilwood region. Even the farm well went dry. This made it necessary for mom to hitch up a couple of horses and haul water for the cattle from a neighbour's well or, alternatively, from the West Prairie River--both of which were about two miles from our home. In this way, the family would have a sufficient reserve of water for the horses, cattle, pigs, and chickens. On those days that water was required, it became mom's job, assisted by Bill and me, to ensure that we had a supply of water. Dad was away for the mid-summer months working on the NAR and Maria was working in a local restaurant. When mom noted that the rain barrels were empty, she said, *"come on, boys, we'll hitch up the horses and bring in a couple barrels of water today."*

In short order the three of us had the two barrels filled with good quality water from a well located on a neighbour's property. The last leg of the return wagon trail took us through a wooded area where the road forked around a large tree. To the right was a less travelled trail developed as an alternate to the main trail which had developed some very deep ruts during the previous year's rainy season. Even thinking about that fork in the road so many years later reminds me of some wisdom which came from the mouth of perhaps the greatest baseball catcher of them all, the New York Yankee's Yogi Berra, who was quoted as saying '*when you come to a fork in the road, take it.*' I believe that his words were prophetic. Mom was sitting in the front seat of the wagon box on a spring-loaded wagon seat. Bill and I sat on the sides of the wagon box keeping an eye on the two barrels of water, which were open at the top but topped off with short planks in order to minimize the spillage.

Suddenly, Prince and Topsy were spooked by something behind them. Whatever it was, they instantaneously broke into a gallop just before they reached the fork in the road. Caught unawares, it was impossible for mom to regain control of the horses. The two barrels of water seemed to be bouncing all over the place, while Bill and I tried desperately to control their action. It didn't seem to help much. Maybe mom thought that the best way to gain control of the horses was to let them run until they ran out of steam. Unfortunately, the unpredictable happened. One horse wanted to take the left fork while the other insisted on taking the right fork in the road. The wagon had no place to go but smack, bang into the centre of the tree which stood big and tall, separating the two forks of the road.

What a mess! The tongue of the wagon glanced off the tree and the left wheel of the wagon struck the tree bringing the wagon and the horses to a sudden stop. However, it seemed that the barrels had a mind of their own. They kept right on going. One barrel just missed mom to her left while the second one bounced off her hip as it was propelled through the front of the wagon box to her right. The cedar boards forming up the perimeter of the barrels were held together by three steel bands and these were no match for the tree. Both barrels collapsed into nothing more than a pile of loose lumber. *"Are you boys all right,"* mom cried out in pain. Having checked to ensure that we were not seriously injured, mom turned her attention to the horses, trying to disentangle them from the restraining harnesses. It took us the rest of the afternoon to pull the wagon away from the tree and to re-assemble the barrels which seemed none the worse for wear. We finally struggled home with the damaged wagon but the water would have to wait for another day.

That fall, school opening was late once again. But the settlers seemed not to mind; they were more interested in Canada's war effort than they were in the status of the local school. Increasingly, the news from the front was improving. For the first time in the war, Canadian troops were being successful. Allied leaders, Prime Minister King of Canada, Roosevelt of the United States, and Churchill of Great Britain met in Quebec City to discuss the progress of the war and to make plans for the future. By September, Italy signed an armistice and left the Axis Alliance even though the Germans continued their tight grip on Italy. By the end of the year, Canadian soldiers captured the Adriatic port of Ortona. On Christmas day, even as carols were sung, the battle raged on.

As 1944 was being rung in, the news kept getting worse for Hitler. News reports confirmed that Canadian infantry and tanks had smashed through the Hitler Line in Italy. This was followed by D-day when some 175,000 American, British, and Canadian soldiers landed in Normandy. The liberation of Europe had begun. The push on Germany continued into 1945. Somehow, and just for a glorious moment, much of this was forgotten when Maurice The Rocket Richard scored, on March 15, 1945, his 50th goal in 50 National Hockey League games. This mark of excellence in hockey would not be broken for many years to come.

During the war years, dad gave as much support as was possible to the war effort. It seemed as though all the Ukrainian pioneers in the region were behind those young boys who were serving Canada and the Allies. For some, it was not without some difficulty since Russia was on the side of the Allies while at the same time it was the spawning ground for the Bolshevik movement which had created so many problems for Ukraine's quest for its independence. In the Old Country, a person's society often extended no further than the village in which he lived and perhaps one or two neighbouring villages. Here, one had to think beyond making a few donations to the church and paying a few taxes. Since many of the communities were new, roads had to be built, school boards and village councils elected, and priests' salaries paid. As a result, a pioneer's whole life often seemed to depend upon politics.

There were those in the Slavic community who were drawn towards socialism. Perhaps the nemesis of some of these political thoughts came to Canada with those immigrants who harboured positive feelings about the equality of man and the supremacy of the worker. In fact, dad had heard of the strength of the communist movement in the Vegreville area of Alberta, in parts of Saskatchewan and in Manitoba. However, despite the pressure of a few neighbours to support a political candidate of socialist leanings, dad would have none of it. He was proud of the Union Jack and always expressed his support for all things Canadian. This attitude was not uncommon within the Ukrainian community, even though their status within the Anglo-Canadian society had, as yet, not been fully established. After all, High Prairie was not exactly in the main stream of political life in Canada. It never did stand witness to strikes and marches, to radical literature, or political rhetoric espousing the virtues of communism or socialism. Even the Ukrainian Social Democratic Party of Canada was not able to catch the ear of the locals.

If dad was not anxious to get involved in the political scene, mom was even less interested. A suffragette she was not! Her world rotated around improving the economic and educational condition of the family. Just about the time that she felt the war was over, she once again began to agitate for improvements to the location of the family's domicile. Andy came of school age and we now had four children attending Prairie River School. For sure, he had it much easier than we did! By this time, he could speak quite a number of words in English and he could use reading materials available at home in preparation for his first class. But, mom wanted better for the family saying, *"Look at some of our acquaintances and how well they are doing. The Nick Halaburda, John Lys and Herman Chemerinski families. Why? Because they have better land than we do."*

"Aren't you ever going to be happy with what you've got, Eva? When is this bossing me around going to stop?"

As coincidence would have it, mom was once again visiting the McCue farm where dad formed up a part of the threshing crew, now with his own team of horses. This gave mom an opportunity to exchange information with other farmers about who was selling land and who was buying and at what price. Mom knew that her children would soon be completing their education at Prairie River School and would have to attend a junior high school in High Prairie. In a discussion with Theodore Basarab, she found out that perhaps their family would be willing to sell the eastern-most quarter section of land from their vast land holdings. *"Besides,"* he added, *"this piece of property, although it has the finest black loam around being only one mile away from the East Prairie River, it does have a considerable amount of quack grass on it which makes it difficult to maximize crop yield."*

At first, dad would have none of it. He disliked being overly influenced by mom, all the while railing about mom's constant grumbling. However, mom would simply not give in. Finally, dad gave in, hoping that he would prove just how wrong she was about this property. That evening they drove over to see the quarter section, which was about three miles east of the McCue farm. No sooner had they arrived than dad knew he should never have consented to this visit. For, like mom, he was very impressed with the property. It was completely under cultivation and the soil looked very productive. However, he wasn't going to make it easy for mom, pointing out all of the reasons why they should not consider another move. But, mom would not take no for an answer, saying, *"At the present, it is too far for the children to walk to school in High Prairie. Without motorized transportation, how will they get to school?"*

Finally, having made the decision to purchase the Enilda property, dad consummated the sale of the Aggie homestead for $650 and concentrated his efforts on raising additional funds through his continued work on the railroad. Meanwhile, at the end of each school day, Bill and I became woodcutters. Our task was to cut, split, and market, for a price of $3, one cord (4' x 4' x 8') of wood each week. Selling the first load of firewood was a bit of a challenge; however, the sale of subsequent loads was much easier. Once a routine was established and a steady clientele developed, the small business venture became quite lucrative. When we learned the value of providing a good service, many of our clients became repeat customers. When delivered, we piled the wood into a neat stack and made sure that it was of high quality weather-dried wood.

As time went on, even mom got involved in the marketing program by putting together a parcel of products such as fresh and sour cream, cottage cheese, eggs and poultry that we could market on a weekly basis along with the wood. The sale of these products defrayed all of the family's living expenses as well as any costs associated with schooling. In turn, all of the monies that dad made went directly towards the purchase of the new farm.

For those families living in the West Prairie School District attendance area in 1944, the news on the scheduled school-opening day was not good. A recent report indicated that 500 one-room schools in rural Alberta, Manitoba, and Saskatchewan would not open their doors to students because of a teacher shortage. Would Prairie River School be next? As parents waited for some assurance that a teacher would be in place for the ensuing year, the news from the war front was much better when Canadian solders liberated Dieppe on September 1.

Eventually, a teacher was put into place at Prairie River School for the 1944-45 school term. Since the demand for teachers far outstripped supply, the school board could not guarantee that the teacher would be there for the full school year. Obviously, the war effort was taking its toll. In mid-winter of 1945, after three months of quiet, Canadian troops again advanced into Germany hoping to meet the Russian Red Army which was now only 100 kilometres from Berlin. It was not until May 7, 1945, that the news of Hitler's death would be beamed across the world as German forces were giving up on all fronts. To a large degree, the final chapter for the Third Reich had been written about three weeks earlier when on April 16 the Soviets launched their final offensive. In nine more days the Russian troops would meet up with the American troops on the River Elbe.

For my parents, the excitement of Canada's successes in the war effort was made all the sweeter with the birth of yet another child. Lily Eva was born on February 12, the last child to be born to my mother at home.

Binder at work, Edmonton district. Source: Provincial Archives, Edmonton, Alberta, B334.

West Prairie School, 1944. Source: High Prairie & Area History Book Society.

Transporting logs to homestead on a sleigh. Source: Glenbow Archives, Calgary, Alberta. NA 3 09190.

Cutting wood mechanically, High Prairie, Alberta, 1952.

26.

Lost in a Blizzard

The unpredictability of Canadian winters

T he purchase price of the Basarab quarter section, municipally described as the *SE quarter of section 16, township 74, range 16, W of the 5ᵗʰ meridian, containing 160 acres,*[29] was $4,000 of which $2,500 was paid in cash and the balance carried for a period of one year at an interest rate of five percent. Its location, six miles east of High Prairie and three miles west of Enilda, was ideal. Well served with municipal roads, adjacent to the main highway and with a soil rating of #1 agricultural, the title to the property was transferred on September 20, 1945, just seventeen years after dad first came to Canada. There was one sad note attached to the purchase; George Basarab was saving this farm for his son, Louis, who unfortunately became a casualty of the war in Germany in 1944, just six months before the celebration of VE Day on May 5, 1945. With a heavy heart, George Basarab decided to sell the property.

Since the farm had no permanent buildings on it, dad decided to dismantle the two buildings previously constructed at the Aggie Settlement and move these to the new location. This was accomplished by cutting into eight-foot wide sections the shingled roofs of the house and the granary and transporting these, by sleigh, to the Enilda property. Similarly, every log of the walls was carefully numbered, dismantled and also transported to the new farm. By the end of March and just before the snows melted, the move of the two buildings was completed.

I can still recall how dad worried about his decision to buy the property at

---

29   High Prairie & Area History Book Society, <u>Trails We Blazed Together, History of Grouard, High Prairie & Surrounding Areas</u>, Herff Jones of Canada, 1997, p. 685.

so high a price, realizing at the same time that he would have to mechanize the farming operation because he would not be able to complete the task in a timely fashion using horses. It seemed always to be contest as to which would come first, the completion of the farming operation or the first snowfall. As dad prepared for the spring planting, he felt confident that the 1946 crop yield, with increasing grain prices, would generate sufficient funds to make good his indebtedness. In the meantime, the family took up temporary residence on the Freeman property. It would not be until the summer of 1946 that the two buildings from the Aggie homestead would be re-assembled and a barn and machine shed added.

As World War II came to a close, servicemen began coming home—at least those who survived the conflict. There was but one more battle to be fought and that was the one with Japan. Without this final victory, World War II could not be brought to its final conclusion. It would not be until the Americans dropped an atomic bomb on Hiroshima that Japan would surrender on August 14, 1945. And, for the first time, dad began to talk about the possibility of buying his first farm tractor; maybe even a truck and more land.

In many ways, the move from Gilwood to Enilda came at a very good time. There was a drastic shortage of teachers which eventually led to the closing of West Prairie School in favour of the Consolidated School in High Prairie. From September, 1944 to February of 1945, the very best that West Prairie School could do was to provide school correspondence services under the supervision of Gladys Williscroft, a young Correspondence School Supervisor. The closure of the school was delayed for a period of time when, in May and June of 1945, Jean McGillis was brought on staff only to be replaced in July and August by Marie Hughes. By 1946, Marie was replaced by Berta Martin (who initially came on staff in 1942) and by George Nelson in 1946-47. However, before the school finally did close, our family had already moved to another school attendance district and we were soon enrolled in a more modern school in the village of High Prairie.

At the time of the move, Bill and I had completed grade four and were promoted to grade five while Andy was promoted to grade three. Anne did better; she skipped another grade of school and was promoted to grade six. For us, the last day at West Prairie School should have been a happy one, but it wasn't. We had come to like the school and the friends we made. Those first years of schooling from 1942 to 1945 would help us formulate some very important habits and learn two important lessons; first, the degree of success *was* directly related to the amount of work invested and the second, not all education took place in the classroom. World War II had left its mark in the battlefields of Europe and in our classrooms. But, all of that was behind us now. The future looked very bright.

When the 1945-46 school year opened, the Consolidated School District in High Prairie informed the parents of children in our immediate area that they would be transported to and from school by a horse-drawn covered van.

During summer months, this van would be mounted on rubber-tired wheels while during winter months it would be mounted on a sleigh. The owner and operator of the van turned out to be Mike Porisky, our next-door neighbour.[30] In all, the van could transport about fifteen youngsters. We found it convenient to walk the half mile from the Freeman farm home directly south through our vacant farm property to the Porisky residence, the start of the van route. There, we would board the van and collect another dozen farm kids on the seven mile route to the elementary school in High Prairie.

The Consolidated School in High Prairie was in stark contrast to the one-room school in Gilwood which housed 24 students from grades one through six. Bill and I were now enrolled in a split class of grade five and six students and in a school that housed over a hundred students under the tutorship of eight qualified teachers. Although my teacher said that this was a better arrangement than was the one-room school, I missed the opportunity of helping a grade one pupil or receiving assistance from a grade six student. However, it did not take me long to begin to appreciate the advantages of the new environment. For one thing, the teacher was able to spend more time with those students who were experiencing difficulties with their studies.

There was something else very different about the Consolidated School. When I looked around at the other students, the ethnic mix was very different from that of my previous school. Where in the past most of the students were first generation Canadians of Slavic descent, we now had a mixture of English, Scottish, Scandinavian, German, Slav, Metis and native students and the parents of many of the students had resided in the district for a number of years or were transplanted from the prairies. At first, this matter of belonging to a minority ethnic group made me feel a bit uneasy. *Would the English students accept me? Would I be treated like a second-class citizen? Belittled and teased?* I recalled my dad saying that other schools in Alberta were experiencing varying degrees of problems with minority groups. *Would I be one of them?* Still, I noted that the village of High Prairie was a very young community and that most everyone came from somewhere. This made it easier for me to fit into a diverse group of students.

As time went on, any student who felt uneasy about their heritage soon discovered that others were experiencing a similar problem, especially the native children. Sometimes a student was criticized by his peers for the way in which he pronounced an English word. At other times, someone would get teased about the manner of their dress or when wearing a homemade shirt. Still, being a good academic student with a keen interest in schooling and athletics helped to ensure that I would fit in quite well in my new environment.

Shortly after I celebrated my eleventh birthday in January of 1946, I was

30 Centennial Book Committee, F.W.U.A High Prairie Local 204, Pioneers Who Blazed The Trail, Mike Porisky Story, 1967, p. 267.

The daily chore of milking cows. Source: Provincial Archives, Edmonton, Alberta.

Consolidated School, High Prairie, Alberta. Source: <u>High Prairie & Area History Book Society.</u>

Horse-drawn school van operated by the Keshen family during the 1940s. Source: <u>High Prairie & Area History Book Society.</u>

looking forward to attending school and playing some outdoor winter soccer. It was an unusually cold week and this particular day was no different. The Freeman house was not too well insulated and early that morning the wind seemed to pass right through the walls as though they were a sieve, all the while making peculiar whistling sounds. Still, the farm house was rather well protected from the northwesterly winds because of its location near a stand of trees, evergreens and willows. As was our custom, the route to the school van would take us directly south from the Freeman home, across our quarter section of land and on to the Porisky residence for pickup and transport to High Prairie. Since not all of us would finish breakfast at the same time, it was not unusual for Anne and Andy to start their walk to the school van in advance of Bill and me.

No sooner had we left the protection of the farm buildings than we were into a good old-fashioned country blizzard. We knew that Anne and Andy were just ahead of us as we tried to follow their tracks. But, we found this to be impossible. Looking behind us, we noticed that our own tracks were quickly obliterated by the blizzard conditions and drifting snow. Although we were but a short distance from our house, we could scarcely see the light from the coal oil lamp. The whole world seemed to be swallowed by the blizzard. What to do? Turn back or continue, knowing that Anne and Andy were somewhere else ahead of us? We looked skyward for some sign of the sun to establish our direction. There *was* no sign of the sun. But for the wind, we would not be able to tell the direction in which we were walking. Here it was nearly eight-thirty and it was still pitch black out there. The storm made it look as though it were the middle of a dark night.

Bill and I huddled for a moment to decide whether we should return to the house or continue our journey. To turn back, we decided, might compromise the safety of Anne and Andy should they get into some difficulty in the blizzard. Not wanting to be called sissies in the event that they should show up at the van and we did not, we made a decision to continue. The snow drifts, in some places, were waist high and progress was slow. Subconsciously, I knew that we should have reached the property line by this time. We again paused to discuss the matter. Finally, when we did reach the fence, we realized that we were completely off course.

Panic set in. In which direction had we wandered? Was it east or west? *"West,"* shouted Bill. That being the case, we continued west along the fence line in hopes of making it safely to the Greer residence located just west of the Freeman farm. Our hands were cold. So were our feet. We were thankful that we wore our fur-lined and hooded parkas. The hoods were pulled tightly over our faces and tied snugly with a cord. To retrace our steps could well be fatal. It was no longer a case of looking forward to helping Anne and Andy; it was now a simple case of survival. Our only hope was to keep moving.

When the fence line took a ninety-degree turn to the north, we knew that we had reached the corner of the Freeman property and were now following the boundary of the Greer-Freeman property line. Still no sign of the sun. As we struggled along the Greer fence line, we peered very hard to the west in the hopes of spotting the Greer farm buildings. No such luck! We stuck to our plan and continued our walk northward. When we reached a grove of shrubs, trees, and willows, we knew that we had reached the north perimeter of the farm. Not only that, but with the increased amount of wind-break, we could now see several feet in front of us. At that point we began to follow the north boundary of the Freeman property in an easterly direction.

We covered the northern boundary of the Freeman property in a relatively short period of time and then made a ninety degree turn to the south. When we finally made it to the house, it was nearly eleven o'clock. Anne and Andy were happy to see us; mom was overjoyed as she applied some coal oil to our frostbitten fingers and toes. Slowly, ever so slowly, the feeling seemed to come back to those frostbitten areas. We were finally ready for some chicken soup and our school sandwiches!

And what of Anne and Andy? Well, Anne proved herself to be a very good decision-maker in a time of crisis. When the two of them reached the fence line, they changed their minds about going on and made a turn to the left following the fence line to the southeast corner, then north to the roadway and back to the house. They were back at the house by eight-thirty, less than an hour from the time they left the house. As for Bill and me, we spent nearly three hours in the blizzard. It was at that moment that I gained a new respect for Anne. This would not be the only time that she would show good judgment.

Since dad was doing some work for the railroad, he did not hear of our heroics for a couple of weeks. When told about the near-tragedy by mom, he looked at us with a twinkle in his eye. Even though he said nothing, I knew that he must have been very proud of us. Later, mom told us that he expected nothing less.

At that point, I thought that the cold weather and bad luck were well behind me. But, that was not to be. Dad had already decided that he would need about 4,000 board feet of lumber to build new structures on the farm. Today, a farmer might go directly to a lumber outlet and purchase the required supplies. But, in those days, a farmer was more apt to find a way to saw his own lumber from a stand of fir trees on his own property or from that of his neighbour. Such was the case with dad. Discussions followed and in a few days he had the consent of Wasylchuk for the fir logs and another neighbour to saw and plane the logs–all for the price of one thousand board feet of lumber. Needing considerable assistance to fall, trim and cut to length the fir trees, dad announced that the activity would take place during Easter holidays in late March. On the day before the Easter break, he announced, *"All right, boys, tomorrow morning, we'll take our supplies and head on out to the Wasylchuk homestead. Once there, we can stay overnight in the abandoned Wasylchuk cabin or at Badan's."*

Being accustomed to cutting firewood with the Swedish cross-cut saw, Bill and I felt that the planned tasks would not be too much for us. Dad calculated that it would take about two days of work to compile a sufficient number of logs for intended purposes and another couple of days, at a later time, to haul these to a sawmill. In preparation for the trip, mom packed a quilt, pillows, and food while dad loaded some hay and oats for the two horses. As we left home early on March 22, the weather continued to be warm with the temperature hovering around the freezing mark. The weather reports out of radio station CFGP in Grande Prairie were also encouraging for the weekend. But then, how could anyone rely on weather reports? In those days, weather reports were not an exact science.

As the sun broke out of the east, we were just passing through the village of High Prairie. The hooves of the horses made a crunching sound in the snow as they clippity-clopped along. During the eleven-kilometre sleigh ride to the fir stand, I thought about the food mom had packed; home-baked bread, cured bacon, a large pot of soup, pre-cooked ham, coffee, butter, and milk. It seemed as though it might be a trip to a nearby lake for ice fishing rather than on an important work mission. Knowing that the weather can take a turn for the worse, all three of us were warmly dressed in parkas, long underwear, toques, leather mitts with woollen under-mitts, and felt boots. Whenever we felt a little chilled, Bill and I would get out and then walk behind the sleigh swinging our arms across our bodies as if to encourage a better circulation of blood.

The last leg of the sleigh ride took us along the railway, through the whistle stop at Aggie and into the Aggie Settlement. By one o'clock we were on site and ready for a lunch break before commencing our tasks. Earlier, we noticed that the Wasylchuk cabin was in very poor repair; as a result, dad announced that with the warm weather we would sleep in the sleigh overnight. After covering the two horses with blankets, Bill and I started a fire of twigs and deadwood and then heated the soup for our lunch. The talk was about which fir trees might be felled most easily for our purpose and how these would be skidded to a location from which they would later be loaded onto a sleigh for transport to a sawmill.

To prepare water for the horses, dad filled a pail full of snow, melted it and poured the water into a second pail for the horses. Sufficient coffee was brewed to last us the afternoon. In a few minutes, the three of us were busily engaged in falling the first fir tree, trimming the limbs, and cutting the tree into lengths of eight, ten, and twelve feet. As work progressed, we admitted that we were no match for dad. Having spent several years contracting for Northern Alberta Railways, he was an experienced logger and seemed to know just how to make the first directional cut on the lower part of the fir tree to make sure that it fell in the right direction. *"You know, boys, at the rate we are going, we will have finished cutting sufficient logs by tomorrow afternoon. We can be home tomorrow night."*

By evening, we had cut quite a number of logs and skidded some of these to a roadside location. Preparing for supper was a pleasant experience. Once again, Bill and I gathered sufficient wood to keep a fire going as we prepared for our snooze in the sleigh. The supper was all as good as we might have been served at home. Looking up, we could see a few clouds swirling around a full moon. It was a starlit night and I was certain that I could hear the crackle of the northern lights. The horses were fed and watered and we listened to the howling of the wolves. As I peered into the darkness, I imagined that I saw a wolf.

As we turned in for the night, dad made sure that a sufficient number of green logs were put on the fire so as to prolong their burn. Still dressed in all of our clothing and with the sleigh slightly down-breeze from the fire, we felt warm and comfortable in the sleigh-box filled with hay. Dad slept at one end of the sleigh and Bill and I at the other end. The howling of the wolves was incessant. Could it be that they were trying to get a message out to these intruders?

A slight breeze blowing in from the north made an eery whistling sound in the fir trees. I was awakened by a few drops of snow which landed on my face just as dad got out of the sleigh to pile a few more logs on the fire. As we settled in once again, I recalled a western story I had recently read entitled *West of the Pecos*. My thoughts soon turned into a dream. It all seemed so real to me. The cowboys urging their *dogies* on in a cattle drive to Sante Fe, New Mexico. As the cowboys settled in for the night, they were hit by a snow storm. The dream was so real it suddenly awoke me. What I saw chilled me to the very bone. As I peered out from the down-filled quilt, my toes felt as though they were frozen. Suddenly, I was struck by the severity of the wind. *'But, how could this be,'* I thought. *'We are in the middle of the forest. There is not supposed to be any wind!'*

At about the same time, dad and Bill were also roused by the gathering storm. Nearby, the horses whinnied. The howls of the wolves became increasingly mournful. *"Oh, no,"* said dad, *"it sure doesn't look good out there. I'll get this fire going and we'll see how this storm shapes up in a little while."*

"Dad," I remarked, *"this is just like the storm we had earlier this winter when we got lost going to the school van."*

Bill did not need to be reminded. *"You know,"* he said, *"to this day, I still have nightmares about that blizzard."*

Quickly, more short logs and branches were piled onto the fire. At first it was difficult to keep it lit. As a result, its location was moved downwind from the sleigh; the wind that was now fiercely blowing in from the north making the snow swirl around the sleigh. The trees in the forest seemed to whistle a tune and it certainly was not a merry one. *"To try to get to Badan's or to High Prairie may be difficult in this storm. We'd better stay put. Maybe all of this will blow itself out in a couple of hours."*

Dad was correct in his prediction. By eleven o'clock the storm vanished as quickly as it had appeared. However, we were suddenly confronted by another problem; extreme cold temperatures. As a result, dad made the only decision he could make and that was to complete the falling and the cutting to length of the fir trees but to leave the hauling of the logs to another weekend. Once we started to work, we were able to stay warm. The camp fire did not hurt either. By nightfall, dad estimated that we had a sufficient number of logs to accomplish our goal. We were thankful to hear dad say, *"Let's go home."*

Bill and I noted that dad had the foresight of bringing a grain shovel with him. It became very useful on several occasions when we used it to dig the sleigh out of a snow drift. In other places, the snow was so tightly blown into a drift that the sleigh would ride on top of these. When we reached the main highway south of Aggie, we were thankful that the snowplows had done their work, making the going much easier. We arrived at the Freeman farm shortly after midnight.

"Boy, oh boy," commented Bill, *"I am sure as hell going to be happy to get back to school next week!"*

"Yeah," I responded, *"school never looked better. Maybe mom was right when she said that we should be happy going to school. Well, we will be."*

27.

The Mechanization of Farming

As Eva dreams of becoming a Canadian citizen

In contrast to West Prairie School, each day's educational program at the High Prairie Consolidated School was broken down into specific periods of study. This was my first exposure to a structured physical education program, which was conducted in a vacant classroom during winter months because the school did not have a gymnasium. For the more hardy, an outdoor game of soccer played on a field of packed snow was an excellent form of physical activity. In the spring, softball was the game of choice made popular by the returning war veterans who seemed to be in love with the game. For the students, all of this attention to physical training culminated in a district-wide track and field day at the end of May.

For all recent immigrants to Canada and especially for my parents, May 14, 1946, became an important date. It was on this date that the federal government passed the Canadian Citizenship Act which assured citizens in Canada that they would no longer be classified as British subjects. Instead, it would now identify them, for the very first time, *as a member of an independent and sovereign state* rather than a colony of Britain. The new act would take effect on January 1, 1947. Still, my mother would not become Canadian citizen for another decade. Dad had already become a British subject and a citizen of Canada in 1942 under the provisions of the Dominion of Canada Naturalization Act. By the end of World War II the vast majority of Canadians believed that the war had truly confirmed Canada as a sovereign nation and politicians wanted the rest of the world to recognize the country's recently won status. This is why the remaining emblems of colonialism were about to be removed and the symbols of independent nationhood put into place.

Maria was now twenty years of age and mom began to worry, not so much about the family but Maria's future. After all, most girls in the Old Country were either promised in marriage by the time they were twenty or already married. Although Maria had found part-time employment in High Prairie and later in Dawson Creek, the prospects of marriage just weren't there. Well, there was a railroad engineer that courted her; however, she expressed little interest in him. Mom impressed two things upon Maria as she contemplated the future: *'the boy you marry should be of Ukrainian heritage and a good Catholic.'*

When several war veterans returned from active duty, the eligible girls in High Prairie felt as though they had hit the jackpot. In fact, other veterans from outside the region would come to the village in search of good times and it was not uncommon to see a carload of boys from as far away as Peace River come all the way to High Prairie on a Saturday night just to kick up their heels in one of many dance halls in the region. On other occasions, small groups of young people would attend Sunday Mass and then a picnic which followed, in the hopes of meeting a future mate. This was how Maria met Michael Kalyn the man of her dreams.

"You know," Maria said, as she reflected on that chance meeting, *"up until that moment, I had never met anyone quite like Michael. He had more energy than anyone I knew. And my, could he dance! Especially the polka!"*

On occasion, Michael would invite me to come along with the two of them as they roamed the countryside. Wow, that car he drove was a beauty! A 1934 Dodge with a rumble seat in it, always kept immaculately polished. I was impressed with his sense of humour and his ability to tell a good story. At times, it was not uncommon for him to be the butt of his own jokes. He was a devout Catholic and loved to spring into a love song, sometimes in English and at other times in Ukrainian. He was a practical and charming conversationalist with a thorough knowledge of cars, trucks, and farm machinery. I didn't know about my sister Maria, but I liked him. My only question was *what was she waiting for?* Later that fall, the predictable happened. Michael came to High Prairie, not so much to see Maria but to see dad and mom. He came to ask for her hand in marriage. Before dad could answer, mom jumped right in and said *yes.* Even if dad wanted to object, it was no use. The wedding date was set for the next summer.

There was another important occurrence in Canada. Over 35,000 veterans enrolled in 29 universities across Canada following an announcement by the federal government which would allow returning soldiers to continue their education without interruption. The University of Alberta attracted a number of these registrants. When dad heard of this news, he remarked, *"I wish that the Austrian government had provided me with this kind of an opportunity."*

"Well," replied mom, *"that is too late to question what might have been. I want us to work very hard to make sure that our children have an opportunity to attend a university."*

271

Eva Kashuba receives her Certificate of
Canadian Citizenship from the Department
of Citizenship and Immigration, 1959.

John Diefenbaker,
Prime Minister
of Canada, 1957
– 1963.

As dad took in the fall crops, he declared that he was thinking about buying his first farm tractor. Bill and I were thrilled with the idea, especially since we would be getting rid of the task of feeding the horses, cleaning the barn, and harnessing and unharnessing the horses during the cultivation and harvesting seasons. And, speaking of horses, dad seemed always to be reminded of the time that he ran over a bees nest while cutting a stand of wheat. *"All hell broke loose,"* was the way dad described it, *"when the three horses were stung by dozens of bees. In fact, one bee got to me, stinging me in the neck area.*" Eventually, he did get the horses under control but he vowed to mechanize the farming operation as soon as possible.

To raise the extra funds needed for school supplies, skates, hockey sticks, and softball gloves, Bill and I continued to sell firewood, sour cream, fresh eggs, and newly-churned butter to clients in High Prairie. It was right there in High Prairie that I learned about marketing. I learned that to win a client, you didn't have to be the biggest player or have the biggest budget. All you needed was a planned approach to marketing that targets the right customers. I learned that a marketing plan didn't have to be complicated and that the direct sales approach worked best. It was all about relationships by making the customer feel good by paying close, personal attention to his needs. During winter months in High Prairie a warm house was an imperative. Best of all, the main source of heat was firewood. That is where Bill and I came in.

Even before the first snows came, we would launch our marketing program, cutting and splitting chord upon chord of poplar wood. Our best clients seemed to live in *Mocassin Flats,* a name applied to a poorer section of town frequented by Native Indians and Metis. It was here that we decided to concentrate our efforts and develop our own unique *trap line.* In many cases an Indian family wanted a second load of wood but had not paid for the first load. We worked out a payment schedule even though we recognized that the likelihood of being paid for the final load of wood in the spring was somewhat dim. In all, this marketing lesson never left me; *take a reasonable profit and cut your losses when required to do so.*

Bill and I continued to be hooked on the activities in the National Hockey League and every Saturday night we would listen to the immortal Foster Hewitt and his opening, *'good evening, hockey fans in Canada and the United States,'* as the goose bumps would go up and down my spine. This was hockey night in Canada and no activity was important enough to interfere with the love for the sport. Hockey was a way of life and a close friend of ours, Mike Kalita, had a cousin by the name of Alex Kalita who played for the New York Rangers. That seemed to be the only exception we made when selecting the National Hockey League players for whom we would be cheering. No one ever pulled for the Montreal Canadiens and the sporting community in High Prairie was thrilled that spring when the Toronto Maple Leafs beat the Montreal Canadiens four games to two to win the Stanley Cup.

The news that Barbara Ann Scott of Ottawa had won the world figure skating championship did not make much of an impact on local residents. Unless the game was played with a hockey stick, it didn't seem to count for much. Still, there were other events that happened in Canada that our home-room teacher would bring to our attention. News about Canada's first nuclear reactor in Chalk River, Ontario, and the level of pension payments for Canadians who were 70 years of age or older as well as pensions for those 21 or over who were legally blind. She seemed particularly interested in a young Saskatchewan lawyer who, as a Progressive Conservative in Ottawa, spoke most eloquently on the issue of pensions. His name was John Diefenbaker. He would one day become the prime minister of Canada.

The winter of 1947 saw me anxiously waiting for the tractor that dad said he would buy. But, he did not seem to be in a hurry. Maybe he was reluctant to give up on the horses. In the meantime, he knew that wishing accomplished little; the very success of a farming operation often depended on preparation for spring cultivation. One important task that he liked to complete over the winter months was the preparation of seed grain for spring seeding. The best grain of the previous year would be selected, poured into a hopper, and then cleaned by a hand-operated seed-cleaner which filtered the grain through various-sized mesh-screens so as to separate the chaff from the seed grain. I got so proficient at the task that I could operate the seed-cleaner by hand while at the same time reading a book, studying for an examination or daydreaming about some baseball or hockey exploit.

In fact, the seed-cleaning operation and the sale of seed grain became quite lucrative on its own and provided the family with those precious dollars that would soon be needed for the purchase of a tractor. There was another good thing about farming. Nothing seemed ever to be wasted, not even the residue from the cleaned grain. Next to the grain separator was a grain crusher in which oats, barley or wheat would be crushed for use as feed for the pigs, chickens, cattle, and horses. A small amount of our top quality wheat would be set aside and crushed in a grain crusher to be used for domestic purposes in two ways—as morning cereal and as flour for baking purposes. This was accomplished by filtering the crushed wheat through a screen and using the very fine crush as flour and the thicker crush as a morning cereal.

Spring came early and the family was off to High Prairie in the horse-drawn wagon. It was a very special trip. Bill drove the wagon back to the farm while I came back with dad on his brand new Oliver tractor; a beautiful forest green in colour. This would soon become a symbol of the changes that would come to the farming operation. In future, horsepower did not necessarily mean implements powered by horses--it was the number of *horses* under the hood of the tractor and the amount of power it could impart to the draw-bar. Yes, the mechanization of the farming operation came at a time when grain prices were going only one way and that was up, way up.

Everyone in our family seemed to gather around and talk about the tractor. That little green monster took front and centre stage until another event bumped the tractor to the back burner. And that event was the birth of what would turn out to be mom's final offspring. Buddy Walter was born on May 26, 1947. However, unlike the other children, he had the good fortune of being brought into the world at the High Prairie Providence Hospital under the care of the venerated Dr. John Barrett Thornton Wood, a man who dedicated his life to serving the people of the High Prairie region.

"Finally," declared mom, *"now that the pregnancy is over, we can start planning Maria's wedding."*

28.

A Country Wedding

As Maria takes a husband

Love took its course and the date for the wedding was set for August 10, 1947. Naturally, the date of the big day had to be such that it would not interfere with the harvesting operations of our family nor that Michael's family in the village of Reno, near the town of Peace River. It was expected that the Ukrainian-style wedding would bring on a series of celebrations, first in High Prairie and then in Reno. There was another important reason for this date. The wedding reception and dance were scheduled to be held out-of-doors in our front yard and the weather was more likely to be favourable during mid-August. Dad was glad that he had sufficient lumber in stock to construct reception tables and a large deck which would serve as a dance floor. These would be disassembled after the wedding to be used for intended purposes.

Since this would be the first child of the family to be married, great importance was attached to the formal church ceremony to be held in the local Ukrainian Catholic Church and the wedding reception which was to follow. In most instances, the wedding invitations were delivered in person to friends living in High Prairie and by the mail to those living outside the village. In all, over one hundred and fifty guests were invited. However, the number that would attend the wedding reception would very much depend upon the weather.

As might be expected, the wedding triggered a plethora of mixed emotions for mom. For one thing, there was something irreversible about that very act of setting a wedding date and, for another, her closest link to the Old Country would soon be leaving her nest. As Maria's wedding approached, mom must have been thinking about her own wedding which took place just twenty-three years earlier. No doubt Maria would soon be raising her own

Left to right, Koby Hayden, Tony Porisky, Bill Naturkach (best man), Michael Kalyn (groom), Anne Kashuba (maid of honour), Maria (Kashuba) Kalyn (bride), Steven Kashuba

family while mom was still nursing Buddy, now three months old. In a lighter moment she was heard to say to dad that they should not have worried so much about Maria becoming an old maid because, "...*even today, she looks so young.*"

"*Yes, she does. But, how quickly she grew up,*" responded dad.

After the vows were taken, it was off to a studio for formal pictures before attending the reception where mountains of food lay in wait. The family, with the help of neighbours and friends, prepared the traditional Ukrainian cuisine. As was the custom, the whiskey, wine and beer was the responsibility of the bride's parents, although Michael was not shy about pitching in. Throughout, a small band provided the music, mixing traditional Ukrainian wedding tunes with good old country and western music.

Following the reception, guests lined up to present the bride with a gift, a cash donation, and to propose a toast to the young couple. The parents of the bride and groom made their little speeches of blessings and the initial presents and cash donations, followed by members of the bridal party. To show his manhood, the groom would respond to each toast with a drink while the bride kissed the male donors. Naturally, as the evening wore on, the groom soon had his fill of drinks and as a result, and in keeping with tradition, he would toss whatever drink remained in his shot glass over his left shoulder for good luck. The more Michael drank the less accurate was his toss. Some guests went away feeling that they had been in a rain shower. During the evening, the young male guests developed sufficient courage to propose, in turn, a toast to each bridesmaid in exchange for a kiss.

All the while, the musicians played and the guests danced. When the reception line was complete, it was the turn of the wedding party to lead off the formal part of the dance. By this time the groom was well lubricated, discarded any inhibitions he might have had and put on a fine exhibition, first of old time dancing followed by his patented *whirlwind polka* step. Some said that it was the finest exhibition of dancing that they had seen. It was here that he would be crowned the unofficial king of the polka step. It seemed that every girl at the reception wanted to dance with him. He did not disappoint!

The wedding celebration continued into the wee hours of the morning and the Ukrainian wedding songs seemed to get more and more ribald. I am sure that some of those lyrics were not meant for the ears of the younger folk. But then, by morning, it is unlikely that anyone really remembered exactly what was sung or to whom. By noon on Sunday, everyone was back in church for Sunday mass. A wedding just would not be complete without attending Sunday Mass. After the Mass it was back to the farm for the traditional opening of the gifts and more food and drink. Not only did Bill and I have a couple of alcoholic drinks, but so did Andy. In addition, we got into dad's can of Dominion tobacco and rolled our own cigarettes. We lit up and tried to act very grown up. After the wedding we discovered that Andy and a couple of his young friends really tried to make a party of it by stashing a case of beer in the garden. Lucky for them, they only consumed a couple of bottles. When dad investigated the incident, no one would take responsibility for the evil deed.

By late Sunday evening, the wedding was over. The yard looked a bit of a mess with empty beer bottles scattered about, mixed with cigarette butts and paper. Bill and I assisted dad in dismantling the banquet tables and the dance-floor platform. For the newlyweds, it was time to pack up for the one-hour car ride to Reno so that the groom's family and friends might put the finishing touches on the celebration. According to the bride and groom, things never got back to normal until the following Monday. Good thing at that, because by this time the harvest season was in full swing and Michael had a crop to take in.

Sandwiched around the activities of the wedding, Bill and I got to do something for the very first time. Dad allowed us, under close supervision, to take a spin around the yard with the new Oliver tractor. It was a thrill that we will never forget because it marked, for the very first time, a move away from the use of horses to do the farmwork. True to an earlier predication that dad made, this was the first of many moves to mechanize the farming operation. However, these changes were not made without some misgivings and nostalgia and, just for old time's sake, it was not uncommon to see dad hitch the horses to a wagon to take advantage of a mode of work and transportation that was quickly losing its importance and effectiveness.

The farm boys in our neighbourhood were extremely resourceful and frequently invented ways to entertain themselves. Several of these boys got together and formed up what they liked to refer to as The East Prairie River Slingshot Club. The purpose of the association was simple; to have fun and enjoyment. Oh, yes, and while having fun, it was not improper to take a few potshots at a muskrat, a prairie chicken, a blackbird, or at those insulators on telephone poles. At the same time, club members liked to keep a record of their *kills* and to brag about their accomplishments. In many cases, verification was difficult. Each member seemed to be the best at this or that. The rubber bands for the slingshots came from inner tubes of tires at a local Chevrolet dealership. Nothing but the best would do. During those hot summer days we would often hang up our slingshots in favour of a bike ride to the East Prairie River. It was here that we laid claim to a very special swimming hole and go skinny-dipping. No one ever thought of wearing swimming trunks; that was for sissies and the townsfolk.

Most of our activities during the summer months took place in our own neighbourhood. To participate in any organized activity beyond the immediate farming community would be problematic. Our family did not have a car or a truck and using the tractor for transportation was out of the question. Our best bet was by horseback or bicycle. The only problem was that the horses were simply plough-horses and not useful for any leisure-time activity. That left the one bicycle which was available to members of the family in accordance with seniority. Although dad rarely used the bicycle, he did have first choice. The best that we could do was to ride double when we were able to get use of the Canadian-built CCM bike. Otherwise, getting from one point to another was done the old-fashioned way--on foot.

For some reason, mom always told us that she did not want to learn how to ride the bike. I think that she took this position because she knew that one bike was simply not enough for all members of the family. Still, Bill and I insisted that she learn how to ride the bike while at the same time making sure that every time she attempted to ride the bike it would develop a mechanical problem. Eventually, she simply lost interest in the bike saying that she had trouble with her balance. We knew better. She must have known how much we liked to ride the bike and did not want to cut into our time for its use.

Although mom gave up on the bike, Andy did not. He was determined that he should have his time on the bike. Reluctantly, we cut him in for a short session from time to time. In the meantime, we impressed upon him how lucky he was to get that much time on the bike where other families would not allow anyone younger than ten to ride one. Bill got it correct when he said, *"You know, Andy, you are only eight years of age and far too young to spend a lot of time on a finely tuned bike."* He seemed to accept this explanation.

Turning twelve meant that I was now of the age to fully participate in all phases of the farming operation. That was the expectation of dad. The same held true for Bill. Naturally I gravitated to certain tasks, especially if they had to do with the operation of mechanized equipment such as driving the *jolly green* farm tractor. Some chores were carried out daily while others but once a week. Daily chores included milking the cows and feeding the pigs, chickens, cows, and horses while the weekly tasks included the cleaning of the buildings which housed the farm animals. I especially disliked having to get up early each day to milk Bossy, the cow specifically assigned to me. I disliked Bossy and, I suppose, she wasn't exactly enamoured with me. She was big and mean and seemed to object to being milked on cold mornings. Having the biggest teats of all the milk-cows, it took quite a bit of strength just to get the milk flowing. At times, I would bribe her with some grain-chop while at other times it seemed that a few lines of a country and western song would put her in a better frame of mind. These chores had to be completed early in the morning before leaving for school as well as later in the afternoon when I got home from school. There was no escaping it; neither the tenderness of my years nor poor performance was a defence against the sharing of responsibilities.

Much of my aversion to doing chores started two years earlier and continued for quite some time. It happened when the family still lived on the Gilwood property and I was required to water the cows and heifers by herding them to the East Prairie River which was about one and one-half kilometres to the west. The necessity for this procedure came about as a result of the dry weather and the farm well going dry. To melt the snow in order to get enough water for the cows was time consuming. Of course, by mid-November and on this particular day the river was frozen over, making it necessary for me to chop a hole in the ice sufficiently large for the five cows and two heifers to get at the water. It is remarkable just how resourceful an animal can be. Each would gingerly approach the open hole, get on their knees, stretch their neck, reach in and drink from the river.

I interrupted this process by roughening the edges around the hole in the ice with an axe so that each bovine would have better footing and not slip into the hole. Were that to happen, I knew that I would have great difficulty in extricating the four-legged creature from the hole in the ice. Just as I was about to perform this task, I slipped into the river. Imagine my surprise and shock. Damn, that water was cold. Thank goodness it was only three feet deep. I scrambled out of there as though I had been shot out of a cannon. I knew that the temperature was well below zero. In a few moments, the lower extremities of my pants began to freeze. They felt as though they were made of two stove pipes.

I abandoned the cows right there and headed up the river bank and across the road allowance to the nearby Kozy farm. When Mrs. Kozy saw me, she didn't know whether to laugh or cry. There stood I, pants frozen, framing the doorway of her home with an axe in my hands. She seemed to know just what to do. Never mind that I felt a little self-conscious standing there in the buff; the heat from that old Franklin stove never felt better. Still, I shivered and shook for the longest time. Mrs. Kozy got me into one of her husband's trousers, a shirt, and parka and helped me round up the cows before seeing me off.

All things seemed to have a silver lining. When I got home that evening, mom didn't recognize me at first. She mistook me for a neighbour. When I explained to her what had happened, she had difficulty suppressing a laugh but did assure me that she would once again convince dad that we should revert to melting snow as a source of water for the cattle. For the time being, the necessity of herding the cattle to the river each day was abandoned.

I must admit that there were several other tasks which I had to perform and which I hated with all of the passion I could muster. Since dad's farming operation included the raising of cattle, pigs, and chickens, it was natural that we would include beef, ham, sausage, and bacon in our diet. Well, cattle did not just happen. There were milk cows, reproduction cows, steers, and heifers. A man had to think about reproduction which meant that each year we would have to take one or two cows to a neighbour who had a bull. That is one job I sort of disliked. Besides, that bull was often unpredictable and I always felt that I was party to an activity that even the cow may not like. Naturally, a farmer did not want to raise bulls. So, I was always called upon to help dad castrate those young bovine so that they would be raised as steers and not bulls. Yikes, that hurt!

The same process applied to pigs. My dad wanted only one boar on the farm for breeding purposes. Those other young piglets had to be neutered. Again, it was my job to hang on to the piglet being neutered. My, could they squeal! Well, given the same circumstances, who wouldn't? I hated this task. There were other tasks that did not meet with my approval. Tasks such as butchering a pig where my dad would strike the creature on the centre of its forehead with a sledgehammer and stick a butcher knife through its heart. Most of the organs would be used in one way or another for food: blood sausage, ham sausage, bacon, ham, and the like. The hardest part was de-bristling the pig after it was butchered. Sometimes, dad used hot water and then scraped the bristles away while at other times he used a bonfire for this purpose. Perhaps the other task I disliked was that of eviscerating chickens and turkeys or the task of pulling off the soft under-plumage of feathers for use as down in pillows and quilts.

Yes, it was at times like this that I lost my love of farming and embraced schooling just a little bit more. School enrolment in the fall of 1947 meant that I was now in junior high school, in a split-class of grade seven and eight students. It now seemed as though I was entering a new era in education. The teacher, a real *looker* by the name of Miss Peggy Roberts, was a recent graduate of the University of Alberta in Edmonton and seemed to bring with her many new ideas about the psychology of teaching and learning.[31] Gone were those teachers who held temporary teaching licenses. The subjects were now almost completely departmentalized which lent a new meaning to how learning would take place, not only during this particular year but for many years into the future.

Much of the talk in High Prairie had to do with Canada's role in accepting displaced persons from Europe as a result of the war. Many of the pioneers knew that Ukrainians were recruited by the Nazi regime to work in the munitions factories during the war and were now trying to find a country, other than a Soviet Bloc country, that would accept them. Given a choice, most would have refused to be repatriated to the Soviet Union. Naturally, those of Ukrainian heritage wanted to know if any of their relatives were working

31 High Prairie & Area History Book Society 825 - 828.

in Germany and if they would be interested in coming to Canada. Many of the *displaced persons* originated with the armed resistance movement in Ukraine during World War II known as the Ukrainian Insurgent Army which struggled against both, the Nazis and, later, against the Soviet re-occupation of Ukraine. As a result, several million Ukrainians moved west during the war years. Those who came under the control of the British, American, Canadian, and French armies felt that they had a better chance of survival. Unfortunately, many of them, as a result of the Yalta Agreement, were repatriated as Soviet citizens, regardless of their wishes. To be labelled a Soviet citizen was to be branded for expulsion or even worse.

Other residents of High Prairie shifted their attention to Newfoundland. It appeared that Joey Smallwood was investigating the possibility of a union with the United States, Britain, or Canada. As time went on, it seemed that the best alternative lay in a confederation with Canada, which would be economically advantageous to Newfoundland. And within our school, the course of studies in Social Studies now began to reflect more and more of what was happening in Canada and around the world. Radar, electronics, atomic energy, and jet engines suddenly brought Alberta into a new era and everyone felt confident that leisure and prosperity made possible by automation was about to visit all Canadians. Even dad could not resist his good fortune. He, too, thought that it was time to enter this new era of machines by purchasing a brand new maroon-coloured Fargo farm truck manufactured by the Chrysler Corporation.

"Now, Eva," he declared, *"we can put the horses to pasture!"*

By now Alberta's population had increased to over 800,000. The pace of social life also increased. As well, the population of Edmonton and of Calgary exceeded 100,000 and even the village of High Prairie was experiencing an increase in population, approaching the astronomical figure of 250 souls. The population shift away from the land to the city was heating up and the percentage of the rural people had fallen to fifty-six percent. Even the older people living on homesteads were following in the footsteps of the younger generation. Those pioneers who had devoted their lives to winning a farm from the forested wilderness were now boarding up their windows and selling their holdings to a neighbour for the comfort of the city.

Suddenly, the village of High Prairie decided that it must provide better for its citizens if it wished to retain them and began thinking about bringing water and sewer services to its residents. These demands were also being driven by newcomers connected with the oil industry who demanded better services. Roads throughout the province were being improved with over 530 miles of bituminous surfaced roads and 9,000 miles of gravelled roads. All of this was required because residents demanded it. Besides, now that dad had his new truck, he wanted to be able to drive it to Edmonton in the near future even though it would be on a gravelled road!

For most of Alberta, the future in agriculture was not meeting expectations. By now, most of the accessible arable land had been settled and even in the

High Prairie region, the land available for homesteading was of a lower grade and too often located in a remote area away from railroads and roads. But, this did not seem to deter dad from thinking about buying another farm and moving away from his complete dependence on grain. '*It is time,*' my dad concluded, '*to develop a better and bigger herd of livestock.*' At a time when Alberta's prospects were somewhat grey, dad was quite happy with the return on his investment. Enterprising Albertans were setting aside their skepticism about the future. They were looking at the coal reserves and its 171,000 square miles of forests. They were also looking at the rivers flowing to the sea and how they might be harnessed for electrical power. In particular, they were looking at the tar sands and how these might be exploited. For decades, drillers had probed the underlying rocks in search of oil and gas concluding that their riches could not elude them forever.

As my parents contemplated developments in Alberta, they must have felt quite confident that their children would have a better life in Canada than they might have had in Galicia. Suddenly, even dad took great pride in the scholastic achievements of his children.

29.

Oil Money Comes to High Prairie

Bringing with it employment and prosperity

When Leduc Well No. 1 belched out a black smoke ring on February 13, 1947, it signalled the oil era in the province of Alberta. The immediate area turned out to be a field of 1,278 wells containing over 200 million barrels of recoverable oil at a time when the Turner Valley oil field in southern Alberta was being quickly depleted. Just as fifty years earlier Alberta's rich soils had proven to be a boom for thousands of prospective farmers, Albertans could now turn to another source of revenue. Where revenues from farming operations were being augmented by revenues from coal and lumber, residents could now look to petroleum products for the next economic boom. And, even more important, the benefits from the oil industry extended to every corner of the province and buoyed every sector of Alberta's economy.

For Albertans, the discovery of the Leduc Field was a very important event. It caused the petroleum industry to mushroom and created dozens of businesses. New housing and businesses blossomed in the nearby town of Leduc and the new town of Devon. The city of Edmonton started to hum with increased industrial activity and soon became a major terminal for the many exploration companies fanning out in all directions. Geophysicists learned how to interpret records that indicated the presence of buried reefs.[32] Seismic crews could be seen all over Western Canada with miniature drilling rigs mounted on their trucks drilling 100-foot holes in which explosives were set off. The resulting vibrations were recorded and analysed for underground formations in the earth's crust.

---

32 Hunter, Bea. Last Chance Well, Legends & Legacies of Leduc No. 1, D. W. Friesen Limited, Edmonton, Canada, 1998, pp. 204 - 208.

Bill Brown, an American who came to Canada from Texas in 1951, is an example of how the oil industry attracted so many young people who gave up their lives to the development of its riches. Although he is now fully retired in the city of Edmonton, he recalls those halcyon days of *"...the oil business which was reflective of a bizarre human enterprise. Imagine,"* he continued, still reflecting upon the excitement of those bygone days, *"someone raises millions to pay someone else to put a steel pipe five miles into the ground in case there is any oil or gas down there. If there is any of that stuff down there, someone gets rich; if not, everyone decides to do it all over again at another location. All over again, that is, if there is any money left!"*

The oil industry, according to Brown, attracted inventors, innovators and people who loved to tinker around with the various bits of equipment that force the oil and gas out of the ground, *"And, I am one of those innovators,"* he added as an afterthought. *"Sometimes,"* adds Lyle Abraham, a man who has also devoted most of his life to the oil industry, *"a simple idea can make a person a millionaire. At other times, an old idea is used in a new way or at a new time making a company take off."* Having successfully served the oil industry for decades, Abraham should know what he is talking about. John Wronko, the retired chief executive officer of a successful oilfield service company is in full agreement concluding that these are important *"...examples of how so many not only made a comfortable living in the oil industry but have profited from such ingenuity and, in many cases, amassed fortunes in Alberta."* In all of this, there is little doubt that every Albertan benefited from the dedication and hard work of oilfield employees.

High Prairie was not immune from the positive and sometimes negative effects of the oil industry and the wealth it generated for Albertans. New towns such as Devon, Red Water and Swan Hills sprang up, proving to be fertile ground for new oil discoveries. As Albertans became more and more mobile with the addition of new paved roads, smaller centres began to die out in favour of larger centres scattered throughout the province. High Prairie found itself in an enviable position; it was simply too far away from any provincial centre to be passed up by local residents. This encouraged local growth and High Prairie's status changed from that of a sleepy village to a vibrant town, making it eligible for provincial funds as additional services were being contemplated by its residents.

Yes, the petroleum economy in High Prairie really began to stir when oil surveyors and seismograph crews appeared in the region in search of oil. They were very thorough, searching every valley and flat, every muskeg and every hilltop, just as hunters and trappers did some one hundred years earlier--except the quarry was no longer the wolf or coyote; it was now *black gold*. In the farming areas surrounding High Prairie, their movements were relatively straight forward, but they were soon asked to penetrate the forests and marshes around Lesser Slave Lake, the Caribou Mountains, the ox-bowed Chinchaga River and Zama Lakes.

By mid-1949, the long-awaited results of this seismographic activity in the High Prairie region were made public. And the news was good, very good. The northern edge of the prolific oil fields angled northwest to Utikuma Lake, Red Earth, Rainbow Lake, and finally to the Zama field. The enormity of this find, along with that of Swan Hills, would ensure the prosperity of Albertans and especially those in the High Prairie region for years to come. The industry's roughnecks were making a very good wage which explained, in part, why so many young men were deserting the halls of learning for the oil patch.

Everywhere in Alberta one could smell the scent of oil which was rapidly transforming the face of the province. Auditoriums, art galleries, and luxurious schools were springing up in every corner of the province, as were expanded university campuses and hospitals. These changes did not go unnoticed with mom, for in them she saw the image of the future for the family. Dad, on the other hand, continued to be consistent in his outlook for the future—more land and more mechanized farming equipment. These two disparate images of what the future held for the family would soon collide.

It is without doubt that the oil industry had a great impact upon dad's farming operations. By the fall of 1948, all of the farm work was now being done by tractor and transportation was no longer a problem either. And, increasingly, I got to drive the farm tractor as well as the truck. But, I had another dream; I wanted to drive that darn truck to a baseball game or to a hockey practice; better yet, maybe to a school dance. Other changes were in the offing for me; where at one time I took great pride in belonging to a slingshot club, the neighbourhood boys now wanted to belong to a rifle club. Instead of shooting birds, we now shot muskrats and ground hogs. To take advantage of the price on the hides of fur-bearing animals, Bill and I developed a trap line in the local area so that we might trap weasels, squirrels, and beaver and sell their hides at a local general store.

For sports and diversion during the winter months, we would clean an area of ice on the East Prairie River and play a friendly game of hockey with the neighbourhood boys. As the weather got colder and it became increasingly difficult to maintain river ice, we turned to playing, in our front yard, a modified game of hockey called *shmockey*. Instead of a hard rubber puck we used a rubber ball so that no one would get hurt. When we ran out of commercially-made hockey sticks, which cost a staggering two dollars each, we would shape a birch-tree-branch in the form of the real thing. When spring came, I turned to baseball, a game being promoted by the likes of Laurie Savill, Leonard Sloat and Benjamin Halbert. It would not be long before our team made it all the way to the provincial juvenile and junior baseball finals.

During my final year of junior high school, I tried very hard to be a part of the in-crowd. And, in those days, being a part of an in-group meant that you pretty well had to do what the other members did. If you did not, you then risked being ostracized by that group and, perhaps, all other groups. In the extreme, one might even risk a severe physical beating by one or more members of the group. Since I had witnessed this happening to two other students, I did the expected and joined a group of my choice, sealing the deal by promptly lighting up a cigarette as part of the initiation ritual. Once a part of the group, there was little to fear from anyone in the school other than the principal, Ed Pratt. You see, he was an ex-football player with a physique to match; he was not a person to be trifled with.

My love for baseball continued and by now I was getting quite good at the game, spending early spring throwing pitches to Bill from a pitcher's mound created in a straw pile near the farm home. In this way, I could start my spring training well before the snows melted. I dreamed of one day being able to throw the *fade-away* as did Christy Matheson in the big leagues. Bill would often complain about his sore and puffy hands, begging me not to throw that baseball so hard. But, it all seemed to pay off. When the baseball season opened in the spring, my pitching arm was in mid-season form. All of this gave me a head start for a starting position on the local baseball team.

During the summer of 1950, I was very much looking forward to helping dad with the farming operation, especially if it involved the operation of the tractor or truck. Sister Anne added to the excitement of the summer when she announced that the boy next door was the man of her dreams, all of which was confirmed when the youthful Carson Porisky asked mom and dad for her hand in marriage. *"But,"* objected mom, *"you are only nineteen. Your sister was twenty-two when she got married. Why don't you wait?"* Anne, of course, was not surprised at this reaction. Shortly, love overcame any objections and Anne and Carson were married. One thing was for certain; the proximity of the Porisky home to ours made it very convenient to do the planning for the wedding.

No sooner was the wedding over than dad decided to make an offer on a piece of property on the village limits of Enilda, bordering the East Prairie River. *"Who knows,"* he was heard to say to mom, *"I do know that my offer is very low. If I can get it at this price, it would be a steal. Besides, I checked out last year's yield per acre on this property. You know what? It was very good."* It appears as though dad wanted to create more work for his new tractor and truck. To his surprise, his offer of $2,200 for a farm with 140 acres of cultivated land was accepted.

Already dreaming of the family's next move, perhaps to Edmonton, mom was not pleased with dad's decision to expand the farming operation. After all, Bill would soon complete his high school program and would want to attend college, followed by the other children. I recall the anger in my mother's voice when she confronted dad with, *"...once a kaszublak, always a kaszublak. Why didn't you talk this over with me before making the purchase,"* continued mom with her attack. Of course, at times like this, dad knew better than to ask mom for her opinion about the purchase. He knew what the answer would be.

It would not be until years later that I would learn that my mother's use of the word *kaszublak,* in a derogatory sort of way, was to insult my dad, much like Poles and Germans did at one time to the kaszub tribe. I recall how my dad recoiled from the remark. Instead of being defensive and counter-attacking my mom he reflected upon her criticism saying, *"you know, maybe my grandfather did come from the kaszubian tribe. Who knows?"*

"Kaszubian tribe? What do you know of your ancestry?"

"Well," responded my dad, *"I remember my grandfather saying to me that his ancestors might have come from the Pomeranian region of Poland."*

"Andrij, I think you are dreaming. It is more likely that your family were Haydamaks.[33] *Besides, you're getting off the topic. Our children need a better education,"* continued mom. Wanting a commitment, she was reluctant to let dad off the hook.

At that time, I did not have the interest to ask my dad about his reference to the kaszubian tribe and, even if I had, it is doubtful that he would have cast any light on the subject. However, research does show that there were as many as two hundred thousand members of the kaszubian tribe of peoples living in the Gdansk region at the turn of the 20th century. Many migrated to the nearby districts as Wejherowo, Puck, Kartuzy, and Koscierzyna while others moved out of this impoverished region of Poland. The question is, did some of these members find their way up the Vistula River to the province of Galicia? Over time, were these interlopers absorbed by the Ukrainian and Polish communities? After all, Grohi was a young community and its first inhabitants must have come from elsewhere. But from where?

Historically, at the beginning of the 20th century, most members of the kaszub tribe were fishermen and peasants. Since they lived in close proximity to the international city of Gdansk, many became germanized.[34] With the construction of the port of Gdynia on their territory, great social and cultural changes began to take place among them. The kaszubs had a distinct Slavonic dialect which differs considerably from the Polish language in that words have a movable accent, often falling on the first syllable. In the Polish language, the accent always falls on the second last syllable of each word.

However, with few exceptions, the kaszubians believed that their dialect came from the Slavs and that their nationality was Polish. Many old time residents of Plazow believed that the Kaszuba name had its origins in the

---

33   The term Haydamaks is a derogatory name applied to those rebel bands that attacked and pillaged the estates of the Polish landlords in Ukraine. It is said that these bands were swelled by the outraged rural population and Cossacks. Haydamak derives from Turkish and generally means robber or pillager. Shevchenko, in his poem *The Haydamaks* thought their actions to be just and that the rebels considered it an honour to bear the descriptive word.

34   Rekowski, Aloysius J., <u>The Saga of the Kaszub People in Poland, Canada, U.S.A.</u>, Book Made Available Through the Kaszubian Association of North America, 2002, pp. 1 - 20.

Kaszuby region of Poland, a region rich in kaszubian folklore.[35] It was here that kaszubian intellects created a literary language which, in many respects, is similar to the Polish language but is quickly dying out, being swallowed up by the Polish, German and Ukrainian languages.

I can still recall mom reflecting on this conversation. She seemed somewhat skeptical about dad's explanation, taking more interest in the future rather than in the past.

Although High Prairie was in the midst of the postwar boom, there were labour shortages throughout Alberta, particularly in the oil patch and in the agricultural industry. Perhaps dad had second thoughts about acquiring more property for fear that he would not be able to cultivate all of the land. The traditional $8 per day was no longer enough to retain a worker. It is for this reason that several pioneers of Ukrainian heritage in the High Prairie region began to search their family trees for the possibility of discovering a blood relative in postwar Europe whom they might sponsor for immigration to Canada. Where my parents fled Poland to escape from the poverty and illiteracy of the earlier Austrian-ruled Western Ukraine, it was now the turn of others to come to Canada; those who had survived the Stalinist and Nazi occupation, genocide, mass terror, political persecution and slave labour in Germany. As the battle lines swayed back and forth during World War II, many Ukrainians fled their homes in Soviet Ukraine or were forced into labour to support the Third Reich's vision of the future. They became known as *Ostarbeiters* or *Eastern workers*.

Researchers claim that between 2.5 and 4.5 million Ukrainian displaced persons were scattered throughout Western Europe at the conclusion of the war. True, there was a concern in political circles as to what these in-migrating political refugees would bring to Canada. Would they introduce dissonance into the organized Ukrainian community in Canada? Still, those farmers experiencing labour shortages or who wanted to connect with family members from Europe paid little attention to these questions of politics. My dad's sister Anna and mom's nephew Vasyl Groszko did become Eastern Workers; Anna in a small German village near Hamburg and Vasyl on a farm in Austria. Interestingly, Anna, after pleading with the German Commandant, was released from bondage in 1943. Vasyl was forcibly returned to Soviet Ukraine in 1945. He had no choice, the Soviets told him, *"Comrade, you are coming back with us to the Soviet Union. Dead or alive. You decide."*

The stories about my Aunt Anna and my Cousin Vasyl Groszko are reminiscent of three other individuals who experienced the horrors of the war and who came to have quite an impact upon me as a teenager. Francis Hayden, whose parents resided in High Prairie, served with the Canadian

---

35 Note: From 1466 to 1772 the kaszubs were under Polish rule. Following the Partitions of Poland, beginning in 1772, Poland disappeared from the face of the map. All of Pomerania came under Prussian rule until after World War I.

Leduc #1 Oil Well in 1947 signalled the emergence of the oil industry in Alberta. Source: Glenbow Archives, Calgary, Alberta. NA-555-5.

Andrij Kashuba was anxious to give up the task of stooking, 1953.

A photograph of Andy Kashuba on the left and Andrij Kashuba on the right, cutting and placing into windrows a stand of wheat. High Prairie, 1955.

Andrij Kashuba moves into the age of mechanization by combining (threshing) wheat from windrows, 1956.

military in Holland. When he came home as a veteran of the war in 1945, he did not come alone; he brought with him a young Dutch bride by the name of Koby. The circumstances under which they met, dated, fell in love and got married captured my imagination. Although Francis was reluctant to talk about the war, Koby was not. From her, I learned a lot about Holland and about the war; about hardship and about sacrifice; about the role of the soldier and of the *sniper*. Even more important, I learned that war was not *always* about war. It was also about people and parties; of good times and romance. And, obviously, she was a romantic at heart. On the other hand, Francis loved to talk about the concept of managing crop rotation and the use of fertilizers, of planting shrubs to control soil erosion and of the most effective way to use pesticides. But, I was not the only one that enjoyed being in the company of the Haydens. My mom spoke very little English, about the same amount as did Koby. Yet, they became good friends, discovering that there was much more to communication than knowing a common language. Mom was heard to remark that Koby was *"like a breath of fresh air."*

Another significant influence upon my life came from Badan's nephew Fred Kulynych and his wife Lydia. Badan was getting well up in years, had a prosperous farming operation going and needed help. He had no family in Canada and wanted to *will* his property to someone other than the government. Although he did have a family in the village of Nova Kamianka in Soviet Ukraine, he lost contact with them years earlier.

Badan's nephew Theodore (Fred) Kulynych turned seventeen in 1941 at a time when the Nazis were already in control of Poland and Western Ukraine. On this particular day, the Nazis put the word out in Nova Kamianka that they needed workers in Germany, to maintain a high level of production in their armament factories. Who would volunteer to go? Which family would allow one or two of their children to make high wages in Germany?

It was not a surprise that Fred Kulynych came to be identified by Nazi officials as being eligible for work in Germany. The only problem was, his father passed away when he was ten years of age and his mother needed his help with domestic chores. It was either Fred or his older brother. After further discussion, the authorities gave his mother the bad news, Fred would have to go but his brother could stay. His mother didn't want either boy to go so she promptly hid Fred in the nearby meadow. However, after only three days of seclusion with little to eat, Fred came out of hiding. His mother had little choice but to succumb to the pressures of the Nazis and allow Fred to become an Ostarbeiter in Germany. Many years later, Fred would recall that moment and how the world caved in around him. First, as a youngster he was forced to learn Polish against his will and now he would have to learn German.

His transport to a location near Dortmund, Germany was in a railway cattle car very similar to that used for the transport of Jews, prisoners of war, criminals and Jehovah's Witnesses to labour and extermination camps. It took the train seven days to reach its destination during which time Fred slept on a bed of straw with little to eat. Upon arrival, he was promptly put to work in a coal mine in Wanne Aikel, six kilometres west of Essen. The year was 1941 and he was among the first to be seconded into forced labour.

Two years later and many miles away in Kharkiv, a similar scenario was to take place. The Nazis gained complete control of the city by 1943 and the German program of seeking young people for Hitler's munition factories continued unabated. Lydia Cherback was, according to Fred, a beautiful twenty year old enrolled in the second year of her medical program at the local Kharkiv Medical Academy. She was fluent in three languages; Ukrainian, Russian and German. And, that is where *her* odyssey starts.

When the Nazis discovered her language skills, they immediately rounded her up for employment in Dortmund, Germany as an Ostarbeiter. However, unlike Fred, her work turned out to be in a private home of a German medical doctor associated with health care. As fate would have it, near the end of the war Fred was charged with the responsibility of allocating rationed food supplies to Ostarbeiters. One of the workers whose credentials he had to check was that of Lydia Cherback. Fred was smitten by her beauty. Years later he was heard to remark that it was love at first sight. They were both twenty-one years of age and the city of Dortmund was witness to a love affair that ended in their marriage on June 23, 1946.

After the war and with the help of the International Red Cross and the United Nations, the newlyweds were sent to a Transit Camp in Germany before gaining entry to England where they ended up as employees in a textile factory. In 1948, their first child, Borys, was born. This, among other factors, caused them to pause and consider their future. Would it be in England? Or, would they have to look at emigrating to a country willing to take displaced persons? It was no surprise to them that a communications network developed among displaced persons in England. One rumour had it that the Canadian Government was amenable to accepting a limited number of displaced persons. Better yet, England was prepared to cooperate with Canadians who wished to sponsor a relative with the goal of immigrating to Canada.

It is with this in mind that Lydia and Fred Kulynych discovered that other displaced persons in England were using any means possible to contact a family member in Canada. Fred was well aware that he had an uncle by the name of Steve Badan living somewhere in Canada. But where? Further research indicated that a personal letter of appeal to a newspaper in Canada might help them find the whereabouts of Badan. In 1947, Lydia wrote a letter to the Nova Shlakh *(New Path)* newspaper in Winnipeg requesting help from readers in contacting a person by the name of Steve Badan. Since the Ukrainian newspaper was widely circulated in Canada, it did not take long for someone in High Prairie to get wind of the request and pass the good news on to Badan. In short order, Fred, Lydia and their infant son, Borys, were on their way to Canada, arriving in High Prairie in 1949. Their search for home was over.

I recall first meeting Fred and Lydia in 1949. Since Badan was our neighbour in the Aggie Settlement, my parents treated the Kulynyches as part of our extended family. I also developed a fond regard for them because they brought into focus so many elements of my own life; the breakup of a family through emigration, the geographic location of our respective ancestors and the tragedy of war. To me, they were a most interesting couple, very knowledgeable about the history of Ukraine and particularly about World War II.

However, Fred and Lydia Kulynych were not the only displaced persons to end up in High Prairie after the war. Other families in the region took the opportunity to bring to Canada a relative or a displaced person. Mike Porisky's nephew Vasyl Porisky was born on December 23, 1926, in the village of Horodziv, Poland. My brother-in-law, Carson Porisky *(Mike Porisky's son)*, his older brother, Walter, and their cousin, Vasyl, were all born in the same village.

It is interesting to note that Mile Porisky emigrated to Canada in 1928 *(the same year as did my dad),* some eleven years after his brother had perished in Russia during the Russian Revolution of 1917. Since this region had a strong White Russian influence, the Porisky family found itself to be buffeted by two opposing forces. On the one side was the pressure from those residents leaning towards the ideals of Bolshevism while on the opposing side, a continued support of the Ukrainian Greek Catholic Church.

Vasyl's father served in the Polish Army in 1939, at which time the Nazis over-ran Poland, taking 170,000 prisoners of war. Wounded, taken prisoner and unable to participate in the war, his father returned to his village of Horodziv in 1941. Meanwhile, Vasyl, as a twelve-year-old and the oldest of eight children, became, in accordance with tradition, the head of the household. It was in August of 1939 that Germany signed a non-aggression pact with the USSR; however, all of this went by the wayside when, on June 22, 1941, the Nazis, calling it Operation Barbarossa, attacked the USSR. Suddenly war had come to Horodziv.

As a fifteen year old, Vasyl initially took a liking to the German soldiers who showered him with candy and gum. However, when a call came out by the Nazis in 1942 for *slave* labour in Germany, Vasyl, on the advice of his mother, feigned injury and refused to go; she suggested that her husband go in place of her son. When Vasyl reflected upon that moment, he admitted that, *"Contrary to the feelings of my mother, I secretly wanted to go to Germany; I wanted something better for myself."* Well, as it turned out, he had no alternative. The Nazis insisted that he go and the fact that he was only fifteen was not a deterrent.

Piled into a railway boxcar with 85 other forced labourers, the trip to Germany took nine days with precious little to eat. *"What a contrast,"* reflects Vasyl, *"to those instances when I received candy from Nazi soldiers."* Arriving in Rohrbach, Germany, he was assigned to a farmer who had two teenagers, a boy and a girl, both of whom had a physical disability. His job was to do the ploughing with two oxen, threshing, taking in the vegetables and assisting with other farm chores. He served the couple through 1944, at which time the Russian Army marched through the region en route to Berlin.

To this day, Vasyl cannot get out of his mind the sounds of war; the warplanes and bombs; machine gun fire and the smell of war. In 1945 he was sent to a refugee camp near the city of Karlsruhe, Germany, along with thousands of other Russians, Poles and Ukrainians. As might be expected, there was little love lost amongst the three groups. Hearing that the Soviets were rounding up refugees for repatriation to Russia and possible expulsion to Siberia, he escaped from the camp and found his way back to the farm he had earlier served. What a relief when the farmer for whom he had worked earlier helped him find work in the nearby village of Inflinger! He stayed on this farm from 1946 to 1948.

As luck would have it, an associate in Inflinger had a copy of the newspaper, *Nova Shlakh* and, in a story that parallels that of Fred Kulynych, Vasyl wrote a letter to the newspaper seeking information about his uncle, Mike Porisky. He did get three letters of inquiry, but none was from his uncle. To his surprise, the next letter to come *was* from his uncle, Mike Porisky, along with the necessary affidavit certifying that Vasyl was, in fact, his nephew. Mike requested that Vasyl be allowed to emigrate to Canada. Vasyl arrived at Pier 21, Halifax, Nova Scotia, in July of 1948.

I first met Vasyl, as a thirteen year old, in 1948 and I can still recall his physical prowess. It was not uncommon during the harvest season to transport fuel from one farming location to another. In those days, the containers for the gasoline were 45 gallon drums which weighed in the neighbourhood of 250 to 300 pounds. When my brother and I were charged with the responsibility of transporting a couple drums of fuel on our Fargo truck to a field operation, it took two of us to accomplish the task. To my surprise, Vasyl was able to hoist a similar barrel of gas onto a Chevy truck singlehandedly. My, was I impressed!

Meanwhile, in 1938 and just before the outbreak of the war, Lena Omelchuk, as an ten-year old, arrived to Canada with her parents from a Polish village some fifty kilometres from Vasyl's village and settled in Onoway, northwest of Edmonton. By 1949, Lena was enrolled in a Faculty of Education program at the University of Alberta. As fate would have it, Vasyl attended the very same wedding shower as did Lena. As she tells it, *"I was immediately smitten by his good looks. When I found out that he loved to dance, I attended every Saturday night dance in the Edmonton region for the next two months in the hopes of meeting him again."*

Eventually, she did meet Vasyl at the Ukrainian National Federation Hall in Edmonton. Looking back, Vasyl wondered why he took dance lessons while an Ostarbeiter in Germany. He now had his answer. With his love for the old time waltz and the tango, he offered up that Lena had *"no chance once I had her in my arms."* They recently celebrated their 52nd wedding anniversary.

(Sadly, Vasyl Porisky passed away shortly after the writing of this story. We all mourn his loss.)

These stories, which took place just after World War II, reflect much of what I learned about the oil industry and the people who devoted their time and talents to ensure that its impact upon the economy of Alberta would pay dividends. I also learned a lot about new immigrants to this province, especially about the Kulynych and Porisky families. From them, I learned a lot about the Nazis and the Ostarbeiters; about displaced persons, and the life and times of their families in Soviet Ukraine.

Much as my parents did before them, I am glad that they found a home in Canada. They all helped to build this great nation of ours and, for that, I am eternally grateful.

Vasyl Porisky and daughter of his German employer, Germany, 1945.

Vasyl Porisky (pictured on the right) serving as Ostarbeiter in a German tobacco field, 1945.

30.

Eva Has a Dream

But, Andrij has a dream of his own

European families are patriarchal in structure and male-dominated. Were it otherwise, a father rearing his family would soon lose face in the eyes of the larger community; he simply would not measure up. However, I do believe that a transformation in this traditional structure really took flight by 1950 in our family. Dad always prided himself in the strength of his character and in his physical prowess but mom was relentless in her pursuit of schooling for her children. Perhaps this had something to do with the principles of democracy and evolving trends in Canada where women became *real persons* as a result of a Committee ruling in England in 1929 and an earlier decision in Alberta which allowed women to vote. I could see that dad hated to give up any of his powers; however, mom certainly had a plan of her own. This was Canada and in Canada it was the expectation that the woman of the household would have something to say about how the family was reared. More and more, it looked like the first half of the century belonged to dad while the next half would belong to mom.

Prior to 1950, dad was the breadwinner, king of the castle and the architect of all major decisions. This element of influence and control encompassed the workplace, financial planning, the home and the community. In the meantime, mom tended to raising the children, cooking and sewing. But, I would soon learn that mom, too, had a stubborn streak. She did not want to continue to ride in the back seat of the family car--being a *back seat driver* was no longer good enough for her. She now wanted to sit in the front seat so that she would have a better view of the world around her while assisting dad with mapping the best route to ultimate success. In fact, there were times when it looked like she wanted to grab the steering wheel right out of dad's hands.

I am sure that mom spent a lot of time trying to figure out the best way to convince dad that the family should abandon farming in favour of Edmonton. *'What'* she must have thought, *'if the boys said no to farming as a career choice?'* Dad must have sensed this because he gave Bill and me more and more liberties in the use of the farm truck as a means of transportation to leisure-time activities such as hockey practice and Friday night dances in the hopes that this would encourage us to stay on the family farm as opposed to post-secondary education. In a couple of instances when he did not grant us the use of the truck and we wanted to get to a *sock-hop* or a dance, we would physically push the vehicle away from the farm yard and start it only when we were some distance away from the house so as not to wake our sleeping parents.

By 1951, World War II had been over for six years and many of the pioneers who claimed High Prairie as their home in the 1920s and 1930s were now quickly approaching retirement age. An increasing number of local residents were planning on leaving their farming operation in exchange for part-time work before retiring or pulling up stakes completely for an urban centre. In other cases, families turned to home ownership in Edmonton and then providing room and board to university students. Some realized this dream by selling all of their property while others saw the advantage of renting their farm, knowing full well that the price of the land would continue to go up. Perhaps with some of these ideas in mind, my parents decided to motor to Edmonton in their new car to visit a neighbour who had recently moved to Alberta's capital. Could it be that mom had a plan and, unwittingly, dad was becoming a participant in the adventure? *"Do you realize, Andrij,"* ventured mom en route to Edmonton, *"we have been married for twenty-six years and this is our first holiday?"*

"You don't say," chided dad, *"you've never had it so good."*

The highway from High Prairie to Edmonton received many improvements during and following the war and was now referred to as *the high-grade highway* because its surface was higher than was the surrounding terrain. Highway engineers said that this would decrease the incidence of snow drifts during winter months and muddy conditions during the rainy spring and summer months. When we got to Westlock, I was intrigued by what I saw. Imagine, a road so smooth that the car did not kick up any dust or gravel. My dad said that it was a new form of asphalt paving. Arriving in Edmonton, my parents were surprised at how Edmonton had grown since their last visit. Much had changed for them as well. Where last they travelled the route to High Prairie via rail, they now made the trip by car which cost nearly two thousand dollars. Edmonton was now replete with modern paved roads and a large number of multi-storey buildings. Not only that, but there was evidence of a building boom in all sections of the capital city, moot testimony to the prosperity of a post-war Alberta. This phenomenon was in sharp contrast to the village of High Prairie, which was just now talking about bringing water and sewer services to its residents. In Edmonton, these services were the standard.

Although our stay with friends was relatively short, my parents simply loved all of those newfangled gadgets, which seemed to be a part and parcel of every home in the city. These ranged from household appliances such as a natural gas stove, a toaster, washer and clothes dryer, to the most important of all--indoor plumbing and a toilet. For certain, ten years earlier dad would never have taken so kindly to these creature comforts preferring to get up in the morning to stoke the old wood-burning heater and use the outdoor *biffy*. However, a transformation seemed to be taking place.

Mom saw the trip as providing her with an opportunity to broach the topic of eventually moving the family to Edmonton and, to my surprise, it seemed as though dad was prepared to at least listen. On our return trip home, my parents talked about technological advances and the many conveniences home owners had in Edmonton; advances that they did not have on the farm. They seemed especially intrigued with the black and white television signal being received in Edmonton, suggesting that this signal would soon be received in colour. There was one other observation that I made--in High Prairie we could listen to one radio station while Edmontonians could tune in to any one of a number of radio stations. This made conversations all the more interesting when people could talk about international affairs; talk of Communist North Korea invading South Korea which would soon lead to the Korean War and of the Federal Government repatriating the Constitution of Canada. In all of this, it seemed as though the seeds for what was to happen to the family in the future were sown on the trip to Edmonton.

As we neared Enilda on our return journey, the conversation turned to the Indian Reserves and Metis Settlements that were common in the region. During harvest season, it was not uncommon for local farmers to recruit labourers from the Sucker Creek Indian Reserve. In fact, the relationships between the aboriginals and the settlers was very positive and it was not unusual to find a Ukrainian family that had been befriended by an Indian. But, there were problems as well. During those earlier days when the white man first came to Western Canada, it was a common practice to barter for furs. Before too long, traders noted that the preferred item of barter was whiskey. Unfortunately, it was soon obvious that the Indian did not hold his liquor too well. This resulted in social problems and the federal government revised the Indian Act in 1951 to more accurately reflect the evolving circumstance of the Indians throughout Canada by giving them more control over their resources and their own destiny.

Being promoted from grade nine to grade ten was never a worry of mine; after all, with very few exceptions, all of my grades were *highly satisfactory*. Since mom insisted that I attend university upon graduation from high school, I enrolled in matriculation courses consisting of mathematics, physics, chemistry, English and French. However, during that first year of high school, a terrible thing happened--I discovered girls. It happened in a physics class and her name was Patsy Smith. I can still feel those tingles run up and down my spine as we held hands. I did not anticipate this kind of impact upon me. Some said it was the hormones while others said that it might be *puppy love*. As for me, I was not in a position to define this feeling. All I knew was that I wanted to learn how to dance and that this was the girl I wanted as my dance partner. She sure looked good to me.

Something else happened the next spring as I was completing my grade ten program. John Dubeta, the high school principal, got word from The Army Survey Establishment that the Commander of the detachment was coming to High Prairie High School for the purpose of recruiting four high schools for their topographical survey crew. When Major Cunningham arrived at the high school he told the principal that he wanted *'four students who are bright and physically fit'* and that is why, according to Mr. Dubeta, I got invited to apply. Upon being a successful candidate, I was informed that the centre of operations would be in the small community of Faust, thirty miles east of High Prairie and that my role would range from being a chainman, rodman and barometer operator to a cook's assistant.

How could I refuse? This meant that I could leave school in mid-June and not return until mid-September. And, the pay at $125 per month was not all bad. Our camp was set up in a matter of days and by the end of the month, my inservice training was over. The army contingent consisted of Major Cunningham and three corporals while the civilian component included a camp cook who also doubled as a packhorse operator and four high school students. Our means of transportation was an army jeep and, where necessary, horseback. The summer was chock-full of memories and my favourite was the operation of a two-way shortwave radio on which I could contact another crew in Saskatchewan or Army headquarters in Ottawa. I can still remember our call code, VDG241 or verbally as, *'this is Victor Dog George 241 calling Victor Dog George 248. Do you read me. Over.'*

Cunningham informed us that the purpose of our work was twofold: first, to provide the details necessary to the creation of accurate maps to be used by the military as well as the general public and second, to provide information to the Army about the topography of the region for purposes of national defence. At first, we would establish elevations along one route using a level and then run a level line parallel to it, several miles apart. Elevations between these two base lines would be determined after barometer readings were recorded and interpreted. I was amazed at how well the topography showed up in the aerial photographs under a stereoscope and how the crew could establish elevations throughout the region using barometer readings. There was no doubt in my mind as to the usefulness of this information.

I learned many things during that summer, the most important of which was the value of teamwork and being able to rely on your co-worker for support. On one particular two-day 20-mile barometer route, Tony Porisky and I got caught in heavy rainfall. The trekking through the dense forest of fallen and the burnt-out logs was slow and difficult. The first sign of trouble took place when Tony fell and broke his compass. Since we had only one compass, our ability to determine the correct route was gone. Worse yet, we could not rely on the sun due to the rain and heavy cloud cover. As a result, we made a decision to camp overnight.

But, the next morning's weather was no better. We had to rely on our knowledge of the aerial photographs that we had viewed before commencing our route, studying the direction of the flow of the creeks and determining the growth of moss on trees which are normally on the north side. By the end of the second day we still had not reached a road or a cut-line that would help us determine our location. Worse yet, we ran out of food and water. It would not be until the third day that we would finally stumble upon a trail which took us to a homestead. Of course, the homesteader did not have a telephone and the best he could do was point to us in the direction of Faust. Major Cunningham was glad to see us, informing us that it was the policy of the Army to send out a search party if any member of the survey crew was overdue by more than 48 hours. Since we were overdue by only 24 hours, we did not qualify for a rescue party.

After each barometer line, the two-man team could take a couple of days off to plot the barometer readings on a large map at base camp, do their laundry, and maybe even drive to Faust in the army jeep to play some pool or go for a swim in nearby Lesser Slave Lake. I enjoyed those days off and liked to play pool while Corporal Jones would have a few beers in the local hotel. On one such occasion, Corporal Jones consented to drive this young Indian woman, who happened to live near our camp, to her home. Much to my surprise, I do believe that he seduced her right there in front of the jeep under a large tree in her family's front yard while all the while a light rain continued to fall. I can still see the water dripping off his beret during the encounter. A week later the Corporal said that he had to make a sudden trip to the High Prairie Providence Hospital. *"Why, Corporal,"* I asked, *"are you making this trip? You don't look sick to me."*

"Oh, yes, I am, Carson," he responded. *"I have the drips. The dose."*

At the time, I didn't know what he was talking about until some time later at which time I learned that the Corporal had contracted a sexually transmitted disease; perhaps gonorrhea and had to get some treatment for it. Apparently, the slang for it was the drips, the dose, or clap. As a young man out on his first job, the summer was full of first-time experiences which were extremely useful to me in later years.

Although my love for baseball suffered because Faust did not have a baseball team, I did manage to spend some time in High Prairie to pursue my first love. There was one other important change during that summer. It was the last time that my parents really had to provide me with any funds for *personal* use. During the ensuing school year, I did graduate from grade ten, but with only one *highly satisfactory* grade and it would be in mathematics; all other grades were *satisfactory* with one notable exception, French 10, which I barely passed. Still, that didn't seem to matter because by mid-June,

I was back under the employ of the Army Survey Establishment. However, instead of Faust, it was now Fort St. John, British Columbia, with a new crew which included a bright university student from Winnipeg by the name of Gerry Hardy and Bohdan Slabij, Doug Morden, and Donald Hayden, all from our local high school. In many respects, the work was similar to that of the previous year except that we now had a new survey instrument called the theodolite, a surveying instrument for measuring horizontal and vertical angles.

Even though the centre of operation was the town of Fort St. John, our field camp was set up many miles from the town, sometimes near Hudson Hope on the Peace River and at other times on the Halfway River, a tributary of the Peace River. The topography of this region was far more hilly than was the case with the Faust region and I could see why Cunningham wanted to make use of a theodolite. The summer, as well, brought many new experiences, not the least of which was the service of a full-time camp cook and a professional guide/horse packer who had four horses at his disposal. His name was Jim Simpson, a well known and respected cowboy, rancher, guide, part-time songwriter and western troubadour. I can still recall his performance on radio in Dawson Creek to sing a song we wrote entitled *The Boat's Gone Up The River.*

Unlike the Cree Indians of Faust, this region was sparsely populated by Beaver Indians, who did use Cree-type tipis but whose customs, I was informed, were quite different. As well, it was good ranch country and it was not unusual to see wildlife, including the odd black and grizzly bear. It would be on one of these occasions that Don Hayden and Doug Morden, after completing their barometer line, would come across a mother bear and her two cubs near our encampment. Why she did not attack, I'll never know. As Doug and Don ran towards my tent yelling *'get the gun,'* I could see the bear slowly loping behind them, perhaps to make sure that they did not harm her two cubs. My, those two boys were a couple of frightened puppies! I got that high-powered rifle in a hurry but, as the bear stopped to observe, I went back into the tent, got a couple of pots, and started to bang them. The mother bear stood on her hind legs, observed me for another moment and then, with her cubs in tow, sauntered off into the forest.

To establish our second camp site, we had to cross the fast-flowing Halfway River. Jim Simpson swam his three horses across the river, picked up a small boat stashed on the opposite bank of the river for crossing purposes and used it to transport our gear across the river. Before we set out with the first load of gear, Simpson told me of the importance of docking the boat on the opposite bank and assigned me the task of holding a rope which I would use to secure the boat once we reached the opposite bank. We loaded about 200 pounds of gear and with Jim Simpson at the oars and Doug Morden at the rear of the boat, we set off. Half way across the swollen and fast-flowing river, things began to happen. The oars were anchored on each side of the boat by U-shaped blocks of wood. I guess Simpson put too much force into his rowing because one of these blocks snapped right off its mooring. Having the use of only one secured oar, Jim's ability to control the direction of the boat was lost and I knew that if he did not get control soon, we would be in grave danger when we hit the rapids, about a mile downstream. Jim quickly handed one paddle to Doug Morden while he used the other. In a crazy zig-sag way we made it to shore at which point I jumped out of the boat to secure it. But, in doing so I lost the rope and the force of my jump propelled the boat back into the river. My, you should have heard them yelling at me! Luckily, Jim was able to grab a willow on the bank and hang on until I rescued them.

On another occasion, we crossed the river by riding double on Sim Simpson's horse, one at a time, until all of our crew had crossed the river. That horse of Jim's was an excellent swimmer, yet we did learn that a week earlier a geological party at this same location, led by a packer on horseback, tried to swim their equipment across the river on three pack horses. Well, they lost their pack horses and equipment. Having regard for this incident, I felt most fortunate to have survived the crossing.

But, all was not peaches and cream. When we established camp on the west side of the Halfway River, the rains came for a solid week and the utility boat was torn from its mooring, thereby leaving us unable to get supplies from Fort St. John. To make matters worse, our two-way radio went on the blink making it impossible for us to contact army officials. The only food we had for two weeks was venison, river trout, and bannock; a favourite Indian flatbread made of flour or oatmeal and fried on a griddle. My, were we glad to get back to civilization. Still, that is not to say that the summer was totally devoted to work. We played baseball on the local team, dated local high school girls and even had the odd beer at the Pomeroy Hotel.

For whatever reason, it appeared as though the north generated many interesting stories and Fort St. John was the heart of the prospecting industry. It was not unusual to come in contact with prospectors; an unusual lot--always dreaming of the big find, be it iron ore, coal, or gold. One such prospector got my attention because he used a large husky dog as his pack animal. On this particular occasion, I watched as he came out of the bar, not too steady on his feet, then physically attack his dog. Just as suddenly, he stopped beating his husky, gave it a big hug and started to cry. I did not know what to make of the scene.

Our summer survey crew finished its tasks by mid-September and much like the previous summer, the friends that I had made were very special to me and we would remain close buddies for a very long time. We were like family, sharing our deepest hopes and aspirations; our fears, strengths and weaknesses. It seemed as though each of us ended up with a girlfriend before we left for High Prairie. I had a crush on a high school girl by the name of Hazel and considered her to be my girl. As for Hazel, I believe that it was simply a summer romance. The fact that I was so infatuated with her seemed not to matter. I even corresponded with her for a time. But, in the end, it all seemed so hopeless. By the time I settled in for my grade twelve program, she informed me that she was getting married the following summer, saying in her letter, *'why don't you come to Fort St. John for my wedding.'* Didn't the girl know that I was in love with her? Sadly, the romance was over.

That fall, I had decided that any further work that I undertook would have to be in my home town of High Prairie. With two summers of work experience under my belt, I realized that during that period I had made enough money for all of my personal needs and now needed to concentrate on my studies, hockey during winter months, and baseball during summer months. Oh yes, and I would have to put some time aside for dad's farming operation, if that did not interfere with my love of sports. Dad, of course, had other ideas.

There seemed to be two places that young people hung out in High Prairie: Eng's Café and Borsky's pool hall. The bus depot was a favourite of those students who wanted to hang out in the evening or drop in during the school day for an ice cream, a soda, or apple pie with ice cream. Next door was the Spalding Hotel, and the café patrons would wait for bar-closing time at which time, sure as hell, a fight would break out and they would have a ringside seat. But, that would not have been my favourite activity. No, sir. I preferred Borsky's Pool Hall, owned and operated by Alex Borsky. It was here that I learned how to play pool and the two most popular games were kelly pool and snooker. Everyone knew that you could not go into the pool hall unless you were eighteen years of age. But, that did not stop me or my brother Bill. And, I suppose Borsky was more interested in collecting the twenty cents per game than he might have been in our ages.

Prior to my second summer with the Army Survey Establishment, I turned seventeen in January of that year and frequently played pool during the winter months. It was a time in the history of the village that many young employees were being recruited into the oil patch and it was not uncommon for some of these boys to try their luck at pool. The province's vast natural resources were attracting companies from all over the world. In excess of $100 million was being spent in the Edmonton area alone. And, there were rich oil reserves in the High Prairie region to provide sought-after raw materials for such diverse industries as pulp and paper mills in the Peace country and chemical refineries in Edmonton. I must admit, some of those oil patch boys had little chance of beating me in a game of pool, especially if they had a drink or two before entering the pool hall. It got to the stage where I would make several dollars in an evening; sufficient funds for my schooling needs and even the odd taxi ride to our farm home. On days when the oil boys were not in, the take-home pay was not so good. There were other players in town that were much better than I. Naturally, I avoided them like a plague.

There were two individuals who cut short my career in the pool hall; a trucker by the name of Stan Parker and mom. Stan was a gambler of note, preferring the game of poker over pool and, recognizing that I was gaining a reputation for playing a solid game of pool, he gave me a lesson in psychology, saying, *'You know, you've been beating up pretty badly on a couple of those oilfield roughnecks. Remember, Carson, never kill the goose that lays the golden eggs. Take a little and give a little.'* I have never forgotten those words of wisdom.

The second important lesson came as a result of the actions of our school principal, John Duchak. One day he motored to our farm home to tell my parents that Bill and I were spending too much time playing pool and, as a consequence, our studies were suffering. *'On three occasions,'* he said, *'I picked them up in the poolroom during school hours and transported them back to school.'* He told my parents that we were university material and it was his hope that we would mend our ways. It is unfortunate that we were not aware of this conversation because the next day and right in the middle of a Kelly-pool game my mother burst into the pool hall with broom in hand– not just an ordinary house broom, but my prized curling broom. She seemed intent on having our scalps. Bill and I hightailed it out of there through the back door. Embarrassed, the amount of pool we played thereafter was very limited.

Earlier, our high school hockey team had come under the tutelage of John Duchak. He was no ordinary coach and even though the composition of our team was mediocre, our play seemed always to exceed expectations. Somehow, he always got the most mileage out of us. As I remember one incident, I was playing defence on our high school team against a fine team in the French community of Falher. It was an outdoor rink and Duchak told me that they had an outstanding player by the name of Jean Cote. Why, by the end of the first period the score was *four* to *zip* in their favour and the four goals were scored by Cote. Turning to me, Duchak said, *'Carson, it is your job to slow him down,'* I knew immediately that he was referring to their high scoring forward and I needed very little encouragement. I feared Duchak more than I did the referee or the opposing players. When I cross-checked Cote, even the five-foot high boards surrounding the ice-rink could not save him or stop his momentum. I guess his home must have been close to the rink because he disappeared into the night. No, we did not win the game but I never forgot the incident. With the emphasis on winning at any cost, my enthusiasm for the game diminished.

My work with the Army Survey Establishment now complete, I needed a part-time job while attending school. Russel Popel, the son of friends of my parents, was the manager of the Northland Utilities power plant in High Prairie. Powered by four huge diesel engines, the plant provided electrical power to the village and surrounding area. Since I practised or played baseball most every day, Len Sloat, the club manager, helped me nail down a part-time job at the plant during the late fall of that year. I loved the work because I could do the night shift, four to twelve, which also freed me for my sports activity. The pay of $125 per month was excellent as were the working conditions. My role was to monitor the power consumption in the village and increase or decrease the amount of power being generated by disengaging an engine during low consumption or starting one up during high consumption and then synchronizing it with the others to produce more electricity.

The work was so good at Northland Utilities that I decided to accept a full-time job during my second year of grade twelve by working the graveyard shift from midnight to eight in the morning. Of course, things did not always go that well for me. Instead of sleeping during the evening hours in advance of my graveyard shift, I often spent time playing baseball in those late summer months or socializing during winter months. Naturally, my grades suffered. On one occasion I must have fallen asleep during my graveyard shift only to be awakened by a frantic manager. Apparently Popel got a call from a customer at six in the morning, mad as hell, saying that the power was out. Sure enough, a rain storm hit High Prairie at five in the morning causing a lot of folks to consume much more electricity than was the norm. Had I been awake, I would have noticed the need to cut in another diesel engine. Imagine my embarrassment when I was rescued by Popel! Still, I learned from that experience that making a mistake was not all bad. I was the talk of the town for a week or two. No one had power that morning and I was the one to blame.

My memories of 1952 are all the more vivid because it was the year that King George VI died and was succeeded by his daughter, Elizabeth. It was also the year that Canada's first TV station, CBC/CBFT signed on the air in English and in French. What I liked most was that this was the year that the school district recruited a new kind of high school principal by the name of Benjamin Gold Halbert. His son Tom and I became close friends, played sports together and became life-long friends. Ben Halbert was an excellent educator, drilling us for hours at a time in preparation for a final examination saying that there was nothing wrong with memorizing a lot of facts. Throughout, he promoted sports in the community and nothing was more important to me than sports, except, perhaps, Shirley Trump. Shirley was the daughter of the local train master and she stole my heart. But, the romance suddenly came to an end when another suitor told me that he would break my arm if I ever even came close to her again. I thought long and hard about sports and my arm; my pitching arm. Finally, I said to myself, 'go ahead, you can have her.'

With the decision to quit hockey, I turned to curling by joining the high school curling club. I loved the game and quickly became very good at it. In grades ten and eleven I played third on a curling team. During my final year in high school, I skipped my own team and naturally Tom Halbert was on my team. In those days, the ice was natural as opposed to being artificial as is the case today. It was inconsistent and a team sometimes needed some luck to end up on the winning side. To make matters worse, the curling rocks were not matched and were owned by members of the curling club. I shall always recall that I used the rocks belonging to someone with the initials *FP* engraved on them. Well, during that final year of high school we fought our way to the Peace Country finals and I found myself in a game to represent the region in the provincial finals. When, after seven ends the score was 11 - 3 for the Peace River team, most everyone left the McLennan rink except for Halbert and a few of our fans. Maybe Halbert recalled Yogi Berra's famous words, '*it ain't over until the fat lady sings,*' and held out some hope. We scored 3 in end number eight to make the score 11-6, three more in end number nine to make the score 11-9 and stole three more in end number 10 to defeat the Peace River entry by a score of 12 to 11. Imagine the surprise in Peace River when their local paper falsely published an article entitled, '*Kashuba Defeated in Curling Finals.*'

It would also be a time when, under the leadership of Halbert, I would first compete in the provincial juvenile baseball playdowns and the following year in the Alberta junior baseball playdowns. Although we lost the finals both years, I got to play with some of the finest baseball players in all of Alberta while continuing to dream of one day playing in the big leagues.

Several other important events took place in 1952. Bill would graduate with a high school diploma and weigh the options available to him for post-secondary education and a career. Eventually, he made a decision to enrol in a business program at MacTavish Business College in Edmonton, saying that he was influenced in his decision by a classmate who earlier enrolled in the College. It would be the same summer that Bill would be involved in a near tragedy; an incident that would cause dad to reconsider his insistence that his sons inherit and continue with the farming operation. It happened while Bill was cultivating some land on the Enilda property. To dad's surprise, Bill arrived home shortly after the lunch hour, on foot and not on the tractor. "*You're home early. And, your clothes. What happened?*" asked dad.

"*I've had an accident, and the tractor, cultivator and I ended up in the river,* " explained Bill.

"*Ended up in the river? The hell you say. How did that happen?*"

Bill went on to explain how he had fallen asleep on the tractor and failed to make a turn at the end of the field, continuing over the bank and into the river. To everyone's surprise, except for a few bruises, Bill escaped injury. Apparently, it was shear luck that the river bank was not very precipitous and only about twelve feet above the water table. In fact, the five feet of water cushioned the impact of the tractor's plunge. If nothing else, the cold water wakened Bill who managed to scramble to shore. It would take Carson Porisky's powerful D6 Caterpillar tractor to recover dad's tractor and cultivator. Suddenly, the incident was precisely the ammunition mom needed, saying that it was God telling her that the family should abandon the farming operation. She used every argument in her arsenal to argue her case, from the cost of room and board in Edmonton to the fact that the younger children would soon be attending university. She applied more and more pressure on dad to embrace the inevitable.

Getting admitted to the University of Alberta in those days was easier than it is today. All a student needed was an average of sixty percent with no failing grade in a matriculation subject. However, there was one barrier to my application; my grade twelve French grade was less than fifty percent. Not only that, but I also received a failing grade in French when I wrote the supplemental examination in August. Still, the University of Alberta did admit me in the fall of 1954, or so I thought. However, in mid-October I was informed by the Registrar that my high school grades were too low to continue in the Bachelor of Geology program. After discussing the matter with my high school principal, Ben Halbert, I switched my program to education. *"Besides,"* added Halbert, *"Tom is already enrolled in the program."* Up until that moment, I had never considered the possibility of becoming a teacher. *'Strange,'* I concluded, *'how a career decision can be made as though by a flip of the coin.'*

To this day I am thankful that I did enrol in the one-year teacher-training program, not only for the content of the courses which prepared me for the tasks which I was about to undertake but also for the life-long friends that I made. Two members of that class, Tom Halbert and John Benson went on to successful careers in educational management. In particular, it was John's interest in sports that brought us together and I can still recall playing basketball, football and volleyball with him as well as attending fight cards in Calgary, Edmonton and Barrhead. From time to time John would come to the fights, satchel in hand imitating a medical doctor while I would accompany him as a photographer. Thank goodness we did not have to practice any of our magic. It was also the year that I introduced John to Glenda, the girl that he would soon marry.

In addition to the University of Alberta, there were many other important things to remember about the summer of 1954; some pleasant and others rather sad. Statistics from the previous year showed that 8,000 Canadians had come down with poliomyelitis of which 481 died. I recall that at least two students at High Prairie High School came down with the crippling disease. But, there was good news, too. The Salk vaccine was developed to successfully fight polio. It was also the summer that the British Empire Games were held in Vancouver and England's Roger Bannister would run the first-ever 4-minute mile.

As I considered the events that got me to the University of Alberta, I had to admit that without the influence and persistence of my mother, I would have remained on the farm helping my dad accomplish his dream.

Steven Kashuba on army jeep while serving with the Canadian Army Survey Establishment, Fort St. John, British Columbia, 1952.

Graduation picture, Steven Kashuba is in the back row, 3rd from left. High Prairie High School, 1954.

31.

Andrij Throws in the Towel

Agrees to move to Edmonton

Having graduated from the University of Alberta with a teaching certificate, I was encouraged to learn of the number of teaching positions available to graduates. In fact, school superintendents descended upon the Faculty of Education from all parts of the province with the hopes of signing a new teacher to a contract. After some thought, I signed a contract with the Westlock School Division with the hopes of being assigned to a school in Westlock and then put the whole matter aside so that I might pursue summer employment with the Department of Highways and *sandlot* baseball–especially tournament baseball.

Labour Day weekend came all too quickly. As I packed my two suitcases on Sunday morning in preparation for the trip to my assigned school in Jarvie, twenty miles north of Westlock, I felt good about the fact that Bill would drive me to my destination that afternoon, well in advance of my first day of teaching on Tuesday morning. But, trouble developed quickly when Bill informed me that he could not start his car. I called the bus depot, only to be informed that the bus scheduled for Jarvie and points north had just left. Worse luck when the passenger train bound for Peace River had also left that morning. There being no other means of transport, I decided to *thumb* my way to Jarvie. The trucker who picked me up seemed genuinely happy to have someone to talk to, even though conversation was difficult in that noisy cab. I was thankful that the Chairman of the School Board had made arrangements for my room and board.

I began my teaching duties with a split grades 1 and 3 class, but within a couple of weeks was moved to a split grades 6 and 9 class. I completed my first year of teaching on a Letter of Authority from the Minister of Education allowing me to teach high school subjects without the necessary qualifications. That first year of teaching taught me a lot about survival in a small community where everyone knew your business. I recall dating a grade twelve student who also took Chemistry 30 from me. Looking back, I am not surprised that this immediately caused a problem and after some discussion with school principal, Mrs. Newnham, I dropped the idea of dating *any* student. Mr. Newnham, a veteran of World War II, also gave me some sound advice saying, *"...running a class is the same as commanding a company or platoon in the army. Never let your subordinates get too close to you; always keep some distance between yourself and the foot soldiers."* I have never forgotten his advice.

But, there were other lessons to be learned. I soon discovered that teaching was a complex and tough job. Suddenly, I had a great admiration for all those who taught me, going so far as to entertain the idea of calling at least one of them to apologize for not being a better student. During that year it seemed as though I taught just about every subject from grades one through twelve. In those instances where I was not prepared to teach the subject matter, I relied on a team approach in the presentation of course content, thereby harnessing the strengths of the students themselves. And, since the age spread between the grade twelve students and me was rather small and our relationships quite positive, I had little difficulty in motivating my students.

A one-year teaching contract brought me an annual salary of $2,150 or a monthly cheque of just over $150. After paying income taxes and professional dues to the Alberta Teachers Association, my annual take-home pay was just over $1,800. With monthly living expenses in excess of $65, very little was left over as disposable income. To help me get around in the rural community, I purchased a 1951 Ford car for $650 which added another expense of $50 per month, financed through a loan company at six percent per annum. I remember the pride I took in that car and how I wanted to share my joy with the world. Since the car had a damaged muffler, I replaced it with a straight pipe. My, that beast suddenly became noisy and I could not go anywhere without the whole world knowing of my whereabouts. In self-defence, I installed a new muffler so that I could drop off my date without waking her parents and the neighbourhood. Thank goodness for the occasional invitation to dinner, otherwise it is doubtful that I could have survived the year without taking out another loan.

In addition to my teaching duties, I served on the Village Council, started up a Square Dance Club and scheduled gym night once a week for pickup basketball. For leisure time activities, I joined a curling club in nearby Fawcctt and referred basketball games in the local gymnasium. In the spring, I coached the track and field team and joined the local baseball club during which time I developed a close friendship with Wilf Willier, a full-blooded Cree Indian who worked for Northern Alberta Railways. *'Finally,'* remarked our coach, Carl Winniski, *'with this pitcher-catcher battery, we have a competitive baseball team.'* All too soon the school year was over and

I would have to consider what I wanted to do, not just during the summer holidays, but in the future as well.

But, I needn't have worried about the future. Bill called me from the Department of Highways and had me on my way to Calgary before the end of June. The first order of business was to check in at the regional office in Calgary, located in the Old Court House, deliver the truck to a survey crew in Cochrane and return to Calgary for my deployment. I started my duties as a gravel checker for the Department just south of Calgary, but that did not last long. The Highway Inspector, Jim Flynn, liked the quality of my work and promptly promoted me to the position of field-office manager in Calgary. For me, that was an excellent move because I now had sufficient time to play baseball with the Strathmore baseball team. My catcher was a University of Alberta student by the name of Alan Warrack who, in due course, would enter politics and serve in Premier Peter Lougheed's cabinet.

I have a suitcase full of memories of that summer, the fondest of which is my initial stint as a relief pitcher with a semi-pro baseball club by the name of Brookman Dodgers. But, even this memory is shunted aside as I recall playing in a baseball tournament and relieving pitcher Wally Laschuk in the fourth inning with the bases loaded and then getting *fifteen consecutive strikeouts* to win the game 2-1. To this day, I still cherish that article which appeared in the Calgary Herald highlighting this special feat.

In those days, highway construction was strictly a summertime activity and by late October all activity came to a halt. Upon my return to Edmonton, I looked for a career other than teaching and, since I took a liking to office work which involved the basic principles of accounting, I accepted a job with Deloitte, Plender, Haskins and Sells, an Edmonton chartered accounting firm. At that time, a person could pursue the Chartered Accounting designation without first having to complete a baccalaureate degree. Each Saturday I attended formal accounting classes, wrote periodic accounting examinations and got myself deeply immersed in the world of debits, credits, financial statements, and accounting audits for the princely sum of $125 per month. However, when it came to working late into the night on those corporate tax returns, my love affair with accounting began a downhill slide.

Not only was 1956 a pivotal year for me, it was also a very important year on the world's stage when Canada provided free transportation to refugees from the failed Hungarian Revolution and many of those immigrants found their way to Calgary. Earlier, it was the Russian tanks that doomed the revolution and Canada was now trying to help those who escaped the terror. As I witnessed the breakup of Hungarian families, I was reminded of an earlier scene where my parents left their homeland for a new start. As the year came to a close, it was Secretary of State Lester B. Pearson who tried to broker a peaceful solution to the conflict involving the hostile British,

French, Israeli and Egyptian forces in the Suez Canal region. At the same time, another soon-to-be famous Canadian, a tough talking Tory leader by the name of John Diefenbaker began to spin his magic. I first met Diefenbaker in a political rally in Red Deer in 1961 and, after a brief conversation, became a fan of Diefenbaker and a lifelong member of the Progressive Conservative Party. My, I sure did love his oratorical style!

As the income tax season was coming to a close in April of 1957 and the frequency of my trips to Lamont, Mundare and Two Hills to undertake accounting audits decreased, I suddenly developed, once again, a yen for the out-of-doors. Paper tapes upon tapes of countless numbers fed into a hand-operated adding machine or a comptometre were starting to get to me. With just a little bit of coaxing from Bill, I was once again on my way to Calgary with the Department of Highways. But, it was not just the work with the Department that attracted me, it was once again baseball, first with the Brookman Dodgers and then with Strathmore and Carstairs. I particularly enjoyed tournament baseball and I can still recall being on the mound for the final game of a tournament which was broadcast live by Henry Viny. Those were heady moments! But then, those moments were also intermingled with failure. Later that summer, Baz Nagle, who played baseball with Brookman Dodgers as well as football with the Calgary Stampeders, invited me to attend their football training camp. And, even though I was in great physical condition, I cannot say that I enjoyed the experience as Baz put us through the daily regimen. At the end of the first week, I had the distinct honour of being the first prospect to be cut loose by the football club.

Still, most of my evenings were free and I wanted to earn more money so that I might pay off the debt on the newly-purchased 1952 Chevy. Having reached the age of twenty, I applied for a chauffeur's licence and took a part-time job with United Taxi Cab Company. When, in the future I enrolled in a psychology course at the University of Alberta, I often recalled my experiences driving taxi. It was here that I learned a lot about people; how to provide a first-class service in order to qualify for a large tip and how to be especially nice to female passengers who became my most generous *tippers*. But, I also discovered that not all clients were honest. Some refused to pay while others would try to short-change me. At times it was stressful and even dangerous work. On one occasion I picked up two male passengers who wanted to be taken to the *chicken restaurant* where, they said, they had a couple of *chicks* waiting for them. Darned if I knew how to get there and they, being inebriated, were of no help. An argument broke out between them and then a fist fight which frightened the hell out of me. In the process, they broke the side window and the windshield. What to do? I kept my two-way radio on so that the dispatcher could hear what was happening. Quickly, I drove to the nearest police station where both passengers were promptly arrested. The damage to the interior of the car was considerable. That, for the time being put an end to my career of driving taxi.

Stationed over the winter of 1957-58 in Carstairs with the Department of Highways, I was glad to be close to the nurses' residence in High River and my girlfriend, Jean Mason. In the spring of 1958, I was transferred to Fort Saskatchewan as an office manager and played baseball with the Fort Saskatchewan Red Sox, one of the finest amateur teams in the province. I had not considered a career change, but with the burgeoning student enrolment in the local high school and a teacher shortage, I was asked by the principal if I would consider accepting a teaching position. The pay scale at the Clover Bar School Division was among the best in the province and the new high school looked very inviting. So, I said, *why not?*

I shall ever remember that first day of school. It was morning recess and the Superintendent of Schools, Mr. Walker, had just introduced me to the 8th grade class. In the hallway, I heard someone call, *"Hey, Teach."* As I looked around, I was surprised to note that a student in my class had addressed *me* as *Teach*. Being caught off guard and not knowing what to say, I sauntered over to the area occupied by a small group of boys. One of the students told me that the culprit's name was Ted Bachleitner. He was big and tall and at that moment I wondered what he was doing in grade eight. He looked down at me and called out to another student, *"Hey, Jim Fisher, come and sit on my forearm."* Jim Fisher did just that and Ted promptly lifted him straight upwards to shoulder level, held him in that position for several moments, then set him down very slowly. As he set him down, I heard him say, *"I hope, Teach, that you and I never have a problem."* Well, to tell you the truth, we never did have a problem.

With the coming of spring in 1959, Dr. Walter Buck, a well-known local dentist, took over the duties as manager of the Fort Saskatchewan Red Sox. He must have suspected that I enjoyed teaching and that the students looked upon me as a role model so he took it upon himself to encourage me to get my butt back to university. Not only that, but Walt also wanted to make sure that I heard him correctly by inviting me to play a round of golf at the local nine-hole golf course. At that moment, I was not so much interested in my career as I was in golf for, even with a borrowed set of golf clubs, I liked the game. I liked it enough that I asked my landlord, Scotty Walker, a transplanted Scot and a player of note, to give me a golf lesson. As I reflected upon Walt's plea, I thought about all of those positive teaching experiences and decided to accept his advice.

Meanwhile, momentous things were happening with my parents and my siblings in High Prairie. During the time that I attended university, taught in Jarvie, and worked in Calgary, my parents were not asleep at the switch. No sir. Obviously, mom had worked her magic and following a couple trips to Edmonton during that period of time and, with the help of a family friend by the name of John Sernyk, dad purchased a vacant building lot on 80th Avenue and 114th Street, just a stone's throw from the University of Alberta, and promptly took out a building permit in 1957. Of course, dad did not immediately abandon the farm; instead he contracted the construction of the home to John Sernyk, who lived near the construction site, with the understanding that the home was to be completed by the summer of 1958.

The new home in Edmonton was sufficiently large not only for the family but to house as many as six students in the lower level. Although it was true that those same suites were contrary to Edmonton's Land Use Bylaw, city officials turned a blind eye to such use because the University of Alberta was experiencing phenomenal growth and faced a drastic shortage of housing for its students. As a consequence, my parents were able to continue with the farming operation in addition to operating a modest rooming house. Taking into consideration that the cost of the dwelling was less than ten thousand dollars and that the revenue was upwards to $500 per month, my parents found the venture to be a money-making proposition. By 1959 my parents established, in essence, two homes–maintaining the existing one in High Prairie while at the same time moving the family to the new home in Edmonton. All of this meant that Alice, Lily and Buddy could now enrol in St. Mary's Catholic High School in Edmonton.

From 1959 to 1962, dad would return to High Prairie during the farming season and return to Edmonton for the winter months. By this time he knew that neither Bill nor I was interested in farming. Meanwhile, Andy completed his high school and immediately got a job in the oil patch where wages were very high. Having regard for all of these developments, dad sold the family farms to Carson Porisky and began the final move to Edmonton. I am sure that it was with great reluctance that he gave up the only way of life he had come to know since coming to Canada. To him, change must have come with many misgivings as he turned his attention to life in an urban centre and part-time employment in a cabinetry shop, a role that he would continue until his retirement in 1967.

In the meantime, upon completing my one-year teaching contract in Fort Saskatchewan, I moved back home in pursuit of my degree in education to find that mom had already adjusted to life in the city as a duck might to water. My dad was somewhat slower in accepting a mode of daily activity that was quite foreign to him, yet, he did make the adjustment and seemed to be very happy helping mom in the daily operation of the rooming house. Most every day, just before the supper hour would find him in control of the television to watch professional wrestling, which, incidentally, he believed to be the real thing. In fact, I recall the day that he got so excited about a wrestling match that he attacked a recliner and virtually knocked the stuffing right out of it.

There was little doubt that changes were taking place in our family during the late 1950s and early 1960s but there were also great changes taking place in all of Canada. To solidify Canada's position as a nation bent on international trade, the St. Lawrence Seaway officially opened in 1959 under the leadership of Canada's Prime Minister, John Diefenbaker. In 1961 and to the delight of political pundits, the President of the United States, John F. Kennedy and his wife Jacqueline visited Canada. It would also be the year that the 2-millionth immigrant entered Canada since the close of World War

II and the following year, the 7,700 kilometre-long Trans-Canada highway opened providing a major motor route to rival the Canadian Pacific Railway which was completed some 85 years earlier.

Some of these accomplishments by Canadians provide a backdrop to what Andrij and Eva had achieved. Taking stock of all that happened since my parents arrived in Canada, I had to conclude that their present circumstance was testimony to the fact that dreams do come true and that all things are possible in this land called Canada. And, in the final analysis, they accomplished their dream in a relatively short period of time.

As events unfolded, my parents were preparing for a life of retirement while I was contemplating a journey of a different kind. It all came about at a time when mom took great pride in her new home and the role she played in the career choices of her children. She seemed particularly proud of her three youngest, Alice, Lily and Buddy. Alice was about to graduate from MacTavish Business College with outstanding grades and Lily and Buddy were both working hard on their baccalaureate programs at the University of Alberta. All she wanted was the best for each child, no more and no less. And, strangely enough, by the time the family completed its move to Edmonton, all dad could do was smile smugly when mom was heard to say, '...*finally, Andrij, I have to admit that my dreams have come true.*'

Although it may be true that mom realized her dream in 1961, exactly thirty years after first coming to Canada, it is also true that through a strange coincidence of history, thirty years later Ukrainians the world over would also realize a dream of gargantuan proportions.

Here is how it happened.

A colourful bus stop shelter near Lviv, Ukraine, 1998.

Religious shrine located at entrance to Plazow, Poland, 1997.

A photograph of a bride and two bridesmaids taken in the Carpathian Mountains in 1967 is reminiscent of mom's special day in 1924.

Sharon Kashuba and Anna Grokh crossing a brook on a path leading to Aunt Anna's home in the village of Loshniv, 1998.

*Kashuba family home,
Edmonton, Alberta, 1958.*

*Family pride, L to R are Anne Kalyn, Andrij Kashuba, Buddy
Kashuba, Lynne Porisky, Maria Kalyn, John Kalyn, Michael
Kalyn; front row, L to R, Jeannie Kalyn, Eva Kashuba, Lorainne
Kalyn, Irene Kalyn, 1958.*

*The Kashuba
siblings: Back
row—Buddy,
Andy, Steven,
and Bill; Front
row—Alice,
Anne and Lily,
2002.*

PART 4

A SEARCH FOR THE VILLAGE

32.

Ukraine, Free at Last

Thanks to glasnost and perestroika

Millions of Ukrainians the world over, and especially those living in Ukraine, awakened on August 24, 1991 as if from a dream. For it was on this day that Ukraine declared itself an independent state taking its rightful place among the nations of the world. With so little being written or heard about Ukraine during the Soviet era, many Canadians didn't even know that Ukraine existed. *Perhaps*, they thought, *Ukraine is simply a part of Russia.* Suddenly, there was the realization that Ukraine was a buried nation for much of its history. Travel to and within the country was restricted for many years and little was written about its rich history and culture. But, to shake the Russian bear from its back was not easy. In fact, the process of democratizing Ukraine may take much longer than anyone thought possible and flies in the face of those who said that the move from a *planned economy* to a *market economy* should be as easy as learning to walk.

Having been to Soviet Ukraine in 1967, I came to understand that there was *the nation that the West saw based upon the limited amount of reliable information* while on the other hand there was the *Ukraine as presented in the Soviet press; a sanitized form of misinformation.* The time had suddenly come for *all Ukrainians* to resurrect the nation of Ukraine; to ferret out the truth from fiction about its history. Yet, because the nation lay behind an Iron Curtain, it was difficult to get at the facts with any degree of certainty. Soon, however, the truth about what happened in Ukraine since the Bolshevik Revolution, suppressed for so many years, was about to be uncovered, *thanks to Gorbachev and his perestroika and glasnost.*

Emerging Ukrainian leaders taking up the challenge of leading Ukraine out of the darkness soon discovered that centuries of economic and political dependence on Moscow had sufficiently crippled the new nation to such a degree as to render it incapable of full and meaningful nationhood. Ukraine had just emerged from three centuries of colonialism and seventy years of totalitarianism; a nation with severe economic, ecological, transportation, communications, and energy problems. But, to those living in Ukraine as well as the offspring of those who had emigrated to other lands, the fear of short-term pain would not deter them from pursuing full-fledged nationhood.

Up until that time, my involvement in the Ukrainian community was minimal, at best. However, a series of seemingly unconnected events would soon have an impact upon my future plans. It was several years earlier that my dad promised his youngest sister, Anna, that he would bring her to Canada for a visit. In 1988, my mother felt duty-bound to fulfill dad's wish and, as the Christmas holiday season approached in 1990, we were informed that Aunt Anna Grokh would soon be winging her way to Edmonton. All of this was confirmed when we received a telephone call from a bus company in Quebec enquiring as to whether or not we were the family that brought Anna to Canada. To everyone's shock, Anna was aboard a Greyhound bus en route from Montreal to Toronto. How did this happen? Why was she on a bus and not on an aircraft? Apparently, mom purchased a return ticket for Anna from Lviv to Canada via Moscow. Somehow her travel agent neglected to book the final leg of her flight to Edmonton. Anna was now stranded on a bus, unable to speak a word of English and only a few dollars to her name. Were it not for the help of a generous stranger, the outcome might have been very different.

Despite these problems, Anna's arrival in Edmonton was very timely because Sharon and I had visions of one day flying to Poland in search of my dad's village and I hoped it would be my Aunt who would provide me with the information necessary to start my search. After all, she *was* born in Grohi, the same village as was dad. But, getting *any* information from Anna *at that time* was impossible. Perhaps it was because she was brought up under communist rule and learned well how to keep her thoughts to herself. Maybe it was because my extended family in Ukraine came under the scrutiny by the KGB following my misadventures in 1967. Meanwhile, Poland had gained its independence in 1989 and, as a result, travel to that country was now possible. However, I wanted to travel to both countries, Poland and Ukraine. The question was, *would Ukraine be next to gain its independence, thereby enabling me to obtain the necessary documentation?*

It was during this same time frame that another important event was unfolding in our community. The Alberta Branch of the Ukrainian Canadian Congress (UCC) which represents the Ukrainian community before the provincial government on issues of history, culture and education, was busy planning a big celebration for the fall of 1991 to commemorate the centennial of the arrival of the first Ukrainian pioneers in Canada. There was much work to be done in preparation for the celebrations and I consented to head up a committee to oversee the production and distribution of specially-designed souvenirs for the occasion. As Gene Zwozdesky, the Executive Director of the celebrations, John Shalewa and I deliberated on the most appropriate

Mikhail Sergeyevich Gorbachev, President of the Soviet Union, 1989.

His Holiness John Paul II made a pastoral visit to Lviv in 2001, the seat of both the head of the Ukrainian Greek Catholic Church and the Archbishop of the Roman Catholic Church. During his visit he blessed the new Ukrainian Catholic University.

mix of souvenirs to be produced by Peter and Alice Kmech's firm, Creative Concepts, it seemed to be the precise moment that Mikhail Gorbachev was pushing ahead with his *perestroika* in the Soviet Union. Suddenly, my work as a first-generation Ukrainian-Canadian took on a new meaning.

It is without doubt that thousands of Canadians of Ukrainian descent played a role in Ukraine's march to independence by working tirelessly in providing assistance to Ukrainians through formal government channels, participation in the affairs of the Ukrainian Canadian Congress, and by supporting the Rukh movement in the months immediately following Gorbachev's ascendancy to power in 1985. In fact, many believe that the emergence of Rukh in 1989 in support of *perestroika* was instrumental in Ukraine's march to independence.[36] When Mikhail Sergeyevich Gorbachev[37] came into power and declared that he would pursue a policy of *glasnost and perestroika*, Ukrainian-Canadians applauded his ascendancy and saw this as an opportunity to address two important issues; *the impact of the Chornobyl nuclear explosion on Ukrainian children and Ukraine's inexorable march towards full independence.*

From an historical perspective, Ukraine's status had remained relatively static for seventy years from 1920 to 1991. Her gross national product in the realm of mining, agriculture, manufacturing, infrastructure, provision of services, and all those other components that make up a nation's gross

---

36   Motyl, Alexander J. Dilemmas of Independence, Ukraine After Totalitarianism, Council of Foreign Relations Press, New York, 1993, pages 43 and 44.

37   Mikhail Sergeyevich Gorbachev became the President of the Soviet Union in 1989 and was awarded the Nobel Peace Prize in 1990. Best known for his policies of perestroika and glasnost, he did much to spearhead the breakup of the Soviet Union.

Leonid Kuchma,
the second President of an
independent Ukraine, July,
1994 to January, 2005.

Viktor
Yushchenko,
President of
Ukraine, 2006.

national product could have been attributed to the direct involvement of the Soviet Union through its domestic and foreign policies over those many years. What then was the legacy that the Soviet Union left behind after its seventy years of suppression of Ukraine? One must conclude that the Soviet Union was interested mainly in massive developments, particularly as related to nuclear energy and cared little if rivers became polluted and ran like *multi-coloured rainbows*. So what if the collective health of a nation was put at high risk? Did they really care about the sanctity of the individual? Just what were the results of those wayward policies? Birth defects in the geographic area of Chornobyl continued to be alarmingly high and cancer-causing pollutants exceeded acceptable norms many times over in some areas and lead and zinc were found in the soil. Other poisons from smelted ores were also present; among them arsenic, mercury, and cadmium. This resulted in immune-system abnormalities in children, predisposing them to viral infections and other diseases. Researchers have also found that chromosome damage was widespread.

And, who knows which among all of those maladies might have contributed to the development of President Mikhail Gorbachev's perestroika in those critical years of 1985 to 1991 which gained so much notoriety and ultimate success? Yet, one begins to wonder whether all of that heartache about nation-building on the part of so many was worth it, *for in the final analysis, did not all Ukrainians end up with damaged goods?*

One thing seemed clear; things could only get better for Ukraine and its inhabitants. For those living in this pillaged land, this was their home and the mass exodus experienced in Western Ukraine a century earlier would not occur again. As the events leading to Ukraine's independence are examined more closely, one man above all others will be recognized for putting a choke hold on the Russian Bear and wrestling him to the ground. And, what is interesting to note, he was not of Ukrainian heritage but rather *the Soviet Union's Mikhail Sergeyevich Gorbachev.*

Gorbachev was not born a reformer, recognizing at an early age that it would be suicidal to express opposition to the ruling proletariat. As a result, even as a young Komsomol Youth member, he had determined that he would work to change the political system from the inside and not the outside. Perhaps, as he looked around at a rapidly aging Kremlin leadership, he might have echoed the sentiments of another dissident who toasted his young colleagues with, '*Comrades, we shall outlive them...*' Gorbachev must have known that it would only be the true believers that would last long enough to change the system. To anyone who knew him, he was a true Stalinist. Even his wife, Raisa, believed this of him. For sixteen years as the leading Party official in his native city of Stavropol in southern Russia, Mikhail was able to listen to critical ideas while at the same time leaving the impression that he would ultimately play the Party loyalty card.

In 1978 Leonid Brezhnev brought the young Gorbachev to Moscow and put him in charge of agriculture at the age of forty-seven; *the only member of the Politburo under the age of fifty.* Good luck and timing in 1985 had much to do with how the ten members of the Politburo selected the next leader. Brezhnev, Andropov, and Chernenko all seemed to die in quick succession and three of the ten members were not able to attend a hurriedly-called meeting by the then acting deputy, Mikhail Gorbachev. With the old guard missing from the meeting, it was not a surprise that the youthful Gorbachev was elected as the new Party leader and the following day unanimously elected as General Secretary. The record shows that his first brief address to the members of the Politburo had to do with *democracy, reform, change, and economic dynamism.* '*To do anything else,*' concluded Mikhail, '*would be to deny the Soviet Union membership in world leadership.*'

Even though he was only five foot ten, he radiated energy and self-confidence and to foreign leaders he stood very tall. Given sufficient time, he felt that he could convince anyone of anything while at the same time leaving the impression that he was the defender of the faith. It was his view that the Politburo had to *blend communism with a good measure of capitalism.* To accomplish this feat, he first had to convince the Politburo that he was a dedicated communist while at the same time confiding in Raisa that '*Russia cannot continue living in the old way.*' Even though Gorbachev knew that he could comfortably be the Party's leader for upwards to twenty years, he insisted on reform and refused to quit.

The magnitude of his undertaking cannot be denied. He had no road maps to follow, no rough guidelines, and no friends in high places to advise him. It was no longer a case of tinkering with the edges as it were, it was now a matter of spearheading fundamental changes in the very basis of the Soviet economy. Mikhail also knew that he could not communicate his future vision for Russia for to do so would tip his hand and allow his opponents to have the very ammunition that might topple him.

Even as the Politburo was putting into place those pre-conditions necessary to a free market economy, old party-liners were blaming Gorbachev for betraying their nation even though he garnered the *Man of The Decade* award from Time magazine in January of 1990. Russians blamed him for the breakup of the USSR and for turning their nation from a proud superpower into a charity case that constantly looked to foreign aid. Others blamed him for not moving far enough and fast enough and both groups said that they would never vote him into public office again. In retrospect, he left office without a solid base of political support while at the same time being recognized as the most successful reformer in Soviet history.

What then was the premise of Gorbachev's *uskoreniye or acceleration policy* in Ukraine? How was he able to describe Brezhnev's legacy as that of stagnation and not be drummed out of office? The answer, in part, lies in his ability to communicate effectively not only with members of the Politburo but also with the masses. Despite apparent difficulties, Gorbachev pushed ahead with perestroika on two fronts, the political and the economic. In order to accomplish this, he determined that he would have to democratize the whole process and widen the decision-making process.

As fate would have it, a most unfortunate event would take place that would have far-reaching repercussions, not only in Russia, but particularly in Ukraine. It would be on April 26, 1986 that a nuclear reactor blew up in Chornobyl and Gorbachev found himself involved in the cover-up of the nuclear accident. The Soviets tried their best to minimize the health dangers at home and abroad and it was not until two weeks later that Gorbachev would, on national television, admit to the disaster while at the same time saying that, '*the worst danger is over and the situation is under control.*' More than any other single event, it would be the disaster at Chornobyl and the way in which the Soviet Union handled the nuclear disaster that would come to haunt its leaders.

By 1987 Gorbachev's democratization plan seemed to stall. Old party-liners prevented him from bringing in younger mavericks. Even Moscow's Party leader, Boris Yeltsin, resigned his position in the Politburo while at the same time criticizing Gorbachev for his '*bullying reprimands.*' As Ukrainians watched, Yeltsin became the first political leader to rise to the top in the Kremlin by running against the Communist Party. To them, this was testimony to the fact that it was now possible to have competitive elections and win. Yeltsin, in turn, continued to criticize Gorbachev by arguing that his reforms were not radical enough and quit the Party leadership in October of 1987. The question for Ukrainians was obvious; would this development in Moscow help or hinder the cause of political and economic reforms in Ukraine?

As 1987 ended, no one would be able to predict whether reform would continue or completely collapse. After four years of perestroika, many felt that his reforms had weakened the Soviet system in such areas as democratization, economic performance, unrest by minority nationalities, and foreign policy. Yeltsin, in his campaign in Moscow declared that, *'the rouble of a janitor should be worth the same as the rouble of the Party leader.'* This gave Muscovites the feeling that the elections were not fixed in advance. As the elections of 1989 drew closer, some real problems developed in the Ukrainian cities of Kharkiv and Lviv. On March 12, forty thousand protesters in Lviv staged a rally to boycott the elections. In the end, even though most elected to parliament were communists, the elections marked the beginning of the multi-party system and the doom of communist rule.

If nothing else, the elections fuelled the nationalist movement throughout the USSR. And, the Baltic states of Latvia, Lithuania, and Estonia led the way. I vividly recall the visit to Edmonton in 1975 of my uncle, Damian Groszko of Liepaja, Latvia and his excitement to be able to move about our community without being censored. It was an opportunity to talk about democracy in Canada as opposed to the empty words used by Soviet authorities to define the same concept. He must have taken some of these political thoughts with him when he returned to Latvia for his family became directly involved in Latvia's struggle for independence. I was delighted to learn in 1989 that it was Damian's son-in-law, Karlis Straupeniece, a popular musical director, who, joined by his wife Mariann and their daughters Ilze and Liene and a large group of young and old, marched in the streets of Riga in support of the country's cause. The independent candidates for elections attached themselves to popular fronts which became a transparent name for independent parties, something that was outlawed.

Ukraine took its cue from the Baltic states and quickly created its own popular front movement. Popular front candidates declared themselves to be communists but most were really separatists at heart. Once elected in 1989, these new deputies would use the Soviet parliament as a means to push for Ukrainian independence. Suddenly, the new parliamentarians could develop a strategy for *all* of Ukraine. In the meantime, Gorbachev seemed not to mind this small group of candidates offering up their objections to government policies. However, even though the small group did accept that they could not change the system in the Soviet Union *did not mean to say that they could not effect change back home!*

Suddenly, the Ukrainian popular front candidates stationed in Moscow began to gear up for independence back home. Gorbachev belatedly realized that he would be unable to reform communism. In the end, it was either communism *or* reform *but not both.* When Congress convened for the first time in May, outbursts and questions were the rule of the day. Gorbachev was being challenged at every opportunity and from every quarter of the Soviet Union. As these events were televised for the very first time, the Soviet people suddenly realized that democracy, in fact, was taking root. Unfortunately for many, politics was one thing but the economic decline was something else. Many objected to food shortages. Gorbachev's foreign policies made their problems worse and the problem seemed to come to a head when a half million Soviet troops came home from Eastern Europe; unemployed and with no place to live. All of this led to public unrest and demonstrations and the eventual downfall of Gorbachev himself.

There is no doubt that Pope John Paul II, who was elected in 1978, was instrumental in bringing democracy to Eastern Bloc countries. Although it is true that Josef Stalin once said of the Pope *'how many divisions has he'* would not be around in 1989 when the Pope would be able to influence the hearts and minds of fifty million Roman Catholics in Eastern Europe, thirty million of them living in Poland. For, in the final analysis, the crusade for democracy would not be pacified by Gorbachev's reforms or crushed by Stalin-like repressions. Following the Pope's visit to Warsaw in 1979, the Solidarity movement would help Poland break free from the chains of communist oppression in ten years. In the meantime, the struggle would quickly spread to Poland's neighbour, Lithuania and the other two Baltic states of Latvia and Estonia and finally spread across the USSR and break the Soviet Union into fifteen independent nations.

Even though Lithuania is a small nation, it would be the nation to spearhead the struggle for independence. It all started when the Communist Party of Lithuania broke away from the Communist Party of the Soviet Union and it would be the first nation to declare its independence from the Soviet Union and lay the groundwork for other Soviet Bloc countries. Of the countries that belonged to the Soviet Union, it would be the Baltic States that would be the most pro-West. They were the nations that had the greatest Western influence, the most independent-minded, and, geographically, the closest to the West. All of this was possible despite the fact that in all three Baltic states a large portion of the population was, in fact, Russian or non-Baltic.

As events unfolded, it would be a combination of factors, starting with the Pope's visit to Poland, that would create a spark for independence for nations which formed up a part of the Soviet Union. However, it would be Ukraine that would play the critical role in the eventual breakup of the USSR. This became critical because Ukraine, aside from Russia itself, was the largest Soviet republic with a territory the size of France and a population of fifty million which was fully sixteen percent of the Soviet Union's population. Ukrainian nationalist Maksim Strikha defined it this way, *'Ukraine is indispensable to the Soviet Union. If Lithuania leaves, there will be a Soviet Union. If Ukraine leaves, there will be no Soviet Union.'*

As for Ukraine, much as a sibling might, it seemed as though it was not in a hurry to leave the comfort of the Soviet Union. In part, this attitude came from the fact that the nation was split along geographic lines. From Kyiv east, the Russian language, the Russian Orthodox Church, and the large Russian minority population predominated and favoured a continuation of a union with Russia while in the west, particularly in Lviv, the sentiment was the opposite. For it was here that the Ukrainian language, the Catholic Church, and the Ukrainian majority population prevailed. It was also here that the people pressed for independence.

As the world-wide Ukrainian diaspora and significant organizations such as the Ukrainian Canadian Congress and Rukh would soon find out, even the pro-Moscow eastern Ukraine which dominated the republic was about to make a u-turn. With the communications linkages now opening up between east and west, even residents of East Ukraine began to shift their opinions and beliefs. To a large part, much of this became attributable to the Chornobyl nuclear disaster. Perhaps it was Les Honchar, a popular Ukrainian writer who put it best when he said, *'Yes, the officials come here every day from Moscow to visit Ukraine. The problem is, they bring with them their own food while at the same time telling Ukrainians that there is no danger of radioactivity here. If that is the case, why do they bring their own lunch baskets?'*

Unravelling what had happened on Ukraine's road to independence, it is clear that the appearance of Rukh *(Ukrainian People's Movement for Restructuring)* as a popular front in Ukraine in 1989 was instrumental in getting the ball rolling. At its founding meeting in Kyiv it already had the fundamental elements of economic reform, political reform, mass support, internal unity, and church support in place. Even more important, the Rukh movement, with 280,000 active members at its birth, was not limited to Ukraine. The movement would soon become equally strong in Canada and in the United States. And, it was economist Vladimir Chernak who declared, *'We all want to move from a free-market economy to a free Ukraine. That is our destiny.'* And it was Father Nikolai Negoguz who put it all in perspective when he said, *'God gave us Rukh as a tool to lead us out of the bondage we now have. Ukraine is our land of promise.'* The Ukrainian blue and yellow flag seemed to be everywhere.

For decades, most Russians were convinced that it was their duty to protect its republics and could not understand why the republics were seeking to break away from the Soviet Union. They concluded that these republics were ungrateful for Moscow's past subsidies and would soon come back into the fold. In part, this became the rationale for letting some of the ingrates such as Lithuania, Latvia, and Estonia go their own way. Even Gorbachev underestimated the depth of anti-Soviet sentiment. The Berlin Wall was now down and Eastern Europe was breaking away from the Soviet Union. Some even said that *'East Germany did more in a month of freedom than the Soviet Union did in five years of perestroika.'*

Soon after, the leaders of Belarus, Russia, and Ukraine signed the Belovezhsky Treaty on December 8, 1991 which helped to bury the Soviet Union and ensure its demise. The three Slavic leaders agreed to do away with the Central Soviet Government. Their three republics would become independent, but continue to cooperate as one political, economic, and military region. When confronted with the context of the treaty, Gorbachev had no alternative but to resign. He could no longer be the president of a country that no longer existed. On December 24, 1991 Yeltsin met with Gorbachev to talk about the transfer of power. It was agreed that Gorbachev would resign on December 25, 1991 and that the Soviet government would cease to exist on December 31, 1991. Thirty minutes after he resigned, the red Soviet flag with the communist hammer and sickle came down from the Kremlin walls and in its place flew the red-white-and-blue flag of reborn Russia.

After all of these years of communist rule, only one thing was clear; without the ruthless use of deadly force to seize and maintain power in Russia and Ukraine none of this would have been possible. As my parents once said in their newly adopted land of Canada, *'there is no way that a repressive communist regime can compete with the democracies of the world. Sooner or later the corrupt system will whither and die.'* What really stuck in the craw of Ukrainians was the low prestige of the Ukrainian language and culture. Policies since World War II resulted in a decrease in the number of Ukrainian books being published and it seemed that fewer Ukrainian students were seeking entry into post-secondary school institutions. Ukrainians suddenly realized that admission policies of universities favoured children of white-collar workers, the majority of whom were Russian. Ukrainians wanted their own children to have increased opportunities to pursue higher learning.

Yet, despite some of these shortcomings, it is without question that Gorbachev's policies of glasnost and perestroika *(hlasnist and perebudova in Ukraine)* propelled the Ukrainian Writers' Union to actively promote the rebirth of Ukrainian culture and language. With the support of noted writers, native-language societies were created and writers who went underground during the Stalin and Brezhnev eras suddenly came out of hiding and published new works that spoke openly about historical events which had previously been banned from public discussion. Much as Shevchenko had done years earlier, these writers would light a fire under Ukraine's quest for independence and play a leadership role in Ukraine's vision of a future. It would be a stroke of genius that the Taras Shevchenko Ukrainian Language Society under the leadership of Dmytro Pavlychko would realize its dream when in October of 1989 Ukrainian would be declared the state language.

In Edmonton, the Ukrainian-Canadian community came to the aid of Rukh's popular movement for restructuring by way of financial and vocal support. Perhaps the most important impetus to all of this came from an almost spontaneous appearance of a number of newspapers, journals, bulletins, and flyers all of which added to the mosaic of Ukraine's rich history; a history that the Soviet Union had earlier tried to bury. Suddenly, documentary evidence was made available about national tragedies in Ukraine and how the nation was pillaged, first by the Germans and then the Russians during the war and especially news of the Great Ukrainian Famine which was imposed by Josef Stalin during 1932-33 and which was later to be declared as genocide.

For those in the Ukrainian diaspora who had always envisioned a great struggle and plenty of bloodshed as Ukraine moved towards complete independence found both, joy and disappointment. Sovereignty seemed to come in with a whimper. Rukh held its first national congress in Kyiv in 1989 and began planning for the elections to Soviet Ukraine's Supreme

Soviet *(Verhovna Rada)* which were scheduled for March of 1990. As events unfolded, pro-Rukh candidates won over 100 seats in the elections out of a total of 450 and promptly joined forces with the democratic wing of the Communist Party *(Democratic Bloc)* and were instrumental in having the parliament declare Ukraine as a sovereign state on July 16, 1990.

By 1991 the Soviet Union ceased to function as a unit and Leonid Kravchuk, who had been a staunch communist, suddenly sensed the sentiment of Ukrainians and embraced nationalism for Ukraine. To consolidate his new sense of importance, Kravchuk embarked on foreign trips as head of an independent state. However, it would not be until August 24, 1991 that Ukraine's position would be crystallized, the same day that conservative political forces in Moscow staged an unsuccessful putsch to overthrow Gorbachev. Again, Kravchuk acted decisively by spearheading a resolution to declare Ukraine an independent state while at the same time *calling for a referendum on independence to be held on December 1, 1991. Presidential elections were also scheduled for the same date.*

Of course, Kravchuk took heart from the results of the December 1, 1990 referendum where the results left no doubt in anyone's mind when fully 92 percent of the voters in Ukraine voted for independence and even in Eastern Ukraine, which contained a strong Russian minority, over 80 percent voted for independence. Ukrainians saw in Kravchuk a person who was ready to champion their cause and 62 percent voted him in as Ukraine's first president.

Looking back over the 20th century, August 24, 1991 turned out to be the sixth time that all or some significant part of Ukraine had declared itself to be independent. The first instance of such a declaration took place in Kyiv in 1918 followed closely by a declaration of independence in Lviv the very same year. Neither declaration could be sustained; nor could the third one which was declared in Kyiv in 1919. The same fate befell the declarations of independence during the course of World War II in Khust in 1939 and in Lviv in 1941. *All of these declarations seemed to come at a time of civil war or at a time when Ukraine was being invaded by a foreign power.* It is interesting to note that in the first five of the six instances of a declaration of independence, *never was the general population consulted as was the case in 1990.*

Without question, the biggest single factor working in favour of independence for Ukraine had to do with the power of mass media. Every move that Ukraine made towards democracy was being watched by the world and what the world saw seemed to meet with its approval. True, Ukraine suddenly had its share of problems. Rather than sitting back and constantly griping about communism and the Russians, Ukrainians suddenly had to do something for themselves. Important questions confronted the newest of nations. It had to take a decision as to whether or not it wanted to be a member of the Commonwealth of Independent States (CIS) and just as quickly it wanted to embrace reforms and move towards a market economy.

Above all else, one thing was abundantly clear; these problems now belonged to Ukraine. She would no longer have to go, hat in hand, to Moscow for approval.

The trident (tryzub) would once again be raised as the official coat of arms of Ukraine. It consists of a gold trident against an azure background and dates back to the ninth century when the Rurik dynasty adopted it as their coat of arms. In 1992 the Ukrainian Parliament would choose the national anthem music composed by Mykhailo Verbytsky in 1863 where the first line of the anthem states, *'Ukraine has not perished, neither her glory, nor freedom...'* The Ukrainian-Canadian community in Edmonton joined millions of others in celebrating the birth of a new nation.

As I considered Ukraine's new status and the disintegration of the Soviet Union, I also hoped that my status as a persona non grata would meet a similar fate. Only then would I be able to undertake, in earnest, a search for my dad's village in Poland and my family in Ukraine.

The national symbol and official coat of arms of Ukraine is a gold tryzub (trident). Various versions of the tryzub are used by Ukrainian organizations.

33.

My Return to Ukraine

Through a border crossing that defies description

What seemed impossible just a short time earlier really happened when Ukraine, without shedding blood, gained its independence in 1991. By coincidence, it would be the same year that the Ukrainian Canadian Congress would recognize the many contributions made by Ukrainian immigrants since first coming to Canada in 1891 by unveiling the Ukrainian Centennial Pioneer Monument on Alberta's Legislative grounds on September 24, 1993. Opportunities for trade and economic development were opening up with Ukraine and, at the provincial level, a boost was given to Ukrainian bilingual programs. It was now over twenty-five years since I was last in Soviet Ukraine and I hoped that my expulsion had run its course. Since Canada was the first nation to support and then accept Ukraine's declaration of independence, I felt confident that as Canadians, Sharon and I would receive preferential treatment.

A telephone call to the Ukrainian Embassy in Ottawa confirmed that their office had nothing on file which would prevent me from getting a visa to travel to Ukraine. As a result, we planned our

Unveiled on September 24, 1993, the Ukrainian Centennial Pioneer Monument commemorates the arrival of the first Ukrainian pioneers to Canada in 1891.

trip for the fall of 1997. Dr. Roman Petryshyn, the Director of the Ukrainian Resource and Development Centre at Grant MacEwan College arranged for a letter of invitation from Yuri Konkin, the manager of the College's foreign office in Kyiv. At the same time, we applied for travel visas to the Czech Republic and Poland.

The shrill sound of the jet engines seemed somehow to be out of synch with the sunny and cloudless October day as we lifted off from Edmonton's International Airport for a flight to Calgary before boarding an international flight to Frankfurt, Germany. In a way this would not be a new experience but rather a continuation of the search I began thirty years earlier; a search for my dad's village that was so rudely interrupted by Soviet officials in 1967. Sharon, by virtue of her work on her family history and the publication of an annual newsletter entitled *Meister Memories,* was also anxiously looking forward to the journey. An associate, John Benson, Board Member of the Family History Centre in Edmonton, provided me with some timely thoughts and advice about genealogy and family searches.

The eight-hour flight to Germany gave me plenty of time to reflect on the meaning of this journey. I tried to imagine what life would be like in Ukraine today in contrast to 1967. *What would the village of Plazow look like?* Historically, this is where the East meets the West; the imaginary line between the Catholic and Orthodox worlds. *Would this phenomenon be reflected in the community? How would I undertake the search for my dad's village of Grohi?* For centuries, the stretch of land surrounding my grandfather's village had been the scene of confrontations between the East and West; a land where the various nationalities lived and fought both, together and against each other. At the end of World War II, the Ukrainian nationalists fought a bitter and cruel two-year battle for the right of independence. In April of 1947, the Ukrainians not already deported by virtue of Stalin's dictum of 1944, were forcibly resettled, either in the USSR or in the former German regions of Poland. *Only the evacuated and burnt-out villages remained. And, this was the region that attracted my thoughts.*

If newspaper reports about the democratization process in Ukraine were accurate, I would then have to ask the question, *how can a people switch from a communist state watching them to its inhabitants now watching the state? Would its people have the foresight to fight for the rule of law, for civilian control of the military, and for all of the forms of democracy? Would Ukrainians understand the idea of rights and know that a country can be governed by laws and not raw power? Could they conceive of a police force that was accountable and its courts impartial?* In my own mind I was suspicious that communist rule in Ukraine had poisoned everything, including its institutions, officials, citizens and culture. *How could one forget that the Soviet Union, over the years, murdered, starved, and worked to death upwards to 60 million people?* I really wanted to experience whether or not members of my family in Ukraine and Poland were able to let go of history and cope with the effects of a lingering communist poison.

Researchers tell us that the most productive years for an individual occur between the ages of twenty-five to fifty. Reflecting upon this statistic, I had to admit that for me and my siblings this time frame occurred between the date of my last visit to Ukraine and the date of the present trip. True to form, not only did my parents realize their dream of success in Canada but so did their children, now adults and approaching retirement. It is without doubt that the work ethic of my parents took root with their children. The question could now be asked, *how well did all of my cousins do under the yoke of communism?* In other words, *did the communist regime live up to its promises?*

Looking back to November 12 of 1994, Sharon and I recalled a special occasion when over 100 family members celebrated my mother's 90th birthday. It never ceases but to amaze me that in so short a period of time two people through their marriage and the marriage of their children, grandchildren and great grandchildren could increase in number so quickly! Some said that this particular circumstance was a reflection of *Eva's Dream*. The only sad note was that my dad was not with us to enjoy that very special day. I'm sure that he would have been as proud as was mom. Still, the members of the extended family recognized that without the work and *dedication of my mother in a free and democratic country*, none of this would have been possible.

As future events unfolded, the 1997 trip to Europe would be the first of several trips that Sharon and I would make to Poland, Ukraine, and Latvia– the countries that were home to twenty-eight of my first cousins and their families. When I told my mother that the purpose of our trip was to visit her village of Plazow *and* dad's village of Grohi, she immediately insisted that we abandon the idea. *'After all,'* she explained, *'Andrij's village was burned to the ground by the Polish nationalists in 1945, immediately after the war.'* Knowing that mom, even though she did have several nieces and nephews living in Poland, harboured some unhappy memories of Grohi and of the *zealous nationalists*, I elected not to pursue the matter with her. However, it was an important mission for me. What were the pre-existing circumstances that caused the nationalists to torch the village? Identifying the *bygone* village for which I was searching was one thing; finding its true place and meaning in the context of the history of my family was quite another. I was about to discover just how illusive was the search for a small village that no longer existed. Thankfully, the political situation was now sufficiently stable in Ukraine and in Poland to undertake the special purpose of the journey.

We knew and understood what happened economically and politically in Canada during our lives and now we were about to learn first hand from immediate family members about their experiences in Ukraine, Poland and Latvia during that same period of time. *What place did religion have in their lives during the communist era and now? What was life like during the Soviet Regime? Over the years, who were their political leaders and what impact did they have upon the current political climate?* And finally, I wanted to know their understanding of the *concept of a free market economy and democracy.* Their responses would help me understand the degree to which the information they had been fed had been *cleanitized.*

Yes, for Ukrainians, the one dictator most often identified with Soviet Ukraine during and after World War II was Josef Stalin. When he died in 1953, an era of tyranny also came to an end. However, millions of Russians minimized his crimes and emphasized his achievements. In this way they could still embrace everything they had been taught and continue to believe that although he had made mistakes, he had turned the Soviet Union from a rural backwater into an industrial giant and a military superpower. The years following his death led to some contradictory tendencies in Ukraine; some wanted to fully integrate Ukraine with the Soviet system while many others wanted to loosen the stranglehold on all Soviet Republics. When in 1954 the Crimea was ceded to Ukraine, it seemed as though it was a signal of support for Ukraine even though the majority of the residents in Crimea were Russian.

It was clear that Stalin's successor, Nikita S. Khrushchev who became the First Secretary of the Central Committee, wanted very much to institute a program of de-Stalinization by encouraging writers to express a point of view even though it might have been contrary to earlier expressed interpretations of history. This new attitude helped Ukrainians reclaim their past, as it were, by correcting some of the earlier views about Ukraine's history as presented by the Soviet Union. All of this had an immediate impact upon the arts, painting, decorative design, music, and theatre. In conjunction with this, the economy of Ukraine began to grow. Industry flourished and power stations sprung up along the Dnipro River and a natural gas find south of Lviv helped to accelerate economic growth.

Even with the advances in the hydroelectric and natural gas industries, uncertainty of supply caused the Soviet Union to turn to nuclear power plants in the 1970s. Under Khrushchev's leadership, the Machine Tractor Stations were abolished and their equipment sold to collective farms and soon nearly one-third of Ukraine's arable land was planted with corn. Less and less of the arable land was seeded to rye. This ill-fated plan led to crop shortages in the Soviet Union making it necessary to import grain from Canada. This, along with other factors, resulted in Khrushchev's removal from office in 1964 to be replaced by Leonid Brezhnev. This effectively ended the period of change and experimentation headed by Khrushchev. Until 1984, Brezhnev emphasized stability and order and liked to refer to his policies as embodying the three concepts of rastsvet (*flowering*), sblizhenie (*drawing together*), and sliianie *(merging);* a concept that came from Lenin and Stalin.

For Ukrainians, the policies of Brezhnev meant only one thing–an emphasis on one Soviet nation (*sovetskaia natsiia*) and the Soviet people (*sovetskii narod*), just about the time when Khrushchev left the impression that Ukrainians would have their day in the sun. In essence, the policies of Brezhnev caused the Soviets to *circle the wagons* and to resist change. In particular, the ruling Soviets felt that too many members of the Party were flirting with decadent western ideas and singled out Ukraine for encouraging a *bourgeois nationalism*. This explains why any westerner visiting the Soviet Union during the 1960s would have been watched very closely to ensure that western ideas were not being encouraged.

I must have qualified on all counts when I visited Russia in 1967. After all, I was a *westerner with western ideas*. Naturally, I was not the only person being watched by the KGB. Ukrainian writers and authors had to go underground to publish their ideas, stressing the promotion and implementation of the Helsinki Accords on Human Rights. By the 1970s, the so-called Helsinki group of Rudenko and others began speaking out boldly and in political terms about Soviet society so that Ukrainian cultural and political aspirations could be realized. Their positions suggested a federation for Ukraine; others wanted independence for their beloved country. Despite how radical these ideas may have seemed, these political activists felt that change was possible within the framework of the rights guaranteed by the Soviet constitution. Even though their ideas were frowned upon by Soviet authorities, the writers and political activists knew that the international community would look with favour upon these innovative ideas being bandied about, not only in Ukraine and Russia, but also in Poland and Czechoslovakia. *Unlike the Stalin era, political arrests and political trials did little to stem the flow of ideas in Ukraine; many of these aimed at independence.*

Coincidental with my trip to Ukraine in 1967, the first wave of trials dealing with accused dissidents such as Dziuba and Moroz were just completed. Their prison terms, many Ukrainians said, were in violation of the Soviet legal code. In the years that followed, other dissidents and political writers were arrested and tried because they were active in *samvydav,* the underground publishing industry. It didn't matter. They were at the front of the Ukrainian cultural revival and it seemed that the march to independence was no longer reversible. This eventually led to Ukraine being granted greater economic self-management, support for its cultural interests and more tolerance for political dissidents.

What Brezhnev soon discovered was that the removal of political activists did not solve the Soviet Union's problems. Even the Greek Catholic Church, despite its abolition in the late 1940s, continued to function underground and lent its support for a free and independent Ukraine. Some would even say that between 1960 and 1991, it almost seemed possible to be Ukrainian and a Soviet citizen while living in Ukraine and that the Soviet Union had given up on its attempts at the russification of the Ukrainian population despite the increasing dominance of Russian forms in the political, social, and cultural life in Ukraine. *In fact, it would be the eastern cities in Ukraine that would embrace Ukraine as a nation*, a situation that would have been very welcome in Western Ukraine at the close of World War I when Ukraine might have gained a greater measure of independence.

The 1970s and 80s brought a considerable amount of urbanization to Ukraine. Contrary to what Russia predicted would happen, an increasing number of persons claiming Ukrainian as their mother tongue continued to increase from 30 million in 1959 to over 37 million in 1989. Even dissident writers in western democracies issued dire warnings about the demise of the Ukrainian language and, ultimately, the death of Ukraine's hopes for independence. *All of this highlights one important phenomenon and that is that a nation's hopes and aspirations for independence are very difficult to suppress.* In fact, a closer look at a census taken in Ukraine in 1970 shows that over 95 percent of Ukrainian citizens were conversant in the Ukrainian despite the intrusion of the Russian language. Even the Russian minority in eastern Ukraine expressed a desire to be a part of a Ukrainian nation at a time when the Marxist-Leninist ideological imperative called for the *withering away* of the Ukrainian language.

Of great interest to me was the question of the changes which had taken place in Ukraine and Poland since my dad immigrated to Canada. For, as history shows us, when World War II ended in 1945 the real problems for Soviet Ukraine began. Germany and Austria had within its borders over 16 million foreign workers, refugees, and prisoners of war and, it is estimated that over 2.2 million of these were Ukrainians. One of these Ostarbeiters was my cousin Vasyl Groszko, now living in Lviv, who spent several years in Austria before being repatriated. He was only thirteen years of age when he was co-opted by the Nazi regime to work for a family in Austria. After all hostilities ended, the Soviets sent in repatriation missions composed of officers and propagandists to convince these Soviet citizens to return home, *either honourably or in a pine box.* Not all of these citizens returned to a communist regime. As many as 220,000 ended up in Europe, Canada, and the United States as political refugees. To add to the confusion, many of these refugees were from that part of Galicia which was now within the borders of Poland and embraced the Ukrainian Catholic faith while most were from Soviet Ukraine where the predominant religion was the Orthodox faith. Not only that, but a number of prisoners of war located in Italy did, in fact, fight on the side of Germany.

As a part of the Ostarbeiter group, Vasyl Groszko was to say years later that, *'after the war, the Austrian family wanted to adopt me as their son. They begged me to stay and I really wanted to become an Osterreichisch or what the Austrians called an Ostfluchtling; a refugee from Eastern Europe.'* All of this meant that many foreign workers had positive experiences while working in Austria or in Germany and may have stayed behind were it not for the Soviet authorities who insisted that they be repatriated. This anxiety on the part of the Soviets to ensure that its citizens returned to their countries of origin stemmed, in part, from the realization that the Soviet Union had lost an estimated 11 million combatants and 7 million civilians. Further, because Ukraine was in the war zone, it was particularly hard hit by fatalities, losing 1.4 million military personnel and 4.1 million civilians. During the war, an estimated 3.9 million Ukrainians were evacuated eastward by the Soviet Union in 1941 and 1942 to escape the rapid German advance. Later, the Germans, through their Ostarbeiter program, compelled 2.2 million Ukrainians to work in Germany in forced labour.

As noted earlier, Ukrainian borders were re-established after World War II and, as a result, Eastern Galicia extended nearly to the San River and as far west as the Buh River. In essence, it was because of Soviet prestige that Soviet Ukraine's territory increased by 165,300 square kilometres and 11 million additional citizens. However, the leaders also conceded that national minorities, wherever they lived, would be of particular concern and that decisive action was needed. This is how the decision was made to undertake population transfers. The largest departure out of Soviet Ukraine was that of nearly 1.3 million Poles from eastern Galicia and Volhynia along with 53,000 Czechs. *To countervail this, 500,000 Ukrainians arrived from Poland in addition to the 12,000 from Czechoslovakia.* These transfers were in addition to those returning from Germany and Austria as part of the Ostarbeiter program who were either POWs, survivors of concentration camps, forced labourers, or refugees. In all, nearly two million Ukrainians were returned, some willingly and some, like my cousin Vasyl, by force.

More recently, Germany established a $7.9 billion fund to compensate survivors who laboured in German concentration camps or on farms and factories during the war. However, survivors, such as Aunt Anna, now living in Ukraine, were experiencing more difficulty in filing their claims than did those living in the West.

Immediately after World War II, all of the remaining members of my Ukrainian family living in the County of Lubaczow, Poland, were re-located to Lviv, Ternopil and surrounding areas in Soviet Ukraine. In all, I lost only one member of my family to war and that was Oksana, dad's sister, who left Grohi to work in France in 1938, just before the outbreak of World War II. Despite efforts to locate her, she was never heard from again.

Research and statistics show that *not all of those who were repatriated survived.* Tens of thousands were summarily executed by the Soviets while others were considered to be politically unreliable and were sent to labour camps in the Soviet Far East or Central Asia. In addition, some 250,000 stayed in Germany, Austria, and other western European countries. Many of these emigrated to Canada and the United States in the years that followed. As events unfolded after World War II, the Soviet Union recognized that Ukrainians living in Galicia had become westernized and would be unlikely to accept Soviet indoctrination. The Soviet challenge was to rebuild the economy while at the same time resisting the military movement offering resistance to the Soviet troops. However, a small Ukrainian Insurgent Army (UPA) was particularly prone to frustrating Soviet attempts at relocating Ukrainians living in Eastern Poland.

This particular action forced the Soviets, in the spring and summer of 1947, to forcibly move 140,000 Ukrainians, including Lemkos living in the Carpathian region, to Silesia and Prussia *(western and northern regions of Poland)*. By 1948, the UPA had nearly exhausted itself and became a part of the Ukrainian diaspora scattered throughout Europe and North America. Still, the biggest problem for the Soviets seemed to be their conclusion that the Greek Catholic Church in Galicia had to go. After all, to them it was a creation of Poland set up to undermine the *true* Orthodox faith of the Rus people. The Soviets wanted very much to uphold the tsarist and Russian attitude that Orthodoxy was the *only acceptable religious orientation for all East Slavs*. Finally, in 1948 the Ukrainian population in the Przemysl eparchy was dispersed and the Greek Catholic Church forced to join the Roman Catholic Church of Poland.

Planning a trip to Galicia in 1996, after Ukraine gained its independence, was quite different from the journey I had taken earlier in 1967. With the breakup of the Soviet Union, it seemed unlikely that I would have to worry about the twenty-five year expulsion imposed upon me by Soviet authorities. Sharon and I landed in Frankfurt, Germany just about the time that the first fall frost would be visiting Ukraine. Our rental car was a new Opel[38] and the customs officials were just as efficient and thorough as might be expected. Not much seemed to have changed since Sharon and I were last in Germany in 1972 for the Munich Olympics. The German drivers on the autobahns continued to act as though they were speed demons.

From Frankfurt's efficient international airport, it did not take us long to reach Ansbach, the homeland of Sharon's paternal great-great-grandparents. Our next stop was the Czech border which, just a few years earlier, was the Czechoslovakian border--but that changed when Slovakia broke away. Our destination was the beautiful city of Prague, an experience that I had in 1967 and now wanted to share with Sharon. Much as I did in 1967, we booked into the Grand Hotel Europa in Wenceslas Square, the Square which was the centre of anti-Soviet sentiment three decades earlier. In November of 1989 about 500,000 students and citizens gathered in the square to protest the policies of the former communist regime. After a week of demonstrations, the government capitulated, thereby bringing to power the first democratic government in forty years.

When we reached the Polish border crossing at Cieszyn the following day, it felt as though we were going back in time. For whatever reason and without warning, the designated border crossing was closed to vehicular traffic. Military police and police dogs were in evidence everywhere. To make matters worse, the officials refused to give us directions to the alternate border crossing. Noticing the problems we were experiencing, a Polish national driving a black Mercedes befriended us and escorted us to another border crossing. The traffic was backed up and it took the better part of two hours to clear the border. Once across the border, we refuelled at a convenience

---

38   In 1997 it was difficult to rent a car in Germany for transport to an Eastern Bloc Country since these cars became a target for thieves and unscrupulous *chop shops* where the parts from a dismantled automobile brought premium prices in Ukraine and Russia.

store, purchased some Polish zloty and set our sights on the city of Chrzanow to visit our neighbour's daughter, Dorothy Dalba, now teaching English as a Second Language in a secondary school.

We spent that night at Dorothy's apartment located in a large residential high-rise. For her, I am certain that it was a sleepless night. She worried the whole night through about our car, telling us that no car was safe in Poland, especially if it was a German model. *'You know Steven,'* I recall her saying, *'car thieves love German cars. These cars are stolen and transported to a Soviet Bloc country or end up in a chop shop.'* The following day we journeyed to the state Museum in Oswiecim and visited the infamous Auschwitz and Birkenau extermination camps where nearly two million citizens, mostly Jews, were put to death during World War II.

The two-lane highway taking us Chrzanow to Lviv was shown on our Polish map as a freeway, however, there were only two lanes; the other two lanes were formed by the ever-popular but small Polish cars driving on the shoulders of the highway. The rolling countryside to Jaroslaw reflected a multitude of fall colours and somehow made me feel as though I was coming home. After all, Jaroslaw is only thirty kilometres from Plazow and the scene of several major battles during World War I that my dad often talked about. Wherever we stopped to take in a scene of harvesting or to talk to Polish workers, they immediately seemed to take note of the German automobile plates--to which they did not take too kindly. When they discovered that we were from Canada, they suddenly had a personality change.

As we approached the border crossing into Ukraine near the town of Przemysl, I was reminded of border crossings in the Soviet Union in 1967. The first challenge was one of simply getting out of Poland. With a traffic backed up well over two kilometres, we recalled the words of Rudy Pisesky, our Edmonton travel agent, who said that were we to encounter such a situation, we should go to the head of the line since we already had valid visas for Ukraine. Noticing our foreign plates, we were approached by four young thugs *(later we were told that they were border bandidos who seemed to have immunity from prosecution)* who wanted DM200 to take us to the head of the line. When we told them that we were Canadians, they demanded US$150. We refused. Time seemed to drag when, out of the blue, I heard someone saying in Ukrainian, *'It's too bad that this couple is German. If they spoke English, I could help them.'* Well, it didn't take me long to convince him that I spoke Ukrainian and needed his assistance. He introduced himself as Father Prokh from Lublin and said that he was on his way to Lviv for a conference.

Although it may be true that we were dealing with the residue of the communist regime, it does not necessarily follow that the border officials did not believe God. In fact, they did listen to the clergy. And, it would be the priest that would take us to the head of the line, uninterrupted by the border hoods. Still, it took us well over two hours just to cross the Polish border and another two hours to cross the Ukrainian border. One or two of the officials wanted to make small talk. Others simply milled around. Eventually, I was

338

told that a new shift of officials was coming on duty. Upon request, an official allowed me to take a peek at the computer screen. To my surprise, there was my name along with a long entry in Russian with a reference to 1967. When I asked the official about the contents, he chuckled, saying, *"Oh, don't worry about that. Your file contains some KGB information about your visit in 1967; information that is no longer relevant."* I wondered why the KGB neglected to remove this file after they said they would.

Having checked our car registration, automobile insurance, health insurance, international driver's licence, and the letter of invitation we had received from Ukraine, the officials seemed ready to wave us on. Yet, there was that imperceptible delay. What were they waiting for? Of course, I believe that I had the answer but was most unwilling to play the game. I suspected that even the officials at the border were not above accepting a small bribe. After all, we had heard that officials, whatever their station or role, felt that they were entitled to these kinds of small rewards. Obviously, they must have been waiting for their just rewards. Much as I hated to do it, I did slip them a few American dollars. Actually, the rumour mill had it that even the *border banditos* did not pocket all of their ill-gotten gain--sharing it with the border guards. Little wonder that they seemed to be immune from reprimand!

By this time it was dark out; very dark. And, in the absence of any street lights, the sheer darkness of the night was accentuated. An official instructed us to drive to Lviv without ever stopping for anyone except the police who would be easily identifiable by the clothing they wore. *'In this way,'* said an official, *'you will avoid the border banditos.'* No sooner had we left the border than we came upon a police check-stop where, in the dark, I nearly ran over one of them. Having examined our documentation, and giving us another warning about stopping, we were soon on our way again. As we drove through a number of small villages, we were amazed at the number of young people walking along the highway, pathways, and streets.

The sheer stupidity of the process used to admit visitors with a valid visa into Ukraine made me hot under the collar. Still, I was happy to have kept my temper in check because, as I discovered from future visits to Ukraine, border crossings at Uzhorod, Homel and Rava Ruska were no different. Perhaps it would be more correct to say that the intent of the border crossings was always the same but the officials would, from time to time, make one slight change or add a wrinkle or two. Eventually, I left it up to Sharon to figure out the process and I would end up jumping from one station to the next, showing an official this numbered piece of paper or that note. At one point I recall asking Sharon, *"...just how did you figure out the process for this crossing?"*

"Oh, that's simple," was her response, *"I simply watch what the others are doing and get you to follow the same process!"* I noted that the officials rarely used official forms. Upon entering the border zone, my vehicle would be given a number on a small piece of paper torn from some other document. This small piece of paper would be handed to another official and sometimes

replaced by a second piece of paper at which time I might be required to register my vehicle in a small *field* office. Then, it was on to another location to present my visa for examination followed by another location for my car and health insurance. Sometimes I would be charged for the use of their roads and always for car insurance for the duration of our stay in Ukraine. The same procedure was applied for health insurance, even though I assured them that I was fully covered by my employer. In some cases an official would provide me with a receipt. At other times he wouldn't, leading me to believe that these funds would rarely find their way into the national treasury.

We finally arrived at our destination of Lviv at about 2200 hours. The road leading into the city was in bad need of repair and the streets in Lviv were in awful shape; much worse than I had remembered them. Very little construction was in evidence anywhere and finding our way to Hotel Dnister was no picnic. It appeared that with the disintegration of the Soviet Union, the city was left to fend for itself. Obviously, it was not doing very well.

When we checked into Hotel Dnister, we informed the clerk that we had not eaten since leaving Radom, Poland. *"Unfortunately,"* said the clerk, *"our restaurant closed at ten. The only thing I can suggest is a small restaurant on the 8th floor."* We followed her directions to the 8th floor restaurant and decided that Lviv was not ready for prime-time tourism. The restaurant, but for a few athletic-looking young men, was empty. It looked a little odd in that the floor-area was rather small, done in hardwood and faced a small stage. We hurriedly ordered a small meal and sat down to a soda. Suddenly, I understood the meaning of the pole in the middle of the small stage when an attractive but scantily-dressed dancer made her entrance. Embarrassed as we were, we were still happy to get a meal.

Lviv's attitude toward hard, western currency had not changed. Our hotel cost us well in excess of US$150 per diem which included breakfast served in that slow and inimitable Soviet style and still very clearly reflected the power of the American dollar--to what they refer as hard currency. To store our car in the hotel compound was another US$13 per night. However, when we awoke in the morning to bright sunlight flooding the beautiful downtown park, we quickly forgot about the culture shock and the excessive costs. Lviv is the region's cultural capital and was once a part of the Austro-Hungarian and Polish empires and, even though it is 750 years old and a bit down on its heels, it still displayed elements of its Renaissance glory days when Germans, Poles, Ukrainians, Armenians, Venetians, Hungarians and Jews mingled on its streets.

For me, the task at hand was quite simple. I wanted to find various members of my family--especially those that I met in 1967. Even though it was thirty years later, it was as if time stood still. Now that the veil of Soviet secrecy had been lifted, I looked forward to the joy of meeting family members without fear of being arrested.

Yet, I would soon discover that although the veil of secrecy may have been lifted, old attitudes refused to die.

Left: *Photograph of Oksana Kaszuba (Dutkevich), lost in France at the outbreak of WWII.*

At the entrance to the infamous Auschwitz death camp is a sign, "Arbeit Macht Frei" (Work Will Set You Free), Oswiecim, Poland, 1998.

34·

A Search for Family

Meeting cousins for the very first time

My fifteen uncles and aunts were all born shortly after the turn of the twentieth century and, at the time of this visit to Ukraine, only two of them were still living; one on my maternal side, (mom's sister, Oksana Medvid of Kamianka Buzk) and one on my paternal side (dad's sister, Anna Grokh, who had visited us in Canada in 1991). Our plan was to first visit these two aunts and then undertake a search for *the children of the remaining fifteen uncles and aunts. In addition, I wanted to initiate a search for my extended family in Poland[39] and most of all I wanted to find the exact location of the burnt-out village of Grohi.*

From Aunt Anna I had earlier learned that she lived in a village by the name of Loshniv. At the time, I did not ask her as to what raion (county) or oblast (province) the village was located, but I should have. Before leaving for Lviv, I did write her a letter telling her the most likely date that we would be in Loshniv. When we arrived in Hotel Dnister (*Intourist Hotel in 1967*), I tried to telephone her only to be told that either she did not have a telephone or that the telephone she did have was strictly for local use. As a result, we decided to drive to her home without first contacting her.

Since the return address on a letter from Aunt Anna had the word Ternopil on it, I immediately assumed that Loshniv was either a small village on the

---

39   Note: Reference is being made to the family of my grandfather, Ivan Groszko (see chapter 6, **The Groszko Family**), whose daughter, Maria (my aunt), married Mariusz Mazurkiewycz. One of their daughters, Izabela (Mazurkiewycz) Kopczacka, now lives in Plazow and it would be Izabela that would help us with the search for the village of Grohi.

outskirts of Ternopil or a subdivision of the city. Our map of Ukraine was of no help because it did not show the village at all. *"But,"* I said to Sharon, *"don't worry. I'll be able to ask someone along the way."* In retrospect, I should have worried for, in the first instance, just getting out of Lviv was a nightmare. Finding the highway that would take us to Ternopil was no picnic either. I suppose it had a lot to do with Ukraine's highway markings. Sharon could not read the Cyrillic print and I had great difficulty in reading any of the small signs at highway speeds.

As we left Lviv behind us, I tried to assess the extent to which democracy was taking hold in Ukraine. Brought up under the Soviet regime, it seemed as though the people we met were very reluctant to talk openly about themselves, their family, politics or religion. It was as though the sceptre of totalitarianism still hung heavily over their heads. Maybe they were reluctant to talk to a stranger whose command of the Ukrainian language was suspect. To get through some of the villages required that we go through the occasional police check-stop and our rented foreign car with German plates was a magnet for attention. A Canadian flag and a couple of Canadian car stickers seemed not to help much.

The fall colours of the countryside were back-dropped by the drabness and sameness of the Soviet-style buildings yet in sharp contrast to the beautifully-finished and artistic bus stops along the way. The city of Ternopil was a two-hour drive east of Lviv and en route we stopped at a service station *(which in itself was a rare sight)* to seek directions to the village of Loshniv. An employee said that he had never heard of the village but thought that we were on the right highway. When we stopped at the eastern outskirts of Ternopil to make another enquiry, we were once again given directions to proceed *straight ahead* only to discover at another police check-point that we were on the road to Khmelnytsky and not Loshniv. So, it was back to Ternopil and finally the right highway. As I considered our missteps, I had to admit that there were dozens of small villages along our route and very few, if any, locals knew all of their names and locations. For most residents it looked as though their world did not extend beyond the next village.

The highway to Loshniv took us through several small villages and two more police check-stops--all of which reflected, perhaps, the last vestiges of a crumbling communist empire. When we finally arrived at the turn-off to Loshniv, I was impressed with the beauty of a lazy brook meandering through a meadow where cattle grazed and domesticated geese and chickens were in evidence everywhere. It struck me that in the midst of poverty was a beautiful and peaceful scene. Yet, when I spoke to a local resident tending to her cow, she seemed not to reflect the joy and happiness I felt. She spoke of hard work and the lack of opportunity for economic advancement. The mode of transportation seemed to be on foot, on bicycle or horse-drawn wagon

Loshniv Valley,
Ternopil Oblast,
Ukraine, 1998.

and, from time to time, via a beat-up Lada. New cars were as rare as hens' teeth and when you saw one, they seemed to be immune to speed limits *or* the niceties of the road. At police check-points, they were waved through without having to stop.

We followed a paved but deteriorating road into Loshniv, which was about six kilometres off the main highway. A light but steady rain began to fall when we stopped to ask a woman about Loshniv and whether or not she knew the Grokh family. *"Yes,"* she said, *"I live in the next village beyond Loshniv. I know most of the families in Loshniv and I know Anna Grokh."* Not only that, but she offered to take us to my Aunt's home. We drove about four hundred yards down a dirt road to a small grain mill, beyond which we could not drive. The workers told us that Anna Grokh lived less than one kilometre up a trail in the extreme portion of the village. We walked the remainder of the distance by way of a small, muddy path past several villagers harvesting their sugar beets or gardens. There being no culvert or bridge over a small brook, we carefully crossed it by way of a large fallen log. Our guide seemed to be able to cross the brook like a mountain goat; however, the progress for Sharon and me was somewhat slower. We arrived at a second brook where the water was far deeper and fast-flowing; however, the crossing was made easier by a suspended metal bridge. The lane leading to Anna's home seemed to be the domain of domesticated geese and chickens, and there was no lack of goose-poop. Our guide seemed oblivious to all of this while Sharon, in her recently tailored black pant-suit, chose her steps with great care.

We met Aunt Anna's son, Zenoviy *(my cousin)*, his wife Anna, their daughter Oksana and their son Andriy, who were all helping Babcha with her gardening. Later, we discovered that Anna did not live alone; she lived with her teen-aged grandson, Andriy, who had developed a speech impediment at an early age as a result of an accident which affected his ability to speak. Shortly, Aunt Anna arrived from her garden to a joyful, yet tearful reunion. The food, in the form of preserved meats, mushrooms, potatoes and chocolates, was immediately spread on the table along with a variety of alcoholic and non-

344

alcoholic drinks. As we sat around chatting over a meal, Aunt Anna told us that prior to the relocation of the family, the home belonged to a Polish family that was relocated to Poland. *"You know,"* added my Aunt, *"the Polish family continues to covet this home and land. They have visited me on a couple of occasions. I like them. However, I have never returned to my home village of Grohi in Poland."*

Even though my Aunt seemed reluctant to talk about her experiences, our conversations had to do with the relocation of the Grokh family from Poland. Perhaps she feared some sort of reprisal should she say anything negative about those earlier communist authorities or their regime. *"Yes,"* I said to my Aunt, *"I am somewhat aware of the history of this region during World War I. What I want to know is how you and the residents of Grohi survived World War II and deportation after the war."*

"Oh Lord, Steven," was her reply, *"They were such difficult times. Even thinking about them brings tears to my eyes. It is such a sad part of our history."*

"Would you rather not talk about it?"

"No, no. I'll be all right."

"I would like to know more about your childhood years. About the villages of Grohi and Plazow. I want to know about your time as an Ostarbeiter in Germany during the war and about the German occupation of your village."

"Well, the small village of Grohi had about twenty families living in it. Every family knew one another and I have many happy memories of my childhood. I was born in 1924, two years before your older sister Maria. I attended school in Plazow."

"What about the Nazi attack on Russia under the code name 'Operation Barbarossa,' what do you know about that?"

"Yes," confirmed my Aunt, *"I was seventeen years of age in 1941 when Hitler's armies passed through our villages on their march to Moscow. I can still recall how joyfully many Ukrainians greeted the German soldiers."*

"Joyfully? Why did they greet them with joy?"

"Because, we looked upon them as our liberators from the domination of the Poles and we certainly did not want to fall under the yoke of the Russians. But, as the war progressed, our kind thoughts about the Nazis turned to horror. In 1942 I was taken from my home and became a slave labourer in a small town near Hamburg, Germany."

"How long were you in Germany as an Ostarbeiter?"

"Well, interestingly enough, I was able to write my family while working in Hamburg and my mother took ill in 1943. She needed my help. I begged the Nazi authorities to return me to my village."

"And, did they?"

"Yes, to my surprise they did. And, in 1944 the Russian Armies pushed the Nazis out of our region. And, soon after, the war ended. What is interesting, as you may know, the village in which I grew up was under Polish rule from

1919 to 1939 and the Polish borders extended well east of the city of Lviv. After the war, the Polish border was established at its present location but the villages of Grohi and Plazow, both of which consisted of a majority of ethnic Ukrainians, found themselves to be in Poland once again."

"So, what happened in Grohi right after the war?"

"The Soviet authorities reached an agreement with the Polish government that all Ukrainians living in Poland in the border region should be re-located to Soviet Ukraine and the Poles living in Soviet Ukraine, in the border region, should be re-located to Poland."

"That's quite an undertaking. What happened then?"

"Well, the Poles living in this region were re-located to Poland and the Ukrainians living in Poland were re-located to this region. Three of my brothers and I moved to this region from Grohi. Those members that had land and a home in Grohi were given a similar amount of land and a home in this region. Well, maybe not all of them."

"Is this how," I asked Anna, "all of dad's brothers and sisters ended up in this region of Western Ukraine? Is this why so many of my relatives now live here?"

According to my Aunt, not every member of my family wanted to re-locate from Poland to this region. But, they had no choice in the matter. There were many other Ukrainian families living in the Carpathian Mountains. They did not want to leave either. They hid out for months which stretched into years. Some were harboured by Poles while others found their way to other parts of Poland. Eventually, the Soviet government did resettle many of these families to Southern Poland recently vacated by Germans who were relocated to East Germany. Others ended up in or near the city of Szczecin and in the Pomeranian region of Poland. *"I am not an expert on Polish-Ukrainian relations, Steven, but I do know that during the inter-war period, relations between the Poles and the Ukrainians were already violent and became worse during and immediately after World War II."*

She went on to tell us about how the two groups fought back and forth, with the Poles forcing assimilation upon its minorities and the Ukrainians rebelling against it. Hence, the violent actions undertaken by the Ukrainian radicals negatively affected the Polish leadership's view of the Ukrainian minority. As a result of all of this, the Polish government welcomed ways to remove the problematic population at the end of World War II. *"After all, polonization was not met with success and evacuation of the Ukrainian population served as the next best option for creating a nation of one people in Poland."*

The Polish government, when faced with the opportunity to participate in the transfer of minority populations with the Soviet Union in 1944, agreed in the hope of solving its nationality conflict. Feeling betrayed and angered by the violent reaction of the Ukrainian population, the leadership adopted a resettlement campaign. Ukrainians were deported voluntarily and forcibly, as the Polish government set out to retrieve its nationals and to achieve its goal of a homogeneous state. Frustrated by its loss of land at the end of World War II, Poland's attitude towards its national minorities worsened. As a result, the population transfers that took place between Poland and the USSR from 1944 to 1946 marked only the beginning of the evacuation of Ukrainians from southeastern Poland.

On September 9, 1944 an agreement between Poland and the USSR was signed regarding population transfers. The agreement stipulated that people of Ukrainian nationality living in Poland should be evacuated to Soviet Ukraine while Poles in Soviet Ukraine should be repatriated to Poland. The view that national minorities had been one of the major causes of world War II was a predominant notion among many European countries at the time. The terms of the agreement stated that the evacuation was voluntary. *"However, contrary to the agreement,"* pointed out my Aunt, *"in 1945 the Polish authorities began to apply pressure and to use violence in order to persuade Ukrainians to leave Poland."*

Resulting from this agreement, about one million Poles were relocated to Poland between 1944 to 1946 while about 520,000 Ukrainians were deported from Poland to Soviet Ukraine. However, there remained one big difference; the Poles wanted to escape from the harsh conditions under which they suffered in the Soviet Union whereas many Ukrainians in Poland were forced to leave their ancestral homes they had occupied for centuries. Many did not want to leave but the brutality to which the Polish government resorted in order to remove Ukrainians testifies to its eagerness to resolve the minority conflict. In particular, the Polish Army began the process of forcibly relocating the Ukrainians from the districts of Lesko, Lubaczow, Przemysl and Sanok. Those Ukrainians who remained behind in these regions after 1946 came under the purview of Poland's *Operation Wisla* and relocated to Western Poland.

"You know," explained my Aunt, *"a band of Polish nationalists, right after World War II, served notice on the Ukrainians living in my village of Grohi that we must leave immediately. If we did not do so, we would be shot on the spot."* According to Anna, her two brothers, Mikhailo and Dmetro, just barely escaped with their lives. Sadly, during this siege in 1945, the village of Grohi was burned to the ground by the Poles. In the process, several Ukrainians were killed. In the nearby village of Plazow, my grandmother, Tetyana Groszko was among those reluctant to leave the village and refused to seek refuge with a Polish family. She was subsequently attacked by the marauding Poles and drowned in her farmyard well.

It would be the dense forest surrounding the tiny Ukrainian village of Gorajec, located about five kilometres to the south of Cieszanow, that would provide a relatively safe hiding place for a number of Ukrainians from nearby villages. Among this group was Aunt Anna. Once the crisis with the Polish nationalists was over and the Ukrainian *refugees* felt relatively safe to come out of hiding, those who survived the attacks by the lawless and marauding Poles were assisted by Russian and Polish authorities with a safe passage to

Soviet Ukraine.

According to Aunt Anna, a part of the resettlement policy stated that those who had a home and land in Poland would be relocated to a similar circumstance in Soviet Ukraine. This meant that the Soviet government had to relocate a like number of Poles with similar real property holdings so as to make the exchange as equitable as possible. Those who did not have buildings or land in Poland ended up in a similar situation in Soviet Ukraine. To carry out the re-settlement program was not easy. Initially, there was the matter of identifying *just who was Ukrainian*. As a result of mixed marriages, this process became very complicated. Once ear-marked for re-settlement, the most difficult part was the matter of saying goodbye. Some were transported by train or truck while others elected to hitch up their horses and make the journey by wagon. On average, the distances travelled were in the neighbourhood of one-hundred kilometres.

On our walk back to our car, Aunt Anna negotiated the mud as sprightly as a champion skater and, as we approached the mill, she commented that one of the daughters of Mikhailo Kaszuba lived across the brook. Just about that time Anna called out to a figure in a field of beets and, lo and behold, the person turned out to be Mikhailo's daughter, Stephania. We all met at the mill for our last conversations and goodbyes. At the same time, Anna presented us with a couple of bottles of liqueur, some preserves, chocolates, apples, walnuts and dried mushrooms.

With many thoughts running through my mind, we hurriedly left Loshniv to drive our guide to the next village. She said that it was en route to Ternopil and that the road was a shortcut to the main highway. To this day I regret the decision to take her home. The road got muddier and muddier and increasingly rutted. Although her village was only five kilometres from Loshniv, it seemed much farther. We dropped her off and continued on the small road to the main highway only to find that the distance was far greater than we anticipated and the road now became a tractor trail beside a wheat field. We thought of turning back but we knew that it was nearly impossible to make a u-turn on the narrow and muddy road. In fact, I envisioned having to approach a kolhosp in the vicinity to be rescued by a farm tractor. When we finally arrived on the main highway, our car was a mess.

We arrived at Hotel Dnister at ten o'clock, fully three hours late for dinner at the home of Dr. Vera Pirogova, the Dean of Nursing at the Lviv State Medical University. When we telephoned her, she immediately sent a taxi to pick us up. Located near a park in what appeared to be the wealthier section of Lviv, we were surprised at how well appointed was her home. Joined by her husband, son, mother and close associate Ludmilla Hdulevych, we spent the evening talking about our respective countries and about the City of Lviv. At one o'clock in the morning Vera called a taxi for our return trip to the hotel, asking that we call her upon our arrival. This request sounded strange to me, but I did not question her.

As our taxi drove through a large park near the downtown area, the driver suddenly stopped, motioning that he had a flat tire. I got a bit nervous about this unscheduled stop especially when I noted that he had dialled someone on his cell phone and that the conversation had nothing to do with car trouble. Obviously, he was not aware that I spoke Ukrainian and, as I listened to his conversation, the alarm bells went off. It appeared as though he was acting as an accomplice to a heist. I stepped out of the taxi and checked the tires. For certain, none was flat. I suddenly grabbed him by his arm and told him, in Ukrainian, to get his butt back into the taxi and take us back to the hotel. This, he did. When I called our hosts at two in the morning telling them what had happened, they sounded as though they were not surprised. Little wonder that Vera wanted me to call her back with assurances of our safe return to Hotel Dnister. I was thankful that we got home safely. At the same time, the incident served as a reminder of the dangers that confront a traveller in a foreign country

We spent the balance of the week pouring over the telephone directory seeking out my relatives who lived in Lviv. Once we made contact with one member of the Kaszuba family, we were able to build on our knowledge and contact other members. Perhaps the most interesting experience was the appearance of a gentleman at our door claiming to be my cousin, a son of my missing Aunt, Oksana *(Kaszuba)* Dutkevich. He had the right last name, but related? No sir! Still, I thought that he was quite enterprising. After several more telephone calls, we did meet the right Dutkevich family when the voice at the other end of the telephone told me that his mother perished in France during World War II. To my surprise, Ivan and Yaroslav Dutkevich had never met their cousins who lived just minutes away from them in the city.

With the time remaining in Lviv, we asked my cousin, Vasyl Groszko, to join Sharon and me for a short trip to Buzk to pay a visit to Olha Abranik, whom I met in 1967. She was overjoyed to see us and pointed out the very table at which I sat when confronted by the KGB. In short order we got caught up on all the news and *you can imagine my delight when she informed me that she regularly corresponded with our half-cousin Izabela Kopczacka in the village of Plazow and that it was Izabela who tended to grandmother Tetyana's grave.* Learning of this was of great importance to me because we planned to drive through Plazow on our way back to Frankfurt in search of family and my dad's village. We completed the day's trip by driving to Kamianka Buzk and visiting my Aunt, Oksana Medvid and her three daughters, Marika, Olha and Iryna.

Before leaving Lviv, with a promise to return in the near future, Vasyl and Maria Groszko packed a lunch big enough to last at least three or four days. A number of my relatives gathered at the Dnister Hotel to see us off. I didn't know what to say to the pleas of a couple members of the family who expressed a desire to emigrate to Canada. I doubted that they were aware of the procedures and the difficulty of qualifying for such an undertaking. They sounded disappointed that I was not able to lend encouragement to their pleas.

Vasyl Groszko escorted us out of the city in his Lada and pointed us in the direction of Rava Ruska, the border crossing into Poland. This time we knew what to expect and how to avoid the border hoodlums.

After all these years, our destination, finally, would be the village of Plazow. And, my cousin Izabela Kopczacka was in for quite a surprise. So was I.

The tiny village of Gorajec, surrounded by a dense forest served as a relatively safe haven for Ukrainians being persecuted by marauding Polish nationalists at the end of World War II. Photographed in 2007.

The Ukrainian Catholic Church in Gorajec survived not only World War II but also the political crisis immediately following the war. Photographed in 2007.

The still-popular horse-drawn wagon, near Ternopil, Ukraine, 1997.

Aunt Anna Grokh, Steven Kashuba and Anna's granddaughter, Oksana Grokh, next to Anna's home in Loshniv, 1998.

Grandmother Tetyana Groszko's grave, Plazow, Poland. 1998.

351

35.

The Village Was Right Here

"And I witnessed its torching..."

O n a late afternoon in October Sharon and I checked into Motel Jawa operated by Jan Wazny in the town of Cieszanow, just ten kilometres west of Plazow. I recalled mom talking about Cieszanow as being close to her village and being the repository for the region's Roman Catholic Church records. Later that evening we drove to Plazow with a great deal of anticipation to have a look, for the very first time, at my mom's *home village*. Having escaped me on both legs of my journey in 1967, I had to admit that this moment was not without a great deal of anticipation and emotion. At the outskirts of the village was the beautiful religious shrine which reflected the reverence that the locals had for religion. The first landmark that we recognized in Plazow was the *Dormition of the Blessed Virgin Mary* Ukrainian Catholic Church which was featured in a book titled *Churches in Ruin*. Just beyond the church, we stopped to talk to an elderly gentleman who seemed to be out for an evening's stroll. *"Dzien dobry,"* I said to him, hoping that he would be able to understand my version of Polish. As he responded, I asked him, this time in Ukrainian, *"Sir, do you know the name Kaszuba?"*

He seemed uncomfortable with my question and took a long time before he responded, in Polish, *"no, I do not know the name."*

"Have you heard the name Groszko?"

"Yes, yes I have. Some years ago. I don't know that the name exists in this village today."

"Is there a village near Plazow by the name of Grohi?"

"No, I have never heard of it?"

"How long have you lived in Plazow?"

"Well, I lived here most of my life and I am seventy years of age."

As I considered his responses, I wondered if he knew more about my family name and about the village of Grohi than he was prepared to admit. However, not wanting to be argumentative or raising any suspicions, I thanked him and left. At the other end of Plazow, I spotted another villager in his back yard and decided to ask him the same questions. His responses seemed to mirror those of the first villager except he contributed something that caught my attention, *"...yes, although I am relatively new to this village, I did hear that there once was a village by that name. Just northeast of here, I am told."*

When I asked him about the family name *Kaszuba,* he thought for a moment and then shook his head to say *no.* He had the same response to my question about the *Groszko* family. *"Do you know a resident by the name of Izabela Kopczacka,"* I then asked him.

"Yes, I do know Izabela. She lives in that house right over there," as he pointed to a house, a barn and a chicken coop. *"Do you want me to take you to her home?"*

"No, no. It is almost dark out and I don't want to disturb the family. Would you tell my cousin, Izabela, that Kaszuba is staying in Cieszanow and will be here tomorrow to meet her."

When we arrived in Plazow the following day, the first thing we noticed was that Izabela's neighbours were lolling about out-of-doors as though to witness our arrival. Had the two villagers we met the previous evening spread the word that Kaszuba was coming to their village the next day? What else did these two villagers tell their neighbours? With these thoughts in my head, we arrived at the Kopczacki residence to the barking of two dogs and the appearance of Izabela and her husband at the gate. I introduced myself and Sharon, telling her that I was her cousin and that Olha Abranik of Buzk told us all about her. True to Polish custom, Izabela greeted us with hugs and kisses and ushered us into the house where she had a lunch waiting for us. Only then, it seemed, was she ready to talk about the family. And, talk we did. All afternoon. We talked especially about her father, Mariusz Mazurkiewycz *(my uncle)* and the fact that he was the son of the mom's oldest half sister, Maria Groszko.

"I am so proud of my father! He played the organ in a Polish Catholic Church in Cieszanow for forty years and was recently cited by Pope John Paul II for his work."

"My mother told me that Mariusz had two brothers, both of whom became Catholic Priests."

"Yes, I do have two uncles who are priests. One of them is still living in Lublin. In fact, it was your mother who would send funds from time to time to help with their education."

I listened to Izabela as she spoke proudly about her family and I was especially surprised to hear that mom helped Izabela's uncles with their educational expenses. She then took us to another subdivision of the village where the original Mazurkiewycz home still stands and is occupied by her son, Konrad, his wife Bernadette and their three children. Konrad is in the process of constructing a new home on the property.

We then visited the local graveyard in search of tombstones that might reflect my heritage. There were a couple of Groszko and Horoshko grave markers but no Kaszubas. At that point, Izabela motioned to us saying, *"this is the grave of your grandmother, Tetyana Groszko. If you are looking for any Kaszuba tombstones, you might be able to find one in the old Ukrainian graveyard across the road."*

"Who," I asked Izabela, *"tends to my grandmother's grave? It is beautifully maintained."*

"I come here often to tend to the graves of family and that includes Grandma Tetyana."

That, above all else, really solidified my relationship with Izabela. With promises to return the next year, we said our goodbyes and walked across the road to examine the Ukrainian cemetery in the hopes of finding a grave marker with the name of a family member. True, the names were written in Cyrillic letters, but we were unable to find any Groszko or Kaszuba grave markers.

After leaving Plazow, we drove towards Narol and asked a couple of farmers hauling sugar beets about the village of Grohi. *"Yes,"* one farmer said, *"it was there, just beyond the forest, about one kilometre to the south."* We thanked them and collected a small jar of soil to be taken to Canada and sprinkled over my dad's grave. As we drove through Narol, I was reminded of the wagon road that my parents took to Belzec for the start of their journey to Canada. When we arrived in Belzec, we wanted to visit the site of the extermination camp that was located right next to the railway station and pay our respects to all those who lost their lives.

En route to Frankfurt and our return flight to Canada, I had to conclude that Izabela and the villagers we met *likely* knew more about Grohi than they were prepared to admit. Why, then, did the *oldtimers* clam up at the very mention of Grohi and Kaszuba? Did it have something to do with guilt? Memories of atrocities?

Shortly after we returned to Edmonton, I asked our neighbour, Sophia Dalba, to write a Christmas letter *in Polish* to our cousin Izabela and make a special request--*would Izabela be able to find a World War II survivor in Plazow who might remember the village of Grohi?* To our surprise, we got a letter back telling us that she had been successful. *"What a pleasant surprise,"* commented Sharon. Perhaps Izabela saw just how persistent I was in seeking answers to my questions about my family and the village of Grohi and decided to help. As fortune would have it, not only did Izabela find an individual in Plazow who remembered the Kaszuba family name, she also told us that this individual was born in the village of Grohi. I immediately drove to the St. Basil's senior's residence with a question for my mom, *"do you know of anyone who was born in Grohi that might still be living in Plazow?"*

She thought for a moment and then said, *"yes, there might be one person born in Grohi who would still be living."*

"If there was such a person, would you know his name?"

"Well," responded my mom, *"I do not know his name off hand. However, if someone mentioned his name, I would be able to tell whether or not he lived in Grohi."*

"Well, mom," I ventured, *"would you know the name Kruczko? Michal Kruczko? Does that ring a bell?"*

"Good Lord," exclaimed my mom, *"that is his name. I remember him as though it were yesterday. He was just a young lad when I left Plazow."*

I was elated to discover that my mother remembered the family name Kruczko because Izabela, in her letter to me said, *"The gentleman who can help you is Michal Kruczko. Michal was born in Grohi and now lives in Plazow. He is 79 years of age and would be prepared to take you and Sharon to the site of the village of Grohi."*

Before we left for a return trip to Poland and Ukraine in 1998, my mother gave me what I considered to be some useful information at the time. *"You know,"* she revealed, *"I heard a rumour that during the war the Kruczko family declared themselves to be Polish. With the exception of his grandmother or grandfather, I know that they considered themselves to be of Ukrainian heritage when I lived in Plazow. But, the family may have concluded that it was politically important to say that they were Polish."*

In the context of the Soviet policy of relocation in 1944 and 1945 and the Poland's Operation Wisla in 1947, I could see why the Kruczkos would want to declare themselves to be Polish. It appeared as though the family, attached to the land for a very long time, wanted to stay in Plazow, regardless of the cost. *Suddenly, I knew that I had found the key to unlocking the mystery of the disappearance of the village of Grohi and, his name was Kruczko.* The time before our next trip to Poland and Ukraine seemed to drag very slowly.

Much as we did the previous fall, we lifted off from the Edmonton International Airport in mid-April bound for Frankfurt. We made arrangements to rent a car from Auto Europe before we left because it was considerably cheaper to sign the contract in Canada rather than in Germany. Auto Europe would not allow us to take an automobile into Eastern Europe with an automatic shift saying that it was a prime target for thieves. As a result, we were provided with a new Astro with a manual shift transmission. Our route would be through Berlin, the Kashuby region of Northern Poland *(Pomerania),* Lithuania, Latvia, Belarus, Ukraine and then back to Frankfurt via Plazow in Poland. By taking this route, we planned to visit my cousin, Mariann Straupeniece, in Broceni, Latvia. The border crossing into Poland at Szczecin was very efficient. However, the transport truck line-up to get into Lithuania extended several kilometres. We managed to get to the head of the line and within a couple of hours were clear of the border en route to Riga. By the size and number of potholes in Lithuania, it was obvious that the country was in dire need of improvements to its infrastructure.

By prior arrangement, we met Mariann's daughter, Ilze, a medical student in the local Latvian University, over breakfast at Hotel Riga, an old but elegant ex-Intourist hotel. I could not help but smile as I met Ilze for the first time. I recalled having sent her mother a nice pair of winter boots the previous year only to get a letter, in return, asking me '...*why did you send me an old and worn pair of army boots?*' To me, it looked obvious as to what happened– someone intercepted the parcel and exchanged an old pair of army boots for a brand new pair.

From Riga, the three of us motored to Broceni where we met my cousin, Mariann, and Ilze's sister, Liene. Since I met Mariann in Lviv in 1967 after my ill-fated visit to the village of Buzk, we had a lot to talk about. Her father, Damian Gruszko who passed away two years earlier, was an ethnic Ukrainian and, as a result, Mariann knew some Ukrainian. In addition, the language of instruction in her school had been Russian and, with a knowledge of these two languages in addition to her mother tongue of Latvian, we were able to communicate. It was less of a problem with Ilze and Liene in that both were taking English as a second language. While visiting, we also had the pleasure of meeting Maria Spichka, a woman who lived in Broceni but was born in Ternopil and volunteered to write the letters from Mariann to my mother in Ukrainian. Another interesting person we met was Mirdza, the local English language teacher, who wrote the letters to me, on behalf of the Straupeniece family, in English. Although our visit was short, it was heart-warming to meet another cousin and her family.

Early the next morning, Sharon and I went to the Belarus Embassy to purchase our transit visas for Belarus, which would provide us with a shortcut to Ukraine. To our surprise, the line-ups were over two blocks in length. We jostled our way to the head of the line, amidst numerous comments, complaints and criticisms where an official told us that those waiting in line were making application for exit visas, in part because thirty-five percent of those living in the country were non-Latvians, were not allowed to vote in their federal elections and could not hold federal jobs. Although the government was working on new legislation to permit them to gain citizenship, the line-ups reflected the present reality. I was told by a Ukrainian in the line-up that it seemed as though the government *wanted them to leave!*

Our drive through Belarus en route to Minsk reflected considerable poverty, yet evidence of a strong communist influence by virtue of the many statues of Lenin on entry points to state farms. As I entered Hotel Minsk to confirm our reservations, I felt that this was my lucky day for at the entrance to the hotel I picked up a 200 rouble note on the sidewalk; *finder's keepers,* I suppose. However, my joy was short-lived when I exchanged US$30 and received over one million roubles! The 200 rouble note, I discovered, was worth less than two cents! Minsk had been rebuilt since my last visit and now portrayed wide and stately streets and many Soviet-style buildings re-constructed in the image of those they replaced. Of interest was the Museum of the Great Patriotic War which portrayed the horrors of World War II. It went a long way towards explaining Belarus' apparent obsession with the war. Most disturbing were the photographs of partisans being executed. It is a curious twist of history to think that all the suffering by Belarusians served only to liberate the people from one regime of terror and deliver them to another oppressive regime.

Our route to Lviv took us through Homel and the region of the Chornobyl nuclear disaster. Experts claim that this region of Belarus was worse hit than any other region, with 70 percent of the fallout landing on its territory and around one-fifth of its area seriously affected. By 1990, two million people, 20 percent of the country's forests and well over 250,000 hectares of agricultural land had been contaminated. It was hard to imagine that so beautiful an area, dissected by the grandeur of the Dnipro River, could have become so contaminated.

When we arrived in Lviv and checked into Hotel George, we made plans to visit those Kaszuba and Groszko relatives that we did not get a chance to meet the previous fall. But, most of all, I wanted to once again drive to the village of Loshniv, home to so many of my relatives, and pay a visit to Aunt Anna. I had some good news for her.

Aunt Anna greeted us warmly before sitting us down to dinner. We were joined by several members of her immediate family and the conversations were upbeat, even though the economic conditions in Ukraine continued to look a bit sour. About the time we were getting into her best Armenian cognac, I decided to inform my Aunt that, *"yes, after visiting a couple more relatives, we shall be driving to Plazow once again before flying to Canada."*

"By the way, Stefan," enquired my Aunt, *"did you get to meet any of your mother's family while in Plazow last year?"*

"Yes, I did. We met my cousin, Olha Abranik of Buzk who told us about our cousin Izabela Kopczacka who lives in Plazow. By the way, Auntie, Sharon and I have a surprise for you. Finally, we will search out the village in which you were born, Grohi."

"You will? How in the world will you ever find it?"

"Well, I have some very good news for you. We wrote to Izabela and she gave us the name of a resident of Plazow who will take us to the village. You may even know the person."

"You say that I may know the person? Who is he?"

"His name," I enunciated carefully, *"is Michal. Michal Kruczko."*

The very mention of the name of Michal Kruczko must have had quite an impact upon my Aunt. I looked at her. At first she turned white. Then she got her colour back and seemed to turn as red as a beet. It was as though she was suddenly incapable of putting her thoughts together or uttering a word. When she did, even I was surprised at the vitriol that seemed to be attached to the name Kruczko. *"You know,"* she finally exclaimed, pointing the palms of her two hands heavenward, *"I hope that a bolt of lightning strikes him. Kruczko is no more than a turncoat. A traitor."*

"A turncoat? A traitor? How's that?"

"He was no more than a Ukrainian hoodlum who joined a local Polish partisan group during the war. He turned on local Ukrainians in Plazow and Grohi like a mad sow."

"Do you mean to tell me that he was not of Polish heritage but became a Polish national?"

"That is exactly what I am saying. He is a dangerous person who would turn on his own mother."

Suddenly, I realized why the two villagers that we initially met in Plazow were reluctant to talk about the Kaszuba family or the burnt-out village of Grohi. It must have started when I told them that my name was Kaszuba, from which they may have concluded that I was in Plazow to seek some sort of revenge or retribution. This, however, did not explain why my cousin, Izabela Kopczacka, would not have known of the existence of the Kaszuba clan and of the village of Grohi. Did she hide something from me during our first visit? These thoughts were suddenly interrupted by my cousin, Maria Hrabovska *(daughter of my uncle, Mikhailo Kaszuba)*, who got into the conversation with a great deal of emotion, saying, *"it was Michal Kruczko who identified the homes of all Ukrainians living in Grohi making it easier for the Polish partisans to rout them. In fact,"* my cousin continued as though the flood gates had suddenly opened, *"my father had just built a new home in Grohi. He was most reluctant to leave the village. It was Kruczko who came after my father and had he not jumped out the window of his home, he would have been shot on the spot by Kruczko's henchmen."*

"What is most shocking about all of this," added Aunt Anna, *"is that the Kruczko family resided in the village of Grohi. In fact, the Kruczkos were our neighbours."*

"And, what about the Kruczko home in Grohi?"

"Well," she said, *"just to solidify his own contention that he was an ethnic Pole, I was told that he set fire to his own family home in Grohi. Yes, those nationalistic Poles burned to the ground every home in that village to the ground. I have never been back to the village since."*

To me, it was obvious that the memories of the deportation were very painful for my Aunt. As a result, I put aside any further questions in favour of asking her daughter-in-law, Anna Grokh, to put in writing a summary of the experiences of my Aunt as well as *all members of* the Kaszuba family during the time of deportations. That report describes, in considerable detail, how each member fared during those fearful days and supports the belief that upwards to 120 Ukrainians in the immediate area were killed by the Polish nationalists. Anna's parents and her brothers and sisters initially hid in the nearby forest and then took refuge in several nearby villages in advance of a return to law and order. During those dark days of 1944 and 1945, my grandmother Tetyana Groszko was killed and thrown into the family well when she refused to go into hiding with the Polish members of the family living in Plazow. Both my grandfather Andriy Kaszuba and my grandmother Maria Kaszuba died as a result of fear and stress; some saying that it was as a result of heart attacks brought on by the lawlessness of the day. However, most family members did take refuge in villages near Cieszanow before receiving protection of Soviet authorities prior to deportation.

As for the residents of Plazow, the story is told in an article written in a Buzk newspaper in 1996, entitled *Semi-Centennial Tragedy of Plazow*. Not only does the article deal with the proud history of the village of Plazow when Ukrainians, Poles and Jews lived in harmony, but it especially speaks to the horrors of events during the final stages of World War II in 1944 and 1945 when '*armed robbers came to Plazow from a Polish villages in the region and took away cattle, horses, shoes, coats; everything they saw*' with the belief that a favourable completion to the war was in sight and that Poland would once again emerge as a sovereign nation. The author goes on to say that, '*our part of village hesitated to leave. Some of us did not believe that something bad may happen. But, at last we decided to go. It was too late; the Polish bandits from the other villages attacked the Ukrainians in Plazow and in the forest. They took all of our belongings.*' The article brings to life the names of members of my extended family and what happened to them— names such as Goroshko, Klymus, and my grandmother, Tetyana, '*who was killed for no reason*' and how '*in the evening my cousin and I went to see what was going on in the village. When we came to the well, where the Poles threw the dead bodies of two tortured women, there were a lot of people who tried to take them out. At night I could not sleep thinking about how the Poles selected various means to torture and annihilate ethnic Ukrainians.*'

I thought long and hard about Michal Kruczko and about the cruelty of history. Most of all, my thoughts turned to the deportation of so many Ukrainians from Polish territory to Soviet Ukraine in 1944 and 1945. At the same time, Poles living in Soviet Ukraine were relocated to Poland. While it is true that many ethnic Ukrainians were killed in Poland during this period in history, one must not forget the Volhynian massacre. It was a tragedy that is shocking and an example of the entire evil that took place between Poles and Ukrainians during that time frame. For, it was in the village of Poryck *(recently renamed Pavlivka)* that 300 people were brutally murdered in June of 1943. Then, in July of the same year, units of the Ukrainian Insurgent Army simultaneously attacked as many as 167 Polish settlements, murdering, according to Polish authorities, nearly 10,000 Poles.

Considerable friction between the population and the occupying forces was generated in 1944 when the Soviets pushed the Nazi forces west out of Galicia and Ukrainians suddenly realized that the German aggressor was no better than the Russian or the Pole. There were numerous instances where the Germans publicly executed tens and even hundreds of persons in order to control the population by fear and terror. On the heels of this terror, the occupation of western Galicia by Polish and Soviet forces suddenly brought three disasters; lawlessness during the change in position of the front lines, the expulsion of the local Ukrainian population east to Soviet Ukraine and, in due course, the deportation of the remainder of the Ukrainian population to the northern and western territories of Poland.

According to Aunt Anna, *the lawlessness encountered during the movement of the front lines presented an opportunity for the criminal elements to flourish. Suddenly, your normal law abiding Poles, expecting the return of a Polish State, felt supreme and perpetrated vicious deeds on the Ukrainian population.* There are numerous examples of forceful deportations when a company of Polish soldiers would enter a village, give the population two hours to pack and load their belongings onto wagons and then escort them to the nearest railway station. Once the population became aware of this procedure, many would flee into the forest to escape deportation. Sometimes, they would flee a convoy en route to a railway station and take up residence in a village from which the population had already been deported. In other cases looters would raid a village prior to a deportation and rape the young girls as well as the older women. Whatever was left was all too often pillaged by the Polish soldiers themselves. *"It is difficult to imagine,"* pointed out my Aunt, *"the hatred that was present where Polish men went so far as to murder their own wives of Ukrainian ancestry."* To many Ukrainians, it seemed as though they were reliving the events that took place centuries earlier by the marauding Tatars. The Polish army deported whole communities and murdered those who would not cooperate. To prevent the return of the inhabitants, the army burned whole villages. In order to prevent belongings from falling into the hands of looters, some villages were burned by the departing population. In 1946 the Polish government issued an edict whereby the government became the owner of all possessions belonging to Ukrainian communities--including churches and parsonages.

To further complicate matters, one must not forget the fate of all the workers (Ostarbeiters) returning home from occupied Germany after the war. Thousands of them were transported east by trains which never did stop in the western part of Galicia but continued east across the border to Soviet Ukraine thereby saving the Polish government considerable expense. By the time the crisis had ended, fully sixty-five percent of the Ukrainian population had been deported from Polish territory. Although there are many monuments erected to the memory of soldiers who died during the deportation period, it is a pity that so little is written and said about the pain and suffering encountered by those being relocated from both sides of the border.

A few days later as Sharon and I drove to Plazow and our visit with Izabela, I reflected upon what my mother said of Kruczko. Somehow, it seemed as though there were two perceptions of him; the one held by my mother and the other as expressed by those living in Loshniv. In fact, when my mom recalled Michal, she had a mischievous twinkle in her eye. Could it be that mom had mixed feelings about the Kaszubas of Grohi? Did it have something to do with how she was treated by Andrij's parents? Maybe, in a strange sort of way, Michal Kruczko's heritage reflected, to some degree, that of my parents; a mixture of Ukrainian and Polish. *"This burning of the village,"* I asked

Sharon, *"do you believe that it might have had something to do with my great-grandfather coming to Grohi from the Kaszuby region of Poland?"*

"What do you mean? Do you believe that to be true? Do you really believe that those patriotic Poles stopped long enough to consider such complex questions?"

"Maybe the Polish nationalists wanted to kill two birds with one stone, as it were. Not only did they remove the kaszubs from the village but also the village itself."

"Maybe," responded Sharon, *"that is stretching the truth a bit, don't you think?"*

To further add fuel to the nationalistic ambitions of the Poles, the very name of the village, Grohi, a Ukrainian word meaning garden peas, might have been offensive to them. The Grokh family was among the first to settle in the new village and the village bears the family name. Having married into the Grokh family, it is little wonder that my Aunt Anna felt so strongly about what happened to her village. Yet, even though the memories of Grohi seemed always to be with Anna, she was reluctant to talk about the ordeal. Like so many displaced or relocated Ukrainians, survival and the welfare of the immediate family came first. Other members of my extended family in Western Ukraine exhibited the same attitude. One thing was clear, it seemed as though Anna and my cousin Maria wanted in the worst way to get their hands on Kruczko. I do believe that they would have done him great physical harm had they been able to get their hands on him. *"I hate that man,"* reaffirmed Maria.

When we arrived in Plazow, Izabela and her son, Grzegorz, were waiting for us. However, before setting out in search of Grohi, Grzegorz and Izabela drove us to Lubaczow where we met, for the very first time, two other Polish cousins and their families. To my delight, one came bounding across her front yard exclaiming, *"You are definitely a Groszko. I would have recognized you anywhere!"* Her obvious joy at meeting me set the stage for the rest of the day. Back at the Kopczacki residence in Plazow, Izabela provided each of us with knee-high galoshes, saying that, *"we will walk to the location of the village of Grohi which is about two kilometres from the edge of Plazow."* According to her, we would be traversing a region that had no roads, was soggy and wet, and required the use of rubber boots.

As I was being introduced to Michal, I had great difficulty in suppressing some conflicting feelings. Like an experienced prize fighter, he, too, slowly took my measure. Our meeting was somewhat reserved and cautious. Yet, despite the significant role he may have played in the relocation of my family, I wanted to give him a benefit of a doubt. Since Michal was born in Grohi, I was not surprised to note that he actually understood Ukrainian. *"This,"* I said to Sharon, *"confirms that he must have learned Ukrainian when he was a child."*

As some of the tensions dissipated, Michal asked about my mother, *Ewa Groszko.* By the manner in which he raised the question, I could tell that he had positive feelings about the Groszko family; however, that seemed not to be the case with the Kaszuba name. Not until much later into our walk to the village would he even utter the name. And, strange as it may sound, I sort of took a liking to him. I liked the way in which he stood and walked, as though he were still in the military. I liked the formal way in which he addressed me as *Pan Stefan*. During the process of meeting Kruczko, I made a mental note of his current age of 79 and calculated that he was twelve years of age when mom left Plazow and twenty-six years of age at war's end. As time went on, some of the reserve between us seemed to whither away in the light afternoon breeze.

Grzegorz and I left our cars at the outskirts of Plazow from which point the five of us set out on foot in search of the village of Grohi. We walked past two or three small farmsteads at the edge of Plazow and then traversed a small meadow before picking up what seemed to be trail long overgrown by shrubs and grass. To the right and left, the area was thickly forested by majestic pine which formed up a part of the national forest reserve. The trail we followed, if you could call it that, was barely discernible. Yet, Kruczko seemed to know well the whole area. As I observed him, I recalled how his hands actually shook when I first met him. However, as the morning wore on, it seemed as though he became more comfortable with me. He must have concluded that I was not here for the purpose of retribution but rather in search of my roots. *"You know,"* he said to me, *"I believe that I am the only surviving resident of Grohi who lives in this region."*

"What happened to all of the others?"

"Well," he responded, *"nearly all of the residents of Grohi were ethnic Ukrainians. After World War II they were re-located to Russia."*

"To Russia, Pan Kruczko? Where in Russia? Siberia?"

"No, no, Pan Kaszuba. They were relocated to an area not so far from here. Most of them went to Ternopil."

Wanting to impress upon him that Ukraine and Russia were not the same countries, I remarked, *"you mean that the ethnic Ukrainians were moved to Ukraine, don't you?"* He seemed to understand my intent and did acknowledge that the local residents were relocated to Soviet Ukraine. Somehow, he looked far younger than his seventy-nine. His pace was brisk and I noted that Sharon and Izabela had some difficulty in keeping pace. For certain, he was physically fit. As I looked around in wonder, I had to admit that the trail leading to Grohi showed the signs of nearly a half century of growth. Having covered about one-half of the distance to Grohi, we came across a meadow. *"It was here,"* said Kruczko, *"that your family had some agricultural land, and nearby, some grazing land for the cattle. Their garden plots were next to their homes. In fact, your family owned more than its share of land in Grohi."*

The last portion of the trail once again took us through a forested area. We crossed one small brook by scrambling over a couple of fallen logs. I asked Michal if this was the brook that my dad fished. *"No,"* was his recollection, *"this is a smaller brook that feeds into the larger brook which flowed through the village of Grohi."*

Observing a couple of deep depressions, I enquired, *"What are these Pan Kruczko?"*

"Oh, those are small trenches or fox holes dug by the local partisans in defence of this area during the war. The Germans lost a number of their soldiers in these woods. In hand-to-hand combat, they had no chance. Our partisans knew this area like the back of their hand." I listened with interest as he added, *"...you know, Pan Kaszuba, we did not lose many of our residents during the war. This forest provided an excellent hiding place for us."*

"What about the Ukrainians?" I asked of him. He seemed not to hear my question.

Other than the one large meadow, it was hard to imagine that anyone had ever lived here. Ahead of me, I could see Kruczko surveying the heavily treed area next to a brook. *"It was right here,"* I heard him say, as he made a half-circle with his hand in the air.

"Right here? What was right here," I asked.

"The village. Yes. The village was right here," was his response.

As I looked around shading my eyes against the streaks of sunlight penetrating the tall pine, I would never have known that we had reached the site of the village of Grohi. Completely enveloped by large evergreens, it took a considerable amount of careful examination to visualize what would have been the homes and the garden plots of a number of villagers. *Looking around, I noticed two mature apple trees that would have been planted many years ago. Planted perhaps by my grandfather and my dad following World War I, but now completely surrounded by the larger pine trees. I paused in awed silence, perhaps at the very spot where my grandfather's house had existed.* I looked at the brook pressed up against the pine, a brook that my father had talked about so lovingly. Just as my dad had described it, the homes of the villagers were framed by the meandering brook. This was home to my parents when they were first married and the yard where my sister Maria would have taken her first steps. I found it difficult not to wonder about the mystery of life's journey itself. A sense of quietude and fulfilment settled over me. In some small way, I had attained a life-long dream.

Our guide, Michal Kruczko, seemed also to be in a world of his own as he walked along the bank of the brook. I wondered as to what he must be thinking. Would it be about how the ethnic Ukrainians living in Grohi were treated by the Poles? Would it be about Josef Stalin and his decision to order all ethnic Ukrainians out of this region? He must have sensed my thoughts saying, *"You know, Pan Kaszuba, my grandmother was Polish but my grandfather was Ukrainian. For whatever reason, my parents declared their allegiance to Poland just before the war. Naturally, I was obliged to do the same. It might have been the other way around. They could easily have*

Monument to those who perished in the Belzec extermination camp, Belzec, Poland, 1998.

declared themselves to be ethnic Ukrainians. My family was, in some ways, very similar to the Groszko family."

I knew that this was now history. A part of my heritage. I was also told that Michal had married a Polish girl during the war. For him, perhaps the process of polonization was now complete. And yet, I sensed something else in his voice. As he described the village in more detail, I could see a tear welling up in his eyes. Without doubt, he had a lot of pleasant memories about his childhood and the Ukrainian friends he once had. But, these pleasant memories, for the moment, were being shunted aside. My being here representing the Kaszuba family must have brought to the surface those memories he had tried so hard to suppress. No doubt he was wrestling with the memories of his past and I wondered if he would ever be able to completely forget what happened to the village.

"So, Pan Kruczko, the village of Grohi was right here. What about my grandfather, Andriy Kaszuba. Where was his home?" He considered my question for a long time.

"Follow me, Pan Kaszuba." We walked a short distance and he stopped next to an old apple tree. *"There. Right there was your grandfather's house."*

As I walked around what would have been the perimeter of my grandfather's house to finally stand on the banks of the brook, I was struck with the thought of just how all of our hopes and dreams were so much alike–be it for the Kaszubas, the Kruczkos or the Kopczackis; thoughts that somehow seemed to be embodied in democratic ideals. Yet, it seemed also to be true that language and religion could quickly undo so many of our lofty ideals. I asked Michal about the other families that lived in Grohi. He confirmed much of what my mom had told me about the number of families that once lived in the village. When I asked him, *"do you remember Mikhailo Kaszuba,"* there was a long pause and I knew why. He *nodded* without responding. Finally, he said, *"follow me."*

No more than fifty yards to the north of my grandfather's home, Michal identified the location of Mikhailo's home. As he pointed out the location, the words of my Aunt Anna, now living in a free and independent Ukraine, struck me like a thunderbolt, '...*you know, Stefan, a neighbour was visiting my brother Mikhailo. Suddenly, Mikhailo's young daughter Maria burst into the home crying out, 'the Poles are coming, the Poles are coming!' Mikhailo and Maria jumped through the open window and ran into the nearby forest. They stayed in the forest until the next morning and only then did they venture back into the house. And, you know what they found? The neighbour was still sitting in is chair. Shot several times through the chest. Several others in the village were also shot.'*

I recalled asking my Aunt, '*and what of your mother and father? Where were they?'*

'*Well, they heeded the warnings of others in the village. They accepted that it was not safe in Grohi. As a result, they sought refuge in a nearby village. Of course, they never returned to Grohi. There was no village to return to. It was torched the very next evening. Mikhailo's family got out of the village just in time. I lost my mother and father during those horrible days. My mother is laid to rest in a village near Plazow while my father is buried in another village. I never had a chance to say goodbye.'*

I visualized how the rear window of the home faced the brook and the dense forest beyond and how my uncle, his wife and child exited through that window when they heard the hoof beats of approaching Poles.

"*Did you have anything to do with the burning of this village?'*

Kruczko's answer was thoughtful and measured, "*well, many Ukrainians believe that I had something to do with the burning of the village.*"

"*What about your own home? Who torched your home in the village?*"

For a long time, it looked as though he was about to answer my question, but he never did. Perhaps he wanted to keep the rumour alive that he *was* involved. Maybe the Poles preferred it that way. Returning to our cars, I thought long and hard about Grohi and about Kruczko. I wondered if my Aunt Anna was fully aware of his role in the torching of the village. Was she aware that the village would have been burned to the ground even if Kruczko had not been a willing participant?

On the flight back to Canada, I finally understood why Michal Kruczko seemingly wrestled with his conscience when we were in the village of Grohi. He was obviously trying to reconcile his own past with the feelings he had about me and the circumstances of the moment. Although it is said that the sins of our forefathers come to visit upon us, I could only conclude that Michal would have to come to grips with the actions *he and his family* took during the expulsion of Ukrainians in 1944 and 1945. A number of Ukrainians from the region did hide in the forest surrounding Grohi, rounded up in 1947 and relocated to other regions of Poland as a part of Operation Wisla. *Did Michal Kruczko have anything to do with the relocation of these Ukrainians?*

Sharon and I did return to Plazow in 1999 at which time we once again met with Michal Kruczko and his wife. Except that this time, *we knew*, as they say, *the rest of the story*. Somehow, it seemed as though Michal had aged considerably since our meeting of one year ago. I had heard a lot about forgiveness from other people. This was the first time in my life that I wrestled with the thought of forgiving someone, not so much for myself, but for the members of my family whose lives were impacted by Michal Kruczko and the Polish nationalists. But then, I couldn't decide in my own mind whether the attacks on the small and defenceless village were perpetrated by locals out of control or as a result of events in Volynia in 1944.

I tried placing myself in Kruczko's shoes. *What would I have done differently? Looking at my own heritage,* didn't my dad serve in the Austrian and Polish Home armies? Wasn't he just one step away from entertaining the possibility of declaring himself as being a Polish national? And, what about my Uncles Mikhailo and Dmetro? Didn't they also serve in the Polish Army after World War I? What would have stopped *them* from declaring their allegiance to the nation of Poland? Would it be their Ukrainian Catholic religion? Their heritage? Certainly it would not be the language. After all, most Ukrainians in the region *were* fluent in Polish.

En route to Riga, the Hill of Crosses near Siauliai, Lithuania is an unforgettable sight. Standing upon a small hill, hundreds of thousands of crosses represent Christian devotion and memorial to Lithuania's national identity, 1998.

But, none of this seemed to matter. Taking stock of events as they unfolded, the answer was obvious: *the end of World War II did little to quell the desire on the part of local nationalists to seek revenge upon ethnic Ukrainians.* Common sense was in short supply and gave way to mass hysteria. *Polish authorities did not embrace the concept of democratic rights for minority groups. You were either a Pole, or you were not.*

In the final analysis, *it seemed* as though no members of my extended were lost as a result of *any direct action of Michal Kruczko*. His actions, more than anything else, reflected the political circumstance of the day where the ultimate goal of the Polish nationalists was to rid the landscape of ethnic Ukrainians. Perhaps the lawless Polish bands were reacting to what happened in the Volynian region of Soviet Ukraine where Polish villages were

Operated as a kolhosp under the former communist regime, it is now a state farm operated by the Oblast of Ternopil.

Maria Kaszuba, Ivan Kaszuba, Steven Kashuba, Oksana Grokh during a visit to a state farm in Suhostav, 1998.

At site of memorial to Latvia's greatest war heroes, L to R are Sharon Kashuba, Karlis Straupeniece, Ilze Straupeniece, Mariann Straupeniece, Liene Straupeniece-Kravinska, Klavs Kravinski, Janis Kravinski, Liepaja, Latvia, 1998.

Izabela Kopczacka and Sharon Kashuba in the yard of the original Mazurkiewicz home, Plazow, Poland, 1998.

Michal Kruczko, Steven Kashuba, Grzegorz Kopczacki, and Izabela Kopczacka; setting out in search of the village of Grohi, Plazow, Poland, 1998

Izabela Kopczacka and Steven Kashuba in the front yard of the burnt-out Kaszuba home, Grohi, Poland, 1998.

Two apple trees planted in the Kaszuba front yard by Andrij and his father in 1918 to commemorate the conclusion of World War I, Grohi, Poland, 1998.

Traditional Ukrainian greeting in Lviv for Alberta's Premier, the Honourable Ralph Klein and Minister of Education, the Honourable Gene Zwozdesky, 2006.

A youthful Nicole Kashuba participates in a Ukrainian dance program, Edmonton, 1982.

burned to the ground by Ukrainians. In fact, it could well be that some of the members of the Polish bands operating in the County of Lubaczow were the very survivors of attacks by Ukrainian armed bands in 1944 in Volynia.

One can only speculate as to what might have happened to my Uncles Mikhailo and Dmetro had they remained behind in the village. For example, the tragedy of Grohi is rife with rumour. Some say that Michal Kruczko actually warned the villagers about the impending attacks before joining an armed Polish band himself. However, my cousin Maria Hrabovska (Mikhailo's daughter) is firm in her belief that Kruczko was actually a member of the band that attacked her family and participated in the torching of the village. In particular, Maria refutes the notion that Kruczko's actions were *some sort of a response to the terms of the agreement reached between Poland and Russia for the repatriation of Ukrainian citizens to Soviet Ukraine.*

In the end, one can argue that Michal was as much a victim of ethnic tensions as were members of my family.

I recall the day that Michal Kruczko led us to Grohi. I can still see him standing on the bank of the brook, deep in thought. Somehow, our lives became intertwined at that moment. I reflected upon the brook and the fresh spring-water in the heart of Plazow that provided sustenance for so many people over the years. Surely, this was the fountain of life that signified birth, rebirth, and renewal. The playing out of this small drama brought home to me the devastation and pervasiveness, not only of world conflict but also of ethnic conflict. Even for a Canadian who was far removed from World War II by time and distance, its impact upon me was very real. On the one hand, the conflict of ethnicity between our respective families saddened me, yet I had to admit that my family was also very lucky. Although the village of Grohi was set ablaze and wiped off the face of the earth, at least most of the villagers survived.

As Sharon and I left Plazow, I hoped that Michal Kruczko would find some peace in all of this. Much like Symon Petliura before him, Kruczko was a hero to some and a villain to others. 'Yes,' I concluded, *'there once lived a village. Now the only things that remain are the two apple trees planted by my dad and my grandfather—standing among the tall pine in witness of the tragedy of Grohi.'*

EPILOGUE

Ukraine: The Road Ahead

Some say that the burnt-out ashes of Ukrainian villages located in Poland at the end of World War II helped to accelerate the birth of present-day Ukraine. Perhaps it *was* one of the penalties that Ukrainians had to pay to re-awaken, coalesce and consolidate their national psyche to a sufficiently high degree to seek political stability and reach out for complete independence.

However, not only did Ukrainians suffer loss of life and psychological scars of relocation as a result of the nationalistic actions of individuals and government policies, but so did the Poles. When it comes to burning, pillaging and killing, neither group can claim innocence.

With the memories of these events still imprinted upon the minds of many, it is little wonder that on the eve of the 2004 presidential elections Ukrainians reflected upon the nation's declaration of independence in 1991 and looked forward *to an escape from communist rule and the adoption of democratic freedoms*. Although it is true that Ukraine, at least on paper, is a free and democratic republic, what then is it that is keeping the nation from making any great strides towards attaining the attributes of a democratic state?

I have talked to Ukrainians in their homes and their gardens; to professors in the halls of learning and to university students on Prospekt Svobody. It is as if they are waiting for something positive to happen in their economy; something to give them hope. Yet, it seems as though there *are* obstacles. As the nation looks forward to the future, it will have to continue to deal with a heritage which made it an integral part of tsarist Russia and then a part of the Soviet Union. Its most poignant legacy may well be the Chornobyl nuclear disaster, however, even more important is the totalitarian ruin left behind as a result of the dissolution of the Soviet Empire. After all, who among us would have predicted that having lived under the yoke of totalitarianism for so long would have left Ukraine less than capable of facing the complexity of change.

While Ukraine strives to create a national identity of inclusiveness where all ethnic groups feel a part of the nation, Ukrainians must themselves exhibit these same attributes. After all, other nations see Ukraine as Ukrainians see themselves; a nation where fully twenty percent of its residents live in small villages and see themselves as having a special relationship with the rich, fertile, and abundant soil which provides for their basic needs. *In the soil they see the stability that they had sought for so many years and within the village they see the embodiment of hard-working families who are reliable and honest.*

All of this brings me, as it were, to a closing of the circle. My parents left Poland in the prime of their lives in search of political and religious freedoms, yet they developed a profound respect for the democratic principles emanating from Vienna, the capital of the Habsburg Empire. Somehow, these principles remained with them even though they left their beloved homeland behind. *Much as the story started with the notion of democracy, it now seemingly ends there.*

As I contemplate what the future holds for individual members of my family in Ukraine, it is without doubt that their hopes and aspirations are closely tied to the state. They are well aware that apathy and corruption often stand in the way of attracting multi-national corporations and small business ventures. In fact, recent opinion polls conducted by Ukraine's Social Monitoring Center and Institute of Social Studies find that nearly eighty percent of the respondents believe that government officials are on the take and forty percent of these respondents personally paid bribes during the previous year. As a result, many are of the opinion that ordinary people on meagre salaries or pensions are called upon to pay bribes to medical personnel for treatment, to staff to admit children into higher education, or to minor bureaucrats to issue vital documents. Their defence for bribery is often a case of paying for one's services. In the absence of being able to collect taxes, there has to be another mechanism which can be used for the payment of services. Although it is true that corruption does exist, there is also some hope that change is in the offing.

In the final analysis, the Soviet Union may have disintegrated but the ideas and the fears of that regime are *not* tucked away in the past. Even though the days of Stalin are gone, his shadow continues to fall over the Ukrainian population where the experiences of communist rule have poisoned everything. No one seems to be immune from the pervasiveness of a system of government that everyone thought was buried. This is what Ukrainian institutions, officials, citizens, and the national psyche are confronting. Before the future for Ukraine can be mapped out, its inhabitants must first confront the sceptre of the hammer and sickle.

Western Canada provided a haven for many immigrants from Eastern Europe who fled famine, dictatorship, economic and political turmoil. It is now time for Canadians to realize that the nascent economy of Ukraine is *coming out of hibernation.* As I close my search for family roots, I do so with a deep sense of humility. I have had the good fortune to exchange ideas with many individuals from whom I have learned that one should never go to his ancestral homeland with an inflated ego. I have visited secondary and post-secondary school institutions and noticed the absence of computers, calculators and high-tech facilities. Yet, the teacher-centred classrooms did not seem obsolete. In fact, it may well be the very absence of high technology that made the product—the student graduate—all the more ready for the challenges ahead.

I am glad that I did not jump to conclusions and preach a child-centred approach to the education of their youth or introduce western teaching methodologies that would be completely out of place in Ukraine. I am glad that I did not propose a system of education that would require massive funds *not currently available in Ukraine.* Most of all, I am glad that I did not request my colleagues to raise funds for the purpose of purchasing outdated computers to be sent to Ukraine only to find that these were incompatible with their infrastructure.

Finally, I have learned that Ukraine has far more to give me than I have to offer. When prescribing what is best for Ukraine, one must first sit amidst the ruins for a long time and feel the pain and injustice of history.

ONCE LIVED A VILLAGE

Selected Bibliography

Andrushyshen, C. H. and Watson Kirkconnell. The Poetical Works of Taras Shevchenko: The Kobzar (Translated from Ukrainian). University of Toronto Press, Toronto, Canada, 1977.

Berton, Pierre. The Last Spike. McClelland and Stewart Limited, Toronto, Canada, 1983.

Berton, Pierre. The Promised Land, Settling the West 1894 – 1914, Pierre Berton Enterprises Ltd., Anchor Canada edition, 2002.

Byfield, Ted. Alberta in the 20th Century, Volume Six, Fury and Futility, The Onset of the Great Depression. United Western Communications, Edmonton, Canada, 1998.

Centennial Book Committee, F. W. U. A. High Prairie Local 204. Pioneers Who Blazed The Trail, A History of High Prairie & District. South Peace News, High Prairie, Alberta, Canada, 1968.

Clark, Alan. The Eastern Front, 1914 - 18. The Windrush Press, Gloucestershire, England, 1971.

Cristall, David. Mundy Map Co. Adapted from Mundy's Indexed Map of Alberta, The Peace River Country in the Thirties, Mundy Map Co., Edmonton, Undated.

Eames, Andrew. Berlin. APA Publications (HK) Ltd., Thomas Allen & Son, Markham, Ontario, Canada, 1993.

Ellwart, Jaroslaw. Kaszuby. Przewodnik Turystyczny, Wydawnictwo, Gdynia, Poland, 2001.

Federal Government of Canada, Department of the Interior, Surveyor General. Diagram Showing the Numbering of Legal Subdivisions of Surveyed Lands. Ottawa, Canada, 1915.

Haythornthwaite, Philip J. A Photo History of World War One. Arms and Armour Press, London, England, 1994.

Haywood, John. Atlas of World History. Andromeda Oxford Ltd., Abingdon, Oxfordshire, England, 1999.

High Prairie History Book Society. The Trails We Blazed Together, History of: Grouard - High Prairie & Surrounding Areas. Herff Jones, Winnipeg, Manitoba, Canada, 1997.

Himka, John-Paul. Galicia and Bukovina, A Research Handbook About Western Ukraine, Late 19th - 20th Centuries, Occasional Paper No. 20. Published by Alberta Culture & Multiculturalism Historical Resources Division, 1990.

Hogan, David J. Editor in Chief. The Holocaust Chronicle. Publications International Ltd., Lincolnwood, Illinois, The United States, 2001.

Holmes, Richard. The World Atlas of Warfare. Viking Penguin Inc., Middlesex, England, 1988.

Hunter, Bea. Last Chance Well, Legends & Legacies of Leduc No. 1. D. W. Friesen Limited, Edmonton, Alberta, Canada, 1998.

Iwanusiw, Oleh Wolodymyr. Church in Ruins. A Publication of St. Sophia, Religious Association of Ukrainian Catholics in Canada, St. Catharines, Ontario, Canada, 1987.

Kaye, Vladimir J. Early Ukrainian Settlements in Canada, 1885 - 1900. University Press for the Ukrainian Research Foundation, Toronto, Canada, 1964.

Keegan, John. The First World War, Vintage Canada Edition. A Division of Random House of Canada Limited, Toronto, Canada, 2000.

Kolasky, John. Two Years in Soviet Ukraine. Peter Martin Associates Ltd., Toronto, Canada, 1970.

Kordan, Bohdan S. And Peter Melnycky. In the Shadow of the Rockies, Diary of the Castle Mountain Internment Camp, 1915 - 1917. Canadian Institute of Ukrainian Studies Press, The University of Alberta, Edmonton, Alberta, Canada, 1991.

Lozynsky, M. Halychyna v rr. 1918 - 1920. Vienna: Institut Sociologique Ukrainien, 1922.

MacGregor, J. G. A History of Alberta. Hurtig Publishers, Edmonton, Alberta, Canada, 1979.

Magocsi, Paul Robert. Ukraine, A Historical Map. University of Toronto Press, Canada, 1985.

Magocsi, Paul Robert. A History of Ukraine. University of Toronto Press, Canada, 1996.

Makowski, William. The Polish People in Canada, A Visual History. Tundra Books, Montreal, Quebec, 1987.

Motyl, Alexander. Dilemmas of Independence, Ukraine After Totalitarianism. Council of Foreign Relations Press, New York, 1993.

Naulko, V. I. Etnichny sklad naselennya Ukrayinskoyi RST (Ethnic Composition of the Population of the Ukrainian SSR). Kyiv, 1965.

Noble, John. Russia, Ukraine, & Belarus, A Lonely Planet Travel Survival Kit, 1st Edition. Lonely Planet Publications, Hawthorn, Australia, 1996.

Potichnyj, Peter J. Poland and Ukraine, Past and Present. The Canadian Institute of Ukrainian Studies, The University of Alberta, 1997.

Potrebenko, Helen. No Streets of Gold, A Social History of Ukrainians in Alberta. New Star Books, Vancouver, British Columbia, Canada, 1977.

Prior, Robin and Trevor Wilson. The First World War. Cassell, Wellington House, London, England, 1999.

Readers Digest. Condensed from the New York Times Magazine by Paul Goldberger. June, 1995.

Rekowski, Aloysius J. The Saga of the Kaszub People in Poland, Canada, U.S.A. Book Made Available Through the Kaszubian Association of North America, 2002.

Salmaggi, Cesare and Alfredo Pallavisini. 2194 Days of War. Arnoldo Mondadori Editore S.p.A., Milan, Italy, 1977.

Sevirsky, David. Stout Hearts. Dmitry Medvedev, Foreign Languages Publishing House, Moscow, 1948.

Subtelny, Orest. Ukraine, A History. University of Toronto Press, Toronto, Canada, 1988.

Subtelny, Orest. Ukrainians in North America. University of Toronto Press, Toronto, Canada, 1991.

ISBN 142511841-0

Edwards Brothers Malloy
Oxnard, CA USA
July 9, 2013